*Economic Resources and
Policies of the South*

THE MACMILLAN COMPANY
NEW YORK · BOSTON · CHICAGO
DALLAS · ATLANTA · SAN FRANCISCO

MACMILLAN AND CO., LIMITED
LONDON · BOMBAY · CALCUTTA
MADRAS · MELBOURNE

THE MACMILLAN COMPANY
OF CANADA, LIMITED
TORONTO

ECONOMIC RESOURCES
and POLICIES of the SOUTH

Calvin B. Hoover

CHAIRMAN, DEPARTMENT OF ECONOMICS, DUKE UNIVERSITY

B. U. Ratchford

PROFESSOR OF ECONOMICS, DUKE UNIVERSITY

New York · THE MACMILLAN COMPANY

To the Memory of J. M. BROUGHTON, *late Governor of North Carolina and Senator from that State, First Chairman of the Committee of the South*

and

To the Memory of E. J. COIL, *late Director of The National Planning Association.*

PREFACE

This book owes its existence to the organization of the National Planning Association Committee of the South which took place in Birmingham, Alabama, November 21, 1946. The Committee then consisted of fifty-five leading citizens of the South. The late Honorable J. Melville Broughton, formerly Governor of North Carolina and later United States Senator from that state, was elected Chairman of the Committee.

Governor Broughton stated at the initial meeting, "It is the view of the Association, shared by its eminent Board of Trustees, that an adequate study of economic conditions of the South, expertly conducted, under the general supervision of a Southern Committee of agricultural, business, labor and educational leaders, would be of inestimable value to the South and, indeed, to the nation as a whole. . . . The nation needs a strong, economically prosperous South. Only the South can give an adequate response to this challenge. . . . It is obvious that much of the economic future of the South lies in industrial and agricultural research. At long last we are beginning to substitute the research laboratory for the wailing wall."

The NPA Committee of the South authorized a number of research projects and one of the authors of this study was appointed Director of Research. During the years following this initial meeting a number of these research projects have been completed and the results published. These research projects were carried out by economists and sociologists at various southern universities and governmental agencies. As a matter of procedure these reports were customarily reviewed by the individual members of the Committee of the South in the form of preliminary drafts and at meetings of the Committee. Assistance of the greatest value to the authors of the research reports came from the suggestions and criticisms of the members of the Committee, themselves experts in a wide range of fields. In all cases, however, the authors of the reports and not the members of the Committee of the South are solely responsible for their contents. This is true of this study as well.

The NPA Committee of the South was from the beginning particularly desirous of having a study made of alternative economic policies for the South. The Director of Research agreed to undertake this study. It quickly became apparent that an analysis of economic policies for the South could not be carried out intelligently without adequate information concerning the economic resources of the South. These basic data had never been gathered into a form which would be usable for the purposes of analysis of policy. It was also clear that an analysis of these economic resources must precede the analysis of policies. There could be no doubt that no one man could hope to accomplish this dual task.

In consequence, a two-man team (Hoover and Ratchford) undertook the combined job. In this study Ratchford has been responsible for most of the research on resources and he also has done a considerable portion of the work on policies as well. This means that Ratchford has done much more than half of all research and writing. This was made possible by a sabbatical leave granted for this work by Duke University. All research and writing represent the closest possible collaboration. We have consulted daily and indeed hourly over almost every line in the book. The intimacy of our collaboration reflects some twenty-five years of association in research, in teaching, and in governmental service.

In the course of our research we became progressively aware that a study of the economic resources and economic policies of a region, such as the South, should properly have had the services of at least a dozen economist-specialists to deal with the various aspects of the study. However, no such specialists exist for a number of these aspects. Furthermore, even if specialists on all aspects of the study could have been found, unless these men could have worked together intimately for a year or more, integration of the results would not have been feasible. Under existing circumstances it was a question of doing the job by ourselves or not at all. Consequently, in this book we are frequently dealing with matters where even experts might fear to tread, while we assuredly are not experts on all the matters with which we have had to deal.

Our work on the book was interrupted by a tour of duty with the Economic Cooperation Administration in Paris during the summer of 1948. This experience was most useful, however, in sharpening our understanding of the problems of international trade as they affect the South.

Our work was further complicated, but enriched as well, by the request of the Council of Economic Advisors to the NPA Committee of the South for a study of "The Impact of Federal Policies on the Economy of the South." We agreed to lay aside our larger study in order to undertake this. We were able to draw upon a large part of the research we had already done. Consequently we were able to complete the Report to the Council by the Spring of 1949. It was published by the Joint Congressional Committee on the Economic Report in July, 1949. We have been astonished and greatly heartened by the widespread interest in this report and by the unexpectedly large demand for it after publication.

The criticism and suggestions which we received from so wide a range of individuals on the Report was of great value to us as we turned once more to the task of completing this book. The Report was written from one limited standpoint, that of federal policy. Limitations of space and time prevented us from presenting in the Report either comprehensive analysis of policies or the great volume of statistical source material contained in this book. Furthermore, we are able herein to take up many topics which were considered in the Report either very sketchily or not at all. Some material from the Report, although much amended and altered, has been included in this book. In final result this book is some five times as large as was the Report.

We are indebted to the editors of the *Southern Economic Journal, The Journal of Politics* and the *National Tax Journal* for permission to use material previously published in these journals. We are also indebted to the *New York Times* for permission to quote several long passages.

We are particularly indebted to Colonel E. W. Palmer, President of the Kingsport Press, who succeeded the late Senator Broughton as Chairman of the Committee of the South and to Mr. E. J. Coil, Director of the National Planning Association for their advice, criticism, and encouragement which have been of inestimable value to us. The advice and suggestions of Mr. William Davlin were always useful. We are likewise under obligations to all the members of the Committee of the South for the same reasons. The members of the staff of the National Planning Association have been helpful in many ways. In particular, Mrs. Virginia Parker was of great assistance to us in one stage of preparation of the manuscript. We are indebted to Mrs. Pauline Everett for secretarial services in preparing the manuscript for publication. Dr. Frank Welch, Dr. H. Brooks James, Mr. C. Brice Ratchford, Dr. Wylie Kilpatrick and Dr. Charles T. Taylor and others have read portions of the manuscript and have made valued suggestions. The technical advice of Dr. Frank Hanna has been of great service to us in connection with the analysis and presentation of statistical data. Many others have aided us by furnishing suggestions of statistical information.

Since we have worked without a statistical staff, it has not been possible to process the statistics as much as might be desired. We have used the statistical data to show the broad trends in the economic life of the region; we have not generally been concerned with statistical refinement. On account of the large volume of statistical data used, the task of verification has been a difficult one and there may be some errors in detail. We have, however, made a particular effort to verify data on which important conclusions are founded. Figures are frequently rounded to the nearest thousand or million. When percentages were computed, they necessarily were rounded to the nearest per cent or tenth of a per cent. For this reason, figures do not always add up precisely to the totals shown.

All data from the 1947 *Census of Manufactures* were taken from preliminary reports. In some cases these data were revised in the final reports, but it is not believed that these revisions were large enough to affect any of our conclusions.

We have not found it feasible to analyze what has sometimes been called the "economics of race" in the South. Statistical data in the field of economics are rarely broken down by race. Indeed, the tendency seems to be to give less, rather than more, statistical information on a racial basis. This perhaps reflects the viewpoint that race differences should be de-emphasized. The Committee of the South is, however, instituting a series of case studies on practices in the employment of Negroes in southern industry. It is hoped that this study will be available within the next two years.

We have likewise not dealt with the basing point pricing controversy in our discussion of southern industry. A separate study of this subject is being made for the Committee of the South by Professor George Stocking of Vanderbilt University.

We are profoundly grateful for the financial assistance furnished by the NPA Committee of the South and the Research Council of Duke University which has made this study possible.

For all conclusions and for all errors and shortcomings in this book we are solely responsible.

CALVIN B. HOOVER
B. U. RATCHFORD

Durham, North Carolina

TABLE OF CONTENTS

LIST OF TABLES

LIST OF CHARTS

I PHYSICAL RESOURCES

In the voluminous literature on the South which has appeared in recent decades, viewpoints have varied widely on nature's generosity to the South. Some have pictured nature as a fairy godmother, strewing her gifts lavishly over the South, and making of the region a land flowing with milk and honey. Others have depicted nature more as a niggardly stepmother, giving the South mainly mountain crags, barren hillsides, and swampy marshes. In a comprehensive, factual survey of the South's assets which are, or may be, of significance to economic production it will be seen that neither of these extreme pictures is true. Since anything approaching a full catalog of resources would require a volume in itself, this survey must necessarily be brief and general.

LAND AREA AND USES

For the purpose of this study the South is composed of the 13 states which stretch from the Potomac to the Rio Grande; namely, Alabama, Arkansas, Florida, Georgia, Kentucky, Louisiana, Mississippi, North Carolina, Oklahoma, South Carolina, Tennessee, Texas, and Virginia. These states contain 843,812 square miles or 540,040,000 acres of land area, which is 28.3 per cent of the land area of the United States. In some respects these states do not constitute a homogeneous region, since they vary widely in respect to certain characteristics. But historically, geographically, and climatically they constitute the most logical combination of states for a study of this kind. One consideration in particular dictates this selection of states; each of them is vitally con-

1

cerned with the production of one or both of the two great staple cash crops of the region—cotton and tobacco.[1]

While the study covers all 13 states, the problems which we regard as peculiarly southern and which receive most of our attention and emphasis are those which concern the southeastern states and especially those east of the Mississippi River. The southwestern states of Oklahoma and Texas, and especially their western parts, present problems of their own, and we are not able to deal with those in a comprehensive or adequate way. Consequently, the views and conclusions expressed here apply primarily to the Southeast and only to a less and varying extent to the Southwest.

TABLE *I* LAND AREA OF THE SOUTH BY MAJOR USES, 1945

	AREA (THOUSANDS OF ACRES)		PER CENT OF TOTAL	
	SOUTH	NON-SOUTH	SOUTH	NON-SOUTH
Total Land Area	540,040	1,365,522	100.0	100.0
Forest Land:				
Commercial	195,200	265,844	36.1	19.5
Noncommercial	35,775	127,009	6.6	9.3
Total Forest Land	230,975	392,853	42.7	28.8
Crop Lands	162,072	363,039	30.0	26.6
Pasture and Range	99,773	509,711	18.5	37.3
Other	47,264	99,675	8.8	7.3

SOURCE: Compiled from Forest Service, U. S. Department of Agriculture, *Basic Forest Statistics for the United States as of Beginning of 1945*. Washington, 1946.

Table *I* shows how the land area of the South was divided among different uses at the beginning of 1945 and gives comparative figures for the remainder of the United States. These figures show that, proportionately, the South has half as much pasture and range land, a little more crop land, and about 50 per cent more forest land than the rest of the nation. Somewhat more than half of the nation's forest

[1] Florida is an exception to this generalization. Indeed, in many other respects Florida does not behave economically like a southern state, but for several reasons it is not feasible to exclude Florida from this study. While the 13 states named above will be the subject of this study, it will frequently be necessary to depart from that grouping. Often it will be advantageous to use the data or conclusions contained in studies which used a different grouping. For example, the Bureau of the Census defines the South to include the above 13 states plus Delaware, Maryland, the District of Columbia, and West Virginia. Odum, in his *Southern Regions*, defined the Southeast to include only 11 states; the 13 on our list, less Oklahoma and Texas.

lands, and almost three fourths of its commercial forest lands, are in
the South.

These figures are affected considerably by the inclusion of large
areas of prairie lands in the western parts of Oklahoma and Texas; if
those are omitted the results are changed substantially. On this basis
the percentage figures for the South become: total forest land, 56.5;
commercial forest land, 55.4; noncommercial forest land, 1.1; crop
land, 29.2; pasture and range land, 3.5; and other, 10.8. The significant point here is that, omitting the western parts of Oklahoma and
Texas, somewhat more than half of the land area of the South is in
forest land, almost all of which is in commercial forests.

SOILS

The land area of a region has significance largely in relation to the
quality of the soils which make it up. In an agricultural economy the
soil qualities which are important are those which contribute to its
ability to produce crops, pasture, or forests. On the question of the
quality of southern soils there has been an especially sharp difference
of opinions, probably because the South offers such a wide variety of
soils. There is support for almost any view, depending on whether one
looks at the fertile lands of the Shenandoah Valley and the Mississippi
Delta or at the red hills of Georgia and the wind-eroded plains of
Oklahoma. Some have referred to the South as a Garden of Eden but
one recent committee said that the Cotton South has "soils that with
few but important exceptions are mediocre in quality, highly erosive
under intensive cultivation, and badly damaged by past practices."[2]

It is not possible here to give any adequate description or appraisal
of southern soils nor to compare them in detail with other soils.
Rather, a few general observations must suffice. It is doubtful whether
much of the South ever had deep, fertile, heavy soils such as those
that cover most of the Middle West, although the Delta area is an
exception to this statement. Further, much of the land has a considerable slope, so that erosion started almost as soon as the forests were

2 *Study of Agricultural and Economic Problems of the Cotton Belt,* Hearings before
Special Subcommittee on Cotton of the Committee on Agriculture, House of Representatives, 80th Congress, 1st Session, July 7 and 8, 1947. This volume is composed
principally of nine reports by committees which had worked for two years on various problems of the cotton states. It contains a wealth of data and analysis dealing
with southern problems. It will be referred to frequently in the pages which follow
under the title, *Economic Problems of the Cotton Belt.*

cleared. Fairly heavy rainfall plus the wide prevalence of row crops which leave no cover on the soil during the winter have contributed to the erosion which has washed the top soil from millions of acres of southern crop lands. In addition, the soil over millions of acres along the coast is thin and sandy; it leaches easily and will hold humus only with difficulty. Finally, there are other millions of acres in mountainous areas, and in swamps and bogs along the coast. Some of this is suitable for forests in its present state, other parts of it can profitably be drained, but some parts of it probably can never be put to any profitable use.

The net conclusion is that the South has some areas in which the soil is of top quality, but that in most areas the soil is of medium or poor grade and requires considerable effort to maintain its fertility and to protect it against erosion. For many years the Soil Conservation Service of the U. S. Department of Agriculture has been engaged in an extensive survey to classify the soils of the nation. This survey includes all lands, whether or not in farms, and takes into consideration the principal physical conditions which influence productivity, such as soil type, topography, rainfall, and temperatures. In this classification, the top three grades are considered suitable for continuous cultivation; class I land requires no special practices other than maintenance of fertility and good physical condition, class II land requires moderate use of special practices, while class III land requires intensive use of special practices. Other categories cover land which generally is not suitable for continuous cultivation. Table *II* shows the amounts of southern lands falling into the three top grades

TABLE *II*   CLASSIFICATION OF LAND IN THE SOUTH AND CERTAIN OTHER AREAS[a]

REGION	THOUSANDS OF ACRES			PER CENT OF TOTAL LAND AREA		
	CLASS I	CLASS II	CLASS III	CLASS I	CLASS II	CLASS III
South[b]	22,535	64,903	127,999	4.2	12.0	23.7
Middle States[c]	36,974	58,602	61,274	12.8	20.3	21.3
United States	78,025	203,462	284,182	4.1	10.7	14.9

[a] See text for an explanation of the meaning of the different classes.
[b] In Arkansas, Louisiana, Oklahoma, and Texas only land in farms has been classified; this probably does not affect the figures for land in classes I and II but might cause an understatement of land in class III.
[c] Illinois, Indiana, Iowa, Michigan, Minnesota, Missouri, Ohio, and Wisconsin.
SOURCE: Soil Conservation Service, as adapted in *Economic Problems of the Cotton Belt*, p. 625.

and gives comparative figures for a group of the best farming states of the Middle West and for the United States as a whole.

In comparison with the states of the Middle West, the South has only a third as much of first quality land, a little more than half as much second quality land, and somewhat more of third quality land. In comparison with the whole nation, the South has about the same proportionate amount of land in the first two grades and about 50 per cent more in the third grade. But the percentages for the United States as a whole are based on the total land area, which includes many millions of acres of arid and mountainous land in the West which cannot be used for production of any kind.

In addition to having relatively poorer soils, the South has suffered more from erosion than the Middle West. In 1934, 63.2 per cent of southern land had lost 25 per cent or more of its topsoil by man-induced erosion and gullying, compared with 45.5 per cent in the Middle West and 73.0 for the United States as a whole.[3] In the matter of soil the South is not bankrupt but for a farming area it is distinctly deficient in the best grades of soil and in many, if not most, places it is true that the people must try ". . . with inadequate machinery and equipment to wrest a living from the relatively mediocre, highly erosive, and rapidly deteriorating 6 to 10 inches of topsoil at their disposal."[4]

Because southern soils are relatively poor, southern farmers must buy large amounts of commercial fertilizers. In 1947 they bought over eight million tons of fertilizers, or about 55 per cent of the national total, at a cost of some $375 million.[5] With only about a fourth of the nation's cash farm income, southern farmers must pay from 55 to 60 per cent of the nation's fertilizer bill. While the outlay for fertilizer is generally a wise investment, it nevertheless represents a toll imposed by the low quality of southern soils.

CLIMATE

Perhaps the most distinguishing physical characteristic of the South is its climate. In some respects it is the South's greatest asset, but it also imposes certain disadvantages. The whole question of the effects of climate on the culture and economic activity of the region is a most

---

[3] *Economic Problems of the Cotton Belt*, p. 625.   [4] *Ibid*, p. 562.
[5] Bureau of Agricultural Economics, U. S. Department of Agriculture, *Agricultural Statistics*, 1948, pp. 606, 609.

significant and fascinating study, but one which can be given only summary treatment here.[6]

The climate varies considerably from one part of the region to another but a few generalizations may be made with a fair degree of accuracy. No part of the region is subject to prolonged cold; sub-freezing temperatures usually last only a few days at a time, and the extreme southern parts of the region rarely experience ice or frost. On the other hand, very high temperatures of 100 degrees and over are not so common as they are in the Middle West. In brief, the region has long, warm summers and short, mild winters. The growing season varies from six months at the northern part of the region to eight or nine months at the southern part. Over most of the South outdoor farm work is possible during at least a part of every month of the year.

For agriculture the mild temperatures and the long growing season permit the growing of a wide variety of crops and in the extreme southern parts allow two, and even three, crops to be grown in a season. Perhaps one of the greatest defects in southern agricultural development has been the failure to take advantage of this asset. The two great traditional crops of the South—cotton and tobacco—require the greatest labor during the warm and often humid months of summer, which sap the energy of man and beast, and call for almost no labor during the season which is most suitable for intensive physical exertion.[7] Also, the soils, which are neither frozen nor covered by snow, are extensively eroded by heavy winter rains unless well protected by cover crops.

For industry, the mild temperatures mean lower fuel bills for heating and fewer interruptions to transportation by snow and ice. In the early days, cotton spinning was facilitated by the prevailing high humidity but today humidity is generally regulated artificially. The high humidity is a disadvantage to certain industries, such as flour milling, which requires a dry atmosphere. The long summers, with their warm and humid days, impair worker efficiency to some extent and many industrial plants are now installing air conditioning equipment.

Except for the western parts of Oklahoma and Texas, the whole region has an average annual rainfall of 40 inches or more; some

6 For an excellent treatise on this subject see Rupert B. Vance, *Human Geography of the South,* Chapel Hill, University of North Carolina Press, 1932, especially Part III.   7 Cf. Vance, *op. cit.,* p. 371.

parts have as much as 60 or 70 inches. This is adequate to provide for the needs of almost any crop and it is usually well distributed throughout the year. Because of its great expanse and diverse topographical features, the whole region rarely suffers from climatic extremes at the same time. For example, the year 1930 was a bad drought year for several sections of the South, 13 weather stations reporting precipitation more than 20 per cent below normal. But at the same time seven stations reported above-normal precipitation, two reported a deficiency of less than 10 per cent, and five had deficiencies of between 10 and 20 per cent. Except for Florida and possibly certain parts of Texas, no part of the region is subject to the regular recurrence of destructive storms.

RECREATION FACILITIES

High levels of income and the increasing prevalence of paid vacations are making the entertainment of vacationers a major business. Through a combination of its climate, location, and geographical features, the South is in a peculiarly favorable position to profit from this trend. The phenomenal growth of Florida has resulted, in a large part, from the capitalizing of this opportunity.

To the traveler, the South can offer a wide assortment of attractions. As summer resorts there are the beaches of Virginia and the Carolinas, the Blue Ridge and Appalachian Mountains with the highest peaks east of the Rockies, the caverns of Virginia and Kentucky, and scores of rivers and inland lakes. For winter attractions there are the sand hills of the Carolinas, the beaches of Florida and the Gulf Coast, the hot springs of Arkansas, the ranches of the Rio Grande Valley, and many other watering places throughout the deep South. The fisherman can get deep-sea fishing off the Florida coast and in the Gulf of Mexico or fresh-water fishing in the many rivers and lakes. The hunter can find quail and deer in the lowlands of the Carolinas and Georgia, deer, bear, and wild boars in the mountains of North Carolina and Tennessee, and other kinds of game in other sections. Those interested in historic spots will be attracted by Williamsburg, Charleston, New Orleans, and many historic battlefields throughout the South.

With its extensive frontage on the Atlantic Ocean and the Gulf of Mexico, the South contains more than half of the nation's coastline, including nearly all that is suitable for winter resorts. Its mountains offer the best scenery in eastern America and are within easy reach of the great centers of population. It has millions of acres of submarginal land which can be, and some of which have been, bought cheaply for private game preserves and hunting estates. With all these assets the South should develop a business here which would rival cotton as a source of income. A survey made in Tennessee in 1941 indicated that receipts from tourists in that state for the one year were in excess of $100,000,000.[8] At the present time, with much higher prices and far more travel, the receipts for the whole region must be many times that amount.

MINERALS

In minerals, as in several other fields, the South has a wide variety of assets and some of these assets are substantial. But many minerals are present only in token amounts or in qualities too poor to permit profitable use.

There are two ways of indicating the importance of minerals to a region. One is by the use of figures on the volume and value of annual production. The other is by the use of figures on estimated reserve deposits. The annual figures do not indicate how soon the deposits will be exhausted. Further, when operations are on a small scale, governmental agencies frequently have to withhold data for a particular state to keep from disclosing data for an individual company. The figures on estimated reserves are necessarily subject to wide margins of error; they usually do not indicate availability under different price levels and technological conditions, and, unless accompanied by voluminous technical details, do not indicate the quality of the reserves.

Table *III* shows, for 1945, the production in the South of all minerals which were economically significant. In value, petroleum accounted for almost exactly half of the total of $2,615,713,000. The total for fuels, including petroleum, natural gas, natural gasoline, and coal, was over 85 per cent of the value of all mineral production. Total southern production was 32.1 per cent of the United States total, a figure somewhat larger than the South's proportion of land or population, and one which represented a considerable relative increase from

8 Cited in *Economic Problems of the Cotton Belt,* p. 579.

TABLE *III*   MINERAL PRODUCTION IN THE SOUTH, 1945

MINERAL	UNIT OF VOLUME	VOLUME	VALUE (THOUSANDS OF DOLLARS)	PER CENT OF U. S. PRODUCTION BY VOLUME	BY VALUE
Barite	1	371	2,990	53.3	55.9
Bauxite	2	943	5,494	96.1	97.6
Cement	3	16,969	27,819	15.7	15.9
Clay Products	—	—	19,411	—	22.5
Clay, Raw	1	6,999	24,550	37.6	61.7
Coal	1	113,246	372,522	19.7	21.0
Feldspar (Crude)	2	177	1,043	47.5	51.6
Iron Ore	2	7,470	18,070	8.5	7.4
Lead	1	17	2,939	4.8	6.4
Lime	1	770	5,337	13.0	11.6
Magnesium Compounds	5	171,936	2,818	31.9	29.1
Natural Gas	4	2,708,070	439,406	69.9	53.5
Natural Gasoline and Liquified Petroleum Gases	6	3,256,589	134,927	69.7	68.7
Petroleum	3	1,082,071	1,318,001	63.2	63.0
Phosphate Rock	2	5,527	22,326	95.2	93.2
Salt	1	2,969	7,957	19.3	17.3
Sand and Gravel	1	33,818	24,742	17.7	20.5
Stone	1	32,366	38,889	21.1	21.7
Sulfur	2	3,833	61,300	100.0	100.0
Zinc	1	89	27,528	19.1	34.3
Total Mineral Production	—	—	2,615,713	—	32.1

Code for Units of Volume: 1—thousands of short tons; 2—thousands of long tons; 3—thousands of barrels; 4—millions of cubic feet; 5—thousands of pounds; 6—thousands of gallons.
SOURCE: Compiled from *Minerals Yearbook*, 1945.

the 24.5 per cent of 1929. This increase was probably due in part to the great emphasis on fuel production during the war.

TABLE *IV*   MINERAL PRODUCTION IN THE SOUTH BY STATES, 1945
(*In Thousands of Dollars*)

STATE	VALUE	STATE	VALUE
Alabama	111,158	North Carolina	14,457
Arkansas	62,772	Oklahoma	282,859
Florida	24,995	South Carolina	5,043
Georgia	19,393	Tennessee	60,199
Kentucky	268,858	Texas	1,360,694
Louisiana	298,842	Virginia	84,081
Mississippi	21,816		
		Total	2,615,167

SOURCE: *Minerals Yearbook*, 1945.

Table *IV* shows mineral production by states. More than half of the production was in Texas, while the four states Kentucky, Louisiana, Oklahoma, and Texas accounted for almost 85 per cent of the total. Coal was the principal product in Kentucky, while petroleum and natural gas dominated the figures in the other three states. In Alabama the chief products were coal and iron ore; in Virginia it was coal, in Florida, phosphate rock, and in Mississippi, petroleum and natural gas. In the other states production was distributed among many minor minerals such as the clays, sand and gravel, and stone.

It is exceedingly difficult to present, within brief compass, any discussion of mineral reserves which is significant and at the same time accurate. Bare figures alone are not sufficient since they must be based upon many assumptions and limited by various qualifications. Some reserves or possible reserves have not been surveyed. Where reserves do exist their economic significance or "recoverability" will depend on the state of technology for processing them, the price level, their location in respect to markets, and other factors.[9] Within recent years the Bureau of Mines and the Geological Survey have produced the most comprehensive survey of our mineral resources, especially the reserves of strategic minerals, that we ever had.[10] Nevertheless, those agencies frequently refer to the incomplete and unsatisfactory nature of our knowledge of mineral resources and impose many quali-

TABLE *V*   ESTIMATED RESERVES OF CERTAIN MINERALS IN THE SOUTH
(*As of 1944*)

MINERAL	UNIT OF MEASUREMENT	AMOUNT	PER CENT OF U. S.
Bauxite	Millions of long tons	128	100.0
Coal	Billions of short tons	928	22.4
Iron Ore	Millions of long tons	2,061	37.6
Natural Gas	Billions of cubic feet	118,297	80.0
Petroleum	Billions of barrels	14.1	70.2
Phosphate Rock	Millions of long tons	5,206	40.0
Sulfur (Native)	" " " "	60	100.0
Titanium (In TiO$_2$ content)	Thousands of short tons	6,680	75.8

SOURCE: Computed from *Mineral Position of the United States*. Some of the data are partly estimated.

9 As industry expands in the South, it should increase the "availability" of some southern minerals. With industry providing a nearby market, it should be feasible to extract certain minerals which could not be profitably worked if they had to be shipped a long distance to market.
10 *Mineral Position of the United States*, printed as an appendix in *Investigation of National Resources Hearings* before a Subcommittee of the Committee on Public Lands, U. S. Senate, 80th Congress, 1st Session, May, 1947.

fications on their findings. A regional study of this kind is faced with an additional difficulty in that many of the figures are not broken down by states.

Subject to the above limitations, an attempt has been made in Table *V* to compute estimated reserves of a few of the more important mineral resources of the South. They should be accepted only as rough indications and not as exact amounts.

Since petroleum accounts for about half of the mineral production of the South, the reserves of that mineral are especially important. The figures show that the South had some 14 billion barrels of proven petroleum reserves, or about 70 per cent of the national total. In recent years production in the whole country has ranged from 1.7 to 2.0 billion barrels, with over 60 per cent, or well over a billion barrels, coming from the South. The ratio of southern production to the total has been rising; from 1859 to 1944 it was 56.1 per cent; in 1939, it was 60.5 per cent; in 1944, 62.5 per cent; and in 1946, 63.6 per cent.

There has been much controversy over the adequacy of our petroleum reserves and how long they will last. No attempt will be made here to settle that controversy. On the basis of the present rate of consumption, which is rising steadily and rapidly, present proven reserves are sufficient for only about 15 years. On the other hand, new reserves are constantly being discovered and for the past 20 years proven reserves have risen steadily despite rapidly rising consumption. In this connection, a few excerpts from the study mentioned above are pertinent:

> The experience of the past 5 years indicates that it is becoming increasingly difficult and costly to find new reserves.
> In each year from 1937 to 1943, the number of oil wells completed and their initial daily production have declined, although this trend was reversed in 1944 . . . .
> Much oil in new fields remains to be discovered and in deeper strata of known fields; but the number of new fields to be found, whatever they may be, is definitely limited, and each newly found field leaves one less to be discovered.[11]

With natural gas the South has about 70 per cent of current production and about 80 per cent of estimated reserves. At present rates of production the known reserves would last about 45 or 50 years.

11 *Ibid,* pp. 277, 282.

Since the war several pipe lines have been built for, or converted to, the transmission of gas and consumption has increased greatly.

Regarding petroleum and natural gas there are several basic facts which are of vital interest to the nation and especially to the South. First, in recent years there has been an enormous increase in consumption, occasioned to a considerable extent by the substitution of these commodities for coal. Several factors have caused this substitution; higher consumer incomes, strikes in the coal mines, technological developments calling for the use of liquid fuels or gas, and controls or pricing practices which held down the prices of oil and gas below their competitive levels. Second, oil and gas are increasingly important industrial raw materials for the production of a great many goods, such as synthetic rubber. Third, as fuels, oil and gas are of vital importance to the great and growing industrial system of Texas and adjoining states. Since there is very little coal or water power in that area, that system would be severely handicapped if those two fuels should become exhausted.

The South has ample reserves of iron ore, with some two billion tons, or nearly 40 per cent of the national total. Again, these are the amounts considered usable with present practices. Two characteristics limit the value of southern ores. First, none of them is equal in quality to the best grades of Lake Superior ore. Second, most of them are taken from underground mines whereas the Lake Superior ores are mined from open pits.[12] However, it seems to be fairly well established that the best grades of Lake Superior ore are approaching exhaustion. When they are gone it will be necessary either to use lower-grade domestic ores or to import ores from abroad. In either case the South will have a good opportunity to profit from the change. If poorer ores are used, the South has a good supply of second grade ores and moderate amounts of steel-making equipment in Alabama, Kentucky, Tennessee, and Texas. If imported ores are used, the South can offer good water transportation, good sites, and abundant supplies of the other raw materials which go into steel.

While the South has only about 40 per cent of the country's phosphate rock, it accounts for over 90 per cent of the current production.

[12] This not only increases their costs but it limits the possibility of expanding production in time of emergency. Thus, while the production of iron ore in Alabama increased somewhat during the war, it did not keep pace with the increase in the country as a whole; as a percentage of national production, Alabama's production fell steadily from 11.5 in 1939 to 7.3 in 1944. *Ibid*, p. 253.

This is one case in which the South benefits from its location and transportation facilities. The principal deposits outside the region are in Idaho and Utah. The chief use of phosphate is in fertilizer, and fertilizers have been used most in the South. Also, water transportation is important here and the Florida fields have an advantage in that respect. As the use of fertilizers west of the Mississippi increases, the western deposits will probably be developed further.

Titanium, a mineral derived from several sources, assumed considerable importance during the recent war. It is important chiefly as a source of white pigment for paints and many other products. It is also used as an alloy for steel and aluminum, and for other industrial purposes. More than half of the nation's reserves are in Virginia, with small amounts in Florida and North Carolina.

Reserves of coal, the South's third most important mineral, are sufficient to last for an indefinite time and apparently the South can expect a continued and stable production of this item if demand holds up. The South has all the nation's reserves of bauxite and native sulfur which are usable under normal peacetime conditions and with present techniques, although in both cases there are alternate sources which can be developed if the need is sufficiently great.

In summary, the South has a wide variety of mineral resources, several being of major importance. Two of the most important— petroleum and natural gas—are being continuously depleted. An increasing industrial demand in the region will probably lead to increased production from known reserves and perhaps to the discovery and development of new reserves.

WATER RESOURCES

The combination of the South's heavy rainfall, long coast line, and many rivers gives it an abundance of water resources. These are important to both industry and agriculture as a transportation route, as a source of power and food, and as a supply of an important raw material to industry.

Water still provides the cheapest transportation route, especially for many of the heavy raw materials which the South produces. No other large section of the country has such extensive facilities for water transportation as the South; in 1929 it had 61.4 per cent of the nation's navigable waterways. Nine of the states reach tidewater, most of them for an extensive frontage, and have five of the best harbors in the country—Norfolk, Charleston, Mobile, New Orleans, and Houston-Galveston. These states have direct access to international shipping, deep-water coastal shipping, and shallow-water shipping over the Inland Waterway and the numerous bays, gulfs, and sounds. Five of the states are served by the Mississippi River and its major tributaries. Oklahoma is the only state which is not on the coast or on a major stream, and even it has several good-sized rivers.

Much of the South's water-power potential is due to the unique coincidence that one of the highest parts of the southern Appalachians —that part just north of the point where the three states of Georgia, North Carolina and Tennessee come together—has a very heavy rainfall, frequently exceeding 70 inches per year. As this water rolls down to the Atlantic Ocean or the Gulf of Mexico it creates a great potential horsepower.

In 1941 it was estimated that the southern states had 5,555,000 horsepower of potential water power available 90 per cent of the time, which was over a third of all potential water power east of the Rocky Mountains. To utilize this power there were installed in southern states, on January 1, 1946, 4,455,000 kilowatts of hydrogenerating capacity; this was 30 per cent of all hydrogenerating capacity in the United States and represented an increase of 111 per cent over 1929. During the same interval hydrogenerating capacity outside the South increased by 72 per cent. Total generating capacity in the South in 1946 was 10,428,000 kilowatts, or approximately 21 per cent of the national total.

The great increase in southern generating capacity between 1929 and 1946 was largely due, of course, to the development of the Tennessee Valley Authority. This brought a large reduction in electric rates and was directly responsible for the location of large aluminum plants and other important industries in the Valley. Although rates had dropped considerably before 1940, they declined further after that date; the average revenue per kilowatt hour sold to commercial and industrial firms in the South was 1.44 cents in 1940 and 1.16 in 1944. For the whole United States the comparable figures were 1.61 cents and 1.29 cents. On rural sales of electricity the figures for these two years were: South, 4.04 and 1.64; United States, 2.48 and 2.45.[13]

[13] *Economic Problems of the Cotton Belt*, p. 676; *Statistical Abstract of the United States*, 1946, p. 480.

This supply of cheap and abundant power is an important asset to both industry and agriculture. Water resources are important in two other respects. Before the war they supported in the South a commercial fishing industry which employed about 40,000 people, and produced annually some 800 million pounds of seafood which was worth about $23 million. Finally, an abundant and reliable supply of water is essential to many industries, especially chemical industries of the kinds which are locating more frequently in the South. In some cases the purity of the water is a controlling factor, as was true with the paper company which located at Brevard, N. C., to produce cigarette paper just before the war. That plant was located at the edge of a large national forest and was assured of the volume and purity of the water it needed. This case well illustrates the importance to industry of both water and forests.

FOREST RESOURCES

It was noted above that, except for the western parts of Oklahoma and Texas, over 55 per cent of the land area of the South is classified as forest land. This fact, combined with the abundant rainfall and the long growing season, could hardly fail to produce a large amount of timber in the South. Most virgin forests were cut over years ago, but growing conditions are so favorable that most of the cut-over land, almost unaided by man, has restocked itself and is now covered by a substantial amount of second-growth, or even in some cases, third-growth, timber.

The South has over 40 per cent of all commercial forest area and almost half of the saw-timber area.[14] Because the southern lands have been cut over, however, they contain only about 30 per cent of the total timber stand. Only with respect to the hardwoods, in which they have a little more than half of the total, do the southern forests compare favorably on a volume basis. The striking advantages of the South show up most clearly in the figures for annual growth; the South receives well over half of the total growth in softwoods and about half for the hardwoods. In both cases there is a large advantage in trees of saw-timber size. The South's saw timber is being rapidly exhausted, while growth and drain are about equal for timber of all

14 See Chapter XI for statistical data on forests.

sizes. In 1945, the South produced a little more than a third of the nation's softwood lumber and almost two thirds of the hardwood. In the consumption of pulp wood, which still represents a comparatively small part of all timber used, the South had nearly half of the national total. No figure is readily available, and perhaps none can be supplied, of the value, on the stump, of the timber harvested in the South each year. In 1948, the estimated *cash* income received by *farmers* for timber products was $151 million. The value of the timber products they used in the form of fuel, fence posts, lumber, etc. was probably even greater than that. In addition, there was the value of timber harvested by owners other than farmers. Altogether, these make timber one of our major crops, although as yet we have put little effort into cultivating it.

Naval stores, principally turpentine and rosin, are forest products unique to the South and come mainly from Georgia and northern Florida. Before the war, southern production of these items was normally about two thirds of world production and ranged from $40 to $50 million in value per year. From 40 to 50 per cent of the production was exported.

Although the South has large forest resources, they could easily be much larger. The principal obstacles to a greatly increased forest yield are several major forms of waste. The first is the waste due to poor stands of trees or understocking. Most people who travel through the South gain an impression of millions of acres of idle land, usually containing a few scattered trees, often of the scurb variety. Statistics confirm this impression; the South has nearly three fourths of the poorly stocked commercial forest lands of the country, amounting to over 54 million acres. In addition, much land in the other categories is far from adequately stocked. The Forest Service estimates that not over one fourth of southern forests are well stocked (defined as having 70 per cent or more of the stand required for full stocking).[15] This form of waste is especially important because it means that we are allowing the forces of nature, which could be producing extra millions of cubic feet of timber for us each year, to go entirely to waste. There are some signs of improvement; the character of forest management is improving and the number of seedlings planted annually in southern states is increasing steadily and rapidly.

15 Forest Service, U. S. Dept. of Agriculture, *Gaging the Timber Resources of the United States, Washington,* 1946, p. 22.

A second form of waste is the loss due to fire, insects, and disease. Fire losses are notoriously heavy in the South. Most of the fires are preventable and losses could be cut sharply if more funds were available for fire control. With 42 per cent of the nation's forest area and some of the most difficult problems to contend with, the South spent in 1945 only about 28 per cent of the funds going for forest fire control.

A third form of waste is that incurred in harvesting and processing timber products. The Forest Service estimates that 35 per cent of all timber cut is wasted completely and another 22 per cent is used for fuel—much of it inefficiently.[16] These losses are due to poor cutting practices, wasteful and inefficient manufacturing processes, failure to use by-products, and other similar practices. The presence of many small sawmills and processing plants is a major cause of this waste.

On any basis of comparison, its forests are one of the South's greatest assets. In the growing of timber the South has outstanding advantages, including climate, location, topography, and transportation facilities. Up to the present, southern forests have not received the attention, the effort, nor the funds their importance would justify.[17]

TRANSPORTATION FACILITIES

In addition to its extensive system of water transportation, the South has 63,460 miles of railroads, which is 27.9 per cent of the total for the United States. Also it had, at the end of 1946, 146,900 miles of hard-surfaced paved rural highways, or 29.4 per cent of the national total. It will be noticed that in both these cases the South's proportion of the mileage is very close to its proportion of total land area. These mileage figures, however, do not make any allowance for extra tracks of railroad or extra highway lanes. If these were included the South's proportion would probably drop somewhat.

In 1947 the 13 southern states spent for highway construction and maintenance $430,100,000 or 34.4 per cent of the total for the country. At the same time the number of motor vehicles registered in these states was 8,830,400, which was only 23.3 per cent of the national total. These facts largely explain the high motor fuel taxes in the South. Roughly those taxes are 50 per cent higher in the South than

16 Forest Service, U. S. Dept. of Agriculture, *Wood Waste in the United States,* Washington, 1947, p. 1.
17 See Chapter XI for a more detailed consideration of forest resources and policies.

in the rest of the country; the median rates were 6 cents per gallon in the South and 4 cents per gallon elsewhere, and the weighted average rates probably would not be far from those figures. It is more difficult to compare registration fees for motor vehicles, but from some computations which have been made, it appears that those fees are also somewhat higher in the South.[18] With smaller registrations and the prevailing low incomes, it is inevitable that these costs should be higher in southern states if highway expenditures are to be maintained at levels comparable to the rest of the country.

SUMMARY

The final picture which emerges from this thumb-nail sketch of the South's physical resources is a fairly encouraging one. Soils present the least encouraging part of the picture, partly because of relatively poor initial endowments, partly because of the erosion and misuse which have occurred during the past two centuries. In minerals the South's principal dependence is on petroleum and it appears that the reserves of that mineral will be substantially depleted during the next 20 years. The region has abundant reserves of coal and substantial supplies of iron ore, sulfur, phosphate rock, and several other less important minerals. Land transportation facilities are maintained approximately on a parity with the rest of the country even though at considerable effort. The South has clear and substantial advantages in its climate, its attractions for vacationers, its water resources, and its forests. If existing assets are used intelligently and if the natural advantages are exploited fully, the South should be able to bring its income up more nearly to the national average.

[18] *Economic Problems of the Cotton Belt,* pp. 599, 681–83.

II HUMAN RESOURCES

A functioning economy consists of people using natural resources and the equipment which they have constructed or acquired to carry on economic production. The preceding chapter surveyed the natural resources of the southern region. Capital goods also were mentioned in that chapter and will be discussed further in later chapters. The purpose of this chapter is to give a brief survey of the people who inhabit the South; their numbers, occupations, and characteristics.

POPULATION GROWTH SINCE 1900

First, it might be well to look at some of the longer-term population movements in the South. Table *VI* summarizes the figures for the growth of total population, distributed between white and Negro, since 1900 and gives comparative figures for the Non-South.

From 1900 to 1948, the population of the South increased from slightly less than 22 million to almost 40 million. The latter figure was approximately the same as the figure for the total population of the United States in 1870. Since 1900, the South's portion of the nation's population has varied from 27.2 per cent to 28.8 per cent. These figures are remarkably close to the 28.3 per cent which represents the South's part of the total land area of the country. This means that the density of population here is about the same as in the remainder of the country as a whole. Again, however, it must be remembered that large areas of the Non-South are almost uninhabitable; if these were omitted, the South would have a somewhat lower population density than the remaining regions as a whole. The South, however, is predominantly a rural area and its population density is high in comparison with rural areas in the rest of the country. In 1940, the density of rural population (using rural population and total land area less "other" in Table *I*) was 31.4 per square miles in the South and 16.8 in the Non-South. If the Mountain States, which include most of the semiarid land, are omitted the figure for the Non-South would be 27.4 per square mile.

As noted below, birth rates in the South are, and have been, considerably above the rates in other regions. Yet despite this fact, in each of the first three decades of this century the rate of population growth in the South was slightly less than in the remainder of the nation. As a result the South's proportion of the total population declined. Between 1930 and 1940, this trend was sharply reversed because of the drastic decline in migration. But during World War II migration was heavier than ever before and in the eight years from 1940 to 1948 the South lost more migrants, both absolutely and rela-

TABLE *VI* POPULATION OF THE SOUTH, 1900–1948, COMPARED WITH POPULATION OF NON-SOUTHERN STATES

(In Thousands)

YEAR	SOUTH	PER CENT INCREASE	NON-SOUTHERN STATES	PER CENT INCREASE	SOUTH AS PER CENT OF TOTAL U.S. INCREASE
1900					
White[1]	14,386	—	52,775	—	21.4
Negro	7,527	—	1,307	—	85.2
Total	21,913	—	54,082	—	28.8
1910					
White	18,012	25.2	64,132	21.5	21.9
Negro	8,327	10.6	1,501	14.8	84.7
Total	26,339	20.2	65,633	21.4	28.6
1920					
White	21,111	17.2	74,136	15.6	22.2
Negro	8,441	1.4	2,022	34.7	80.7
Total	29,552	12.2	76,159	16.0	28.0
1930					
White	24,996	18.3	85,918	15.9	22.5
Negro	8,806	4.3	3,085	52.6	74.1
Total	33,772	14.3	89,003	16.9	27.5
1940					
White	27,751	11.2	91,053	6.0	23.4
Negro	9,262	5.2	3,604	16.8	72.0
Total	37,013	9.6	94,656	6.4	28.1
1948[2]					
Total	39,674	7.2	106,439	12.4	27.2

[1] "White" includes all except those classed as Negro.
[2] Estimate for total population excluding armed forces overseas.
SOURCE: Compiled from reports of the Bureau of the Census.

tively, than in any previous decade. Estimates of the population for July 1, 1948, give the South the lowest proportion of the national population since 1900.

Migration from the South has been heaviest among the Negroes and consequently their numbers have increased slowly in the South. In every decade southern whites have had a higher rate of growth than whites outside the South. The result has been a slowly but steadily changing composition of the population in the direction of more whites and fewer Negroes. Table *VII* summaries these changes for the four decades.

CHART *I*   POPULATION OF THE SOUTH (MILLIONS)

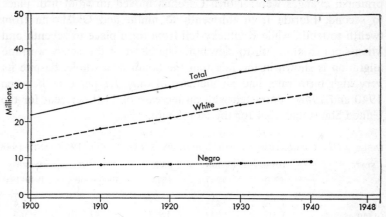

TABLE *VII*   POPULATION CHANGES IN THE SOUTH AND NON-SOUTH, 1900–1940

YEAR	SOUTH			NON-SOUTH		
	WHITE[1]	NEGRO	TOTAL	WHITE[1]	NEGRO	TOTAL
		(*In Thousands*)			(*In Thousands*)	
1900	14,386	7,527	21,913	52,775	1,307	54,082
1940	27,751	9,262	37,013	91,053	3,604	94,656
Per Cent Increase	93.	23.	69.	73.	176	75.
Composition of Population—per cent:						
1900	65.7	34.3	100.0	97.6	2.4	100.0
1940	75.0	25.0	100.0	96.2	3.8	100.0

[1] "White" includes all not classed as Negro.
SOURCE: Compiled from reports of the Bureau of the Census.

Although the whole region showed an increase of 69 per cent from 1900 to 1940, the rate of growth varied widely from one part of the region to another. World War II caused still further changes, most of them accentuating the differences which had previously existed. Exceptions to this generalization are found in Oklahoma, Tennessee, and Virginia. Table *VIII* shows that between 1900 and 1940, one state had an increase of less than 40 per cent while six others had increases of between 40 and 50 per cent; all of these except Tennessee and Virginia experienced declines, or very small increases, in population between 1940 and 1948. Oklahoma was the only state which had an unusually large increase between 1900 and 1940 and a decline after 1940. With the exception of Texas, in first place and Tennessee in fourth, every state has changed its relative position since 1900. The principal changes were: North Carolina moved up from fifth place to second, Florida from thirteenth to ninth, and Oklahoma from twelfth to tenth, while Kentucky fell from third place to seventh and Mississippi from eighth to eleventh. The effect of the heavy wartime migration is shown in the fact that the South as a whole, despite its very high birth rate, had an increase of only 7.2 per cent between 1940 and 1948, contrasted with an increase of 11.0 per cent for the United States and 12.4 for the Non-South.

TABLE *VIII*   POPULATION OF THE SOUTH BY STATES, 1900, 1940, AND 1948

STATE	TOTAL POPULATION		(000)	PER CENT	INCREASE
	1900	1940	1948	1900–1940	1940–1948
Alabama	1,829	2,833	2,901	55	2.4
Arkansas	1,312	1,949	1,937	49	−0.6
Florida	529	1,897	2,430	259	28.1
Georgia	2,216	3,124	3,167	41	1.4
Kentucky	2,147	2,846	2,858	33	0.4
Louisiana	1,382	2,364	2,591	71	9.6
Mississippi	1,551	2,184	2,114	41	−3.2
North Carolina	1,894	3,572	3,798	89	6.3
Oklahoma	790	2,336	2,295	196	−1.8
South Carolina	1,340	1,900	1,982	42	4.3
Tennessee	2,021	2,916	3,179	44	9.0
Texas	3,049	6.415	7,371	110	14.9
Virginia	1,854	2,678	3,051	44	13.9
Total South	21,913	37,013	39,674	69	7.2

SOURCE: Computed from reports of the Bureau of the Census.

BIRTH AND DEATH RATES

Traditionally, birth rates have been high in the South. This fact has often been pointed out and discussed so it is not necessary to labor it

TABLE *IX* BIRTH RATES PER 1000 POPULATION IN THE SOUTH AND THE NON-
SOUTH FOR CERTAIN YEARS

(*Adjusted for Underregistration*)

ITEM	1930	1937	1940
Median Rate:			
South	26.6	24.1	25.1
Non-South	19.2	17.5	18.4
United States Average	20.7	18.5	19.4
Number of Southern States			
above U. S. Average	11*	12*	13

* Texas not reported.
SOURCE: Computed from the Bureau of the Census, *Vital Statistics Rates in the United States, 1900–1940*, Table AG, p. 101.

further here.[1] Table *IX* gives a summary of the data on birth rates by states for three recent years. It shows that, on the average, southern states had a birth rate of about 6.5 per 1,000 above non-southern states, or about a third higher. There are several reason for this but perhaps the two that are most important are: (1) the average age of the southern population is lower than that of the Non-South, which means that there are more women of childbearing age per 1,000 of population; and (2) the population is still predominantly rural and birth rates are almost always higher in rural areas. During the period covered by these figures, which saw a decline and then a rise in birth rates throughout the country, there was no noticeable tendency for the differential between the South and the Non-South in birth rates to change.

It is more difficult to present an accurate account of comparative changes in mortality. The figures for crude death rates would seem to indicate not only that the South has lower rates but also that it has made substantially more progress in lowering the rates since 1930 than has the rest of the nation. Table *X* gives the data on crude rates.

These crude rates, however, are somewhat misleading. The South has, as is shown below, a substantially younger population than the rest of the country. For that reason it would be normal to expect a lower death rate. To afford a valid comparison, the data must be adjusted to take into account the varying age composition of the population. When the rates are so adjusted they are known as "Age-

[1] See, for example, J. J. Spengler, "Population Problems in the South," *The Southern Economic Journal*, April, July, and October, 1937; and Rupert B. Vance, *All These People*, Chapel Hill, University of North Carolina Press, 1945.

TABLE *X*   CRUDE DEATH RATES PER 1000 POPULATION IN THE SOUTH AND THE
NON-SOUTH FOR CERTAIN YEARS

ITEM	1930	1937	1940	1944
Median Rate:				
South	11.5	11.0	10.4	9.3
Non-South	11.5	11.5	11.1	10.7
United States Average	11.3	11.3	10.8	10.6
No. Southern States				
below U. S. Average	4	9	10	12

SOURCE: Computed from reports of the Bureau of the Census.

Adjusted" or "Standardized" rates. The Bureau of the Census has
adjusted the rates for two of the years given and they are shown, by
race, in Table *XI*.

TABLE *XI*   AGE-ADJUSTED DEATH RATES PER 1000 POPULATION FOR THE SOUTH
AND THE NON-SOUTH, BY RACES, 1930 AND 1940

ITEM	1930		1940	
	SOUTH	NON-SOUTH	SOUTH	NON-SOUTH
Median Rate				
All Races:	14.4	11.9	12.3	10.2
White	11.7	11.5	10.3	10.1
Nonwhite	20.2	21.8	16.8	16.1
U. S. Average Rates:				
All Races		12.5		10.7
White		11.7		10.2
Nonwhite		20.1		16.2

SOURCE: Computed from the Bureau of the Census, "Age-Adjusted Death Rates in the
United States, 1900–1940," Table *1*.

It will be noted from this Table that the South, instead of having
a lower death rate, has a somewhat higher rate than the Non-South,
although the South made about the same progress as the remainder
of the country between 1930 and 1940 in lowering the rate. Further,
the difference in the rates for the white population in the two regions
is so small as to be insignificant.

In many respects the best measure of mortality are the figures on
life expectancy or "average future lifetime" at different ages. The U. S.
Public Health Service has computed life tables showing such figures
based on the experience from 1930 to 1939. Table *XII* gives a few
of those figures. For the region as a whole and for each race and sex
separately, life expectancy is almost, if not entirely, as great as in the
rest of the country. In the South Central states it is greater for the

nonwhite population at all ages and for whites after the first year. In the South Atlantic states it is slightly lower at nearly all ages for both races but a considerable part of this is due to the heavy infant mortality in the first year, and notable progress is being made in reducing this.[2]

TABLE *XII*   LIFE EXPECTANCY IN YEARS BY RACE AND SEX FOR SELECTED AREAS AND AGES IN THE UNITED STATES, 1930–1939

	SOUTH ATLANTIC	EAST SOUTH CENTRAL	WEST SOUTH CENTRAL	UNITED STATES
At Birth:				
White Males	59.6	60.6	60.3	60.6
White Females	64.2	64.2	64.4	64.6
Nonwhite Males	48.2	50.7	52.2	49.4
Nonwhite Females	50.9	52.9	54.4	52.1
At Age 3:				
White Males	61.5	62.4	62.2	62.0
White Females	65.4	65.3	65.7	65.3
Nonwhite Males	51.7	53.5	55.2	52.7
Nonwhite Females	53.5	54.9	56.4	54.5
At Age 40:				
White Males	29.2	30.5	30.4	29.6
White Females	32.4	32.8	33.5	32.3
Nonwhite Males	23.7	25.6	26.5	24.6
Nonwhite Females	25.4	26.5	27.6	26.1

SOURCE: U. S. Public Health Service, *United States Abridged Life Tables, 1939.* Washington, 1947, p. 314.

The high figures for life expectancy in the South are somewhat remarkable in view of the low income of the region and its deficiencies in doctors, nurses, hospital beds, and medical facilities generally. Probably the rural nature of the population is the most important factor accounting for this since rural areas almost invariably have a more favorable mortality rate than urban areas.[3]

While interregional comparisons by race and sex are not unfavorable to the South, it is true that the figures of life expectancy for non-

2 Between 1945 and 1947, infant mortality rates were reduced 18.8 per cent in the South Atlantic States, 16.1 per cent in the East South Central States, and 13.2 per cent in the West South Central States, compared with 13.9 per cent in the whole United States. U. S. Public Health Service, "Infant Mortality by Race and by Urban and Rural Areas," (Vol. 31, No. 12) September 20, 1949. Washington, 1949, p. 152.
3 Cf. L. I. Dublin, A. J. Lotka, and M. Spiegelman, *Length of Life,* rev. ed., New York, The Ronald Press, 1949, pp. 72–79. Vance observes that the "remarkable gains in the preservation of life during the past generation have advanced the urban population to the point occupied by rural people at the beginning of the century." *Economic Problems of the Cotton Belt,* p. 927.

whites are substantially lower than those for whites. Since the South has a much larger nonwhite population than the rest of the country it follows that any composite figure for life expectancy for the region as a whole would be low in comparison with the Non-South. In other words, while in most parts of the South Negroes have a higher life expectancy than in the Non-South, the large proportion of Negroes in the South pulls down the region's over-all average because their expectancy is lower than that for the whites.

The combination of high birth rates and moderate death rates gives the South a high rate of natural increase of population which has led some to refer to the region as the "Seed-Bed of the Nation." Vance has made some computations for 1930 to show the "Index of Net Reproduction per Generation" for the native white population in different parts of the country.[4] His results are as follows: Southeast, 1.27; Southwest, 1.25; Middle States, 1.08; Northeast, 1.00; and Far West, 0.79.

The operation of these forces was accentuated and dramatically portrayed during World War II. Birth rates were up, death rates continued to decline, and migration was on a scale never before reached. According to Census estimates, between April 1, 1940 and July 1, 1948 the states of the South had a natural increase in population (excess of birth over deaths) of 5,762,000 out of a national total of 13,982,000.[5] With about 28 per cent of the population in 1940, the South accounted for 41.2 per cent of the nation's total natural increase in population. Net migration from the region was equal to a little more than half of the natural increase—2,960,000—and 2,467,000 went to increase the civilian population of the region. The remainder, about 335,000, represented the net loss to the armed forces.

Perhaps it is not too far-fetched to suggest that the South's principal —and most expensive—crop is its crop of human beings. In normal and boom years this crop is "harvested" when the South "gives away" to the rest of the nation, through migration, thousands of young men and women, principally between the ages of 25 and 35. In depression years the "market" for these "free goods" fails and the South is forced to maintain the excess until demand revives. These considerations

[4] R. B. Vance, *All These People*, Chapel Hill, University of North Carolina Press, 1945, p. 92.
[5] Bureau of the Census, "Current Population Reports," Series p–25, No. 26, August 5, 1949, p. 4.

have been used in the past as justifications for requests that the Federal Government should give special help to southern states in educating their children and caring for their unemployed.

SOME CHARACTERISTICS OF THE POPULATION

The South's population is almost entirely a native-born population. In 1940, of the 11,419,000 foreign-born white residents in the United States, only 453,000 were in the South. This was only 1.2 per cent of the total population and less than 2 per cent of the white population. A large majority of white southerners are descendants from Anglo-Saxon and Western European ancestors.

The southern population is still predominantly rural, although the trend toward cities goes on continually. In 1940 only 34.8 per cent of the southern population was classed by the Bureau of the Census as urban, compared with 65.0 per cent of the population of the Non-South. Vance points out that throughout the depression of the 1930's urbanization and industrialization continued in the South, while it halted in other parts of the country and some of the larger urban centers even lost population.[6] About half of the six million farms of the United States are in the South and the preponderantly rural nature of the population is one of the most important characteristics of the region.

Because of the high birth rates and the normally heavy migration of men and women between the ages of 25 and 35, the population of the South is, on the average, considerably younger than that of the rest of the nation. In 1940 the median ages for the three census divisions which make up the South were, respectively, 24.7, 25.5, and 26.2 years, contrasted with 29.0 for the whole nation, 31.0 for the Middle Atlantic states and 32.8 for the Far West. Table *XIII* permits a fuller comparison on this point by giving age profiles of the whole population of the South and Non-South for 1930 and 1940.

Several interesting and significant points stand out in this Table. First, the sharp drop in the birth rate in both regions is reflected in the smaller figures in the lower age-groups for 1940. Second, the South has a substantially larger percentage than the Non-South in every age-group up to 25 years. Third, the 1940 figures for the South

6 R. B. Vance, *All These People,* Chapel Hill, University of North Carolina Press, 1945, p. 35.

TABLE *XIII* AGE COMPOSITION OF THE POPULATION, SOUTH AND NON-SOUTH
1930 AND 1940

(*In Percentages*)

AGE-GROUP IN YEARS	1930		1940	
	SOUTH	NON-SOUTH	SOUTH	NON-SOUTH
0–4	11.1	8.6	9.8	7.3
5–9	12.1	9.6	9.9	7.4
10–14	11.1	9.3	10.4	8.3
15–19	10.8	8.9	10.4	9.0
20–24	9.6	8.6	9.2	8.6
25–29	7.9	8.0	8.6	8.4
30–34	6.5	7.7	7.6	7.8
35–39	6.6	7.8	6.9	7.4
40–44	5.4	6.9	5.8	7.0
45–49	4.9	6.0	5.2	6.7
50–54	4.2	5.1	4.4	5.9
55–59	3.1	4.1	3.5	4.8
60–64	2.4	3.3	2.8	3.9
65–69	1.7	2.5	2.5	3.0
70–74	1.2	1.7	1.5	2.1
75 and over	1.3	1.7	1.5	2.2

SOURCE: Computed from reports of the Bureau of the Census.

decline more slowly after the age of 20 than do the 1930 figures; this
was due to the fact that migration out of the region was substantially
lower during the 1930's than in previous decades. Finally, the Non-
South has higher percentages in the top age-groups—those above 65
years—but the differences between the regions are not so great as
those which prevail in the lowest age-groups.

The age composition of the southern population has important economic implications. In the first place, it gives the South a relatively
"flexible" population. Since many of the workers are young, many of
them just entering the labor market, it should be easier to channel
them into new lines of activity and thus to meet the needs of a changing economic structure.

On the other hand, this age composition gives more nonproducers
for every worker of productive age. For convenience we may classify
all persons between the ages of 15 and 64 as productive and all persons above or below those ages as nonproductive. On this basis the
South had, in 1930, for every 100 productive workers, 62.4 nonproductive workers while the Non-South had only 50.1. In 1940 the
figures were 55.1 for the South and 43.8 for the Non-South. This fact
is one cause of the low per capita income in the South. In 1940, if
productive workers (as defined above) in the South had produced the

same income as productive workers elsewhere, per capita income in the South would still have been lower by more than 7 per cent.

We may summarize this section by stating that the southern population is almost entirely native born, is decidedly rural, and is comparatively younger than the population outside the South. Each of these characteristics is important in its bearing on the economic potentialities of the region.

HEALTH AND EDUCATION OF THE POPULATION

Low incomes and a relatively large number of people in the nonproductive age groups make it especially difficult for the South to provide properly for the health and education of its people. In a brief survey of this kind it is impossible to deal adequately with a problem so big as this,[7] but it is necessary to give some indications as to how the population is conditioned and affected by health and education factors.

Aside from the death rate, no satisfactory measure of the health of a people is available. There are no data to indicate accurately how much a people is weakened, how much its vitality is sapped, nor how many work days are lost on account of illness, although these are important economic considerations. In the absence of specific information we must note a few general indications.

The National Health Survey showed that there was a definite and inverse correlation between incomes and the number of days lost per person per year from illness; the higher the income the fewer days lost by illness.[8] Since incomes in the South are low, this would suggest a higher rate of time lost on account of illness. Further, rejection rates under Selective Service during the recent war were very high in southern states. Between April, 1942 and March, 1943, the rate in every southern state was above the national average and in seven of them it was above 50 per cent, contrasted with the United States average of 39.2 per cent.[9] Rejections on account of educational deficiencies were unusually high in the South, but these were offset in considerable measure by lower rejections because of mental diseases. This points to one aspect in which the South appears to have an advantage. The number of patients in hospitals for mental diseases per 1000 of population in the South is only about two-thirds the number in the rest of

---

[7] For a comprehensive and intensive discussion of the health and education of the southern people, see R. B. Vance, *All These People*, Chapel Hill, University of North Carolina Press, 1945, pp. 335–465.

[8] *Ibid*, p. 365.   [9] *Economic Problems of the Cotton Belt*, p. 803.

the country.[10] Nevertheless, the high rate of rejections is a disturbing factor since it is logical that any physical or mental deficiency serious enough to warrant rejection by Selective Service must constitute a considerable economic handicap to the bread winner.

It is a little difficult to reconcile the fact that the South has only a slightly higher death rate than the rest of the nation but apparently has a considerably lower level of health and physical well-being. Vance explains it in these words: "The Southeast has proved especially vulnerable to diseases that rank low in death-dealing power but high in drain on energy. Among these are malaria, hookworm, and pellegra."[11] It is encouraging that definite methods of eliminating these scourges are known and that considerable progress has been made in reducing them.

In education the South is definitely and substantially below the rest of the country. In 1920 and 1930 the rate of illiteracy in the South was, on the average, at least twice the rate prevailing in the remainder of the nation. In the 1940 census, the question on illiteracy was replaced by one asking for the number of years of schooling. Table *XIV* gives profiles of the population over 25 years of age in the South and in the Non-South in respect to the number of years of school training.

It will be noticed that the South has considerably larger percentages in each group up to the end of grade school. The number of those who had four years of grade school training or less (including unreported) made up more than a fourth of the southern population but only a little over 11 per cent of the non-southern population.

The proportion of those who stopped after finishing high school was 50 per cent greater outside the South, but it is rather surprising that the difference is much less among those who had college training. Taking all those who had had some college training, the South had 9.08 per cent and the Non-South, 10.32, which is a smaller difference than might have been expected. The greatest differences lie in the lower brackets.

Although the South definitely lags in matters of education, this basic fact must be qualified by two pertinent and important considerations. First, the South is making as great, if not a greater, financial effort or sacrifice to improve its educational system than the remainder of the

10 R. B. Vance, *All These People*, Chapel Hill, University of North Carolina Press, 1945, p. 361.   11 *Ibid*, p. 364.

country. Second, the South is making considerable strides in reducing its educational lag.

It has often been pointed out that southern states are spending about as large a proportion of their total incomes for education as is any other part of the country. In 1945–46, for example, total current expenditures for the operation of public schools by state and local governments in the 13 southern states amounted to $555,400,000, which was 1.78 per cent of the income payments in those states in 1945. In the other 35 states current expenditures were $2,152,000,000, or 1.71 per cent of their income payments in 1945.[12] Since the same proportionate amount came from a much smaller total income, the effort or sacrifice involved was considerably greater for the South. Because of these low incomes and the larger number of children, the southern effort produced only $72.21 per pupil enrolled in the South, or a little more than half the $137.87 spent outside the South.

The essence of the South's problem can be summarized in one statement: it has, based on 1945–46 data, 32.7 per cent of the nation's children of school age (5–17 years of age) and 33.0 per cent of those actually enrolled in public schools, but it has slightly less than 20 per cent of the country's income out of which to provide for their education.

There are many facts to indicate that the South is improving the educational training of its children relative to the rest of the country. The South has been increasing its expenditures faster than the Non-South, especially since 1920.[13] In 1900 only 66.0 per cent of the children between 5 and 17 years of age were enrolled in the public schools compared to 75.8 per cent outside the South; in 1940 the figures were 85.4 and 85.2 respectively. In 1920 the average number of days of attendance per child per year was 91.4 in the South or 67.8 per cent of average attendance outside the South. By 1940 average attendance in the South was 86.8 of the average of the rest of the United States. These are all quantitative data but somewhat comparable efforts are being made to improve the quality of southern instruction. The greatest efforts have been made along these lines during the past 25 years and the South is just now coming into a position to reap the fruits of

[12] Federal Security Agency, U. S. Office of Education, *Statistics of State School Systems*, 1945–46, Table 30.
[13] See R. B. Vance, *All These People*, Chapel Hill, University of North Carolina Press, 1945, pp. 416–17.

these efforts. No doubt much of the South's progress in the past 10 or 15 years has been due to this improvement in its educational system.

TABLE *XIV*   YEARS OF SCHOOL COMPLETED BY PERSONS 25 YEARS OLD AND OVER IN THE SOUTH AND THE NON-SOUTH, 1940

| YEARS OF SCHOOL | NUMBER (IN THOUSANDS) | | PERCENTAGES | |
	SOUTH	NON-SOUTH	SOUTH	NON-SOUTH
Unreported and no Schooling	1,289	2,553	6.92	4.55
Grade School:				
1 to 4 years	3,428	3,877	18.41	6.90
5 and 6 years	3,119	5,296	16.75	9.61
7 and 8 years	4,463	21,435	23.97	38.17
High School:				
1 to 3 years	2,663	8,519	14.30	15.17
4 years	1,967	8,585	10.56	15.29
College:				
1 to 3 years	988	3,087	5.31	5.50
4 years and over	702	2,705	3.77	4.82
Total	18,619	56,157	100.00	100.00

SOURCE: Computed from reports of the Bureau of the Census.

EMPLOYMENT AND THE LABOR FORCE

What do the people of the South do, and how is their pattern of employment different from that outside the South? Since this study is primarily an analysis of the economic life of the South, this question goes to the very heart of our problem. The answer to it will go far to explain the economic characteristics of the region.

Table *XV* gives a profile of the occupational employment in the South for 1940, laid along side a similar profile for the Non-South. The greatest differences between the two regions, of course, were in agriculture and manufacturing. In the South a little more than a third of the employed labor force was engaged in agriculture, forestry, and fisheries compared with about one eighth in the Non-South. On the other hand, outside the South more than a fourth of the employed persons were engaged in manufacturing compared with less than one sixth in the South. The only other significant differences were in personal services, in which the South had the larger proportion, and in the transportation, financial, and professional services, in all of which the Non-South had larger proportions engaged. The total number employed in the South was somewhat less than a third of the total

TABLE *XV* OCCUPATIONS OF EMPLOYED PERSONS (EXCEPT THOSE ON PUBLIC EMERGENCY WORK) IN THE SOUTH AND THE NON-SOUTH, 1940

(*In Percentages*)

OCCUPATION	SOUTH	NON-SOUTH
Total Number (Thousands)	12,156	33,010
Agriculture, Forestry, and Fisheries	34.9	12.8
Mining	2.1	2.0
Construction	4.3	4.6
Manufacturing	15.3	26.4
Transportation, Communications, and Other Public Utilities	5.2	7.5
Wholesale and Retail Trade	13.4	17.9
Finance, Insurance, and Real Estate	1.9	3.7
Business and Repair Services	1.4	2.1
Personal Services	10.7	8.2
Amusement, Recreation, and Related Services	0.6	1.0
Professional and Related Services	5.7	8.0
Government	3.3	4.1
Not Listed	1.2	1.6
Total	100.0	100.0

SOURCE: Computed from reports of the Bureau of the Census.

population, while elsewhere it was a little more than a third, thus reflecting again the larger proportion of the southern population in the nonproductive age groups.

World War II wrought considerable changes in these patterns but the details are not available, as yet. We know that agricultural employment dropped sharply, more in the South than outside, and that the number engaged in manufacturing increased greatly. From 1939 to 1947, the number of production workers (wage earners) in manufacturing in the South rose from 1,349,000 to 2,023,000, an increase of 674,000 or an even 50 per cent.[14] The maximum increase at the peak of the war period was considerably greater. It is probable that the war only speeded up and accentuated the long-run changes which have been going on in the whole country for decades. Table *XVI* shows how employment has been shifting steadily from agricultural to non-agricultural occupations in both the South and the Non-South.

In summary, the chief difference in employment inside and outside the South is between agriculture and manufacturing. The other differences, which are not large, arise mainly from the higher incomes which prevail outside the South and give rise to a greater demand for financial, professional, and other similar services.

The total numbers shown as employed in Table *XV* did not con-

14 *Census of Manufactures*, 1947.

TABLE *XVI* EMPLOYMENT IN AGRICULTURAL AND NONAGRICULTURAL OCCUPA-
TIONS IN THE SOUTH AND THE NON-SOUTH, 1920–1940

(*In Percentages*)

| | 1920 | | 1930 | | 1940 | |
OCCUPATION	SOUTH	NON-SOUTH	SOUTH	NON-SOUTH	SOUTH	NON-SOUTH
Agricultural	50.9	17.6	42.8	14.6	34.9	12.8
Nonagricultural	49.1	82.4	57.2	85.4	65.1	87.2

SOURCE: Computed from reports of the Bureau of the Census.

stitute the entire labor force in 1940 by a considerable margin. The
unemployed and those employed on public emergency work made up
a sizeable group. The Bureau of Labor Statistics has estimated that

CHART *II* AGRICULTURAL AND NONAGRICULTURAL EMPLOYMENT SOUTH
AND NON-SOUTH, 1920–1940

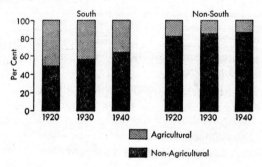

the total labor force in the South in 1940 amounted to 14,372,000,
while that outside the South was 40,406,000.[15] By 1945 it was estimated that the southern labor force had risen by almost three million
to 17,119,000. The Bureau also made a forecast of the southern labor
force for 1950. Using three different assumptions concerning the
amount of migration, it arrived at figures varying from slightly more
than 16 millions to about 16¾ millions. In any event, the South seems
assured of a labor force adequate to meet any likely development
because of the special reserve on which it can draw. The high birth
rates mean that each year there is a large number of boys and girls
entering the labor force. The Bureau of Labor Statistics estimates that

15 Bulletin No. 893, 1947, "State and Regional Variations in Prospective Labor
Supply," Table 1.

between 1940 and 1950, without any migration, the replacement rate of the labor force in the South would be 168; that is, for every 100 persons leaving the force there would be 168 entering it. This compares with rates of 118 in the North and 107 in the West. Normally a considerable number of the southern replacements migrate out of the region, but if there were sufficient demand, most of them would remain.

MIGRATION

The high birth rate, the relatively dense population for an agricultural area, and limited economic opportunities have produced in the South a dynamic, mobile population much on the move. Migration has been the safety valve which has prevented population pressure from reaching dangerous proportions. Vance distinguishes three great population movements in which the southern population has participated. They are: "(1) the expansion westward of the Cotton Kingdom, (2) the great interstate migration to the Northeast and Middle states, and (3) the movement to the region's own cities."[16] The latter movement has caused considerable interstate shifting within the region; after 1880, Florida and Louisiana, and after 1930, Virginia, have benefited consistently from this intraregional movement.

No adequate figures on interregional migration before 1930 are available. Vance has a number of estimates for the 11 Southeastern states going back as far as 1870.[17] They show that the migration of whites became pronounced after 1880 and of Negroes after 1910. Almost without exception the numbers increased each decade and reached a peak in the "roaring twenties," when the Southeast had a net loss of perhaps more than a million and a half people. Some of these, however, went into Oklahoma and Texas and were therefore not lost to the South, as we have defined it.

During the Great Depression of the 1930's the migration of whites out of the Southeast almost completely halted, but the movement of Negroes out of the region continued at a considerable rate, reaching an estimated 425,000. Principally because of the drought, however, there was a large population movement out of Oklahoma during this decade, while Texas also had a small net loss. The region as a whole

[16] R. B. Vance, *All These People*, Chapel Hill, University of North Carolina Press, 1945, p. 110.
[17] See *Ibid*, pp. 109–139.

had a loss during the decade of about 460,000 Negroes and over 300,000 whites for a total loss of about three fourths of a million.

Since each decennial census shows the state of birth and the state of residence for all native-born residents it is possible to strike a balance every ten years which will show the net result of all interstate or interregional migration up to that time as reflected in people then living. Table *XVII* has been constructed to show the net result of migration out of and into the South as of 1940 by regions to which

TABLE *XVII*   NATIVE POPULATION BORN IN SOUTH AND LIVING ELSEWHERE AND VICE VERSA, 1940

REGION	PEOPLE BORN IN SOUTH AND LIVING IN—	PER CENT OF TOTAL	PEOPLE LIVING IN SOUTH AND BORN IN—	PER CENT OF TOTAL
New England	64,360	1.36	81,258	3.90
Middle Atlantic	835,527	17.69	295,569	14.19
East North Central	1,477,132	31.28	578,134	27.76
West North Central	553,035	11.71	646,867	31.07
Del., Md., D. C., and W. Va.	556,283	11.79	357,483	17.17
Mountain	378,861	8.02	78,523	3.77
Pacific	856,663	18.14	44,449	2.13
Totals	4,721,861	100.00	2,082,284	100.00

Net Migration from South—2,639,577.
SOURCE: Computed from reports of the Bureau of the Census.

they went or from which they came. At that date 4,721,861 people who had been born in the South were living outside the region while 2,082,284 people who had been born elsewhere were living in the South. The net loss by migration was thus 2,639,577. In percentages of its native-born population living in 1940 the South had lost 12.01 and gained 5.30, for a net loss of 6.71.

By far the largest number of outmigrants went to the East North Central states, with the Pacific and Middle Atlantic regions as close contenders for second choice. Well over half of those coming into the South came from the two Middle West regions. The total number of inmigrants, which was over 40 per cent of the outmigrants, was considerable and is a factor often overlooked in discussions of southern migration.

With the revival of economic activity after 1939 and later the war boom itself, migration out of the South increased greatly. The abnormally low migration of the 1930's had built up population pressure and, despite the fact that cotton and tobacco prices trebled and quadrupled, the high wages in war plants outside the South acted as a powerful magnet to draw people out of the South by the millions. As noted above, Census estimates show that net migration out of the South between 1940 and 1948 was approximately 2,960,000. So it would seem that the South lost through migration in these eight years more people than it had lost in the whole generation before 1940.

In addition to the large migration out of the region, the war caused very large movements of population within the region, as workers left farms and villages to work in ship yards, war factories, and army camps. Florida, Virginia, Texas, Louisiana, and Tennessee were the gainers in that order; the other states stood still or lost, as can be seen in Table *VIII*.

Those who have studied southern population movements have often been concerned with the quality of the migrants. What kinds of people leave the South and what kinds come in? Often apprehension has been expressed that the South loses the "cream of its human crop" through migration, since those with most ability and initiative, it was thought, will migrate in order to find better economic opportunities. In its questionnaire for the 1940 census, the Bureau of the Census included one question, the answers to which throw considerable light on this problem. Some of the data from the answers have been tabulated and published in two volumes, one dealing with the economic and the other with the social characteristics of migrants.[18] A careful analysis of these data would seem to be worth while, especially since it has been pointed out that the regional shifts in population during these years were similar to those which prevailed during the war as well as to the long-term shifts of the native population.[19]

For its analysis of the educational training of migrants, the Bureau of the Census took those people between the ages of 25 and 34, because those persons are the most mobile and ordinarily have completed their education. Table *XVIII* shows the number of people in this age group in the South who did not migrate between 1935 and 1940 as well as those who came into and went out of the region in those years. The section headed "Per Cent" in Table *XVIII* gives profiles of the educational training of these three categories by express-

[18] See *Sixteenth Census of the United States, Population, Internal Migration 1935 to 1940.*

[19] See Henry S. Shryock, Jr., and Hope Tisdale Eldridge, "Internal Migration in Peace and War," *American Sociological Review,* XII, pp. 27-28 (Feb., 1947)

ing the numbers which had completed various amounts of schooling, in percentage figures.

TABLE *XVIII*   EDUCATIONAL TRAINING OF NONMIGRANTS, INMIGRANTS, AND OUTMIGRANTS 25 TO 34 YEARS OLD IN THE SOUTH,* 1935–1940

(*Numbers in Thousands*)

| YEARS OF SCHOOLING COMPLETED | NUMBER | | | | PER CENT | | | NET AS % OF NON-MI-GRANTS | 13-STATE SOUTH NET MIGRATION | |
	NON	IN	OUT	NET	NON	IN	OUT		NO.	% OF NON-MI-GRANTS
Grade School:										
Less than 5	914.7	5.3	16.3	−11.0	17.11	2.71	5.92	−1.20	−12.4	−1.44
5 and 6	869.2	6.7	23.5	−16.8	16.26	3.38	8.55	−1.94	−18.5	−2.34
7 and 8	1,333.1	29.4	74.2	−44.8	24.94	14.91	29.96	−3.36	−46.4	−4.11
High School:										
1 to 3	998.2	35.7	54.9	−19.2	18.67	18.12	19.96	−1.92	−21.9	−2.49
4	761.6	53.1	55.1	− 2.0	14.25	26.93	20.02	−0.27	− 8.3	−1.27
College:										
1 to 3	285.2	29.2	25.8	+ 3.3	5.33	14.79	9.39	+1.17	+ 0.1	+0.06
4 and over	183.8	37.8	25.3	+12.5	3.44	19.16	9.20	+6.78	+ 8.6	+5.63
Total	5,345.9	197.1	275.2	−78.1	100.00	100.00	100.00	−1.46	−98.8	−2.09

* As defined by the Bureau of the Census, the South is made up of the three subregions, South Atlantic, East South Central, and West South Central; it includes, in addition to the 13 States included in this study, Delaware, Maryland, West Virginia, and the District of Columbia.
SOURCE: Bureau of the Census.

Several striking facts are evident from Table *XVIII*. First, the mobility of the population, at least in so far as interregional movement is concerned, increases with the amount of education. The proportionate number of migrants falling into the two lowest brackets is less than half the number of nonmigrants while with those who had had college training the proportions are reversed. This tends to confirm the apprehension of those who fear that the South is losing most heavily among the best educated. But the second striking fact is that the inmigrants had, on the average, considerably more schooling than the outmigrants. The outmigrants show a definite peak, both absolutely and relatively, at those who had only finished grade school while the peak of the inmigrants is at those who had finished high school. Third, the South had a net inmigration in both groups with college training, and in the top bracket the net inflow was a larger percentage of the nonmigratory population with similar training than was the net outflow in any other bracket. In other words, migration added a larger proportionate number to our most educated group than it took away from any of the less educated groups. So, while the South, in this period, was losing many of its best-educated young men and women, it was gaining more than it lost in the top brackets.

All of the above figures are for the Census definition of the South, which includes Delaware, Maryland, West Virginia, and the District of Columbia. The figures are distorted somewhat by the fact that all the above states except West Virginia had a considerable net inmigration. In order to get net migration for the 13-state South the data for the Census South were adjusted by removing the figures for the above four states. As might be expected, this operation increased the net outmigration in all groups through high school and sharply reduced the inmigration in the college groups, almost wiping out the net for the group covering 1 to 3 years of college training. The total outmigration was increased from 78,100 to 98,800 or from 1.46 per cent to 2.09 per cent of the nonmigratory population. These figures are shown in the last two columns of Table *XVIII*.

On the ground that the figures for Virginia were greatly affected by the expansion of government departments in Washington and that those for Florida were not typical of southern states because of its resort characteristics, the data were further adjusted by removing the figures for those two states (not shown in the Table). The result was to increase further the net outmigration in all groups through high school, to convert the small net inmigration in the first college group into a net outmigration of over 5,000 and to cut the net inflow in the second college group from 5,600 to 2,300. The total net outmigration was further increased from 98,800 to 141,000 or to 3.39 per cent of the nonmigratory population. These two adjustments changed volumes but they did not change the basic pattern whereby migrants into the South, although considerably fewer in number, had considerably more schooling on the average than those migrants who left the South. With the enormous proportions reached by migration during the war years it would seem fairly certain that the South had a heavy net loss in all categories.

The data for the occupation of migrants permit an analysis of occupational employment similar to that for educational training given above. In this case data were tabulated for all employed persons (in

March, 1940) above the age of 14. The figures in Table *XIX* were compiled on a state basis; that is, the figures showing inmigrants and outmigrants for each of the 13 states were added and one total was subtracted from the other to get a balance. For this reason the figures for inmigrants and outmigrants contain many interstate migrants within the South, but the net figures must necessarily represent migrants who came into or went out of the South.

TABLE *XIX* EMPLOYMENT BY MAJOR OCCUPATIONAL GROUPS OF EMPLOYED NONMIGRANTS, INMIGRANTS, AND OUTMIGRANTS OVER 14 YEARS OLD IN SOUTH, 1935–1940

(Number in Thousands)

OCCUPATION	NUMBER				PER CENT			NET AS % OF NON-MI-GRANTS
	NON	IN	OUT	NET	NON	IN	OUT	
Professional and Semiprofessional Workers	463.9	81.7	71.5	+10.2	4.6	11.6	8.6	+2.19
Farmers and Farm Managers	2,265.4	45.8	43.9	+ 1.9	22.4	6.6	5.4	+0.08
Proprietors, Managers, and Officials	663.3	70.6	57.8	+12.8	6.6	10.0	7.1	+1.93
Clerical and Sales Workers	1,042.3	113.2	110.7	+ 2.5	10.3	16.1	13.6	+0.24
Craftsmen, Foremen, Etc.	752.0	74.0	79.5	− 5.5	7.4	10.6	9.7	−0.73
Operatives, Etc.	1,405.2	98.4	133.2	−34.8	13.9	14.0	16.3	−2.48
Domestic Service Workers	725.8	33.4	65.9	−32.5	7.2	4.8	8.1	−4.47
Service Workers Exc. Domestic	562.3	87.9	108.0	−20.1	5.6	12.5	13.2	−3.59
Farm Laborers and Foremen	1,418.7	50.0	77.6	−27.6	14.0	7.1	9.4	−1.95
Other Laborers and Occup. not Reported	816.2	47.6	69.2	−21.6	8.1	6.8	8.5	−2.64
Total	10,113.9	702.6	817.4	−114.8	100.0	100.0	100.0	−1.13

SOURCE: Computed from reports of the Bureau of the Census.

The figures in Table *XIX* are consistent with the figures in Table *XVIII* and tend generally to confirm the conclusions drawn above. Thus the two principal groups in which the South showed net balances of inmigration were the professional and semiprofessional workers and the proprietors, managers, and officials. These are normally the more educated groups. Conversely, the greatest net outmigration was found among the service workers and operatives who normally have less education. Farm laborers are an exception to this generalization, but their immobility can perhaps be explained on other grounds.

Friedman and Kuznets offer figures which help to explain the net inmigration of the more highly educated, better-paid people into the

South. They show that between 1929 and 1936, the incomes of five professional groups did not vary nearly so much from region to region as did the per capita income of the whole population. In fact, they show that when the effect of the size of community is removed, there were small regional differences in the incomes of physicians and dentists, but there was "no evidence of any 'pure' regional differences in the incomes of lawyers, accountants, or engineers."[20] Since there were only small differences in incomes, evidently some of the nonmonetary attractions of the South were sufficient to bring in more than went out among the higher professional and business groups.

In conclusion, it may be in order to point out that both sides of the migration picture should be examined with equal care. In the past attention has been centered primarily on those who leave the South. Normally the South has a large outflow of population but among the better-educated, better-trained groups, which the South needs very much, the movements in and out have more nearly balanced than we have frequently imagined.

SUMMARY

In this chapter we have tried to give briefly some indications of the size, growth, education, health, and occupation of the southern population. Each of these aspects could well be and, indeed, has been elsewhere, the subject of a separate chapter. But the plan of this study requires extensive, but does not permit intensive, study of this fascinating subject.

The southern population is young and mobile. High birth rates and moderate death rates add a large increment to the population each year. In boom years the majority of that increment moves out through migration, leaving the region with a slightly lower rate of population growth than the rest of the nation; in depression years the increment piles up and gives the region a higher rate of growth than other regions. Migration is heaviest among the Negroes; consistently the white population has shown a higher rate of growth than whites outside the South, with the result that the composition of the population is moving slowly but steadily toward a larger proportion of whites and a smaller proportion of Negroes. The population is predominantly rural, with agriculture the chief occupation, though the trends are toward urban-

[20] Milton Friedman and Simon Kuznets, *Income from Independent Professional Practice* (National Bureau of Economic Research, 1945), p. 194.

ization and nonagricultural occupations. The South lags in matters of education, although it is making an effort equal to, or greater than, other regions and is realizing appreciable progress in closing the gap. Inadequate medical personnel and facilities make it difficult to maintain the health of the southern population at the most vigorous or efficient levels; perhaps the greatest need of the moment is for better health facilities. Although the South does lose some of its best human resources through migration, it also gains substantial numbers of people in return, and, on the average, they are better educated and hold better positions than those who leave the region.

III INCOME IN THE SOUTH

In a money economy such as ours, the money income received by individuals is perhaps the best and most comprehensive measure of the economic welfare of the people. It constitutes the best basis for comparisons of standards of living within and between nations. It is not an accurate measure of economic production or of total income generated, but it is fairly closely related to those functions. Further, the data for income payments have been fairly well developed on a state basis in the United States which makes them especially valuable for a regional study of this kind.

The most distinguishing economic characteristic of the South is its low income. It was that low income, more than any other single factor, which caused the region to be labeled "The Nation's Number One Economic Problem." The principal economic problem facing the region, and the central theme of this study, is the problem of how that income can be raised—effectively, substantially, and permanently. For these reasons a study of income is of special significance to the South.

The purpose of this chapter is to trace and examine in some detail the behavior of income in the South since 1929; to search for sources and causes of the changes which have taken place; and to determine, if possible, why income in the South has behaved differently from income elsewhere in the nation.

THE TREND OF SOUTHERN INCOME

The year 1929 is taken as the starting point for this survey for several reasons. First, in this study of the southern economy we are interested primarily in the recent past as indicating trends which may exercise a significant influence on the future. Second, the year 1929 represents the high-water mark in economic production before the decline into the Great Depression. Third, comprehensive and detailed figures on income payments by states are available on a continuous and uniform basis only since 1929.[1] The years 1929 through 1948 make a total of 20 years which span a period starting with prosperity, then declining into the greatest depression of our history, followed by several years of recovery and ending with the period of our greatest war effort and the immediate postwar period of adjustment. Thus these years cover a wide range of economic conditions.

Table *XX* gives the data for total income payments in the 13 southern states for each year since 1929, together with similar figures for the non-southern states. The figures show that in 1930 and 1931, total income payments in the South dropped considerably faster than in the Non-South and that they reached their low-point in 1932 at 56 per cent of 1929—a year before non-southern payments reached their low point at the same level. By 1934, the southern series was seven points above the non-southern series and it maintained a lead of from seven to eleven points until 1940, when the spread began to increase, rising finally to 71 points in 1945, dropping slightly to 68 in 1946, and rising again to 82 in 1948. By the latter year southern income payments were 219 per cent above the 1929 level, while non-southern payments were up 137 per cent.

We get additional light on the progress made by the South in the matter of income by expressing southern income payments as a per cent of national payments. During most of the years under consideration the population of the South was approximately 28 per cent of the total for the nation. In 1929, southern income payments were 15.0 per cent of the total for the whole country. By 1931 they had fallen

1 The series referred to is that compiled by the United States Department of Commerce and published annually in *The Survey of Current Business.* That series is entitled "Income Payments to Individuals" and it "is a measure of the income received by residents of each state from business establishments and governmental agencies." It includes: (1) wages and salaries after deductions for social security and retirement plans; (2) proprietors' income, which is the net income of unincorporated establishments, including farms; (3) property incomes, such as dividends, interest, and net rent and royalties; and (4) "other" income such as relief payments, pensions, bonuses, retirement pay, social insurance benefits, etc.

In 1947, the Department of Commerce revised its national income figures. The net effect was to raise the figures somewhat because of the inclusion of items previously omitted. A similar revision is under way for the figures on income payments by states but it has not been completed and all of the data given here are on the old basis.

TABLE *XX* TOTAL INCOME PAYMENTS IN THE SOUTH AND THE NON-SOUTH, 1929–1948

(Amounts in Millions of Dollars)

YEAR	AMOUNTS		RELATIVES 1929 = 100		SOUTH AS PER CENT OF U. S.
	SOUTH	NON-SOUTH	SOUTH	NON-SOUTH	
1929	12,428	70,189	100	100	15.0
1930	10,210	63,115	82	90	13.9
1931	8,566	53,405	69	76	13.8
1932	6,970	40,462	56	58	15.0
1933	7,225	39,048	58	56	15.6
1934	8,715	44,323	70	63	16.4
1935	9,602	48,956	77	70	16.4
1936	11,170	56,830	90	81	16.4
1937	11,852	60,359	95	86	16.4
1938	11,109	54,936	89	78	16.8
1939	11,764	58,837	95	84	16.7
1940	12,524	63,328	101	90	16.5
1941	15,805	76,464	127	109	17.1
1942	21,453	95,743	173	136	18.3
1943	27,482	114,349	221	163	19.4
1944	30,405	122,901	245	175	19.8
1945	31,177	126,013	251	180	19.8
1946	32,919	138,629	265	197	19.2
1947	36,669	152,543	295	217	19.4
1948	39,649	166,632	319	237	.19.2

SOURCE: Computed from reports of the U. S. Department of Commerce.

CHART *III* TOTAL INCOME PAYMENTS IN THE SOUTH, 1929–1948, AS PERCENTAGES OF UNITED STATES TOTALS

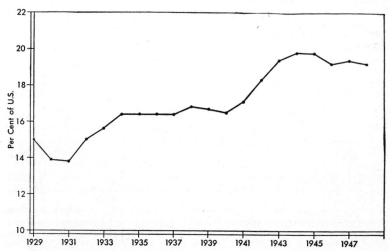

to 13.8 per cent but rose to 16.4 in 1935 and remained at approximately that figure until 1940. During the war years they rose almost to 20 per cent and declined very slightly in the postwar years.

The above discussion has dealt with total income payments. In many respects, per capita figures are more significant than aggregates. Table *XXI* contains per capita income figures for the South and for the remainder of the nation. Since population increased more rapidly

CHART *IV*   PER CAPITA ANNUAL INCOME PAYMENTS IN THE SOUTH AND NON-SOUTH, 1929–1948 (IN DOLLARS AND THE SOUTH AS A PER CENT OF THE NON-SOUTH)

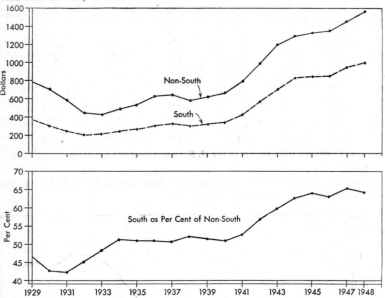

in the South than in the other regions between 1930 and 1940, these figures do not show as large a relative gain for the South as do the aggregates. However, the index figures show the same basic pattern of a substantial gain by the South after 1933. Until 1934, per capita income in the South as a whole was less than 50 per cent of the figure for the Non-South; after that date it was consistently above 50 per cent and rose to 65 per cent in 1947. It may be important to note, however, that practically all of that relative improvement came in two fairly short periods—1932–1934 and 1941–1945. Those were periods when incomes and economic activity were rising rapidly.

In 1929, six southern states had per capita incomes less than half of the average for the whole country; in 1946, only one state was in that category; and in 1948, the lowest state figure—Mississippi's $758 —was 53.8 per cent of the national average. By 1948, average per capita income in the South was 170 per cent above the 1929 level, while in the Non-South it was up by 96 per cent. Measuring from the low points of 1932–1933 to 1948, southern per capita income rose by 395 per cent; non-southern, by 263 per cent.

Since prices varied over a wide range during the years under consideration, the above figures give no accurate indication of the real income received; that is, of the purchasing power of the current dollars received. If we start with 1929 and adjust the income figures for the later years to take into account changing consumer prices, we can obtain some rough idea of the changes which took place in purchasing power.[2] On that basis, we find that the figure for 1932 becomes $274 instead of $203; for 1936, the figure becomes $388, slightly higher than the 1929 figure; and the figure for 1948 becomes $719 instead of $1005. In terms of these deflated or corrected data, the increase in per capita income in the South from 1929 to 1948 was 93 per cent; in the Non-South, 40 per cent. Thus, if these data constitute a reliable measure, the per capita real income or purchasing power of southerners has almost doubled during the past 20 years.

The above data show that the southern states, both as individual states and as a group, have realized substantially greater increases than non-southern states in aggregate and per capita income payments since 1929. In view of this fact, it might well be imagined that the southern states had made some progress in getting away from their traditional positions at the bottom of the scale when states are ranked according to per capita income. Curiously enough, the reverse has happened; in 1948 the southern states were more closely grouped at the bottom of the list than in 1933 or even in 1929. Table *XXII* shows the rankings of the southern states for the years 1929, 1933, 1940, 1944, and 1948. Florida was the highest southern state in most years, ranking 33rd in 1929, 29th in 1933, 30th in 1940, and 27th in 1944. Texas was high in 1948 with a ranking of 34th.

It is not easy to explain this curious result, but apparently three factors have been involved. First, in the past the difference in income

[2] In this operation the index of consumer prices compiled by the Bureau of Labor Statistics, U. S. Department of Labor, was used.

TABLE *XXI*   PER CAPITA ANNUAL INCOME PAYMENTS IN THE SOUTH AND THE NON-SOUTH, 1929–1948

(*Amounts in Dollars*)

| YEAR | AMOUNT | | INDEX (1929 = 100) | | SOUTH AS PER CENT OF NON-SOUTH |
	SOUTH	NON-SOUTH	SOUTH	NON-SOUTH	
1929	372	797	100	100	46.7
1930	302	707	81	89	42.7
1931	251	594	67	75	42.3
1932	203	448	55	56	45.3
1933	208	430	56	54	48.4
1934	249	485	67	61	51.3
1935	272	533	73	67	51.0
1936	314	615	84	77	51.0
1937	331	650	89	82	50.9
1938	307	587	83	74	52.3
1939	322	624	87	78	51.6
1940	340	667	91	84	51.0
1941	423	800	114	100	52.9
1942	568	998	153	125	56.9
1943	715	1198	192	150	59.7
1944	815	1298	219	163	62.8
1945	849	1325	228	166	64.1
1946	855	1352	230	170	63.2
1947	951	1456	256	183	65.3
1948	1005	1561	270	196	64.4

SOURCE: Computed from reports of the U. S. Department of Commerce.

between southern states and other states has been quite large. Second, the non-southern states which in the past years have been close to, or mixed in with, the southern states in the rankings have been states such as Kansas, Nebraska, the Dakotas, and Idaho which derive a large part of their income from feed and food crops and livestock. In recent years the prices of those products have risen more than the prices of other major commodity groups and as a result those states have moved far up the scale of income payments. Finally, there has been a tendency for all states to cluster more closely around the average per capita income for the United States. This is shown by the fact that while the average for southern states was moving up from 55 per cent to 71 per cent of the national average, the non-southern average declined from 117 per cent to 111 per cent. We can get a more accurate and more comprehensive measurement of this trend by computing the index or coefficient of variability (standard deviation divided by the arithmetic mean). This computation, based on the per capita income figures for all of the states, was made for five selected years with the following result: 1929, .3694; 1933, .4246; 1940, .3623; 1944, .2756; 1948, .2139. The figure for 1948 was almost exactly half of the figure for 1933. This indicates that, in relative terms, there has been a significant "closing of the ranks" or a "leveling off of incomes" as between the states. So, while the southern states were moving upward toward the national average, other states with low incomes were doing the same thing, some of them even more rapidly. Consequently, the southern states were not able to attain higher ranks in the order of states.

Table *XXII* also shows the comparative positions of the southern states in regard to per capita income for the selected years. Florida has usually been at the top, with Texas and Virginia usually alternating in second and third places. These three states, which are at the geographical extremes of the region under consideration, have usually been the only states with per capita incomes above 70 per cent of the national average. The four states of Alabama, Arkansas, Mississippi, and South Carolina have regularly shared the four bottom positions on the list.[3] These states did not have incomes exceeding 50 per cent of the national average until the war years and since then have not had incomes above 65 per cent of that average.

Among the southern states, as in the country as a whole, there has been a relative (but not absolute) narrowing of interstate differences in per capita income. Especially since 1940, the states with the lowest incomes have generally experienced the greatest proportional increases in income. Of the six southern states which had the highest per capita incomes in 1929, only one—Virginia—had as large an increase in income between 1929 and 1948 as the region as a whole. The six together had an (unweighted arithmetical) average increase of 145 per cent compared with the regional increase of 170 per cent. On the other hand, the seven states with the lowest per capita incomes in 1929 all had increases greater than the regional average; as a group they averaged 195 per cent. Again, the coefficient of variability will express this trend more precisely. Based on the figures for the 13 southern states, the coefficient was as follows: 1929, .2032; 1933, .2184; 1940, .2242; 1944, .1795; 1948, .1262. Here, also, there was a striking reduction in the variation between states from 1940 to

[3] The District of Columbia is counted as a state for this purpose, and for that reason there are 49 positions on the list.

TABLE XXII SOUTHERN STATES RANKED BY PER CAPITA INCOME PAYMENTS, 1929, 1933, 1940, 1944, AND 1948

(Per Capita Income in Dollars)

Rank in U.S.	State	1929 Per Capita Income	Percentage U.S. Aver.	State	1933 Per Capita Income	Percentage U.S. Aver.	State	1940 Per Capita Income	Percentage U.S. Aver.	State	1944 Per Capita Income	Percentage U.S. Aver.	State	1948 Per Capita Income	Percentage U.S. Aver.
29th	Iowa	546	80	FLORIDA	272	74	Arizona	473	82	FLORIDA*	1053	91	New Hamp.	1261	89
30th	Utah	537	79	VIRGINIA	266	72	FLORIDA	471	82	Arizona	991	85	Idaho	1252	89
31st	Kansas	532	78	W. Va.	265	72	VIRGINIA	450	78	Idaho	990	85	Utah	1231	87
32nd	Idaho	518	76	Arizona	263	71	Idaho	440	77	Iowa	982	85	Vermont	1229	87
33rd	FLORIDA	484	71	Kansas	258	70	Nebraska	433	75	Vermont	977	84	Maine	1219	86
34th	TEXAS	465	68	Iowa	258	70	Kansas	422	73	VIRGINIA	964	83	TEXAS	1192	85
35th	W. Va.	464	68	TEXAS	257	70	TEXAS	413	72	Minnesota	962	83	Arizona	1168	83
36th	OKLAHOMA	455	67	Idaho	242	66	W. Va.	398	69	New Hamp.	941	81	VIRGINIA	1159	82
37th	VIRGINIA	422	62	OKLAHOMA	226	61	S. Dakota	376	65	OKLAHOMA	915	79	FLORIDA	1137	81
38th	S. Dakota	417	61	LOUISIANA	222	60	N. Dakota	368	64	LOUISIANA	890	77	W. Va.	1133	80
39th	LOUISIANA	415	61	N. CAR.	205	56	LOUISIANA	357	62	N. Mexico	830	71	N. Mexico	1125	80
40th	GEORGIA	389	57	GEORGIA	200	54	OKLAHOMA	356	62	W. Va.	817	70	OKLAHOMA	1029	73
41st	KENTUCKY	383	56	KENTUCKY	199	54	N. Mexico	333	58	TENNESSEE	816	70	LOUISIANA	1002	71
42nd	N. Mexico	371	55	N. Mexico	196	53	TENNESSEE	317	55	GEORGIA	804	69	GEORGIA	971	69
43rd	TENNESSEE	349	51	N. Dakota	190	52	N. CAR.	316	55	ALABAMA	781	67	TENNESSEE	955	68
44th	N. Dakota	329	48	TENNESSEE	190	52	GEORGIA	315	54	N. Car.	723	62	N. CAR.	930	66
45th	N. CAR.	309	45	S. Dakota	172	47	KENTUCKY	308	54	KENTUCKY	703	61	KENTUCKY	909	64
46th	ALABAMA	305	45	S. CAR.	167	45	S. CAR.	286	50	S. CAR.	698	60	ALABAMA	891	63
47th	ARKANSAS	305	45	ALABAMA	154	42	ALABAMA	268	47	ARKANSAS	667	57	S. CAR.	865	61
48th	MISS.	273	40	ARKANSAS	152	41	ARKANSAS	252	44		628	54	ARKANSAS	863	61
49th	S. CAR.	252	37	MISS.	123	33	MISS.	202	35	MISS.	577	50	MISS.	758	54
Average Per Cap. Income In United States		680	100		368	100		575	100	*27th	1,161	100		1,410	100
Average for South		372	55		208	57		340	59		815	70		1,005	71
Average for Non-South		797	117		430	117		667	115		1,298	112		1,561	111

1948. It is well to remember, however, that the reduction was in *relative* differences; the *absolute* differences increased considerably during these years.

In summary, southern income dropped more sharply in 1930 and 1931 than did income outside the South, but it recovered a little earlier and rose a little higher after 1932. From 1935 to 1940 income in the South, in relation to the 1929 base, was from 10 to 12 per cent higher than other income. From 1940 to 1945 southern income rose by 142 per cent while income elsewhere was rising by 97 per cent, but in the postwar adjustment period the South's lead was reduced slightly. These developments took place despite the fact that the South is much more heavily dependent on agriculture than the rest of the country and despite the fact that cash receipts from the South's dominant crop—cotton—never regained their 1929 level until 1947 (see Table *XXIV*). After all of these changes, however, the 13 southern states still remain closely grouped at the bottom of the list of states when ranked according to per capita incomes; in 1948 they occupied 13 of the 16 bottom positions.

SOURCES OF CHANGES IN INCOME

Without attempting to determine the ultimate "causes" of the income behavior outlined above, we shall now examine in more detail the different segments of the southern economy in an effort to locate those which are primarily and proximately responsible for the income changes. This procedure should give us, at the same time, a fairly accurate indication of the major changes in the southern economy during the past 20 years. In doing this we shall take the national income pattern as given and concentrate our attention on the factors which caused southern incomes to behave differently from income in the remainder of the country.

The Decline in 1930 and 1931. In 1929 per capita income in the South was less than half the average per capita income in the rest of the nation. Yet in 1930, southern income dropped almost twice as much relatively as non-southern income, while in 1931 it continued to decline at about the same rate as elsewhere (see Table *XX*). The data supplied by the Department of Commerce do not permit a detailed analysis of the source of incomes in these years, but two other series are available which supply considerable supplementary information. They are the series on cash receipts from farming compiled by the Department of Agriculture, and John A. Slaughter's book, *Income Received in the Various States, 1929–1935*.[4] Slaughter's figures do not show as great a drop nor as much difference between the South and the Non-South for 1930 and 1931 as do the Commerce figures, but the directions of change are the same.

It is quickly apparent from Table *XXIII* that agriculture was responsible for the big drop in 1930. Agricultural income was two and and a half times as important in the South as in the Non-South and its rate of decline was almost twice as great in the South. A glance at Table *XXIV* will show further that the trouble was almost entirely with the South's chief crop—cotton. Cash receipts from tobacco and other southern crops held up a little better than cash agricultural income outside the South. The trouble with cotton was a drastic fall in prices. Whereas in the fall of 1929 cotton farmers were selling their cotton at prices between 16 and 18 cents per pound, a year later they were selling at between 9 and 10 cents. In addition, the 1930 crop was smaller by some 800,000 bales, a drop of a little more than 5 per cent. The result was that the cash receipts from the cotton crop (including cottonseed) in 1930 were only 54 per cent of 1929 receipts. Despite a very large crop in 1931—almost 17 million bales—the decline in cash receipts continued because prices continued to decline and reached six cents and below.

In other fields, southern income did not behave very differently from non-southern income. The South had slightly larger declines in public utilities, trade and finance, and services, but it fared somewhat better in manufacturing, construction, and mining and quarrying.

The Upturn. The upturn came somewhat earlier in the South than in other parts of the country. The Department of Commerce data show southern income two points higher in 1933 than in 1932, while

---

4 The first series is compiled and issued by the Bureau of Agricultural Economics. See *Cash Receipts from Farming by States and Commodities, Calendar Years 1924–44*, Washington, January, 1946 (mimeographed), and *The Farm Income Situation*, May, 1947 and June, 1949. Slaughter's book is No. 234 in the National Industrial Conference Board Studies. The concept of income used in these two series is not the same as that used in the Department of Commerce figures and in some respects these two series do not behave in exactly the same way as the Commerce series, but they are sufficiently similar to provide valuable analytical help. Slaughter's concept of production income is defined as follows: "Realized production income, constituting between 90% and 95% of the accountable total, includes all the basic items that are used in all national income estimates with the exception of interest derived from mortgages on owned homes and net rent from residential property." pp. 6–7.

TABLE *XXIII*   INDEXES OF PRODUCTION INCOME* RECEIVED BY SOURCE IN THE SOUTH AND THE NON-SOUTH, 1929–1935

(*1929 = 100*)

REGION AND SOURCE	1929	1930	1931	1932	1933	1934	1935
Total Production Income:							
South	100	89	73	58	58	66	72
Non-South	100	92	76	58	54	60	66
Agriculture:							
South	100	68	51	39	51	62	66
Non-South	100	82	52	33	40	49	62
Public Utilities:							
South	100	94	80	65	60	66	70
Non-South	100	97	86	70	64	66	68
Trade and Finance:							
South	100	93	80	63	55	60	63
Non-South	100	94	82	63	52	56	59
Services:							
South	100	93	80	63	59	65	72
Non-South	100	94	83	65	60	64	70
Manufacturing:							
South	100	92	69	51	54	64	76
Non-South	100	88	68	47	46	56	64
Mining and Quarrying:							
South	100	88	61	48	49	62	66
Non-South	100	82	57	37	36	47	49
Construction:							
South	100	103	68	35	36	43	47
Non-South	100	89	59	28	22	25	30
Governments:							
South	100	102	104	101	95	101	111
Non-South	100	103	104	103	98	103	109

* See text, footnote 4, for a definition of this concept.
SOURCE: Computed from data in John A. Slaughter, *Income Received in the Various States, 1929–1935*. (National Industrial Conference Board Studies No. 234) New York, 1937, Tables 17–23.

Slaughter's figures show it even for the two years, although two of his most significant series—those for agriculture and manufacturing—show substantial improvement for 1933 over 1932. Southern agricultural income made considerably greater improvement than non-southern—12 points compared with seven—while manufacturing income in the South rose three points compared with a drop of one point for the Non-South. In fact, outside the South, income in 1933 showed declines in every field except agriculture, four of them rather substantial; the South showed small gains in three fields besides agriculture.

TABLE *XXIV*   INDEXES OF CASH RECEIPTS FROM FARM MARKETING IN THE SOUTH
AND THE NON-SOUTH, 1929–1948

(1929 = 100)

YEAR	COTTON* SOUTH	TOBACCO SOUTH	OTHER CROPS SOUTH	TOTAL CROPS SOUTH	NON-SOUTH	LIVESTOCK SOUTH	NON-SOUTH	TOTAL RECEIPTS SOUTH	NON-SOUTH
1929	100	100	100	100	100	100	100	100	100
1930	54	85	86	66	82	82	84	69	84
1931	33	52	68	44	54	58	63	47	60
1932	31	39	54	37	40	45	44	39	43
1933	38	60	56	45	51	48	46	45	48
1934	56	93	68	63	55	56	54	61	54
1935	47	94	74	59	58	72	66	62	63
1936	58	94	83	68	74	80	76	71	75
1937	56	124	99	74	79	95	77	79	78
1938	41	115	85	60	64	88	70	67	68
1939	39	103	87	58	72	91	70	66	71
1940	41	88	88	58	75	93	77	67	76
1941	65	120	109	82	100	120	102	92	101
1942	78	185	159	111	134	175	141	127	139
1943	84	203	220	132	175	236	176	159	176
1944	94	288	229	153	179	231	173	173	176
1945	77	346	275	156	210	256	184	182	194
1946	91	368	301	175	241	278	212	201	223
1947	137	390	343	217	300	337	256	247	272
1948	153	358	329	220	297	368	262	258	275

* Including cottonseed.
Actual values for 1929, from which other values may be computed, are (in millions of
dollars): cotton, 1434; tobacco, 234; other crops 589; total crops, South, 2256, Non-
South, 2869; livestock, South, 835, Non-South, 5343; total receipts, South, 3116, Non-
South, 8186.
SOURCE: Computed from reports of the Bureau of Agricultural Economics, U. S. Depart-
ment of Agriculture.

Thus it seems that the early recovery in the South was led primarily
by agriculture and secondly by manufacturing. In agriculture the boost
came principally from cotton and tobacco. Those were the early days
of the AAA and the program had quite an initial success in raising
prices. Between 1932 and 1934, the prices of both cotton and tobacco
approximately doubled. The index of cash receipts from cotton rose
from 31 in 1932 to 38 in 1933 and to 56 in 1934; the index for
tobacco rose even more, from 39 to 60 to 93. The cash receipts from
these two crops were nearly 500 million dollars greater in 1934 than
in 1932. In manufacturing, the South's lead was probably due to the
fact that it produces mainly consumer goods which responded more
quickly to the increased demand and to the NRA control measures of
1933 than did the heavier industries.

Table *XXV* shows the changes which occurred in the income struc-

TABLE *XXV* PRODUCTION INCOME RECEIVED BY SOURCE IN THE SOUTH AND
THE NON-SOUTH, 1929 and 1935

(Amounts in Millions of Dollars)

| ORIGIN | 1929 | | | | 1935 | | | |
| | SOUTH | | NON-SOUTH | | SOUTH | | NON-SOUTH | |
	AMOUNT	PER CENT OF TOTAL	AMOUNT	PER CENT OF TOTAL	AMOUNT	PER CENT OF TOTAL	AMOUNT	PER CENT OF TOTAL
Agriculture	2720	23.3	6000	9.5	1783	21.3	3715	9.0
Public Utilities	1339	11.5	7411	11.8	943	11.3	5060	12.3
Trade and Finance	2049	17.6	12537	19.9	1293	15.4	7342	17.9
Services	1512	13.0	6875	10.9	1090	13.0	4823	11.6
Manufacturing	1668	14.3	16391	26.0	1267	15.2	10460	25.3
Mining and Quarrying	412	3.5	1639	2.6	270	3.2	804	1.9
Construction	354	3.0	2871	4.6	168	2.0	860	2.1
Governments	947	8.1	5250	8.3	1047	12.5	5698	13.8
Miscellaneous	656	5.6	4047	6.4	493	5.9	2639	6.4
Total Production Income	11651	100.0	63021	100.0	8354	100.0	41401	100.0

SOURCE: See Table *XXIII*.

ture of the South and of the Non-South between 1929 and 1935
according to Slaughter's figures. Agricultural income declined in relative importance in both areas, more in the South than elsewhere.
Trade and finance also declined in relative importance, as did construction and mining and quarrying. Manufacturing gained slightly in
importance in the South and declined slightly elsewhere. In both areas
income from governments increased in relative importance by a little
more than 50 per cent.

Interrupted Recovery, 1936 to 1940. By 1936 southern income had
recovered to 90 per cent of its 1929 level while outside the South the
index stood at 81—a difference of nine points. In 1940 the South
enjoyed an income 1 per cent above 1929 while elsewhere it was 10
per cent below— a difference of eleven points. Throughout this period
the South consistently maintained this lead, although its economy
suffered two blows in addition to the slump of 1938, which affected
the whole country. Both of these blows hit agriculture, which had led
the initial recovery, and under their impact agricultural income faltered
and slipped.

In 1937, cotton—the ailing King—was hit by the largest crop in
history—almost 19 million bales. The surplus from this huge crop

depressed prices for the next three years, and despite government price support, cash receipts from cotton dropped from 58 per cent of 1929 in 1936 to 39 per cent in 1939. Then in 1939 the outbreak of the war brought a drastic curtailment of tobacco purchases by Great Britain, the principal foreign buyer, and the index of cash receipts from this crop dropped from 124 in 1937 to 88 in 1940. It is true that by this time the South had begun to diversify somewhat by increasing its production of other crops and livestock, the income from which held up somewhat better. But none the less, southern agriculture was hard hit; until 1937 it had managed to keep fairly well abreast of agriculture outside the South in its recovery from the depression lows, but now it dropped substantially behind.

How, then, was the South able to maintain its lead in the face of falling agricultural income? Of course, it must be remembered that in both areas total income dipped sharply in 1938 but it fell less in the South than elsewhere, so that the South's lead actually increased. In 1939 income rose sharply, in the South to the 1937 level and outside the South to only two points below that level. Figures do not seem to be available for an exact analysis of this movement, but the Census of Manufactures for 1937 and 1939 give a strong indication of the reason for the difference in behavior in the two areas. In 1939 wages paid in manufacturing in the South were only 15 million dollars, or 1.4 per cent, below the corresponding figure in 1937; outside the South they were nearly a billion dollars, or 11.2 per cent, below the 1937 figure. Figures for 1938, if they were available, would probably show even a sharper difference in manufacturing wages between the two regions. If so, they would go far to explain the difference in total income payments in the two areas.[5]

The principal reason why the South fared relatively well in 1938 was the fact that the slump of that year was concentrated principally in manufacturing, and especially in the metals industries. Kuznets estimates that net income originating in those industries fell by 2.6 billion dollars from 1937 to 1938, compared with a fall of 1.7 billions in all other divisions of manufacturing.[6] Since the South contains only a very few metals plants it did not experience as great a decline in industrial activity as did other parts of the country.

5 Kuznets shows that nearly half of the total decline in national income between 1937 and 1938—2.4 billion dollars out of 5.2 billion—was accounted for by the fall in manufacturing wages. *National Income and Its Composition, 1919-1938*, pp. 163, 578.   6 *Ibid*, p. 577.

Fields other than agriculture and manufacturing showed only small changes from 1937 to 1938; trade actually showed a small increase according to Kuznets' figures. Thus it was through a fortuitous combination of circumstances that income was maintained at a relatively favorable level in the South during these years despite the slump in agricultural prices. But it was significant that a region more heavily dependent on agriculture than most other regions could offset a greater decline in agricultural income with a smaller decline in manufacturing income.

The War Period. It was during World War II that the South made its greatest absolute and relative gains in income. During the five years from 1940 through 1944, southern income payments rose from 12.5

TABLE *XXVI* INDEXES OF SELECTED INCOME PAYMENTS IN THE SOUTH AND THE NON-SOUTH, 1940–1946

(1940 = 100)

TYPE OF PAYMENT	1940	1941	1942	1943	1944	1945	1946
Total Income Payments:							
South	100	126	170	215	237	242	255
Non-South	100	121	151	178	192	197	217
Agricultural Income:							
South	100	134	192	215	238	239	272
Non-South	100	146	223	233	251	268	326
Wages and Salaries in Mfg.:							
South	100	135	197	268	298	273	258
Non-South	100	140	200	264	275	243	232
Federal Civilian Payroll:							
South	100	150	302	597	598	569	454
Non-South	100	129	219	350	374	363	309
Military Payments:							
South	100	332	1104	2559	3061	3123	1436
Non-South	100	230	836	2247	3268	3841	1944
Total of Four Components:							
South	100	143	235	349	391	380	322
Per Cent of all Payments	32.8	37.1	45.3	53.0	54.0	51.5	41.3
Non-South	100	142	213	288	312	299	275
Per Cent of all Payments	29.8	35.0	42.3	48.1	48.6	45.2	37.8
Trade and Service Income:							
South	100				184		258
Non-South	100				163		231
Other Income:							
South	100				156		202
Non-South	100				128		170

SOURCE: Computed from reports of the U. S. Department of Commerce.

billion dollars to 29.7 billions, an increase of 115 per cent, while outside the South the increase was from 63.3 billions to 121.5 billions, or 92 per cent. Table *XXVI* shows the index numbers for certain of the more volatile or dynamic types of income payments for the war period and also for the two reconversion years.[7] From these data it will be seen that the South increased its income more each year than did the Non-South.

The one major income field in which the South failed to keep pace with the rest of the nation was agriculture. This was owing primarily to differences in the volume of products rather than to any fundamental difference in the behavior of agricultural prices. In the South there was a gradual decline in the area of crop land harvested, especially in cotton; total acreage fell from 101,781,000 in 1939 to 94,410,000 in 1946, or about 7 per cent.[8] In some cases yields per acre increased, which helped to maintain production, but there was little, if any, increase in the total volume of physical production.[9] On the other hand, outside the 'South there was an increase of about 11 per cent in the area of crop land harvested, which, combined with increases in yields per acre, produced a sharp increase in physical production.

The reason for the reduced acreage in the South was the lack of manpower and equipment. Military demands plus the attractive wages to be earned in factories, shipyards, etc., took laborers off of southern farms by the millions. Further, the mechanization of farming had not progressed as far in the South as elsewhere, and the lack of power equipment did not permit those who did remain on southern farms to increase the number of acres farmed to the extent that it was done in the Middle West, for example. Of course, agriculture was prosperous in the South during the war years and in this respect it did not lag far behind agriculture outside the South. In the total income pic-

[7] After these indexes were computed, the data for income payments by states were revised for the years 1942–46. The revised data for some of the items for certain years are not readily available, and for that reason these indexes have not been corrected to reflect the revised data.

[8] The greatest decline was in cotton acreage, which fell from 22,800,000 in 1939 to 16,695,000. Acreage in corn fell from 32,553,000 to 25,251,000 and tobacco from 1,829,000 to 1,762,000. Wheat, peanuts, rice, and a few other crops showed increases.

[9] For example, tobacco yield per acre increased from 940 pounds per acre in 1939 to 1,180 pounds in 1946 (averages for the United States). After sharp improvements during the 1930's cotton yields per acre fluctuated between 235 and 255 pounds per acre for several years. Thereafter the trend was upward; 1948 produced a record yield of 311 pounds.

ture it just about held its own from 1940 to 1944 (see Table *XXVI*) and this was remarkable in view of the heavy drain of manpower from southern farms.

During the early war years, wages and salaries paid in manufacturing in the South lagged slightly behind similar payments elsewhere, but later they forged ahead. This was probably owing to two conditions. First, in the early period the expansion in industrial production to meet the needs of defence and war took place principally in areas outside the South because those regions had the equipment, the labor, and the skills required.[10] As those facilities came to be fully utilized, as the available labor was all employed, and as it became desirable to decentralize war production for traffic and security reasons, more production was shifted to the South. Second, it was probably true that in the upgrading and other adjustments which took place after the war started, southern wage rates increased more than rates elsewhere.

The index figures for military payments must be used with care since the 1940 base was quite small. The very rapid increase in the figures for the South was due in part to the policy of locating army camps in the southern part of the country; the presence of the troops there attracted many dependents who also drew their pay there. Even if there had not been this shifting of population, however, these payments would still have been relatively more important in the South because, since they were uniform for the whole country, they would have been larger in relation to the low per capita incomes prevailing in the South. The importance of this source of income is shown by the fact that it was responsible for nearly one fourth of the total increase in income between 1940 and 1944, considerably more than any other source. The proportion of military payments made in the South exceeded considerably the proportion of population residing in that region.

As the Federal Government expanded its war activities a larger proportion of its civilian payroll than formerly was paid out in the South. No doubt a part of this was due to the civilian employees of the War

10 At the end of 1942, 10 of the 13 southern states had received less than a proportionate share of supply contracts when measured by value of manufactures in 1939; that is, the ratio of the accumulated value of supply contracts allocated to those states through December 31, 1942 to the value of manufactures in those states in 1939 was below the ratio for the country as a whole. The ratio for the whole country was 141; eight southern states had ratios below 100 and four of them fell below 50. *Survey of Current Business*, June, 1943, p. 13.

and Navy Departments attached to bases and camps in the southern region. Another part probably was due to the expansion of civilian controls; as these expanded it was likely that disbursements for payrolls by states and regions would have to be more nearly in accordance with population than when activities were more heavily concentrated in Washington. In 1940, 18.7 per cent of federal payrolls were disbursed in the South; in 1944, the figure was 27.0 per cent, almost exactly the same as the population ratio.

TABLE *XXVII* SOURCES OF INCOME PAYMENTS IN THE SOUTH AND THE NON-SOUTH, 1929, 1940, 1944, AND 1948

SOURCE	AMOUNTS (IN MILLIONS OF DOLLARS)				PER CENT OF TOTAL			
	1929	1940	1944	1948	1929	1940	1944	1948
SOUTH								
Agriculture	2,513	1,906	4,650	6,549	20.2	15.2	15.3	16.5
Manufacturing	1,562	1,717	5,119	5,994	12.6	13.7	16.8	15.1
Government	1,013	1,591	7,726	6,547	8.1	12.7	25.4	16.5
Trade and Services	3,107	3,157	6,058	10,364	25.0	25.2	19.9	26.1
Other	4,233	4,153	6,852	10,194	34.1	33.2	22.5	25.7
Total	12,428	12,524	30,405	39,694	100.0	100.0	100.0	100.0
NON-SOUTH								
Agriculture	4,425	3,532	9,174	14,464	6.3	5.6	7.5	8.7
Manufacturing	14,737	13,655	37,502	40,152	21.0	21.6	30.5	24.1
Government	5,050	7,815	19,137	22,089	7.2	12.3	15.6	13.3
Trade and Services	17,039	15,958	26,712	45,259	24.2	25.2	21.7	27.2
Other	28,938	22,368	30,376	44,399	41.2	35.3	24.7	26.7
Total	70,189	63,328	122,901	166,363	100.0	100.0	100.0	100.0

SOURCE: Computed from reports of the U. S. Department of Commerce.

The great influence of government payments on the southern economy is indicated in Table *XXVII*.[11] Between 1940 and 1944, they increased by more than six billion dollars and accounted for about 34 per cent of the total increase which took place during those years. In relative importance they doubled, while in the Non-South such payments rose in relative importance by only a little more than a fourth. On any basis of measurement, government payments were the most important factor affecting southern incomes in this period and practically the whole of the increase in those payments came from the Federal Government.

The four sources of income discussed above (agriculture, manufacturing, and federal military and civilian payroll disbursements)

[11] This category includes all income payments by all levels of government—state and local as well as federal.

provided a little less than a third of all income payments in both parts of the country in 1940; by 1944, they were responsible for about a half. Over the interval they accounted for almost 70 per cent of the total increase in incomes in both areas. In absolute amounts, southern income received its greatest increases from agriculture and government, while in the Non-South wages and salaries in manufacturing were the principal source of increase.

Reconversion. Reconversion started in the latter half of 1945 and was fairly well completed by the end of 1946. Naturally the rapid shift from a tremendous war production to peacetime production caused far-reaching changes in sources of income.

During this period income continued to increase over the whole country, but less rapidly in the South than elsewhere. The rate of increase in the South was only a little more than half the rate outside the region. The reasons for this are fairly clearly indicated; a more rapid demobilization of the military, industrial, and governmental war machines in the South than elsewhere, and the food crisis. The faster demobilization was reflected in greater reductions in income from federal civilian payrolls and military payments and by the greater declines in wage and salary payments in the "war industries" in the South. Income from governments in the southern region *declined* by 15 per cent from 1944 to 1948; in the rest of the country it *increased* by 15 per cent. In the two years from 1944 to 1946, wage and salary payments in the "war industries" declined by 54 per cent in the South compared with a decline of 34 per cent outside the region. In the "nonwar industries," however, wages and salaries in the South increased during those same years by 28 per cent compared with an increase of 26 per cent elsewhere. Because the South has a very large proportion of its industries in the latter category, the region suffered a slightly smaller decline in total wage and salary payments in all manufacturing than did the Non-South.

The effect of the food crises is reflected in the figures for agricultural income. During 1945 and especially 1946, all farm prices rose sharply, but the prices of the food crops and livestock rose most. Since the production of food crops and livestock is concentrated outside the South, southern agricultural income lagged behind similar income elsewhere. In 1944, the index of agricultural income in the South was only three points behind the index for the Non-South; by 1947, it was 25 points behind (see Table *XXIV*).

Another factor in the picture was the very small cotton crop of 1946—the smallest in more than 25 years.[12] That small crop made it possible to clear out the stock of surplus cotton and brought about a substantial rise in price. In fact, by the end of 1946 there was in the making a "cotton crisis" which permitted a much larger cotton crop to be sold in 1947 at prices about the same as those prevailing in 1946. This combination raised total proceeds from the cotton crop above the 1929 level for the first time in 1947. The high prices stimulated still larger production in 1948, and prices (and cash receipts) were sustained partly by the price support program of the Federal Government.

During the reconversion period the South did not maintain its relative position in income, but the loss was not great. It was not as great as might have been expected in view of the rapid advances during the war years, the quick reduction in federal payments, and the more rapid demobilization of war plants in the South. The declines came in those fields in which declines were inevitable—in the purely war activities. Perhaps the South made its adjustments in those fields a little more quickly than the rest of the country. In any event, the region resumed its advance in 1947, when per capita income in the South reached the highest point yet attained, both absolutely and in relation to income in the Non-South. In 1948, the absolute gain continued but the relative standing declined slightly.

SUMMARY

Definitely, the South made substantial gains in income between 1929 and 1948. Total income payments in the region increased by 219 per cent during these years compared with an increase of 137 per cent in the Non-South. Per capita income in the South rose from 47 per cent of the non-southern average in 1929 (or 42 per cent in 1931) to 65 per cent in 1947. This is substantial progress, even though the distance to be covered is considerable. Here is one way of looking at it; in 1929 it would have required a doubling of southern income to bring it up

[12] Under certain conditions a short crop might raise rather than lower agricultural income. In 1946 the sharp rise in price did much to compensate for the smaller amount of cotton. There were several reasons why it did not fully compensate for the reduced supply, among which were: (1) a surplus carried over from before the war; (2) increasing competition from synthetic fibres; (3) reduced exports due to the dollar shortage; and (4) the prospect that, with the war over, cotton production would be increased throughout the world.

approximately equal to non-southern income; now that could be accomplished by an increase of 50 per cent in southern income.

It may be well, in closing, to note briefly the principal changes in the income structure which occurred during the period covered by this survey. Table *XXVII* summarizes the data on this point. In relation to the total, agricultural income declined considerably, wages and salaries paid in manufacturing rose somewhat, and income from governments showed a large increase.[13] While agricultural income was declining in relative importance, significant changes were taking place within the total. We may use the figures for cash receipts from farming to make a fairly accurate analysis of the Department of Commerce figures on this point. The greatest change was the great decline in the importance of the cotton crop. Income from that crop (including cottonseed) amounted to 46 per cent of all cash farm receipts in the South in 1929; by 1946 it had declined to 21 per cent but by 1948 it had recovered to 27.2 per cent, or approximately to the 1939 level. Receipts from livestock and products rose from 28 per cent to 38 per cent of the total. Tobacco increased in importance from 7.5 per cent in 1929 to nearly 14 per cent in 1946, but thereafter declined to 10.4 per cent in 1948. Receipts from other crops rose from 19 per cent to more than 24 per cent.

The above changes reflect the far-reaching changes which have been going on in southern agriculture during the past two decades. While it is true that the importance of the cotton crop is greater than is indicated by the percentage figures measuring the cash which farmers get for it, still it is significant to note that in 1948, cash receipts of farmers from that crop were less than 6 per cent of total income payments in the South. The net income from cotton would be somewhat lower, probably around 4 per cent.

While income from agriculture was declining relatively, income from manufacturing was increasing both absolutely and relatively. In 1929, income from agriculture was about 65 per cent greater than income from manufacturing; in 1948, only about 10 per cent greater. If the trends of the past two decades continue, income from manufacturing will soon be the more important.

[13] Government payments include generally all pay and bonuses to civilian and military employees, allowances, allotments, interest payments to individuals, work relief and direct relief payments, old age, survivors, unemployment, and retirement benefits from social security funds, and pension payments by federal, state and local governments. See notes to Table 8, *Survey of Current Business*, August, 1947, p. 11.

Of all the components of income, that coming from governments showed the greatest change. In absolute terms, this segment increased more than sixfold; in relative importance it approximately doubled. In 1948 it was equal to the income from agriculture and somewhat greater than the income from manufacturing. In the years 1946–1948, while federal expenditures were declining, state and local expenditures rose rapidly; in 1949, governmental expenditures increased at all levels. There is little prospect for any substantial net decline in total governmental expenditures in the near future.

There has been little net change in the relative amount of income from trade and services. The decline during the war (in both the South and the Non-South) has been offset by gains in recent years. The relative importance of "other" sources declines as manufacturing and government increase their shares.

As income in the South rises in relation to income outside the region, there is a fairly clear tendency for income in the two areas to become more alike in their composition. In 1948, trade and services and "other" sources were about equally important in the two areas as sources of income. Between 1929 and 1948, there was a narrowing of the differences between the two areas in respect to income from agriculture and manufacturing. Over the whole period, there was no reduction of the difference between the two areas in regard to income from governments, but there was a sharp reduction in the difference between 1944 and 1948. As industrialization slowly increases in the South, it is logical to expect that its pattern of income will become more like that of the rest of the country.

IV BARRIERS TO THE ECONOMIC DEVELOPMENT OF THE SOUTH

There must be basic and fundamental causes for the great gap between southern and non-southern incomes described in the preceding chapter. It is quite unlikely that such causes are either few or simple. Rather, to produce such a large and persistent differential in income, those causes are likely to be numerous, complex, and deeply imbedded in the economy of the region.

In the discussions of the handicaps to southern economic growth which have raged in recent decades, many such causes have been pointed out with varying degrees of validity. In popular and political discussions. many of the alleged causes have been taken over as shibboleths or slogans and it was inevitable that they should often be misstated and misunderstood. Also, once a given factor has been assigned as a cause of southern retardation, there is a tendency to continue using it as an explanation regardless of changes which might have rendered it invalid or reduced its significance. Rather, the tendency has been to publicize it and to seek proof to demonstrate its validity.

The purpose of this chapter is to examine critically the more important practices, institutions, and conditions which have been put forward as barriers to economic progress in the South, to suggest certain others, and to make brief and summary appraisals of their economic validity. We are fully aware that this procedure is unsatisfactory. It often leaves us vulnerable in respect to our treatment of these questions, many of which are highly controversial. We believe that it is essential that these theories be reviewed and appraised critically and together. The space and facilities at our command do not permit a more thorough treatment.

BARRIERS PERTAINING TO THE POPULATION

Productivity. A cause frequently alleged for the southern lag is the low productivity of southern labor. It is not usually specified whether this refers to the innate ability to produce or to actual production. It is certainly true that actual production per laborer has been low, otherwise the lag would not exist. The important question is whether, given favorable conditions, southern labor can produce as effectively as non-southern labor.

In manufacturing, the available evidence indicates that low productivity is not an innate characteristic of southern labor. Man for man, using the same ratio of economic resources and with equally good management, southern labor can produce approximately as efficiently as non-southern labor. The low ratio of industrial capital equipment and the relatively simple processes employed by a considerable proportion of southern industries account for nearly all the low productivity of industrial labor in the region.[1]

In a study of 41 companies which operated plants in both the North and the South, Lester found that 23 of the concerns reported labor efficiency in the South equal to or in excess of labor efficiency in the North. Eighteen comparisons reported labor efficiency lower in the South. In respect to output per man-hour, the showing was even more favorable to the South, "probably due in large part to workloads per employee and to newer plants in the South in some industries." His conclusion was that "differences in labor efficiency and productivity apparently are not a fundamental factor in regional differentials in wage rates."[2]

In their study of new plant location in the South, McLaughlin and Robock report several cases in which employers found southern labor fully as efficient as northern labor even where a high degree of pre-

---

[1] It should be noted, however, that *in the same type of industry* capital equipment does not vary greatly between North and South. Indeed, in some cases southern industry has the newer and more modern machinery. It is simply that industries with high ratios of capital equipment per worker are usually located in the North, while industries with low ratios of capital equipment to labor are usually located in the South.

For a more detailed and comprehensive analysis of this whole subject see Chapter XVI, "Labor and Wage Policy."

[2] Richard A. Lester, "Effectiveness of Factory Labor: North-South Comparisons," *The Journal of Political Economy,* Vol. LIV (Feb., 1946), pp. 74–75. In practically every case where the output per man-hour was lower in the South, the wage differential was greater than the difference in output, so that labor cost per unit was lower in the South.

cision was required, with no report to the contrary. Comments from companies which operate plants in all parts of the country were as follows: a rubber tire company, "Productivity is just as good if not better in our southern plant"; an electric lamp company, "Although we originally had some doubts about labor productivity in the South, our experience has revealed a high efficiency of southern labor . . ."; an automobile company, "In most cases, labor efficiency in our southern plants is higher than in our northern plants."[3]

It is true that industrial plants in the South have a comparatively larger total labor supply to draw from to obtain their workers, so that they may be able to make a better selection than non-southern employers. It is true also that southern manufacturing does not, on the average, require as high a degree of skill and precision as non-southern industry. On the other hand, southern labor does not have equally good opportunities for training nor a heritage of several generations of skilled craftmanship. More and more, southern industry is developing along lines which require more skilled workers and thus far there is no evidence that it has failed to find the labor which can develop the skills required.

Factory workers make up only a minority of all southern workers. What of the productivity of the South's non-factory workers? Outside of manufacturing there is practically no sure method for measuring comparative productivity. However, the Department of Agriculture has developed an index of production which provides at least a rough measure of productivity in agriculture. One recent survey stated that the "three southern divisions have had about 50 per cent of all the farm workers in the nation, and have contributed about one third of the United States production in most of the interwar and World War II years."[4] This means that the southern farm worker produced only half as much as the non-southern worker. Undoubtedly a considerable part of this difference is due to the fact that the southern worker had less land, poorer land, and less machinery to work with. Also, the practice of specializing in cotton or tobacco, with their high peak labor requirements leaves laborers idle for several months in the year.

In other fields, such as trades and services, labor productivity is low in the South but it is impossible to measure the difference with

[3] Glenn E. McLaughlin and Stefan Robock, *Why Industry Moves South,* NPA Committee of the South Report No. 3, Washington, 1949, p. 74.
[4] Sherman E. Johnson, *Changes in Farming in War and Peace,* Bureau of Agricultural Economics, Washington, 1946, p. 59.

any degree of accuracy. Further, it is almost certain that if productivity in industry and agriculture were raised substantially, productivity in these lines would increase, too.

A priori, there is little basis for assuming that southern labor is less productive. True, the milder climate, often hot and humid, tends to reduce exertion and initiative. In certain parts of the country, however, severe weather and the necessity of protecting against the cold may also reduce labor efficiency. Our conclusion is that given equal training, equipment, and managerial ability, southern labor is as efficient as non-southern labor. At least, any difference which may exist is not a major barrier to raising southern incomes.

Health and Education.[5] The innate ability to produce may be affected and qualified by health and education. For this reason the productivity of labor in the South may be affected by the levels of health and education prevailing in the region, although it is extremely difficult to isolate and measure the effects of these two factors.

The average level of education in the South is distinctly below that prevailing in the rest of the country, although the region has made considerable progress in reducing the differential in the past 25 years. Even though no quantitative proof can be cited, it seems fairly certain that this improvement in the level of education was important in enabling the South to make the progress it did during World War II. The millions of southerners who entered the armed forces, who worked in factories and shipyards within and without the region, and who increased agricultural production at home could not have contributed as much as they did if they had had only the educational training which prevailed 30 years earlier. Only in comparatively recent years have most southern states adopted acceptable child labor laws, compulsory school attendance, and school terms of adequate length. The beneficial effects of these measures are just beginning to be felt; they should be even more evident in the future.

Health, even more than education, is difficult to measure and compare between regions. The available fragmentary evidence indicates somewhat poorer health conditions in the South. On the other hand, as noted earlier, death rates are only slightly higher in the South and the difference has been declining.

Presumably good health and educational training enhance productivity. If this were not true, there would be no *economic* reason for

[5] For a more comprehensive treatment of this subject see Chapter II.

striving to attain them. To the extent that they are important, the South labors under a handicap, although it would not appear to be a major one. Since conditions of health and education are, to a considerable extent, functions of income, they are effects as well as causes of the South's low income and they may be expected to improve as incomes rise—as, indeed, they have done in the past 20 years. The conclusion must be that health has probably been a minor but not a major factor in determining per capita income productivity in the South in comparison with the national average. Relatively poor educational facilities have been a factor in the past and continue to be so in diminishing degree.

Migration. As noted earlier, there has been a heavy and fairly persistent outward migration from the South in recent decades. At different times it has been contended that a disproportionate number of the more able and talented people have left the region because of better economic opportunities elsewhere. This, it is argued, is an important cause of the economic lag in the South since if these people had remained in the region they would have used their unusual abilities to increase production and raise incomes.

On *a priori* ground it might appear logical to assume that the South's loss from migration would be somewhat heavier among people of outstanding ability and education. First, Census data show that, generally, mobility is greater among people with more education and from higher-ranking occupations. Second, the Non-South offers a chance to compete for more positions carrying greater responsibility and prestige and commanding higher incomes. As with health and education, this condition is an effect as well as a cause. A substantial increase in the South's income level relative to the rest of the country would undoubtedly go far to stop any drain of talent that might be going on.

In corroboration of the above thesis, one study made some years ago showed that of the 6,015 native southerners living in 1932–33 who had attained distinction, 2,229 or 37.1 per cent, were living outside the region. After deducting the number of distinguished people who had moved into the region, the net loss was 813.[6] Another study

---

[6] Wilson Gee, "The 'Drag' of Talent out of the South," *Social Forces,* Vol. 15 (March, 1937), pp. 343–46. The test of distinction was a listing in *Who's Who in America.* Gee stated further, although without convincing proof, that "the South does not receive man for man the same grade of persons that it sends to other parts of the country."

made a few years later reached the same general conclusion and estimated that the loss of "eminent persons" was nearly three times as great relatively as the loss of white people generally. This study found, however, that the net loss of talented persons tended to decline after 1924.[7]

On the other hand, the analysis of migration in Chapter II shows that between 1935 and 1940, the South had a net gain from migration among persons who had received the most education and who held the more responsible and better-paying positions. This result is not necessarily inconsistent with the above studies since Gee's study was entirely a static one—of the population at a given time— and Geisert's was largely so. The fact that Geisert's static analysis showed a change after 1924 would suggest that the current flow had changed even more and that the direction of the net flow might have been reversed.

Finally, it should be noted that migration is an opportunity as well as a loss. For those who leave the region there is the opportunity to share the more abundant facilities and to compete for the better incomes outside the region. For those who remain there is a reduction in population pressure and more resources per capita available for use.

Aside from the loss of unusual and outstanding talent, there is the financial burden of educating and training the hundreds of thousands of people who are born and reared in the South but who go elsewhere when they reach the productive age. In both of these respects the South is sustaining a loss through migration but it is doubtful if such loss can be described as a major cause of the economic lag of the region. In any event, the total is less than would be suffered if there were no migration.

FACTORS PERTAINING TO NATURAL RESOURCES

Natural resources have been discussed at length in Chapter I. Only the question of the degree to which natural resources have or have not been a barrier to economic development of the South to the national level is discussed in this chapter.

Soils. Because of the dependence of the region upon agriculture, the quality and condition of the soils available to farmers is a factor of major importance to the economic welfare of the South. If one compares the South with the "national average," then the soils of the

7 H. L. Geisert, "The Trend of Interregional Migration of Talent: the Southeast, 1899–1936," *Social Forces*, Vol. 18 (Oct., 1939), pp. 41–47.

South are not greatly below the national average. How can one construct a national average of soil, however? The answer must be that to do so with both precision and meaning is almost impossible. Compared from the standpoint of effective productivity, the soils of the South are vastly superior to the deserts of Nevada or the plains of Wyoming. Compared with the soils of the Middle West, another great area of staple crop production, the soils of the South would in general be rated as poor.

The treatment which they have received in recent decades has reduced still further the productivity of these soils. The years of misuse have greatly reduced the productivity of the soils and the low productivity is now a major cause of low incomes. A concrete demonstration of this is provided by the millions of dollars which southern farmers pay out each year for commercial fertilizers in order to compensate to some extent for the lack of soil fertility. While not much can be done to change the innate qualities of the soils, much can be done to repair the damage of leaching and erosion, and, indeed, a considerable amount is being done. We might conclude that if anything the character of southern soils is somewhat less of an asset to income productivity than is popularly supposed.

Forest Management. About 43 per cent of the land area of the South is classified as forest land; omitting the western parts of Oklahoma and Texas, the proportion is well over half. The virgin timber has been cut from nearly all of this land, and much of the cut-over land has been left to reseed itself or to stand idle. About one fourth of the forest lands are definitely classed as understocked and only about 30 per cent are fully stocked. This means that a very substantial part of the region's land area is, in effect, standing idle and producing nothing. Further, many of the forest lands are not properly protected or managed.

Relatively small efforts applied to planting and caring for forest would yield considerable returns in the forms of timber, flood control, and protection against erosion. A region of low incomes can ill afford not to make such efforts, especially when they could be made during the off-peak season·when a large part of farm labor is normally idle. Another consideration is that in the years ahead more attention must be devoted to the forests in order to insure an adequate supply of raw materials for the lumber, furniture, paper, and chemical industries which provide a large share of the region's industrial employment.

Our forest resources then are a definite asset rather than a liability to the southern economic development.

Minerals and Water Power. It has been pointed out that the South is well supplied with fuel minerals—petroleum, natural gas, and coal—and with sulfur and phosphate rock. Beyond these, the region has deposits of a large number of minerals but in most cases they are so scattered and of such low quality that it is not profitable to work them.

The South is well supplied with water power. A very substantial part of this power is now being used; the region now has a higher proportion of hydrogenerated electricity than the rest of the country. Nevertheless, there are possibilities of further development of hydroelectric power. The TVA has shown what can be done by an integrated, coordinated development in developing latent power possibilities and in building up the demand for current. The remaining potential water power should be studied carefully for possibilities of further development.

Neither minerals nor water power is a barrier but rather an aid to economic development. The power not now being used may be an opportunity of considerable importance. In a region of comparative poverty, it is essential that such an opportunity should not be overlooked.

FACTORS PERTAINING TO INDUSTRY[8]

Capital Funds. In both industry and agriculture, and perhaps in other fields as well, much additional capital equipment will be required if southern income is to be raised to a level approaching the national average. With the low income now prevailing in the region, it is fairly obvious that the South can "catch up" in this respect only very slowly, if at all, if that equipment has to be provided for out of southern savings. This simple fact has led many to conclude that the major barrier to the improvements of economic conditions in the South is the lack of sufficient capital funds. But the problem is not as simple as this and the emphasis on this point has perhaps been misleading.

There are three major ways in which additional capital equipment for the South may be financed. First, and perhaps most important at present, large national companies with headquarters outside the region

---

8 See also Chapter VIII, "Financial Resources" and Chapter XV, "Policies for Industrial Development."

may build and equip plants in the South, using funds derived from various parts of the country. Second, large southern companies may sell securities or borrow outside the region. Finally, large and small southern companies may be financed locally. With the present structure of American industry, by far the largest part of any capital expansion is provided in the form of additional plants built by existing large companies rather than by the creation of new plants by new companies. In recent years such expansion has been financed very largely by retained earnings or other internal funds of the companies. If outside financing is necessary, the companies can place security issues with insurance companies or sell them on the open market. To the extent that southern plants are built in this way, only a part of the funds come from the South. This is the easiest and quickest way for the South to become industrialized. But this way depends upon the initiative and decisions of companies outside the region. There is little the region can do to speed up the process except to give the newcomers full information and fair treatment.

The thousands of smaller concerns in the South must depend almost entirely upon local financing. For them a shortage of indigenous capital funds would be a serious handicap. Whether such a shortage does exist is difficult to say. We know very little about the amount and types of savings by regions and states, and even less about the legitimate demand for investment funds.

It is true that the resources of commercial banks in the South have increased in the past 20 years more than most other measures of economic and financial activity, but the region still ranks lower with respect to them than in respect to most other items such as population, income, or production. Most parts of the region have only rudimentary facilities for assembling and investing savings—such as savings banks, insurance companies, and investment banks. It is certainly true that a considerable part of southern savings leave the region temporarily in the form of insurance premiums, purchases of stock on the New York Stock Exchange, etc. Probably sums greater than these are invested by insurance companies and other national corporations in the South. (This may represent sound practice in any event, since the small savings of the lower-income group in the South, as elsewhere, should be put into sound and seasoned securities or contracts rather than into the equities of small new companies.)

The conclusion which follows is that the South does indeed not have indigenous funds sufficient to finance the capital equipment which it needs, and must have, to raise its income, but that this fact alone is not necessarily serious. Since the South has real economic advantages, funds come in from the outside to finance the large plants, as indeed these funds have been coming South. The real problem lies in providing the necessary funds to finance the many small- and medium-sized companies, which ordinarily must be financed locally. Here the savings may be adequate, but the South does not have the necessary facilities for making them available, and the investment opportunities may not be the kind which are proper and desirable for the savers. It seems logical to conclude that shortage of capital funds for investment in the South has been overrated as a barrier to economic development.

Absentee Ownership. The first method of financing described above, and to some extent the second one, raises questions about the location of ownership. The control of the plants under the first method of financing would be largely in the hands of outsiders. To the extent that earnings were paid out as interest or dividends, there would be a drain of funds out of the region. Even in the second method there would be some control by outside financial interests and some drain of funds. At certain times the drain of funds could be critical and under certain conditions the interests of the company and of the community might conflict. Such considerations have given rise to the contention that absentee ownership is an important obstacle to the economic development of the South.

Clearly there are certain benefits and advantages which accompany the control of a business enterprise. The right to pick the officers and important employees; the power to decide whose products shall be bought, which banks and railroads shall be patronized, and where plants shall be located—all of these carry not only economic prestige and power, but they may also, indirectly and incidentally, give certain financial advantages either to the individual who possesses them or to the company which he represents. If those powers are used to favor interests outside the region, then absentee ownership would not be so desirable as local ownership.

On the other hand, the South has realized substantial advantages from absentee ownership. When a large national concern establishes a plant in the South, that plant brings with it the accumulated technology or "know-how" which the concern has built up over years of operation and the right to draw on the research facilities of the company. It may also bring with it a higher scale of wages than prevails in the region and other employee benefits which are more advantageous to workers—such as health insurance, vacation and retirement privileges, and better systems of personnel administration. They may retain these benefits at the same level in southern as in northern plants, not necessarily because they are compelled to do so, but because it is not feasible to have two different systems in the same company. To the extent that it is more efficient because of larger size, better research facilities, or more competent management, the national company is able to provide the higher levels of worker benefits without impairing its profits. These advantages do not necessarily accompany absentee ownership but they do prevail in some cases.

The above comparison of advantages has been, of course, on the basis of absentee versus local ownership. It overlooks the fact that in many cases there would be no industrial employment at all if it were not financed by outside funds. In such cases outside funds are definitely better than none—unless workers and natural resources are grossly exploited and abused.

There is another significant aspect to this problem of local versus absentee ownership. A very considerable portion of southern industry —more than is commonly realized—was originally owned locally. As the concerns grew and prospered, there was often a tendency for control to be transferred outside the region in two ways:

First, the southern concern might be sold to a national company and be integrated into the larger concern. During the recent war a considerable number of textile mills were sold to outside interests which were building up integrated spinning-weaving-finishing organizations. Second, when a company reaches a certain size, a majority of its stock may be bought by individuals outside the region and most of its financial activities may be transferred to New York, although its operations remain in the South.

The big tobacco companies and the Coca-Cola Company are examples of such developments. Such companies become national concerns and lose their regional characteristics. The region loses the employment opportunities in management and, perhaps not infrequently, some of the top-level officers. In addition, to the extent that ownership remains in the South, southern owners now pay outside brokers, traders, banks, trust companies, etc., for their services in buying, selling, and transferring securities.

It might well be asked what happens to the capital funds which the original southern owners receive when they sell to outside interests. No study of this question has been made and perhaps no worthwhile study can be made. As a conjecture, it is probable that a large part of it goes into the securities of large national companies, into government bonds, annuities, and other similar investments. It is doubtful that any large part of it becomes available as equity capital for southern companies. If this guess is correct, then the region, through these developments, loses a part of the indigenous capital it has accumulated. Once more the conclusion must be that while there are assuredly disadvantages in "absentee ownership," this factor has been overrated in its effect on the economic development of the South.

Infant Industry Status. The technology which plants of outside companies may bring with them calls attention to another major obstacle to the development of southern industry. Modern industrial systems are exceedingly complex, technical, and their various parts are interdependent. Individual companies take a long time to attain maturity as they develop methods, techniques, research facilities, sources of supply, financial connections, channels of distribution, and sales organizations. But an industrial system includes much more than the major industrial firms: There must be a host of smaller companies which design, manufacture, and service equipment; make or process essential parts or raw materials; use by-products; provide specialized engineering, financial, and legal services; and supply many other vital commodities or services.

These auxiliary services cannot be established in a community until industrialization has reached a certain stage. Then they require considerable time to train their personnel, make their connections, and attain an efficient operating basis. All this must be done on a voluntary, unplanned basis by individual concerns searching for profitable opportunities. There will be many delays, many false starts, and many failures. All of these things require many years for full development, and with respect to them the South is several decades behind the more industrialized sections of the Northeast and Middle West. While some of this process can be speeded by integration and cooperative action, in the main it is a handicap which can be overcome only with the passage of time.

Research Facilities. One of the most important of the factors discussed, and one which may be capable of specific improvement, is the amount of research facilities. Because of their small size and comparative immaturity, most indigenous southern industrial companies are conducting little if any research work. Further, many of the largest plants are branches of national companies which maintain their research laboratories outside the region.

According to data of the National Research Council, there were in the South in 1946, 158 industrial research laboratories, or 6.5 per cent of the national total. They employed approximately 5,900 people of all grades, or about 4.4 per cent of the total for the country.[9] Of the total employees, over 2,700 or almost half, were in Oklahoma and Texas and were engaged largely in research for the petroleum companies. In each of three southern states there were less than 50 people of all types engaged in industrial research. A recent study of patents granted in the 50 years from 1893 to 1943 shows that of all patents issued to American citizens, only 3.9 per cent were accredited to residents of nine southeastern states; between 1934 and 1943, the proportion was only 2.9 per cent.[10] There can be little doubt that more research facilities are needed in the region.

One possible way in which this need might be met is by the establishment of nonprofit research centers, either independently or in connection with some large universities or technical schools. Such centers would carry on pure research with the help of public appropriations or endowment income and would do contract research on a cost basis for industrial companies which desire it. Three such centers have been established in the South in recent years.

Managerial Training. Because the South has comparatively few large, locally owned industries and because most of the managerial work for the southern plants of national companies is performed outside the region, there has been little opportunity for the development of trained managers and other policy-forming officers in the region.

9 National Research Council, *Industrial Research of the United States,* 8th Ed. (Bulletin 113), Washington, 1946. The southern total was far below the 8,089 employed by *one* of the largest research laboratories of the country.
10 Southern Research Institute, *A Presentation of Southern Research Institute,* p. 2.

There have been numerous instances in which the founder of an industrial company, who was familiar with all its problems, died leaving neither children capable of taking his place nor other persons trained for the job. Not infrequently the establishment was sold immediately to a larger concern or slowly declined and was eventually absorbed by some other company after years of poor management.

This is a situation which may be capable of improvement by specific and group action. The establishment of one outstanding school of industrial management in this region, perhaps in connection with one of the large research centers, might help to provide a solution for a situation which has indeed constituted a limitation on economic development.

INSTITUTIONAL FACTORS

Freight Rates. Perhaps the barrier to southern progress which has received the greatest amount of popular attention has been the high freight rates. There are a number of reasons why this has been true. First, this cause—especially as it has been presented—seemed a logical one. Second, it absolved the region itself from responsibility for the economic lag and placed the blame on the railroads and the financial interests which control them—always favorite whipping boys. By the same token, it offered a quick and easy panacea if the right law were passed or the correct court decision gained. Third, the question easily and quickly became a political issue; after that the public heard much argument but relatively little factual analysis.

It is true that for several decades freight rates have been somewhat higher in the South than in the North, or Official Territory; just how much higher is discussed below. Also, there have undoubtedly been some cases in which southern producers have been hurt by high interregional freight rates. That is inevitable, North or South, when thousands of freight rates are involved; it is bound to happen even within a region. But it is our opinion that this factor has been greatly overemphasized, and that high freight rates are not now, if they ever were, a major barrier to the economic development of the South.

Basically, there are two reasons for this opinion: First, the difference in rates has not been as great as was popularly claimed. Second, even when the southern rates were higher, they have not been the major obstacle many have imagined—in some cases they actually have been advantageous to southern producers.

It may be well first to discuss one elementary misconception. Some arguments have implied that it was generally cheaper to ship a carload of freight from, say, New York to Atlanta than to ship the same carload from Atlanta to New York, and that this difference existed because of the caprice or evil design of the railroads. In general this simply is not true. As a general principle, freight rates to and from points in the South and elsewhere will be the same. The Interstate Commerce Commission requires that when differences do exist in the rates for movements in different directions those differences must be justified primarily by differences in cost.[11]

The difference in rates has not been presented in its true perspective and its importance has been greatly exaggerated. Most attention has been concentrated on *class* rates, which have ranged some 25 to 40 per cent higher in the South than in Official Territory. But very little traffic, comparatively, moves on class rates. A few historical facts will show why this is true and also indicate the beginning of the present controversy.

Because of the higher class rates in the South in the 1890's, "Southern railroads followed the policy of keeping rates on *manufactured* (italics supplied) goods from the South to the North on a level with those prevailing within Official Territory by granting commodity rates so that products made in the South could reach the large markets in the North in competition with Northern Manufacturers."[12] Thus in the South,

Traffic moving in any important volume, both carload and less than carload, was provided with commodity rates, usually materially lower than the class rates which otherwise would apply. The class-rate structure did not, therefore, reflect the rate level on the great volume of traffic. In the North a somewhat different situation prevailed. The class rates applied on the major part of the railroad traffic moving within that territory, including practically all less-than-carload traffic. Commodity rates were of minor importance. The class-rate level did rather closely reflect the general rate level. The result was that the class rates in the South were considerably higher than those in the North. The commodity rates in the

---

[11] In one case Commissioner Eastman of the I.C.C. said that to have different rates for north-bound and south-bound traffic would be "inconsistent with the principle . . . that 'differences in transportation charges from competing producing points' should be based on 'differences in circumstances and conditions surrounding the *transportation* (italics in original) of the competitive products.'" *State of Alabama v. New York Central R. Co.*, 235 I.C.C. 346.

[12] William H. Joubert, *Southern Freight Rates in Transition*, Gainesville, University of Florida Press, 1949, p. 327.

South on a substantial volume of traffic were on about the same level as, or on somewhat lower levels than, the rates applicable on like articles within the North.

A situation somewhat similar to that within the South existed in connection with the rates between the two territories. . . . Only a small part of the north-bound traffic was subject to the class rates, low commodity rates being applicable on the bulk of that traffic. . . . Prior to the end of the period of Federal control of the railroads (in 1920) they (the Southern railroads) met little opposition to the establishment of such rates, but since that time the northern carriers generally have insisted with success . . . that north-bound rates on competitive commodities be maintained on higher levels than the rates on like commodities within the North.[13]

This pattern of traffic movement according to the type of rates has continued. In a test survey of all carload traffic moving on September 23, 1942, only 1.8 per cent of all traffic in the Southern Territory moved on class rates, 6 per cent moved on exception rates, and 92.2 per cent moved on commodity rates. In Official Territory the percentages were, respectively, 5.8, 17.6, and 76.7. Of the traffic moving from Southern to Official Territory, which is the heart of the controversy, the percentages were, respectively, 0.9, 4.9 and 94.2. On the contrary, on south-bound traffic the percentages were 12.6, 36.3, and 51.1.[14] These are striking differences and they demonstrate how completely traffic out of the South is governed by commodity rates.

Commodity rates have been obtained for most southern commodities (by volumes) moving and in many cases those rates have been so constructed as to reduce or eliminate the territorial differential. In fact, on several important southern commodities, such as aluminum sheet and plate, automobile tires, boots and shoes, cigarettes, and shelled peanuts, the southern rates are substantially lower. That shippers have been able to get satisfactory rates on most of the major southern commodities is indicated by the fact that there have been few complaints about high freight rates on such things as textiles, manufactured tobacco, petroleum products, chemicals, lumber, or furniture. As Commissioner Eastman said in his dissenting opinion on the *Southern Governors' Case,* the case brought

in issue the interterritorial rates on a very limited number (which might also be called "surprisingly small") of southern mineral and manufactured

---

[13] From the majority opinion in *State of Alabama v. New York Central R. Co.,* 235 I.C.C. 265–66.
[14] *Class Rate Investigation, 1939,* 262 I.C.C. 479.

products. Conspicuous by omission are the major products manufactured, mined or grown in the South which account for the greater part of its commerce with the North.[15]

It is impossible to give an accurate and meaningful statement of the difference between the South and the rest of the country in regard to freight rates generally. There are thousands of such rates and the amount of traffic which moves on each varies greatly from one territory to another. One careful study of the problem makes this

CHART *V*   CARLOAD FREIGHT TRAFFIC MOVING SEPTEMBER 23, 1942 IN CERTAIN AREAS BY TYPES OF RATES CHARGED

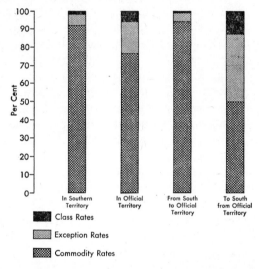

summary statement: "Outbound rates on most of the principal southern manufactured products range between 90 and 110 per cent of corresponding northern rates."[16] That is about as near equality as one could expect, even within a region. Joubert, in his excellent study, concludes that "the level of all freight rates in the South, based upon a weighted average, is probably not more than 5 per cent higher than the weighted average of all rates in Official Territory."[17]

Finally, there is one aspect of this controversy which apparently has never been spelled out. Those who were pushing the southern

15 *State of Alabama v. New York Central R. Co.,* 235 I.C.C. 334.
16 Milton S. Heath, "The Rate Structure," *Law and Contemporary Problems,* Vol. XII (Summer, 1947), p. 414.   17 *Op. cit.,* p. 345.

case wanted interterritorial rates which would allow southern producers to reach northern markets with the same rates, mile for mile, as northern producers. But they did not want the same rates to apply on south-bound traffic. They, and especially the southern railroads, did not want any reduction in rates on south-bound traffic or in interterritorial rates within the South. This was arguing for rate making on the "destination basis" which, as Commissioner Eastman pointed out, "would produce a higher level of rates south-bound than north-bound." Plainly this would be materially to the advantage of the southern producers . . . but it would be inconsistent with the principle of making rates on the basis of cost."[18] Joubert notes that after the Class Rate Decision and the interim adjustments described below, there were complaints from southerners "because the interterritorial rate reductions under the interim adjustment were to apply on traffic from as well as to Official Territory."[19] In brief, the southern case became, at least in part, not a demand for equal treatment but for preferential treatment; for an equal position in northern markets and a preferential position in southern markets.

Thus, while differences in freight rates have existed, their importance has been greatly exaggerated. Most of the "horrible examples" which have been cited have been rates for commodities of minor importance. Such rates may be obsolete and of no appreciable importance to anybody. If there were any considerable amount of traffic to move on such rates, the roads might well revise them or make new ones; the railroads are interested in developing new business along their lines and are willing to consider new rates when it appears profitable to do so. Further, many parts of the South are served by water transportation which has always provided a potent form of competition to keep rail rates reasonable. In recent years the shipper has gained a new bargaining weapon in dealing with the railroads—the motor truck. Whether as a common carrier, a contract carrier, or his own vehicle, the shipper can use the truck either to carry his product all the way to market or to carry it to the water front to connect with water transportation. With some items, air transportation is also becoming a significant form of competition.

High freight rates on interregional shipments are not an unmixed evil to southern producers; in some cases they may give southerners an advantage over northern competitors. As Heath states it, "Rela-

18 See *supra*, footnote 11.   19 *Op. cit.*, p. 379.

tively higher outbound rates on such raw materials as unmanu-
factured tobacco, clay, and hides favor southern industry; and this
is especially so when, as in these cases, the outbound rates on products
manufactured from such raw materials are the same as or lower than
northern rates."[20] If the higher rates are on manufactured goods
coming into the region, they act somewhat as a protective tariff for
the southern producer in the local market. His competitor outside
the region is at a disadvantage because he must pay the high rate to
deliver the goods to the southern market. As southern incomes rise,
that "home market" becomes more attractive and more profitable.
However, the freight-rate structure should not be built upon the principle of "protecting" or benefiting one area as compared with another.
For that reason the elimination of regional differences in rates, such
as is now going on, is to be commended to the extent that it is justified
by cost considerations.

There are other reasons to suggest that freight rates have not had
the importance many attach to them. Again Commissioner Eastman's
dissenting opinion in the *Southern Governors' Case* states a cogent
argument:

> It seems to be agreed that the southern producers had little, if any,
> reason to complain of their rates to the North prior to 1920 . . .
> In light of these facts, it is of interest to note that the statistics in the
> majority report show clearly that the trend in industrial development
> between 1923 and 1929 was markedly better in the South than in the
> North, and that the South suffered less in the subsequent depression.
> This took place in the period in which the interterritorial rate policy of
> the railroads is claimed to have been changed to the detriment of the
> South and the benefit of the North. It will thus be seen that in the earlier
> period, when the rate policy is admitted to have been favorable, southern
> industry (other than agriculture and lumber) was relatively stagnant,
> whereas ever since the changed policy, claimed to be oppressive, was
> inaugurated, industry has been developing considerably faster in the South
> than in the remainder of the country.[21]

Much the same argument could be made with respect to the state
of Virginia, almost all of which lies within Official Territory and thus
enjoys the lower class rates of that Territory. That state has most of
the characteristics shared by the other southern states and in addition
is much closer to the great eastern markets. If freight rates were as
important as many claim, Virginia should be the leading industrial

[20] *Op. cit.,* p. 414 fn.　　[21] 235 *I.C.C.* 341–42.

state of the South. While the state has made considerable progress, there is nothing in its record to indicate that it has enjoyed any special advantage over the other southern states.

Finally, there is the fact that few of the complaints about freight rates have come from leaders of southern industry.[22] In fact, at times it has been difficult to find substantial businessmen who had grievances and who would appear as witnesses. As a group, those men do not seem to have been greatly dissatisfied with the comparative freight rates which they have had.

Any interregional differences in rates which remain are in process of being eliminated. In a series of moves, which have been upheld by the Supreme Court, the Interstate Commerce Commission has ordered railroads to: (1) establish a uniform classification for freight for the whole country; (2) set up a single uniform scale of maximum rates for nearly all of the country; (3) reduce intraterritorial and interterritorial class rates by 10 per cent in Southern Territory and increase intraterritorial class rates by 10 per cent in Official Territory. The latter was an interim adjustment to give relief while the first two changes are being worked out. In the meantime, general freight-rate increases were granted "which were so arranged that they, together with the interim adjustment, might well reduce the differentials to relative insignificance."[23] These moves were made on the basis of studies which showed that the costs of southern roads were no higher than the costs of roads in Official Territory. If this policy of equalizing rates is continued and made effective, it should finally remove this factor from the area of discussion. Even though this issue has been unduly magnified as a factor affecting the industrial development of the South, this new policy is to be welcomed.

[22] In regard to one of the most famous cases—the *Southern Governors' Case*—Commissioner Eastman said, "with respect to some of the products included, the interest manifested in the proceedings by producers and shippers within the South was scant." 235 *I.C.C.* 334.

[23] Joubert, *op. cit.,* p. 379. A number of years have elapsed since the decision of the I. C. C. in 1945 which was intended to eliminate interregional rate differentials. The process of working out rates which will actually eliminate the differentials, while allowing for all other highly technical considerations, is an exceedingly complicated one and has not yet been completed. It appears that several more years will be required to complete the process. Indeed, the process of rate making is so complex that, even with the best intentions in the world, it may prove impossible to convince everyone that differentials have in fact been removed. This is the more likely to be true because what is often really, if unconsciously, desired is not the removal of all differentials but the substitution of differentials favoring a particular region for the existing rates.

International Trade Policies.[24] It has long been the standard argument of almost all southerners that, regardless of its effects upon the country as a whole, a protective tariff was particularly disadvantageous to the South. Indeed the protective tariff was for years considered so devastating a blight on the South as to condemn it to permanent economic inferiority so long as it existed. The reasons for this argument were quite simple. The South has been more dependent on agriculture than other regions and its two principal crops—cotton and tobacco—have depended heavily upon foreign markets. Prices of these two basic crops were determined by conditions in the world market, but southerners had to pay higher prices for many of their consumer goods in the tariff-protected domestic market. Further, the tariff reduced the amount of goods other countries could sell to us and hence reduced the amount of cotton and tobacco they could buy from us. Thus much of the protection accorded to northern manufacturers was provided at the expense of southern farmers.

This was at one time a significant and valid argument and still has some validity. It probably was never so important in accounting for the low standard of living in the South as many of its adherents claimed because it overlooked the fact that, regardless of the conditions of international trade, the low productivity of large amounts of manpower in the production of the two crops prevented the region from attaining the standards of living prevailing in some parts of the country.

Conditions have changed greatly in the past 20 years and the effect of many of those changes has been to reduce somewhat the significance of our tariff policy in determining the volume of our imports and exports. The influence of tariffs upon the volume of international trade has declined throughout the world. Other factors, such as inflation and deflation, exchange controls, quotas, and bilateral agreements, are more potent and direct in their effect on international trade than tariffs ever were. It should be recognized, moreover, that the situation is now vastly more complex than it was 20 years ago. The trade controls now used are so intertwined with domestic, financial, economic, and political conditions in the various countries that the removal of these controls is likely to prove an exceedingly complex and long-drawn-out affair, far more difficult than simple reciprocal agreements to reduce tariffs.

[24] For a fuller discussion of international trade, see Chapter XVII.

Perhaps more significant is the fact that the importance of foreign trade to the southern economy has declined greatly. In the four years 1925–29, the South supplied about 30 per cent of the nation's exports; in the four years, 1945–48, only about 13 per cent. This represents a continuing trend during the whole period. The dollar value of those exports in relation to the value of agricultural production, income payments, and factory production in the South has declined sharply, while in the remainder of the country those ratios have risen. In general, the South is now no more dependent upon exports in general than is the rest of the nation.[25] Some part of the change in the South's status may have been caused by our tariff policy. At any rate, we should undoubtedly have been able to export more cotton, everything else being equal, if our tariff had been lower or nonexistent. The indications are that our policy of supporting the price of cotton and tobacco at levels well above those prevailing in the world markets has in recent years also been a factor in reducing our exports of those products. This policy has also meant that the prices of our cotton and tobacco are no longer determined primarily by the international market. At the same time, increasing incomes have caused a great expansion in the domestic markets for cotton and tobacco. All of these factors have worked to produce this striking change in the relative importance of foreign trade to the South.

Finally, it must be noted that the South has developed quite a substantial interest on the other side of the controversy. Industry has grown in the South, both absolutely and relatively to the rest of the nation. As is true of most new industrial areas, the products turned out by this industry are predominantly of the staple, standardized, and relatively crude types. These products are also produced by many other countries and are subject to keen competition in the world markets. For this reason, it seems possible that if there were a general reduction in international barriers to trade, southern industry might experience a greater increase in competition than would non-southern

[25] The prices of two of the principal agricultural crops are still affected to a crucial extent by our exports of these commodities. The sudden disappearance of the export market for cotton and tobacco would probably be more disastrous to the producers of these commodities than would the disappearance of the foreign market for, say, automobiles. It is easier to see how an increase in domestic purchasing power could compensate for the loss of foreign purchases of American automobiles than to see how a similar increase in domestic purchasing power would offset the loss of foreign consumption of our cotton and tobacco.

See also the chapter on International Trade.

industry. The effects of this competition on the expansion of southern industry are likely to be weighed against benefits to be derived by southern consumers and farmers. An increase in the rate of expansion of industries having a higher ratio of capital to labor would be required as an offset if unemployment were to be avoided.

In summary, the South's specialized interest in our foreign trade policies has substantially diminished. Those policies are still important in their national and international aspects, but the South's interest in them is very much the same as those of the rest of the nation.

Terms of Trade. The typical products of southern economy are agricultural products and the staple, more standardized industrial goods. The producers of those goods traditionally have been numerous and small; usually no small group of them has been able to control production or price. The goods are produced and sold in a fairly competitive market, where prices are free to fluctuate. For this reason, southern producers have not been in as strong a bargaining position regarding the prices of their products and not as able to influence those prices by their own decisions as are northern producers of the more highly processed and differentiated goods.

On the other hand, the goods which are typical of the Non-South, and especially many of those bought by southerners, are produced by the large-scale, mass-production industries in which there are often only a few large producers and which are marked by varying degrees of monopoly or imperfect competition and by industry-wide collective bargaining on the part of labor. Prices and costs are administered and often change only at considerable intervals and as the result of administrative decisions rather than by the action of the market. When demand weakens, the adjustment can be made by curtailing production rather than by reducing costs and prices. Thus, when supply is abundant and adjustments are necessary, southerners have to give more cotton, tobacco, and textiles for their automobiles, tractors, and refrigerators. Since monopolistic or imperfectly competitive prices are usually higher than freely competitive prices, southern products are usually at a disadvantage in this exchange. It is this price relationship that we have designated the "terms of trade" of the region.

This condition is due largely to the later development of industry in the South and to the kinds of industries which have made up that development thus far. It is being corrected to some extent by the development of petroleum, paper, chemical, and other similar industries in the region. It should be noted, however, that to the extent that such industries are monopolistic, their expansion in the whole country is probably less than it would be if they were fully competitive. If the factors of location would normally cause a proportionately larger part of the expansion to take place in the South, then the South is especially handicapped by the presence of imperfect competition.[26]

The terms of trade are also being offset to some extent by the crop control programs applying to cotton and tobacco. Farmers, too, have learned to play the game of "Monopoly" (with the help of the Federal Government) and they seem to like it. It is unfortunately true, however, that this game raises other economic problems which are difficult of solution.

It is true that under the conditions described above the terms of trade are not always unfavorable to the South. During wars and boom periods, agricultural products, raw materials, and the staple manufactured goods advance in price much more than the more complex and highly fabricated goods—in such periods the terms of trade swing in favor of the South. Thus the boom period since 1941 has done much to give the South more favorable terms of trade and has thereby contributed to the relative increase in income the region has enjoyed. Further, the region which has the poorer terms of trade makes its adjustment during periods of depression in the form of price reductions rather than in lower production. This means that employment is better maintained in that region. There may be some offsetting advantage in the higher employment although the result as a whole has been a net disadvantage to the southern economy.

[26] The basing point system of pricing has perhaps been a factor of some importance in discouraging the construction of new plants in the South which would be competitive with those already existing in the North. A study dealing with this subject is being made for the Committee of the South by Professor George Stocking of Vanderbilt University.

V RECENT DEVELOPMENTS IN AGRICULTURE

The South is more dependent upon agriculture than most other sections of the country. Previous chapters have given some indications of the importance of agriculture in the southern economy. The purpose of this chapter is to examine the agricultural segment of that economy in somewhat greater detail to see what are its basic characteristics and what trends have affected it in recent years. A later chapter on Agricultural Policy will interpret these trends and discuss appropriate policies in the light of the basic agricultural resources of the region.

As a background for the discussion to follow, it may be well to list here the more important changes which have been going on in southern agriculture during the past 20 years. They are: (1) there have been large shifts in farm population, with a substantial decline over the whole period; (2) cotton production declined enormously, both absolutely and relatively; (3) the production of most other farm commodities, especially of tobacco and citrus fruits, increased both absolutely and relatively; (4) there was a considerable increase in the number and value of livestock, both absolutely and in relation to the rest of the country; and (5) an inflationary rise of prices greatly distorted all value figures.[1]

BASIC AGRICULTURAL RESOURCES

Farm Population. Some summary data on the amount of resources which have been devoted to agriculture in the South since 1929 are

[1] Although it would be desirable from many aspects, it has not been feasible to deflate all value figures to eliminate the effects of changing prices. An attempt has been made, however, to give enough data on physical quantities to show what has been happening to them.

given in Table *XXVIII*.[2] In the early 1930's farm population increased somewhat as the depression drove thousands back to the farms. Later this trend was reversed and by 1940 the farm population was almost exactly the same as in 1930. Then the war years produced the greatest exodus yet witnessed from southern farms, and in five years the farm population declined by about four million, or one fourth.[3] After the war, as service men returned from the armed forces and as industrial workers in munitions plants, shipyards, and airplane assembly plants were laid off, about half of the wartime loss was wiped out with the return of some million and a half people to southern farms. But the figure for 1948 remained about 1,750,000 below the 1940 figure—or roughly 13,700,000. This was almost exactly half of the farm population of the United States.

Outside the South, the exodus from the farms was not so heavy during the war as in the South, nor was the return flow after the war quite so great.[4] The Non-South had a farm population of about 13,750,000 in 1948. This represented a decline of about 7.5 per cent from 1940, compared with a decline of 11.3 per cent in the South.

The data on farm workers are available only for 1935, 1940, and 1945; they are open to serious question as to reliability and significance.[5] As they stand, the figures seem to indicate that between 1935 and 1945, the number of farm workers in the South declined by about 43 per cent. In the rest of the country the decline was about half as great, or 21 per cent.

[2] These data are taken largely from the *Census of Agriculture* which is made quinquennially by the Bureau of the Census. In this *Census* the data pertaining to a specific point of time, such as population and values, are for some early date in the years ending in "0" and "5," whereas the data for crop production, acreage, yields, and the like are for the years immediately preceding. The concepts and procedures used in this *Census* differ somewhat from those used by the Bureau of Agricultural Economics in the Department of Agriculture, and for that reason there are often considerable discrepancies in data for the same year from the two sources.

[3] The figures of the Department of Agriculture show a loss of somewhat more than three million, or about one fifth. *Agricultural Statistics,* 1946, p. 531; 1948, pp. 542, 544.

[4] Throughout this chapter, where it seems appropriate, comparisons will be made between the South and the Non-South. This is done to afford some basis of comparison and to help to determine whether developments in the South were unique or were merely part of a national pattern. It is not meant to imply that conditions or developments outside the South are a norm or desirable pattern for the South.

[5] The data are supposed to include both family and hired workers, but for the different years they are not comparable as to dates taken, age of workers covered, and the concept of "worker." For a discussion of these points see *Census of Agriculture,* 1945, II, pp. 281–82.

Number of Farms. The number of farms has been affected somewhat by the changing definition of a farm used by the Bureau of the Census. Nevertheless, there has apparently been a considerable decline since the peak was reached in 1935. In the South the number of farms in 1945 was about 11 per cent below the 1930 figure, whereas in the

TABLE *XXVIII* SOME BASIC STATISTICS ON SOUTHERN AGRICULTURE, 1930, 1935, 1940, AND 1945

ITEM	UNIT	1930	1935	1940	1945
Farm Population	Thousands	15,586	16,074	15,585	11,566
Per Cent Change	Per Cent	—	+3.1	−3.0	−25.8
Farm Workers*	Thousands	—	6,561	4,711	3,752
Per Cent Change	Per Cent	—	—	−28.2	−20.4
Number of Farms	Thousands	3,088	3,262	2,857	2,736
Per Cent Change	Per Cent	—	+5.6	−12.4	−4.2
Land in Farms	Mil. Acres	329	361	356	364
Average Per Farm	Acre	106	111	125	133
Crop Lands Harvested**	Mil. Acres	105.6	98.1	99.7	98.5
Average Per Farm	Acre	34.2	30.1	34.9	36.0
Woodland in Farms	Mil. Acres	80.0	105.1	82.9	91.2
Average Per Farm	Acre	25.9	32.2	29.0	33.3
Value of Farms (Land and Bldgs.)	$ Million	11,571	8,198	9,111	12,375
Average Per Farm	$	3,747	2,513	3,189	4,523
Value of Implements and Machinery	$ Million	648	—	657	1,112
Average Per Farm	$	210	—	203	406
Value of Livestock	$ Million	1,415	961	1,255	2,151
Per Cent Change	Per Cent	—	−32.1	+30.6	+71.4
Average Per Farm	$	458	295	439	786
Number of Farms with Tractors	Thousand	119	—	222	385
Per Cent of All Farms	Per Cent	3.8	—	7.8	14.1
Number of Tractors	Thousand	134	—	255	468
Per Cent Change	Per Cent	—	—	+89.9	+83.7

* See text for explanation.
** The figures for these items are for the years 1929, 1934, 1939, and 1944, respectively.
SOURCE: Computed from reports of the Bureau of the Census.

Non-South the decline was only about 2 per cent. Along with the reduction in the number of farms, there has been an increase of about 10 per cent in the total area of land in farms. "Most of this increase represented land used for grazing, reflecting the increasing importance of livestock in this section."[6] These two movements—increasing land

6 *Ibid*, p. 17.

area in farms and declining number of farms—have caused an increase of about 25 per cent in the average size of farms in the South since 1930.

Acreage of Crop Lands. While the total of land in farms increased, the area of crop lands harvested declined. Between 1929 and 1939, the area of harvested crop lands declined throughout the United States —about 10 per cent in the South and about 11 per cent in the Non-South. During the war years after 1939, however, there was considerable pressure to increase farm production, and outside the South the area of crop lands harvested rose, reaching almost the 1929 level by 1946, or an increase of about 15 per cent over 1939. But in the South the decline continued, and by 1946 the figure was some 16 per cent below the 1929 figure.[7] This difference in behavior in the two areas was due to several factors. (1) There was not the same pressure to increase the principal southern crops; for example, throughout the war years there was a large surplus of cotton and strict acreage controls were kept on the tobacco crop. (2) The loss of manpower was much greater on southern farms, probably because the wage differential offered by industrial employment was much greater. (3) The scarcity of power equipment in the South did not permit those who did remain on the farms to increase greatly the acreage cultivated by extra shifts and night plowing as was done in some parts of the country.

Even after the war and the return of a considerable number of workers to the farm, the increase in harvested acreage was comparatively small—from 94.4 million to 96.1 million acres. The latter figure was almost 17 million acres, or about 15 per cent, below the 1929 figure.

The average acreage of crop land harvested per farm increased by almost a fifth from 1934 to 1944, but the latter figure was only slightly above the 1929 figure. The average for the South is still somewhat less than half of the figure for the Non-South.

The increased land made available by increasing total farm land and declining crop lands went principally into pasture and woodland. On the average, southern farms have almost as much woodland as

7 These statements are based on the figures of the Department of Agriculture which, as noted above, are somewhat different from the Census figures. The former show an over-all decline from the 112.9 million acres in 1929 to 94.4 million acres in 1946. See *Agricultural Statistics.*

they have crop land; they have a larger proportion of woodland than any other region except New England. While undoubtedly this land is generally poor in quality and much of it is not well suited for cultivation, nevertheless it is a major resource which thus far has not received the attention it deserves.[8]

The Investment in Agriculture. By 1945, the value of farm land and buildings in the South had risen slightly above the 1930 value; outside the South it was still some 6 per cent below the 1930 figure. The principal increase came during the war years and was undoubtedly caused by the inflation of prices rather than by physical improvements, since it is doubtful that even normal maintenance was possible during the war. The behavior of the prices of southern farm lands is almost paradoxical in view of what has been happening to agricultural production and farm population. In 1948, the Department of Agriculture's index of the estimated value per acre of farm real estate, with 1912–14 as a base, showed the following values for the three census divisions making up the South: 223, 256, and 190. Only one other division showed a comparable increase—the Pacific states with 210. The figure for the whole country was 170. Increases from 1940 to 1948, for the three southern divisions were, respectively, 108, 129, and 92 per cent, compared with 102 per cent for the nation.[9] These inflated values will probably be a major obstacle to necessary agricultural adjustments in the years ahead.

The values of implements, machinery, and livestock in 1945 were also heavily influenced by inflation but there had been some physical increases in these items. All of these series showed greater increases in the South than in the Non-South, both in total and in average per farm, although absolute figures were far lower. The average value of implements and machinery per farm in the South at current prices exactly doubled between 1940 and 1945, while elsewhere it increased by only a little more than 50 per cent. With the value of livestock, however, the situation was about reversed.

The total investment in southern agriculture in the form of land,

[8] See the chapter on Forest Resources for a further discussion of this point.
[9] *Agricultural Statistics,* 1948, p. 530. North Carolina, with an index of 324 in 1948, led the nation by a wide margin. This figure reflected some fantastically high values for tobacco lands. However, net incomes have not been capitalized into land values to the same extent as during World War I. *The Balance Sheet of Agriculture,* 1947, p. 15.

buildings, implements, machinery, and livestock amounted to $15.6 billion in 1945, or an average per farm of $5,715. The corresponding figures for the remainder of the nation were almost three times as large; a total of $44.4 billion and a per farm average of $14,207. On the average, every farmer outside the South had roughly two and a half times as much invested capital to work with as did the southern farmer; in implements and machinery, he had more than three times as much.

Farmers' equities in their property increased more than the rise in values, because farm debts were reduced in the period from·1930 to 1945. Every five-year period saw some reduction in the total of farm mortgages, which declined from almost $2 billion in 1930 to $1.2 billion in 1945, for a reduction of nearly 40 per cent. In the ten years after 1935, the proportion of the mortgage debt to the value of land and buildings was almost cut in half—from 18.9 per cent to 9.6 per cent. The average mortgage per mortgaged farm declined from $1,930 in 1930 to $1,773 in 1945; there was no significant change in the proportion of all farms mortgaged. The decline in mortgage debt plus some reduction in interest rates reduced total interest payments on mortgages from $128 million to $61 million—a reduction of more than 50 per cent. As a proportion of cash receipts from farming the reduction was almost 75 per cent—from 4.1 per cent to 1.1 per cent. After declining for 20 years, the total of farm mortgages showed small increases in 1946 and 1947.

The same movements were going outside the South. Total mortgages on non-southern farms were reduced by 47 per cent between 1930 and 1945. But, even so, in the latter year a smaller proportion of southern farms were mortgaged and the proportion of total mortgages to the value of land and buildings was somewhat lower in the South—9.6 per cent compared with 12.0 per cent.

Farmers increased their equities in other ways. During the war they accumulated large amounts of bank deposits, currency, and savings bonds, while crop inventories rose sharply in value. The Department of Agriculture has estimated that the net equity of all farmers in the nation almost doubled between 1940 and 1945, and that in the latter year, farmers had liquid assets in the form of crop inventories, bank deposits, savings bonds, and currency equal to about two and a half times their debts. The debts included some $1.6 billion of non-real-estate debts, of which almost half a billion were in the South.[10] These data are not broken down by states or regions, but it is only reasonable to suppose that southern farmers shared in this general movement, although perhaps not as much as farmers in some other regions.

THE CHANGING PATTERN OF SOUTHERN AGRICULTURE

Since 1929, southern agriculture has changed greatly as to the acreage of crops harvested, physical production, and cash receipts. It is the purpose of this section to summarize those changes by presenting an analysis of acreage, production and cash receipts by crops for the three years, 1929, 1939, and 1948.

TABLE *XXIX* HARVESTED ACREAGE OF MAJOR CROPS IN THE SOUTH, 1929, 1939, AND 1948

CROP	ACREAGE (In Thousands)			PER CENT CHANGE	PER CENT OF TOTAL		
	1929	1939	1948	1929–48	1929	1939	1948
Corn	30,422	32,553	24,507	− 19.4	27.2	32.0	25.5
Cotton	44,768	22,800	21,173	− 52.7	39.6	22.4	22.0
Hay	10,091	13,041	14,378	+ 42.5	8.9	12.8	15.0
Wheat	8,741	9,182	14,556	+ 66.5	7.7	9.0	15.1
Peanuts	1,325	3,005	4,087	+ 208.5	1.2	3.0	4.2
Soybeans	274	2,647	2,608	+ 851.8	0.2	2.6	2.7
Tobacco	1,826	1,829	1,347	− 26.2	1.8	1.8	1.4
Rice	772	920	1,507	+ 95.2	0.7	0.9	1.6
Truck Crops	772	969	1,034	+ 33.9	0.7	1.0	1.1
Other crops	13,916	14,835	10,951	− 21.3	12.0	14.5	11.4
Total Crop	112,907	101,781	96,148	− 14.8	100.0	100.0	100.0

SOURCE: Computed from reports of the BAE, U. S. Department of Agriculture.

Crop Acreage. Table *XXIX* shows the acreage pattern of the major crops. The outstanding change, of course, was the enormous decline in cotton acreage, amounting to almost 53 per cent. Corn acreage, after showing a sizeable rise in 1939, dropped well below the 1929 figure in 1948. In the latter year, however, it occupied a larger acreage than any other crop. Tobacco, which produces a large value on a small area, was under acreage control during most of the period and showed a reduction of more than a fourth. Hay, wheat, peanuts, truck crops, soybeans, and rice showed large percentage gains. Soy-

10 *The Balance Sheet of Agriculture*, 1947, pp. 2, 54.

beans had the largest relative gain, with 852 per cent, while wheat experienced the largest absolute gain with almost six million acres.

Crop Production. It is more difficult to summarize the changes in physical production, since there is no common unit of measurement. In the case of truck crops, there is no common measure even for the subgroup, so it will have to be omitted from this comparison. Table *XXX* gives the data on physical production for the major southern crops for the three years under consideration. It is readily apparent from a comparison of Tables *XXIX* and *XXX* that there were some

TABLE *XXX*   PRODUCTION OF MAJOR FARM COMMODITIES IN THE SOUTH, 1929, 1939, AND 1948

CROP	UNIT	PRODUCTION			PER CENT CHANGE
		1929	1939	1948	1929–1948
Corn	000 Bu.	586,020	501,464	617,705	+5.4
Cotton	000 Bales	14,096	10,613	12,897	−8.5
Hay	000 Tons	11,313	12,577	15,935	+40.9
Wheat	000 Bu.	105,100	115,078	188,471	+79.3
Peanut*	Mil. Lbs.	929	1,180	2,259	+143.2
Soybeans*	000 Bu.	2,809	4,528	18,381	+554.4
Tobacco	Mil. Lbs.	1,293	1,675	1,690	+30.7
Rice	000 Bu.	34,205	44,722	66,302	+93.8
Citrus Fruits	000 Boxes	18,810	61,117	123,020	+554.0
Apples	000 Bu.	11,007	13,659	10,765	−2.2
Peaches	000 Bu.	14,469	18,181	16,339	+12.9

* Includes only those picked and shelled.
SOURCE: Computed from reports of the BAE, U. S. Department of Agriculture.

large changes in yields per acre. While cotton acreage dropped about 53 per cent, production fell only by 8.5 per cent. Corn production was slightly greater in 1948 than in 1929, although acreage had fallen by 19 per cent. Tobacco experienced one of the greatest increases in yield per acre; with acreage down by approximately a fourth, production was up by 31 per cent. Wheat, hay, and rice also showed much greater increases in production than in acreage. For peanuts and soybeans, the production figures cannot be compared with the acreage figures. Production figures include only that part of the crop which is picked and shelled, while large parts of the crop are used as pasture for hogs. Citrus fruits showed the greatest increase in production of all the commodities.

Farm Output. For the larger aspects of the pattern, the most striking fact is that there were large increases in the production of all commodities except corn and cotton; for citrus fruits, soybeans, and peanuts the percentage increases were very large. All of the increases, except for tobacco, were in the food and feed crops. This represents a very considerable movement away from cash crops and toward a more diversified agriculture which produces the food needed for local consumption. This trend was carried further by the increase in livestock, considered below.

Whether these changes add up to an increase or a decrease in total agricultural production it is difficult to say, since it is impossible to make a direct comparison between bales of cotton and bushels of wheat. The Department of Agriculture has constructed an index of farm output which gives some indication of the movements in physical production. This index is broken down by census divisions; the figures for the three divisions which make up the South (with some additions) are shown for certain years in Table *XXXI*.

TABLE *XXXI*   INDEX NUMBERS OF FARM OUTPUT IN THE SOUTH FOR SELECTED YEARS

(1935–39 = 100)

GEOGRAPHIC DIVISION	1929	1934	1939	1942	1943	1944	1945	1946	1947
South Atlantic	90	85	110	109	109	120	123	133	131
East South Central	96	89	96	115	114	116	120	113	115
West South Central	98	72	102	119	111	126	109	109	123
Average for Southern Divisions	95	82	103	114	111	121	117	118	123
United States	97	79	106	127	124	129	129	134	129

SOURCE: *Agricultural Statistics*, 1948, p. 566.

This index includes the production of livestock as well as crop production. If it is an accurate indicator, the South lagged somewhat behind the rest of the country in physical production of farm commodities during the war but the lag was reduced considerably in 1947. Over the whole period from 1929 to 1947, the average for three southern divisions increased by 29 per cent compared with an increase of 33 per cent for the whole country. While it must be remembered that the percentage figure for the South is computed upon a relatively low beginning figure, nevertheless these figures are significant. They indicate that the South is approximately holding its own in production. This was probably due in part to the fact that the South was beginning to mechanize during these years.

In absolute terms, production per worker in the South has been only about half of the production per worker in other areas. One recent survey makes this observation:

> Gross production per worker in the three southern divisions has been much lower than the 1935–39 average for the United States throughout the entire period (1919–1944). These three southern divisions have had about 50 per cent of all the farm workers in the Nation, and have contributed about one-third of the total United States production in most of the interwar and World War.[11]

Yields per Acre. Yield per acre is an important factor affecting the profitability of a crop which, in turn, affects the pattern of production. Table *XXXII* gives some data on the yields of important southern crops.

TABLE *XXXII*   YIELDS PER ACRE FOR CERTAIN FARM COMMODITIES IN THE SOUTH AND THE NON-SOUTH FOR SELECTED YEARS

COMMODITY AND REGION	UNIT	1929	TEN YEAR AVERAGES 1928–37	1937–46	1948	PER CENT INCREASE, 1929–1948
Cotton:						
South	Pound	151	174*	241	291	92.7
Non-South	"	351	368*	493	532	51.6
Tobacco:						
South	"	712	773	999	1237	73.7
Non-South	"	1028	1030	1133	1210	17.7
Corn:						
South	Bushel	19.3	15.4	18.0	25.2	30.6
Non-South	"	30.1	26.8	38.2	49.8	65.4
Wheat:						
South	"	12.0	11.5	12.9	12.9	7.5
Non-South	"	13.4	13.9	16.7	19.2	43.3
Peanuts:						
South	Pound	701	713	708	706	0.7
Non-South**		—	—	—	—	—

* These figures are for the ten-year period, 1926–35.
** No production outside the South.
SOURCE: Computed from reports of the BAE, U. S. Department of Agriculture.

In 1948, the yields per acre of cotton and tobacco were up 93 per cent and 74 per cent, respectively, above 1929, but peanuts showed practically no change in yield. The yields of wheat, and especially of corn, have been substantially lower in the South for a long time. In

11 Sherman E. Johnson (BAE, U. S. Department of Agriculture), *Changes in Farming in War and Peace,* Washington, 1946, p. 50.

the case of corn, the difference was increased as other areas adopted hybrid varities more rapidly than did the South, although southern yields during the war and since show the effects of this movement. In 1948, only four southern states—Arkansas, Kentucky, Oklahoma, and Virginia—had more than half of their corn acreage planted with hybrid seed. Kentucky and Virginia—the two states with the highest percentages—had yields above 40 bushels per acre which were approximately equal to the national average. The four states together had an average yield of 35.1 bushels per acre. All the other southern states, six of which had less than 20 per cent of their corn acreage planted with hybrid seed, had an average yield of 21.9 bushels.[12]

The wheat yield for the South in 1948 was depressed by a very low yield in Texas, which had a yield about 40 per cent below the 1947 figure. If the data for Texas were omitted, the figure for the South would be 14.8 bushels, which would represent an increase of 23.3 per cent over 1929.

Much research has been concentrated on improving the yield and quality of cotton and tobacco in the South. Those efforts paid off handsomely in the late 1930's; in the case of tobacco, the improvement continued during the war years. The trend in cotton yields has been a striking one. From 1890 to 1915, the yield fluctuated unevenly around a level slightly below 200 pounds per acre. After 1915, there was a steep decline, caused mainly by boll weevil damage. The low point was reached in the years 1921–23 with an average yield of 139 pounds. Then there was a sharp recovery and until 1936 yields fluctuated between 155 and 200 pounds. As methods of fighting the weevil and other improvements were developed, the yield tended to rise gradually. Then in 1937 it shot up to 269 pounds and it has not fallen below 230 pounds since that time. In 1948 a yield of 291 pounds was attained. A substantial and fairly steady increase in staple length has also done much to increase the value of cotton produced per acre.

One intensive study of cotton yields showed that between 1928–32 and 1941–43, average yields increased from 174 to 235 pounds— an increase of 79 pounds, or 45 per cent. The factors causing that increase were listed as follows:

[12] *Agricultural Statistics,* 1948, p. 48; *Crop Production,* December, 1948, p. 47.

Yield changes due to—

	POUNDS LINT PER ACRE
Increased use of fertilizer	25
Shifting of acreage among areas	20
More favorable weather	6
Land selection, better varieties of seed, more legumes turned under, other conservation practices, and other factors	38
Decrease caused by greater boll weevil damage	− 5
Greater reduction from causes other than weather and weevil	− 5
NET INCREASE, 1941–43 OVER 1928–32	79[13]

The problem of increasing tobacco yields has been especially delicate and difficult. The obvious methods of using more fertilizer or switching to heavier, more fertile soils are likely to produce a rank growth which lowers the quality of the leaf and reduces prices. In developing new and higher yielding varieties, special attention must be given to their power to resist the many diseases which afflict the plant. Growers have also had to give heed to the popular demand for milder cigarettes with a low nicotine content. In the face of these obstacles, the increase of more than 70 per cent in the average yield per acre between 1929 and 1948 represents a remarkable accomplishment. The chief causes apparently were "advancing knowledge of fertilizers which permit increased yield without rank growth of poor leaf, and . . . the development of better varieties."[14] The fact that North Carolina, the leading tobacco-producing state, uses far more fertilizer than any other state, as noted below, lends weight to this conclusion.

Livestock Population. In addition to the changes in the crop pattern, there have been important changes in the livestock population. During the 1930's the South increased the number of its livestock steadily and fairly rapidly. This movement was slowed up considerably during the war, but nevertheless from 1930 to 1947 the South showed considerably greater increases in the number of animals than the Non-South. In fact, as shown in Table *XXXIII,* the Non-South actually had fewer sheep, hogs and chickens in 1947 than in 1930, while the

[13] *Cotton,* Hearings before A Subcommittee of the Committee on Agriculture, House of Representatives, 78th Congress, 2nd Session, December 4 to 9, 1944, p. 728.
[14] William H. Fisher (Federal Reserve Bank of Richmond), *Economics of Flue Cured Tobacco,* Richmond, 1945, p. 33.

South had increases in all classes except horses and mules, ranging from 8.1 per cent in chickens to 76.6 per cent in beef cattle. The southern figures are influenced heavily by the data for Texas, which contains more cattle, sheep, and chickens than any other state of the Union.

TABLE *XXXIII* NUMBER AND VALUE OF CERTAIN LIVESTOCK ON FARMS IN THE SOUTH AND THE NON-SOUTH, 1930, 1940, AND 1947

(*Numbers in Thousands, Aggregate Values in Millions of Dollars, Average Values in Dollars*)

ANIMALS	JAN. 1, 1930		JAN. 1, 1940		JAN. 1, 1947		PER CENT CHANGE, 1930–1947	
	SOUTH	NON-SOUTH	SOUTH	NON-SOUTH	SOUTH	NON-SOUTH	SOUTH	NON-SOUTH
Horses:								
Number	2327	11037	2249	8195	1909	5342	−18.0	−51.6
Value	126	819	158	650	140	289	+11.1	−64.7
Av. per head	54	74	70	79	73	54		
Mules:								
Number	4005	1274	3290	744	2415	358	−39.7	−71.9
Value	336	102	396	71	361	29	+7.4	−71.6
Av. per head	84	80	120	95	149	81		
Beef Cattle:*								
Number	10043	25501	13584	29785	17736	37214	+76.6	+45.9
Value	303	1146	326	1016	1034	3075	+241.3	+168.3
Av. per head	30	45	24	34	58	83		
Milk Cows:								
Number	5171	17272	6460	18480	6914	19186	+33.7	+11.1
Value	292	1581	253	1176	663	3126	+127.1	+97.7
Av. per head	56	92	39	64	96	163		
Sheep:								
Number	8024	42479	12437	39670	10612	27959	+32.2	−34.2
Value	61	389	65	264	104	383	+70.5	−1.5
Av. per head	7.60	9.16	5.23	6.65	9.80	13.70		
Hogs:	9342	43896	16238	44837	13961	42940	+49.4	−2.2
Value	90	643	92	384	336	1713	+273.3	+166.4
Av. per head	9.63	14.65	5.67	8.56	24.07	39.89		
Chickens:								
Number (Mil.)	123	346	127	311	133	342	+8.1	−1.2
Value	98	339	64	210	170	514	+73.5	+51.6
Av. per head	0.80	0.98	0.50	0.68	1.28	1.50		

* "All Cattle" less "Cows and Heifers 2 years old and over kept for milk."
SOURCE: Computed from reports of the BAE, U. S. Department of Agriculture.

The much smaller decline in the number of horses and mules in the South than in the Non-South reflects the slower rate of mechanization on southern farms and the greater dependence on these animals for draft power. The same situation also affects the value per head of these animals; it is only with these two classes of animals that the South has a higher value per head than the rest of the country.[15] With all the other animals (which are produced for food), values per head in the South were consistently and substantially below those for the remainder of the nation. This is the more striking because farm prices for grain are usually higher in the South than elsewhere. This differential in animal prices may be due in part to poorer marketing facilities and less competition among buyers, but probably the main cause is the poorer quality of the animals. Better breeding and feeding practices are only slowly becoming established in the South and it will take many years to raise the average quality of animals to a level comparable with that prevailing in other parts of the country. But improvement in the quality of livestock offers one of the surest means by which southern farmers can increase their financial return. For example, if southern cattle had been worth as much per head as non-southern on January 1, 1947, their total value would have been increased by some $456 million, or about 44 per cent.

The importance of more livestock on southern farms goes far beyond just providing an alternative source of income to cotton or tobacco. As mechanization progresses, millions of acres now used to grow feed for mules and horses will become available for other uses; more cattle, hogs, and chickens is probably the best solution to that problem. Further, more livestock provides a better-balanced demand for labor on the farm, tending to smooth out the great peaks created by cotton and tobacco. Finally, more livestock can contribute greatly to a program for rebuilding the soil; soil-restoring legume crops can be used as feed and the manure can be returned to the soil to build up fertility.

Cash Receipts. Estimated cash receipts from farm marketing provide a broad and significant indicator of changes in agricultural patterns. This series sums up the results of most farming operations in terms of one uniform measuring unit; it includes both crops and livestock. It reflects changes in acreage, yields per acre, and prices; it indicates fairly accurately what the farmer finally gets for his year's work. It is true that it is not equally significant for farmers who diversify and

---

[15] This variation reaches its extreme with mules. On January 1, 1947, the value of mules per head varied from $229.00 in North and South Carolina, and $209.00 for the South Atlantic region, to $78.30 for the North Central region and $39.00 for North Dakota. The average for the United States was $141.00. *Livestock on Farms, Jan. 1,* U. S. Department of Agriculture.

grow many of the things they need, as contrasted with those who concentrate on cash crops; that is one big defect of the series. Since the South has been moving somewhat away from cash crops this series probably does not fully reflect all the changes on southern farms in the past 20 years.

Estimated cash receipts from the principal southern crops and livestock products for 1929, 1939, and 1948 are shown in Table *XXXIV*. The outstanding change, of course, was the great decline in

TABLE *XXXIV* AMOUNTS AND PERCENTAGE DISTRIBUTION OF CASH RECEIPT FROM FARM MARKETING IN THE SOUTH, BY COMMODITIES, 1929, 1939, AND 1948
(*Dollar Amounts in Millions*)

CROP	AMOUNTS			PER CENT INCREASE	PER CENT OF TOTAL		
	1929	1939	1948	1929–48	1929	1939	1948
Cotton*	$1,434	$ 552	$2,189	52.6	46.0	26.7	27.2
Tobacco	234	241	836	257.3	7.5	11.7	10.4
Corn	31	31	158	409.7	1.0	1.5	2.0
Hay	17	10	48	182.3	0.5	0.5	0.6
Wheat	95	63	356	274.7	3.0	3.0	4.4
Peanuts	32	35	221	590.6	1.0	1.7	2.7
Soybeans	2	3	36	1700.0	0.1	0.1	0.4
Truck Crops	101	95	264	161.4	3.2	4.6	3.3
Rice	31	28	136	338.7	1.0	1.4	1.7
Sugar	12	16	34	183.3	0.4	0.8	0.4
Potatoes	37	22	54	45.9	1.2	1.1	0.7
Sweet Potatoes	22	16	34	54.5	0.7	0.8	0.4
Citrus Fruits	41	54	90	119.5	1.3	2.6	1.1
Apples	15	9	24	60.0	0.5	0.4	0.3
Peaches	17	14	33	94.1	0.5	0.7	0.4
Other Fruits	35	28	65	85.7	1.1	1.4	0.8
Forest Products	42	37	151	259.5	1.3	1.8	1.9
Other Crops	57	53	233	308.8	1.8	2.6	2.9
Total Crops	2,256	1,308	4,962	119.9	72.4	63.3	61.8
Cattle and Products	254	251	1,211	376.8	8.1	12.1	15.1
Dairy Products	233	187	614	163.5	7.5	9.0	7.6
Hogs	107	121	519	385.0	3.4	5.9	6.5
Poultry and Products	213	143	604	183.6	6.8	6.9	7.5
Other Livestock	53	58	124	133.9	1.7	2.8	1.5
Total Livestock	860	759	3,072	257.2	27.6	36.7	38.2
Total Crops and Livestock	3,117	2,067	8,034	157.7	100.0	100.0	100.0

* Includes seeds.
SOURCE: Computed from reports of the BAE, U. S. Department of Agriculture.

the relative importance of receipts from cotton and cottonseed—from 46 per cent to 27 per cent. Receipts from nearly all other commodities moved up in rank to compensate for this great decline. In relative importance, receipts from tobacco and wheat increased almost 50 per cent, while those from peanuts almost trebled. In absolute terms, receipts from all commodities except cotton and forest products increased by more than 100 per cent; with corn and peanuts, the increases were more than 400 per cent. Despite its big drop, cotton still held first place among receipts in 1948 by a wide margin. Cotton and tobacco together accounted for about 60 per cent of all cash receipts from crops and more than 37 per cent of the receipts from all farm marketings.

Because of the decline of cotton and of the shift to livestock, receipts from all crops increased by only 120 per cent between 1929 and 1948, compared with an increase of 197 per cent in the Non-South. Receipts from crops declined from 72 to 62 per cent of the total, and there was a corresponding increase in the importance of receipts from livestock. Outside the South, there was an opposite, but much smaller trend. Even after these changes, there was, in 1948, still a big difference in the relative importance of receipts from crops and livestock in the two areas. Curiously enough, the proportion between the two was just reversed; in the South, 62 per cent from crops and 38 per cent from livestock, and in the Non-South, 38 per cent from crops and 62 per cent from livestock. The increased emphasis on livestock in the South is reflected by the increase of 257 per cent in receipts from that source, while elsewhere the increase was only 163 per cent.

Cash Receipts by States. Cash receipts also afford a basis for analyzing the geographical shifts in agricultural production within the region. Table *XXXV* gives estimated cash receipts by states, with receipts from crops and livestock shown separately. Texas was in first place throughout with 24.3 per cent of the total in 1948. Oklahoma suffered from the drought and a heavy outmigration of farm population during the 1930's; as a result it lost second place to North Carolina. The other 10 states are fairly closely grouped between the 4.2 per cent of Florida to the 7.4 per cent of Kentucky.

North Carolina and Kentucky and, to a less extent, Virginia, benefited from the great increase in tobacco and improved their relative standings. Florida made a considerable gain, thanks largely to citrus fruits but lost most of the gain after 1946. Alabama, Georgia, and Mississippi lost ground because of cotton, along with Oklahoma.

Interesting examples of the speed with which conditions can change, especially in the turbulent postwar years, are afforded by Florida and

TABLE *XXXV* PERCENTAGE DISTRIBUTION OF CASH RECEIPTS FROM FARMING IN THE SOUTH BY STATES, 1929, 1939, AND 1948

STATE	1929			1939			1948		
	CROPS	LIVE-STOCK	TOTAL	CROPS	LIVE-STOCK	TOTAL	CROPS	LIVE-STOCK	TOTAL
Alabama	7.1	3.3	6.0	4.6	3.6	4.2	6.2	4.0	5.3
Arkansas	7.1	4.0	6.2	7.3	5.4	6.6	8.2	5.1	6.9
Florida	4.2	2.8	3.8	8.3	3.2	6.4	4.8	3.2	4.2
Georgia	8.2	4.3	7.2	7.3	4.6	6.3	7.3	5.2	6.5
Kentucky	4.1	10.7	5.9	5.2	9.7	6.9	5.6	10.0	7.4
Louisiana	6.0	3.1	5.2	6.5	3.3	5.3	5.1	3.3	4.4
Mississippi	8.8	4.0	7.4	7.9	4.1	6.5	8.4	4.1	6.6
North Carolina	9.0	4.3	7.8	14.1	4.6	10.6	13.4	4.7	9.8
Oklahoma	9.0	14.2	10.4	5.7	12.8	8.3	6.9	10.6	8.4
South Carolina	5.1	2.1	4.3	6.3	2.2	4.8	5.7	2.4	4.3
Tennessee	4.4	8.3	5.5	4.6	7.6	5.7	5.4	7.4	6.3
Texas	22.9	30.5	25.0	17.6	31.4	22.7	18.5	32.9	24.3
Virginia	4.2	8.6	5.4	4.6	7.5	5.6	4.5	7.1	5.6
Total	100.0	100.0	100.0	100.0	100.0	100.0	100.0	100.0	100.0

For total dollar amount of totals, see Table *XXXIV*.
SOURCE: BAE, U. S. Department of Agriculture.

North Carolina. Table *XXXVI* gives a few summary figures for the two states.

TABLE *XXXVI* CASH RECEIPTS FROM THE SALE OF CERTAIN FARM COMMODITIES IN FLORIDA AND NORTH CAROLINA, 1945–1948

(*In Millions of Dollars*)

	NORTH CAROLINA			FLORIDA	
	COTTON	TOBACCO	TOTAL CASH RECEIPTS	CITRUS FRUITS	TOTAL CASH RECEIPTS
1945	52.4	359.9	629.1	165.4	384.1
1946	74.1	436.8	753.2	171.9	413.1
1947	89.5	405.4	759.5	80.6	321.6
1948	119.7	377.3	792.0	72.2	353.3

SOURCE: BAE, U. S. Department of Agriculture.

In North Carolina, tobacco prices were maintained at high levels by acreage control and government price supports, but production had to be cut back sharply after 1946. As a result, receipts from tobacco sales declined by about $60 million between 1946 and 1948. But this decline was more than offset by increased receipts from cotton and the state showed a small increase in total receipts. Since, however, the region as a whole had an increase of about 30 per cent between these years, North Carolina's share of the total fell from 12.0

per cent to 9.8 per cent. In Florida, there were no government crop controls or price supports for citrus fruits and cash receipts from that crop declined by $100 million between 1946 and 1948. Nor was there any other one crop which exerted much of a compensating influence. Florida's total receipts declined from 6.6 per cent of the southern total in 1946 to 4.2 per cent in 1948. In cash receipts from crops alone (omitting livestock) Florida fell from third place in the South, with 8.4 per cent of the total, in 1946, to twelfth place, with 4.8 per cent of the total, in 1948.

The above figures for cash receipts have been exclusive of the various government payments to farmers in recent years. In 1939, such payments amounted to $349.6 million in the South, or about 17 per cent of cash receipts from farm marketing; in the Non-South, they amounted to $457.4 million, or about 8 per cent. By 1948, such payments in the South had declined by about 75 per cent to $84.8 million, or less than 1 per cent of receipts from farm marketing. In the rest of the country they had declined to $171.7 million, also less than 1 per cent of receipts from marketing.

Production Costs. Cash receipts do not, of course, represent clear profit to the farmer; he has various costs of production. In the South, because of the relatively poor soil, fertilizer costs are an important item. Just before World War II the southern states were using around five million tons of commercial fertilizer per year, or about 65 per cent of the total for the country. North Carolina alone used over 15 per cent of the national total. During the war the amount of fertilizer used increased to nearly eight million tons, but its use outside the South increased even faster and the South's proportion was reduced to about 60 per cent; North Carolina's part was reduced to about 11 per cent. Since the South paid almost twice as much for fertilizer as all the rest of the country, and since its cash receipts were only a little more than a third as much, it follows that this continuing and necessary cost was a considerable penalty which southern farmers had to pay because of the poor quality of their soil.

Fertilizer, however, represents only one of many items of agricultural cost. It may be significant to notice briefly how all costs behaved during the rapid changes of recent years. In its study of parity income, the Department of Agriculture has estimated all principal costs to farmers by states.[16] In Table *XXXVII* these costs have been ex-

16 See Part VI, Section 1 of the series "Income Parity for Agriculture."

TABLE *XXXVII* FARM PRODUCTION EXPENSES AS PERCENTAGES OF CASH RE-
CEIPTS FROM FARMING IN THE SOUTH AND THE NON-SOUTH, 1929, 1939, AND 1944

	SOUTH			NON-SOUTH		
EXPENSE	1929	1939	1944	1929	1939	1944
Feed Purchase	5.2	6.4	6.8	9.2	10.3	11.9
Livestock Purchased	1.6	2.9	2.6	5.7	7.1	4.7
Fertilizer and Lime	5.8	7.0	4.7	1.4	1.6	1.5
Operating Motor Vehicles	4.0	6.5	3.7	4.7	7.1	4.4
Hired Labor	9.4	13.3	10.1	12.1	12.2	10.8
Maintenance and Depreciation of Buildings and Equipment	9.3	12.8	7.5	12.0	14.1	8.5
Taxes	4.3	4.4	1.8	6.2	6.2	2.6
Interest on Farm Mortgages	4.1	3.2	1.1	5.5	4.1	1.3
Other Expenses	14.0	13.9	10.3	14.8	14.8	12.9
Total Production Expenses	57.7	70.4	48.4	71.6	77.5	58.6

SOURCE: Computed from BAE, U. S. Department of Agriculture, "Income Parity for Agriculture," Part VI, Section 1.

pressed as percentages of cash receipts from farming for the years 1929, 1939, and 1944. In relation to cash receipts, costs of fertilizer and lime were more than three times as heavy in the South as elsewhere, but most other costs were lower. Total production costs, in relation to cash receipts, were substantially lower in the South than elsewhere. This merely means that since the southern farmer was using much less capital and equipment of all kinds, a larger part of what he did receive went to him as compensation for his labor; the non-southern farmer had higher "fixed costs" because of his greater amount of equipment. But the southern farmer's gross income was so much smaller that even the larger proportion going to him for labor left him with far less income than his counterpart outside the South.

Land Tenure Pattern. During the past 20 years there have been important changes in land tenure in the South. The data as they relate to number of farms and acreage of crop lands harvested are summarized in Table *XXXVIII*.

The proportion of farms operated and of acreage harvested by tenants in the South reached record high peaks in 1929–30, but the absolute number of tenants reached an all-time high in 1935.[17] Then in the ensuing years all these series declined sharply to the lowest levels since 1890. The proportion of owner-operated farms increased steadily from 42.5 per cent in 1930 to 57.8 per cent in 1945, and

[17] This is true in so far as the quinquennial data of the Census of Agriculture goes; actually, the peaks may have been reached in some of the intervening years.

the proportion of tenant-operated farms declined correspondingly. The very small proportion of farms operated by managers declined by 50 per cent, but the acreage of those farms increased by almost a million acres. The proportion of farms operated by croppers declined from one fourth in 1930 to one sixth in 1945, and the proportion of crop lands they harvested fell from 16 per cent to 11 per cent in the same period.

TABLE *XXXVIII*   NUMBER OF FARMS AND ACREAGE OF CROP LANDS HARVESTED IN THE SOUTH BY TENURE OF OPERATORS, 1929–1944

TENURE STATUS	AMOUNTS				PER CENT CHANGE,	PER CENT OF TOTAL			
	1929	1934	1939	1944	1929–44	1929	1934	1939	1944
NUMBER OF FARMS—*in thousands**									
Owner	1313	1462	1435	1581	+20.4	42.5	44.8	50.2	57.8
Full Owner	1097	1236	1225	1395	+27.2	35.6	37.9	42.9	51.0
Part Owner	216	226	210	186	−13.9	7.0	6.9	7.3	6.8
Manager	18	15	13	12	−50.0	0.6	0.5	0.5	0.4
All Tenants	1762	1788	1412	1140	−35.3	57.1	54.8	49.4	41.7
Cropper	773	710	540	444	−42.6	25.0	21.8	18.9	16.2
Total	3088	3262	2858	2736	−11.4	100.0	100.0	100.0	100.0
CROP LANDS HARVESTED—*in millions of acres*									
Owner	46.6	45.0	51.7	56.7	+21.7	44.1	45.8	51.9	57.6
Full Owner	34.2	33.7	36.6	39.6	+15.8	32.4	34.3	36.8	40.2
Part Owner	12.4	11.3	15.1	17.1	+37.9	11.7	11.5	15.1	17.4
Manager	1.9	2.0	2.5	2.8	+47.4	1.8	2.0	2.6	2.8
All Tenants	57.2	51.2	45.4	39.3	−31.3	54.1	42.3	45.6	39.9
Cropper	15.8	16.2	12.7	11.0	−30.4	15.0	16.5	12.7	11.2
Total	105.6	98.1	99.7	98.5	−6.7	100.0	100.0	100.0	100.0

* The data on number of farms apply to the status as of January 1 of the following year.
SOURCE: Computed from reports of the Bureau of the Census.

Various forces have operated to produce these changes in tenure. Several forms of financial aid by the Federal Government have helped tenants to become owners or have helped owners to retain ownership when threatened by the foreclosure of mortgages. Between 1934 and 1939, several features of the AAA control program encouraged owners to shift from croppers to hired labor; the effects of this are reflected in the drop from 710,000 to 540,000 in the number of cropper-operated farms. During the war years this situation was reversed and owners, in order to keep laborers, had to offer them a share in the crop. The result was that, in contrast with the preceding period, the principal decline in tenants came in other classes than croppers. In the seven southeastern states the number of croppers declined by only about 7 per cent; in North and South Carolina, they actually increased during these years. The same forces have produced changes in the agreement between owner and operator and "many croppers are now sharing in other crops besides cotton and tobacco and to some extent in livestock as well."[18]

There were significant differences in the changes of tenure as between white and nonwhite operators, especially during the war years. Between 1940 and 1945, the number of white tenants declined by more than a fourth, while the number of nonwhite tenants fell by only about 6 per cent; in several states there were increases in the number of nonwhite tenants. This same trend was evident before the war, although it was not so pronounced. The rate of increase by full owners between 1940 and 1945 was about the same for white and nonwhite operators. The greater decline in the number of white tenants undoubtedly was the result of greater opportunities in non-agricultural employment for whites than for nonwhites.

In the past, the trend toward more farm ownership by operators has been looked on with favor. It indicated a more stable farm population and probably more initiative and income on the part of the operators. But if we assume that we are facing a period of mechanization, this trend may have different implications. We may safely assume that most of these new owners have small holdings. The small size of farms is one of the greatest barriers to mechanization and one of the chief causes of low per capita income in the South. As one of the critics of these pages has commented: "It is the plantations with their croppers that can most easily be recast into the large-scale mechanized agriculture that offers efficiency in the economic sense. More small owner-operators make the change to large-scale operations more difficult."

Just because small owner-operators are more stable and because they have a financial interest in the land, they may make the shift to mechanization more difficult because they do not have the funds with which to buy mechanized equipment nor enough land to use it efficiently—even if they had the ability and the desire to use it, which they do not have in some cases. It is possible that there is here a conflict between the scale of production in agriculture which is economically most efficient and the scale of production which is socially

[18] Southeast Regional Land Tenure Research Committee and Bureau of Agricultural Economics, *Farm Tenure Situation in the Southeast*, Preliminary Draft, p. 14.

more desirable. However, it should be noted that a substantial proportion of the advantages of mechanization and of the advantages of the balanced farm enterprise are attainable outside the plantation sized farm unit. Consequently it is by no means certain that a larger proportion of owner-operators would in fact result in an increase in the proportion of farms which could not utilize the advantages of mechanization.

MECHANIZATION OF AGRICULTURE

In the mechanization of agriculture, the South has lagged far behind the rest of the nation. That remains true despite the exception of isolated areas and despite the higher rate of increase in the use of agricultural machines in the South in the past ten years. This point has been made many times and there is no need to labor it here. Only a few figures will be given as examples.

Table *XXVIII* shows that the value of implements and machinery in the South in 1945 averaged only $406 per farm; outside the South the figure was $1292. In the South in 1945, 385,000 farms (out of a total of 2,736,000) had 468,000 tractors; farms elsewhere had 1,954,-000 tractors. Only one southern farm in seven had a tractor, compared with a little more than one out of every two in the Non-South, but the South had the higher rate of growth between 1940 and 1945—84 per cent compared with 49 per cent.[19] Under the stimulus of high incomes and a shortage of manpower, the South really began to mechanize during the war—but thus far it has only begun.

There have been many reasons for the South's slow progress in mechanization. It is much easier to list them than to evaluate their relative importance and interdependence. First, the South has generally had an abundance of cheap manual labor. Even though it was often inefficient, it was so cheap that it made mechanization unprofitable. Second, the low levels of income which have prevailed in the past have not permitted the southern farmer to accumulate funds with which to buy expensive machinery. Third, the small farms and the hilly terrain which prevail in many parts of the South are not well suited to mechanical operations. It has been only within the past

---

19 In this connection it should be remembered that southern farms have, on the average, less than half as much crop land per farm as do farms in the Non-South. In other words, on the basis of the amount of crop land, the difference is not nearly so great as the comparison given above might imply.

eight or ten years that manufacturers have made a serious effort to develop small, low-priced tractors and specialized equipment to fit these conditions. Fourth, and perhaps the most important of all, the South's two principal crops—cotton and tobacco—are row crops which present unique problems to the manufacturers of agricultural machinery. It has been exceedingly difficult to design machines to cultivate and harvest these two crops. With cotton there has been a partial success, but with tobacco there has hardly been a beginning. In the past, tractors and power equipment could be used only to prepare the seed beds for these crops; cultivation and harvesting had to be almost entirely by hand. Few farmers could afford a tractor for such a small amount of work.

Until recent years, there had been no major change in the methods of growing and harvesting cotton since the perfection of the cotton gin. While machines were being used more and more for most other crops, cotton still relied entirely on the mule and the field hand. This method of cultivation involves two peaks in the demand for labor— the hoeing season in early summer and the harvesting in the autumn. These peak demands for labor require the expenditures of enormous amounts of manual labor and set a rigid limit to the amount of cotton acreage one man can cultivate. It has been estimated that cotton now requires about one fifth of all the manual labor put into all crops in this country. Cotton, on the average, requires about five times as much man labor as wheat, and three and a half times as much as corn, to produce a given income.

Two machines which promise great changes in methods of growing cotton are the flame cultivator and the mechanical cotton picker. The flame cultivator is used only for weed control and can be employed only after the cotton has attained some size and is tough enough to withstand the hot flame which sears the tenderer weeds and grass. To solve the chopping or thinning problem, the farmer may plant the cotton in hills, use a rotary hoe, or, where terrain permits, use check-row planting and cross cultivation. The critical period in this method is just after the chopping operation, before the cotton is tough enough to be flamed. If the weather is bad or if the seed bed has not been carefully prepared, weeds and grass may get such a start that only hand hoeing can eliminate them. But after this period the flame cultivator and tractor-pulled plows can, with reasonable luck, complete the cultivation of the crop without any further hand labor.

It will not do a great deal of good to solve the early summer peak demand for labor caused by the hoeing unless means can be found to meet the peak demand at harvest time. The harvesting of cotton has always been a tedious, slow, and labor-consuming process. Two methods of mechanical harvesting are now in limited use. The first is to strip or snap the bolls from the stalks by means of a stripper. The cotton is then removed from the bolls by special ginning equipment. This method is largely restricted to areas where the climate is dry and the stalks do not attain large size. The quality of the cotton is lowered by the inclusion of much trash, and the special ginning equipment presents a problem.

For 40 years or more work has been in progress on a spindle-type cotton picker which will remove the cotton from the boll without destroying the boll or the stalk. Machines of this type are now being produced commercially in increasing numbers and its success seems assured, although many problems remain to be solved. In 1947, an official of one large manufacturing company stated that up to that time his company had produced "several hundred pickers, by engineering shop methods" and that they hoped to "build more than 1,000 mechanical pickers for the 1948 crop season."[20]

Some of the limitations and defects of the machine at this stage are: (1) it is costly; (2) it is heavy and cannot operate if the ground is very wet; (3) it is not well adapted to uneven terrain or to cotton plants which are too large or too small; (4) the plants must be defoliated before picking begins, which increases costs and problems; (5) mechanical picking reduces the quality of the cotton picked by about one and a half grades compared with hand-picked cotton; (6) it leaves considerably more cotton in the field than does hand picking and (7) it creates special problems in ginning. These problems will probably be solved or reduced in time, but it is a slow process.

It is estimated that at present not more than 5 per cent of the cotton crop is produced under fully mechanized conditions. The potential savings which could be realized if the bulk of the production could be mechanized are indeed impressive. In 1940, it required an average of 191 hours of man labor to produce a bale of cotton in this country. "If fairly complete mechanization of the cultivation and harvesting of cotton could be attained the man hours used per bale

---

[20] Report on the Proceedings of the Beltwide Cotton Mechanization Conference, August 18–19, 1947, National Cotton Council of America, p. 46.

of cotton might be reduced to 65 hours, as a national average."[21] Under the most favorable conditions the number of hours might be reduced to between 15 and 30.

How soon are we likely to achieve mechanization of cotton production and what will be its effects on the South? The progress toward mechanization is likely to be slow for a number of reasons. First, there are a number of technological problems to be solved. The machines must be made more efficient, cheaper, smaller, and more adaptable to use in different kinds of terrain and on different sizes of plants. The principle of the spindle picker has been known and tried for more than 35 years but it is still far from perfect. The grain combine was first introduced in California in 1880 but in 1920, 40 years later, not more than 5 per cent of the American wheat crop was harvested by combines.[22] Second, rapid mechanization would probably displace large amounts of labor which might tend to force down wages, thus reducing the profitability of converting to machinery. Third, further extensive changes in the agricultural situation in the South must be accomplished before mechanization can be profitable except in certain favored areas. In particular, the size of farms must be increased considerably or arrangements must be worked out for the renting or co-operative purchasing of expensive machinery.[23] Finally, as Welch and Miley express it, "vested economic interest in the operation of phases of the old system, sentiment, and the heavy hand of inertia, will delay and hinder rapid shifts even assuming favorable economies associated with such shift."[24]

If and when a fairly high degree of mechanization is achieved, it will produce far-reaching changes in the southern economy. It will be far more than a matter of farmers going out and buying a lot of machines. As one writer has expressed it, "mechanization involves all of the complexities of altering the basic combinations of the land, labor, capital, and management which are available (to the farmer)."[25] It has been estimated that farm mechanization might well cause, by

21 Sherman E. Johnson, *op. cit.*, p. 58.
22 Harold Barger and Hans H. Landsberg, *American Agriculture, 1899–1939*, New York, National Bureau of Economic Research, Inc., 1942, p. 199.
23 In respect to the cotton picker, it has been suggested that ginners might buy two or three machines and custom-pick the cotton of their customers, or even buy the cotton crop in the field.
24 Frank J. Welch and D. Gray Miley, "Mechanization of the Cotton Harvest," *Journal of Farm Economics*, Vol. 27, Nov. 1945, p. 941.
25 C. R. Sayre, "Economics of Mechanization," *Report of the Proceedings of the Beltwide Cotton Mechanization Conference*, p. 5.

1965, a displacement of 2,116,000 farm workers from what might be considered a "normal" level, and a net reduction of 1,183,000 below the 1945 level.[26] The remaining farm population would have a per capita physical productivity two and a half times that prevailing in 1943 and a gross income 65 per cent higher; total physical production would be about 50 per cent above 1943. But these changes would require a greatly increased number of nonagricultural employment opportunities and a market for the greatly increased production of the farmers; if these were not provided, the changes would be delayed or prevented. Farms would be larger and there would be considerable changes in the crop and livestock patterns; there would be fewer row crops and more small grain and cover crops and more livestock.

The story of modern industrial and agricultural society seems to indicate that the individual producer has been able to make significant increases in his productivity and efficiency only as he has gained command over liberal amounts of mechanical power. Southern farmers constitute one of the largest groups which, thus far, has not enjoyed the use of such power. If they are to bring their productivity and their incomes into line with other producing groups in the country they must have that power.

[26] *Economic Problems of the Cotton Belt,* p. 620.

VI THE CHANGING STRUCTURE OF INDUSTRY

The South's portion of the nation's industry has been increasing for a long time. The low point of the past century was reached about 1880, when the South had a little less than 8 per cent of the country's wage earners (approximately synonymous with the current classification of "production workers") in manufacturing. After 1880, the South's share increased steadily except for the decade 1909–1919, and by 1929 the region's proportion of wage earners had almost doubled, standing at 15.1 per cent. In value of manufactured products the increase was about the same—from 5.9 to 11.7 per cent.

Industrial growth in the South, both absolute and relative, has continued since 1929. It is the purpose of this chapter to give some analysis of the changes which have taken place during those two decades. In this analysis we have relied heavily upon the data supplied by the *Census of Manufactures*.[1]

As a background for the more detailed study to follow and to afford some perspective, it may be well to note first the larger aspects of

[1] For a long period before 1939, the *Census* was taken every two years. During the war it was discontinued and was not resumed until 1947. The 1947 data are just becoming available as this is written.

While the *Census* supplies by far the most comprehensive, detailed, and reliable data on manufacturing now available, nevertheless it has its limitations and difficulties. Some of them are: (1) for some years the coverage did not include establishments with annual value of product less than $5,000; (2) some activities on the border-line of manufacturing (such as coffee roasting and gas manufacturing) are included in some years and not in others; (3) if the number of establishments in an area is small, data must frequently be withheld to prevent disclosure of data for individual firms; (4) the classification and groupings of industries have changed from time to time, making it difficult to compare groups from one year to another. When changes in classification are made, the Census frequently adjusts the data for the most recent previous year to make them comparable. In this chapter, the data for 1939 are usually those which have been adjusted in the 1947 *Census;* for earlier years they are usually as originally given.

the changes which have been going on—to get a "preview" of the developments. The summary data in Table *XXXIX* show the main lines of the developments for the past 20 years.

TABLE *XXXIX*   SUMMARY DATA ON MANUFACTURING IN THE SOUTH, 1929, 1939 AND 1947

ITEM	AMOUNTS			PER CENT OF U. S.			PER CENT CHANGE		
	1929	1939	1947	1929	1939	1947	1929–39	1939–47	1929–47
Number of Establishments	35,570	26,516	42,739	16.9	15.3	17.7	−25.5	+61.2	+20.2
Production Workers (000)	1,338	1,349	2,023	15.1	17.3	17.0	+0.8	+50.0	+51.2
Wages Paid ($ Millions)	1,182	1,065	3,981	10.2	12.1	13.2	−9.9	+273.8	+236.8
Value Added by Manufacture ($ Millions)	3,199*	3,124	10,744	10.2	12.7	14.4	−2.3	+243.9	+236.2

* Adjusted by subtracting internal revenue taxes paid on tobacco manufactures to make data more nearly comparable with data for later years.
SOURCE: Computed from *Census of Manufactures*.

THE PREWAR DECADE

The Position in 1929. In 1929, the South had, roughly, a little more than one sixth of the nation's manufacturing establishments, employed a little more than one seventh of the production workers, and paid out slightly more than one tenth of the wages. In value of manufactured products,[2] the South had less than an eighth of the total for the country. The value added by manufacturing in the region was in keeping with the wages paid—a little more than one tenth.

Within the South, the textile industry, including both spinning and weaving, was first in importance. The lumber industry group was second and food manufacturing was third. These three industry groups accounted for about half of the South's total of wage earners. Other important groups were: tobacco manufacturing; furniture; and petroleum refining. North Carolina was the leading industrial state with 16 per cent of all southern wage earners, followed by Georgia with 12 per cent and Texas with 10 per cent. These three states had approximately 38 per cent of the total. The least industrialized states were Oklahoma, Arkansas, and Mississippi, each with less than 4 per cent of the total. The other states ranged between 4 and 9 per cent of the total.

[2] This series is omitted from the table because it is not given in the 1947 *Census* on a regional or state basis.

The Years of Decline. The decade from 1930 to 1939 was marked by three years of precipitous decline followed by seven years of slow and irregular recovery. In the South the decline was not so great as it was outside the South. This smaller decline is apparent in the biennial data of the *Census of Manufactures.* From 1929 to 1931, the southern figures declined at about the same rate as the figures for the Non-South; for the number of establishments, however, the decline in the South was more than twice as great. But from 1931 to 1933 the decline in the South was much smaller; there was actually a small increase in the number of wage earners in the South during this period

CHART *VI*   PRODUCTION WORKERS, WAGES PAID, AND VALUE ADDED IN MANUFACTURING IN THE SOUTH AS PER CENT OF UNITED STATES TOTALS

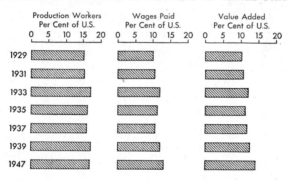

while elsewhere there was a 9 per cent decline. In short, the depression hit bottom somewhat sooner in the South than in the rest of the country.

The reason for the smaller decline and the earlier upturn in the South is fairly evident. The depression of the 1930's hit the heavy industries especially hard and the South had few such industries. Southern industries produce principally nondurable consumer goods, such as textiles, tobacco and food. Declines in those items, while substantial, were not nearly so great as in the production of the metals and machinery. Table *XL* gives some indexes of production for certain industry groups and subgroups. All of these are for the whole United States, but those marked "Typical Southern Industries" include more than two thirds of all southern manufactures. From this table it can be seen that only one industry group of importance—lumber and products (which here includes furniture)—was in the category of durable goods, and production in that group behaved in accordance with the pattern for durable goods. All other major southern industries were in the nondurable group and in none of them did production in 1932 fall below 73 per cent of 1929. In three of the groups, production remained above the average for all nondurable goods. In the durable goods group, production in 1932 typically fell to around 40 or lower.

TABLE *XL* SELECTED INDEXES OF INDUSTRIAL PRODUCTION IN THE UNITED STATES, 1929–1948

(1929 = 100)

						TYPICAL SOUTHERN INDUSTRIES				
YEAR	ALL MFG.	DUR-ABLE MFG.	NON-DUR ABLE MFG.	IRON AND STEEL	MA-CHIN-ERY	TEX-TILES AND PROD.	TOBACCO MFG.	FOOD MFG.	PAPER AND PULP	LUMBER AND PROD.
1929	100	100	100	100	100	100	100	100	100	100
1930	82	74	90	73	77	79	97	99	93	72
1931	67	51	85	46	51	84	91	89	86	52
1932	52	31	75	24	33	76	82	78	73	35
1933	62	41	85	41	38	94	83	82	84	43
1934	67	49	87	46	53	81	91	87	83	44
1935	79	63	97	61	64	99	94	88	96	58
1936	95	82	108	86	81	111	103	97	109	72
1937	103	92	114	92	97	113	107	102	119	77
1938	79	59	102	51	63	90	106	100	106	62
1939	99	83	117	86	80	119	110	107	126	73
1940	115	105	124	111	105	121	114	112	138	79
1941	153	152	153	140	170	162	125	126	164	92
1942	193	211	170	150	262	167	136	133	159	92
1943	235	273	189	156	341	163	139	144	152	88
1944	229	267	184	155	338	157	130	150	150	86
1945	195	208	178	138	264	155	142	149	150	75
1946	161	145	177	113	185	172	162	148	157	90
1947	170	167	185	147	212	173	167	155	169	98
1948	180	170	190	156	213	181	171	157	177	99

SOURCE: Compiled from reports of the Board of Governors of the Federal Reserve System. All series were converted from a 1935–39 base to a 1929 base.

The Recovery Years. Despite the fact that its decline had been relatively small, southern industry recovered as sharply, if not more sharply, in 1933 than did industry in the rest of the country. Two factors helped to account for this fact. One was that the "pre-code boom" in 1933 was especially pronounced in the textile industry. (The industry paid for this with a sharp relapse in 1934.) The other factor was strong upward secular trends in paper, petroleum, and cigarettes which facilitated quick recoveries.

Because recovery was slower in getting under way in the heavy industries and because the nondurable goods had their sharp spurt in 1933, the South did not show as large gains from 1933 to 1935 as did the rest of the country. From 1935 to 1937, however, gains were about equal in the two parts of the country. In 1938 there was a sharp "recession" and again the South fared considerably better than the rest of the nation. The heavy industries were the ones principally affected, while the consumer-goods industries experienced only slight declines. There were recoveries in 1939, but production of durable goods remained substantially below 1937 levels, while in many instances the production of nondurable goods surpassed those levels. As a result of these developments, manufacturing in the South in 1939 showed only insignificant changes from 1937, but in the Non-South the number of wage earners was down by 9 per cent, wages paid were down 11 per cent, and the value of manufactured products was 7 per cent lower.

The Position in 1939. The net result of the changes during this decade was that in 1939 the South, in total manufacturing, was just about back to where it was in 1929. Wages paid were 9 per cent lower and value added was a little more than 2 per cent lower. The latter change was considerably less than the decline in prices, so physical quantities were higher. On the other hand, in the Non-South the number of wage earners was 8 per cent lower, wages paid were down by 20 per cent, and value added was lower by 22 per cent. Relatively, the South had gained substantially in this period.

The textile industry, with 466,000 wage earners, was in first place and had increased its relative importance somewhat. Lumber and timber products were in second place with 203,000 wage earners, but had declined in relative importance. The food products group, with 126,000 workers, was the only other industry group with more than 100,000 workers. The knit goods industries probably had the greatest increase during the decade and in 1939 had over 90,000 wage earners, of which over 78,000 were in hosiery alone.

Among the states, North Carolina was the star performer during this decade, remaining in first place, and increasing its proportion of wage earners from 15.7 to 19.9 per cent of the total for the region. Georgia was in second place with 11.6 per cent. South Carolina and Tennessee showed small gains, but the other nine states had moderate declines. Measured by value of product, Texas was first with 18.5 per cent, North Carolina second with 17.2 per cent, and Virginia third with 12.0 per cent.

THE WAR AND POSTWAR DECADE

Since 1939, southern industry has gone through a full cycle from peacetime production to preparation for war, to full-scale war production, to demobilization, and back again to peacetime production. Although, except for its textile industry, the South did not have many of the facilities needed to produce the goods of war yet, in one way or another, it made a very substantial contribution to war production. The greater part of that contribution was made by the shipyards, the airplane factories, and the munitions plants which were constructed after we were actually in the war. Naturally, such developments as the above caused far-reaching changes in the industrial structure.

General Course of Developments. In the period of preparation and in the first year of the war, the South lagged behind the rest of the country in industrial expansion. Industrial activity in the South was expanding, and fairly rapidly, but not so fast as elsewhere; the reasons for this have already been noted.[3] Later this lag was largely overcome; in some respects, the South had larger gains by 1944.

Broadly, manufacturing employment in the South during the war increased from 1,650,000 to a peak of 2,835,000 in November, 1943.[4] The average for the year 1943 was 2,770,000. This was an increase of nearly 1,200,000, or more than two thirds. Outside the South the increase was approximately three fourths. This great increase in the South occurred at a time when there was a heavy migration out of the region and when large numbers of the men and women most adaptable to manufacturing work were being taken into the armed forces. In view of these facts, it is no wonder that there was a considerable depopulation of rural and farming areas. From the 1943 peak, employment declined to a postwar low of a little less than 2,200,000 in February, 1946, and then rose to about 2,400,000 in 1947 for a net loss of some 425,000 from the wartime peak. In other

---

[3] See Chapter III.

[4] Since there was no *Census of Manufactures* between 1939 and 1947, we must, for the war period, rely upon estimates and computations of various other federal agencies. Some of them are: (1) estimates of employment in manufacturing by the Department of Labor; (2) estimates of wages and salaries from manufacturing by the Department of Commerce; (3) data on industrial consumption of electricity and generating capacity by the Federal Power Commission; and (4) data on new construction by the Department of Commerce. The figures on factory employment by the Department of Labor are different from, and considerably higher than, the employment figures in the *Census of Manufactures*.

words, after reconversion, the South retained about 60 per cent of the wartime addition to its factory labor force.

During the war, wages and salaries paid in manufacturing increased much faster than employment. While employment rose by 67 per cent between 1939 and 1944, wages and salaries increased by 234 per cent. In 1946, when employment was 35 per cent above prewar, wages and salaries were up by 189 per cent. In the rise of total wages and salaries, the South consistently lagged behind the Non-South until 1944; thereafter it remained ahead. There were several reasons for the greater increase in wages and salaries in the South. Upgrading and federal regulations tended to bring the low-wage industries more nearly into line with the others. The big expansion in production in the South came in the midst of the war when the labor supply was short. The projects (ships, airplanes, munitions) were vital to the war effort and had to have labor at any wage.

While employment increased in all industries (after 1943 there were appreciable declines in textiles, lumber, furniture, etc.), the greatest increases came in the war industries. These included iron and steel, nonferrous metals, machinery, chemicals, and others. But the outstanding boom in employment was in the transportation equipment (other than automobiles) group, i.e., largely shipbuilding and aircraft construction. From a total employment of less than 20,000 before the war, this group rose to more than a half a million at the peak in 1943, when it was in second place and accounted for about one sixth of total factory employment. It fell even more rapidly to eighth place in 1946 with less than 80,000, but still it had more than four times its prewar employment. The textile industry declined sharply in relative importance—from 31 per cent of total employment before the war to 21 per cent in 1944. Similar but smaller relative declines occurred in lumber, furniture, and tobacco.

After the war, as is noted elsewhere, the South had a faster demobilization of its "war industries" than did the rest of the country. This was inevitable from the nature of those industries since the need for their products disappeared as soon as the fighting stopped. On the other hand, the normal and permanent southern industries had relatively few reconversion problems and they maintained production somewhat better than did the "nonwar industries" elsewhere. Overall, southern industry had a slight relative decline in the reconversion years and then held its own, with perhaps some slight increase in the postwar years.

Before the war the South had a little more than two workers in the nondurable goods industries for each worker in the durable goods industries; the figures were 68.2 per cent and 31.8 per cent. At the war peak, employment in the durable goods field rose to almost half— 46.6 per cent for 1944—but by 1946 the figures had returned almost to the prewar pattern and stood at approximately 65 per cent nondurable and 35 per cent durable.

Geographically, the outstanding development of the war period was the rapid development of industry in Texas. Before the war that state ranked fourth in factory employment and second in wages paid in the South. Rapid wartime expansion in many lines, especially in the airplane, chemical, and petroleum groups, soon put the state first in both respects. North Carolina had relative losses roughly similar to Texas' gains. By 1947, however, North Carolina had regained first place in both employment and wages paid, while Texas ranked second.

New Construction. Construction activity in the United States has shown very wide variations since 1939. There was the prewar private building boom, followed by the war building boom financed by the government in the early war years, and then a great slump in all construction. After the war, construction reached record new heights to make up the accumulated deficit. In all these changes the South maintained construction at levels considerably higher in relation to prewar than did the rest of the country. From $1,419 million, or 23.4 per cent of the national total, in 1939, southern construction rose to 33 per cent in 1942. In 1948, the total was $3,816 million, which was 26.6 per cent of the total for the whole country.[5]

In private, nonresidential construction, probably the best measure of business and industrial building, the total in the South increased from $154 million, or 19.6 per cent of the national total in 1939, to

---

[5] To a considerable extent the relative gain during the war was the result of heavier expenditures for construction by the Federal Government in the South, but the importance of this factor has frequently been exaggerated. Between July 1, 1940 and June 30, 1945, only 26.6 per cent of all federal expenditures for housing and 30.1 per cent of all federal expenditures for military and naval installations were in the South. Civilian Production Administration, *Facilities Expansion, July, 1940—June, 1945*, p. 43. These proportions are roughly in line with the proportions of population and land area contained in the South, although somewhat greater than the proportion of income received in the region.

$776 million, or 21.7 per cent, in 1948. Public utility construction also is a significant indicator of business expansion, and in addition, perhaps, has some value as a barometer indicating future developments, since public utilities must plan for the future. In relation to prewar, the South had a larger total of public utility construction than the rest of the country in every year after 1939. In 1948, the region had a total of $1,020 million, which was 571 per cent above the 1939 level, compared with an increase of 322 per cent elsewhere. Over the period the region increased its proportion of the U. S. total from 22.3 to 31.3 per cent.

The huge program for the building of war plants and related establishments during the war constituted a special and unique chapter in industrial development. Table *XLI* gives some summary data on that program. Between July 1, 1940 and June 30, 1945, the Federal Government and private industry spent some $26 billion for the

TABLE *XLI*   EXPENDITURES FOR EXPANSION OF MANUFACTURING, HOUSING, AND MILITARY FACILITIES IN THE SOUTH DURING WORLD WAR II BY TYPE OF PRODUCT
(*Absolute Figures in Millions of Dollars*)

PRODUCT	PRIVATELY FINANCED	PUBLICLY FINANCED	TOTAL	PER CENT OF U. S. TOTAL	PER CENT OF TOTAL FOR SOUTH
MANUFACTURING					
Aircraft Engines and Parts	16	336	352	9.3	7.5
Ship Construction and Repair	24	373	397	15.4	8.7
Guns and Ammunition	18	299	317	11.6	7.0
Explosives and Ammunition Loading	3	1019	1022	35.9	22.5
Iron and Steel	88	99	187	7.9	4.1
Nonferrous Metals	76	241	317	21.7	7.0
Chemicals, Coal, Petroleum, Etc.	487	1098	1585	43.4	34.8
Food Processing	239	84	323	7.5	7.1
Other Products	14	38	52	2.3	1.1
Total Manufacturing	965*	3587	4552	17.5	100.0
HOUSING AND MILITARY INSTALLATIONS					
Housing	—	623	623	26.6	—
Military Installations*	—	4163	4163	30.1	—
Grand Total	965	8373	8338	22.1	—

* Per cent of expansion of manufacturing facilities privately financed; South, 21.2; Non-South, 36.8.
SOURCE: Computed from *Facts for Industry*, "Facilities Expansion, July, 1940—June, 1945." Prepared by Civilian Production Administration.

expansion and construction of manufacturing facilities in the United States. Of this amount, about four and a half billion or 17.5 per cent, were spent in the South. In value terms alone, this probably represented about a doubling of the South's industrial plant as of 1939. But it was far from representing a doubling of the South's effective industrial capacity. High wartime construction costs, the nature and location of the facilities and other factors detracted heavily from their peacetime value. Many of the plants have no peacetime use, others can be used only in part, while still others can be converted to peacetime uses at greater or less expense.

One study appraised the South's heritage of war facilities in these words:

> The pattern of war manufacturing facilities expansion in the South was a great deal different from that in the entire country, and generally speaking the differences were not favorable to the South. The industries which had more sound reconversion possibilities and those which would aid particularly in further industrialization accounted for a relatively small part of the industrial expansion program in the South. Of the total value of war manufacturing awards in the South, less than 1 per cent was in plants to turn out vehicles, and barely 1 per cent in machinery and electrical equipment plants, in contrast to 4 per cent and 5 per cent, respectively, for the nation as a whole. Only 4 per cent of the South's expansions (in value) was in iron and steel in contrast to a national figure of 9 per cent. On the other hand, 20 per cent of the southern states' value of war facilities awards was in the explosives and ammunition lines, and 31 per cent in the chemicals line (which included synthetic rubber, aviation gasoline, and other chemicals and products of petroleum and coal) as against 11 per cent and 14 per cent, respectively, for the United States. In general, the explosives and certain chemical plants have major reconversion handicaps, plus the fact that many are held in standby condition by the Government and hence cannot be classed as actual additions to the industrial plant of the area anyway.[6]

In the manufacturing field, well over half of the total expenditures were made in the chemicals and explosives groups. The principal objects of expenditures within the chemicals group were synthetic rubber plants and petroleum refineries. In general, total expenditures for manufacturing were fairly evenly divided between plants and equipment.

6 Frederick L. Deming and Weldon A. Stein, *Disposal of Southern War Plants,* NPA Committee of the South Report No. 2, Washington, 1949, p. 15. The basic studies from which this report was compiled were made by the research staff of the Federal Reserve Banks of Richmond, Atlanta, Dallas, and St. Louis.

Almost a billion dollars of private funds were invested in the expansion of facilities, principally in the chemicals and food processing groups. According to another study, it is estimated that private investments not reported or not connected with the war program during this period amounted to more than $600 million, making a total private investment of over a billion and a half dollars.[7] Presumably these private investments represent solid, permanent additions to the southern industrial plant with good prospects for continued use. The proportion of the total facilities expansion financed by private funds was 21 per cent in the South compared with about 37 per cent outside the South. This was due at least in part to the fact, pointed out in the above quotation, that a larger proportion of the southern facilities did not represent good reconversion risks.

The facilities paid for by public funds represent varying degrees of usefulness. Nearly all of the ordnance plants and a large majority of the aircraft and shipbuilding facilities have no usefulness as such in time of peace; in some cases the buildings and equipment can be converted to other uses, but in many instances they are being dismantled and abandoned or sold for scrap. On the other hand, the iron and steel plants and the petroleum refineries have continued in active use, practically at full capacity, some after sale to private companies and others under lease. A large proportion of the food processing and nonferrous metals plants are also in active use. The synthetic rubber plants constitute a major problem; in the event of another major national emergency they would be enormously valuable, but in time of peace and with an adequate supply of natural rubber their value would be uncertain. In the main the government retains ownership of them and they are being operated under lease at much less than their full capacity since larger amounts of natural rubber have become available.

Rather than doubling the South's industrial capacity, as the gross value figures indicate, the wartime expansion probably did not increase the effective capacity by more than 40 per cent at most.

Changes in the Structure of Industry. The 1947 *Census of Manufactures* provides the best data yet assembled for making an analysis of the changes in our industrial structure over a significant period. The data are conveniently grouped by major industry groups and the 1939 data are adjusted to make them comparable with the 1947 data.

[7] *Economic Problems of the Cotton Belt*, p. 678.

Thus, for this period of important change, we have excellent materials for "before" and "after" pictures of the South's industrial system. Table *XLII* presents such a picture on the basis of employment and Table *XLIII* on the basis of value added by manufacture.[8]

TABLE *XLII* PRODUCTION WORKERS IN MANUFACTURING IN THE SOUTH AND IN THE NON-SOUTH BY MAJOR INDUSTRY GROUPS, 1939 AND 1947

(Numbers in Thousands)

MAJOR INDUSTRY GROUP	SOUTH						NON-SOUTH		PER CENT INCREASES 1939 1947	
	1939		1947		INCREASES		1939	1947		
	AMT.	PERCENT- AGE OF TOTAL	AMT.	PERCENT- AGE OF TOTAL	AMT.	PERCENT- AGE OF TOTAL	AMT.	AMT.	SOUTH	NON-SOUTH
Food and Prod.	126	9.3	202	10.0	76	11.3	676	896	60.3	32.5
Tobacco Mfg.	41	3.0	62	3.1	21	3.1	47	42	51.2	−10.6
Textile Mills	476	35.3	554	27.4	78	11.6	605	593	16.4	−2.0
Apparel	82	6.1	130	6.4	48	7.1	671	844	58.5	25.8
Lumber and Prod.	203	15.0	299	14.8	96	14.2	220	300	47.3	36.4
Furniture and Fix.	49	3.6	75	3.7	26	3.9	140	208	53.1	48.6
Paper and Prod.	37	2.7	66	3.3	29	4.3	233	323	78.4	38.6
Printing and Pub.	31	2.3	46	2.3	15	2.2	293	392	48.4	33.8
Chemicals	72	5.3	120	5.9	48	7.1	204	347	66.7	70.1
Petroleum and Coal	30	2.2	51	2.5	51	3.1	78	119	70.0	52.6
Stone, Clay, Glass	35	2.6	58	2.9	23	3.4	232	348	65.7	50.0
Fabricated Metals	28	2.1	59	2.9	31	4.6	423	763	110.7	80.4
Machinery (Exc. El.)	21	1.6	56	2.8	35	5.2	515	1188	166.7	130.7
Transport. Equip.	22	1.6	68	3.4	46	6.8	523	917	209.1	75.3
All Other	96	7.1	177	8.7	81	12.0	1599	2615	84.4	63.5
Total	1349	100.0	2023	100.0	674	100.0	6459	9895	50.0	52.3

SOURCE: Computed from *Census of Manufactures, 1947.*

All things considered, the analysis of employment or "production workers" is probably the most useful in indicating changes in the

[8] "Value added by manufacture" means roughly the valued added to raw materials by their processing while going through the manufacturing stage. The official Census Bureau explanation of the term is as follows: " 'Value added by manufacture' provides the best census measure of the relative economic importance of manufacturing in different industries and different areas. It measures the approximate value created in the process of manufacture, that is, the contribution of manufacturing establishments to the value of finished manufactured products. Value added is calculated by subtracting the cost of materials, supplies, and containers, fuel, purchased electric energy, and contract work from the total value of shipments.

"Value added by manufacture should not be confused with 'income produced in manufacturing.' The latter figure . . . does not include, as does value added, the amount of capital used up (depreciation) or expenses such as taxes, insurance, rent, etc., which are the contribution of the service industries and other manufacturing activities. Some notion of the relative magnitude of these measures can be obtained from the 1939 figures. In that year value added produced in manufacturing amounted to $18 billion. Of this difference of $7 billion, approximately one-fourth reflected the allowance for depreciation." *Census of Manufactures, 1947.*

TABLE *XLIII*   VALUE ADDED BY MANUFACTURE IN THE SOUTH AND IN THE NON-SOUTH BY MAJOR INDUSTRY GROUPS, 1939 AND 1947

(Dollar Amounts in Millions)

MAJOR INDUSTRY GROUP	SOUTH						NON-SOUTH		PER CENT INCREASES	
	1939		1947		INCREASES		1939	1947	1939	1947
	AMT.	PERCENT- AGE OF TOTAL	AMT.	PERCENT- AGE OF TOTAL	AMT.	PERCENT- AGE OF TOTAL	AMT.	AMT.	SOUTH	NON-SOUTH
Food and Prod.	$ 482	15.4	$1522	14.2	$1040	13.6	$ 3003	$ 7500	216	150
Tobacco Mfg.	245	7.8	463	4.3	218	2.9	105	182	89	73
Textile Mills	633	20.3	2382	22.2	1749	23.0	1185	2952	276	149
Apparel	102	3.3	397	3.7	295	3.9	1284	4026	289	214
Lumber and Prod.	256	8.2	889	8.3	633	8.3	475	1624	247	242
Furniture and Fix.	81	2.6	296	2.8	215	2.8	337	1083	265	221
Paper and Prod.	122	3.9	539	5.0	417	5.5	766	2336	342	205
Printing and Pub.	153	4.9	388	3.6	235	3.1	1612	3881	154	141
Chemicals	302	9.7	1082	10.1	780	10.2	1517	4278	258	182
Petroleum and Coal	175	5.6	642	6.0	467	6.1	522	1375	267	163
Stone, Clay, Glass	93	3.0	289	2.7	196	2.6	763	2018	211	165
Fabricated Metals	69	2.2	307	2.9	238	3.1	1332	4611	345	246
Machinery (Exc. El.)	78	2.5	328	3.0	250	3.3	1959	7489	321	272
Transport. Equip.	68	2.2	333	3.1	265	3.5	1707	5527	390	224
All Other	265	8.5	887	8.3	622	8.2	4795	14738	235	207
Total	3124	100.0	10744	100.0	7620	100.0	21363	63620	244	198

SOURCE: Computed from *Census of Manufactures, 1947.*

industrial structure. Those data are not so much subject to the vagaries of changing wage rates and prices as are the data for wages and value added.

Total employment in the South, between 1939 and 1947, increased an even 50 per cent compared with an increase of 52.3 per cent in the Non-South. This is probably not a significant difference. The southern figure was probably affected to some extent by the fact that southern industry did not receive as much of an impetus from the war, and did not keep quite as much of what it did receive, as did industry in the rest of the country.

The most striking change in the structure of southern industry over the war period was the low rate of increase in the textile industry. In 1939 that industry group had 476,000 workers, or 35.3 per cent of the total, but during this period it had an increase of only 16.4 per cent, contrasted with 50 per cent for the region as a whole and 47 per cent for the next lowest industry group. Consequently, in 1947, the textile industry had only 27.4 per cent of all production workers in the region. Stated in other terms, the textile group had more than a third of the workers in 1939, but it received only 11.6 per cent of the increase in workers during the war period.

Employment in the lumber group increased slightly less than average and in the food group somewhat more than average. These Big Three—textiles, lumber and food—accounted for 59.6 of all workers in 1939 and 52.2 per cent in 1947.

Relative increases in employment—to compensate for the big decline in textiles—were distributed over several groups with relatively small employment in the South. These include paper, chemicals, fabricated metals, machinery, and transportation equipment. The largest percentage increases came in the last three named above, but the absolute numbers involved were small.

Two aspects of the changes in employment may be significant. The first six industry groups listed in Table *XLII* (food, tobacco, textiles, apparel, lumber, and furniture) were the groups with the lowest annual wages in 1947. Each had an annual wage below the average for the region ($1,968) and, with one exception, below $1,850.[9] Those groups had comparatively small increases in employment. In 1939, the six groups accounted for 72.3 per cent of total workers in the South; in 1947, they had 65.4 per cent. On the other hand, the five groups with the highest annual wages, each with an average annual wage above $2,400 in 1947, were paper, printing, petroleum, machinery, and transportation equipment. Except for printing, these all had increases in employment well above average. In 1939 these five had 10.4 per cent of total workers; in 1947, 14.3 per cent. Looked at in another way, the low wage groups had 72.3 per cent of the workers in 1939 and got 51.2 per cent of the increase between 1939 and 1947; the high wage groups had 10.4 per cent of the workers in 1939 and got 21.6 per cent of the increase. The largest increases in employment have come in those groups which pay the highest wages, but this must be qualified by the fact that the numbers in those groups are still relatively small.

The second aspect is that the changes of the past decade have reduced the South's heavy dependence on the textile industry and have produced a more diversified industrial structure. The larger increases of employment in the metals, machinery, and equipment groups are

[9] Annual wages were computed by dividing the total of wages paid by the average number of production workers.

slowly giving the region an industrial structure more like that in the remainder of the nation.

The industrial structure, and changes in it between 1939 and 1947, look quite different when analyzed on the basis of value added by manufacture rather than on the basis of employment. First, the absolute figures increased much more because of the great rise in prices. Value added in the South increased by 244 per cent compared with an increase of 198 per cent in the Non-South. Thus, while the South's increase in workers was slightly less, its increase in value added was approximately one-fourth greater than the Non-South's.[10] Second, the relative importance of the different industry groups is quite different when ranked on the basis of value added. In 1939, textiles had well over a third of the workers but produced only a fifth of the value added. The lumber group loses almost half of its relative importance when compared on the basis of value added. The same is true of apparel and, to a less extent, of furniture. On the other hand, certain groups rank much higher when compared on the basis of value added. These include tobacco, paper, printing, chemicals, and petroleum.

A third aspect of significance is the difference in the character of the changes between 1939 and 1947 when considered on the basis of value added. These arose largely out of the differences in the price behavior of different commodities. Again textiles provide the outstanding example. Despite a sharp drop in relative number of workers, value added in textiles increased by 276 per cent. Undoubtedly this was primarily due to the high price of cotton textiles in 1947; if the Census had been taken in 1945 while price control was still in effect or in 1949 after textile prices had dropped considerably, the results would have been quite different.[11] Tobacco manufacturing affords an equally striking example in the opposite direction. That group had

10 No attempt is made here to make an analysis of the industrial structure based on wages paid, but such an analysis would yield results more nearly like the results from the value-added analysis rather than from the production-worker analysis. Thus, between 1939 and 1947, total wages paid to production workers increased by 274 per cent in the South and 240 per cent in the Non-South.

11 For example, the mill margins of cotton textile manufacturers as computed by the U. S. Department of Agriculture may be taken as a rough indication of the value added by manufacture in those concerns. This figure is the average margin, for 17 standard constructions of cotton cloth, between the value of a pound of cotton and the value of the cloth into which it is manufactured. This figure, in cents per pound, varied as follows: 1939, 11.74; 1945, 20.88; 1947, 54.84; 1948, 47.58; first six months of 1949, 30.46. *Survey of Current Business, passim.*

an increase in value added of only 89 per cent; the regional average was 244 per cent and only one other group had an increase of less than 200 per cent. The cause was a very great rise in the price of leaf tobacco coupled with, first, price controls on cigarettes and, later, a situation which limited price increases.

The groups which showed the greatest relative increases in value added were paper, fabricated metals, machinery, and transportation equipment. In every group shown, the South had greater, and usually considerably greater, increases than the Non-South. In neither region did value added increase as much as wages paid. In the South the increase in value added lagged 10 per cent behind the increase in wages paid; in the Non-South, 18 per cent behind.

Changes under Way in 1947. More current data on industrial changes, and perhaps some indication of future trends, is afforded by the data on expenditures for new plant and equipment in 1947. These are given in Table *XLIV,* together with some comparisons. While these

TABLE *XLIV* EXPENDITURES FOR NEW PLANT AND EQUIPMENT BY MAJOR INDUSTRY GROUPS IN 1947

MAJOR INDUSTRY GROUP	EXPENDITURES IN SOUTH ($ millions)	PER CENT OF U. S.	EXPENDITURES PER PRODUCTION WORKER		PER CENT OF REGION	
			SOUTH	NON-SOUTH	SOUTH	NON-SOUTH
Food and Products	144	17.5	$713	$756	12.4	14.0
Tobacco Mfg.	30	83.3	484	143	2.6	0.1
Textile Mills	186	50.7	336	305	16.0	3.7
Apparel	16	19.0	123	81	1.4	1.4
Lumber and Products	54	31.4	181	393	4.7	2.4
Furniture and Fix.	23	29.9	307	260	2.0	1.1
Paper and Products	110	27.0	1667	920	9.5	6.1
Printing and Pub.	27	11.9	587	508	2.3	4.1
Chemicals	259	31.9	2158	1591	22.3	11.4
Petroleum and Coal	104	26.0	2039	2487	9.0	6.1
Stone, Clay, Glass	51	17.9	879	672	4.4	4.8
Fabricated Metals	21	6.9	356	372	1.8	5.9
Machinery (Exc. El.)	41	7.9	732	402	3.5	9.8
Transport. Equip.	19*	5.4	279	754	1.6	14.3
All Other	74	9.4	418	272	6.4	14.7
Total	1159	19.3	573	490	100.0	100.0

* Partly estimated because of withheld data.
SOURCE: Computed from *Census of Manufactures, 1947.*

are for only one year they nevertheless have considerable significance in indicating the directions in which industry is expanding.

Total expenditures in the South were well over a billion dollars, or more than 19 per cent of the national total. Since the South, on any basis of measurement, had considerably less than 19 per cent of the nation's industry in 1947, this would indicate that there was some relative growth in the region. Tobacco manufacturing is the only industry group in which the South has a clear majority of the nation's production. In this group, five sixths of the new investment in 1947 took place in the South, thus accentuating the concentration already existing. On the other hand, investment in the lumber group was not in keeping with the South's proportion of the industry; this was probably due to the fact that lumber production in the West is much more highly mechanized than in the South. The South's share of the new investment in textiles was roughly equal to its share of that industry. In three other groups—furniture, paper, and chemicals—the South had between a third and a fourth of total national investment. These ratios were high in relation to the groups' importance in 1947 and indicates that relative expansion was under way.

Since the necessary investment per worker varies widely from one industry to another, the expenditures for 1947 have been expressed in terms of production workers for each major industry group. These figures show that for many of the industry groups the expenditures per worker were larger in the South than in the Non-South. This is particularly evident in the case of tobacco, paper, chemicals, stone, and machinery, all of which require large investments per worker. For industry as a whole, there was a substantially larger expenditure per worker in the South than in the Non-South.

In order to show where each region is placing most emphasis in its industrial expansion, the expenditures for the South and the Non-South are broken down by major industry groups. For the South, chemicals were receiving by far the greatest attention; with about 6 per cent of the nation's workers and 10 per cent of its value added, that group was receiving 22 per cent of the new investment. Textiles and lumber were low in new investment, while the food group was roughly in line. Paper and petroleum were receiving large amounts of new investment in relation to value added. In the Non-South, new investment was largely concentrated in the food, metals, machinery, and equipment groups; except for foods, the South has very small stakes in these fields and hence they received little of the new funds in this region.

SHIFTS BETWEEN STATES

In the complex changes of the past 20 years there have been considerable differences in rates of industrial growth between the various southern states. Table *XLV* presents summary data which permit the measurement of those changes from several angles. Generally, the results are essentially the same whether production workers, wages, or value added is used as the basis of measurement.

TABLE *XLV* PERCENTAGE DISTRIBUTION BY STATES OF CERTAIN SERIES ON MANUFACTURING IN THE SOUTH, 1929, 1939, AND 1947

STATE	PRODUCTION WORKERS			WAGES PAID			VALUE ADDED BY MANUFACTURE			EXPEND. FOR NEW PLANT & EQUIP.	
	1929	1939	1947	1929	1939	1947	1929	1939	1947	1939	1947
Alabama	8.9	8.6	9.2	8.6	8.6	9.4	8.1	7.9	8.2	5.7	6.2
Arkansas	3.3	2.7	2.9	3.3	2.3	2.6	2.9	2.1	2.5	2.1	2.6
Florida	4.9	3.8	3.3	4.6	3.4	3.2	4.1	3.7	3.3	3.8	4.3
Georgia	11.9	11.6	11.1	9.3	10.0	10.1	9.2	9.0	9.4	8.6	7.3
Kentucky	5.8	4.7	5.5	7.4	5.8	6.0	6.9	6.0	6.9	4.3	6.7
Louisiana	6.5	5.3	5.5	7.1	5.1	5.8	7.7	6.4	6.4	7.5	8.4
Mississippi	3.9	3.4	3.5	3.6	2.5	2.9	3.3	2.3	2.8	2.7	2.0
North Carolina	15.7	19.9	17.3	13.6	18.6	16.1	14.0	17.4	15.3	14.2	11.9
Oklahoma	2.4	2.1	2.2	3.5	2.8	2.6	4.7	3.3	3.2	2.6	2.2
South Carolina	8.1	9.3	8.7	6.2	8.1	8.3	5.0	5.4	7.4	5.2	5.3
Tennessee	9.6	9.7	9.5	9.8	10.2	9.3	10.0	10.2	8.9	10.8	7.2
Texas	10.1	9.3	12.0	12.8	11.9	14.0	14.4	14.4	16.0	22.9	26.3
Virginia	9.0	9.8	9.4	10.0	10.7	9.7	9.6	12.0	9.8	9.6	9.6
Total	100.0	100.0	100.0	100.0	100.0	100.0	100.0	100.0	100.0	100.0	100.0
Absolute Amounts*	1338	1349	2023	1182	1065	3976	3199	3124	10744	211	1159

* Workers in thousands; dollar amounts in millions.
SOURCE: Computed from *Census of Manufactures*.

Perhaps the most striking aspect of Table *XLV* is the large relative gain[12] made by Texas after 1939, which put that state first in value added and second in workers and wages. North Carolina and, to a smaller extent, Virginia and Tennessee, had large gains between 1929 and 1939 but substantial losses after 1939. Certain states had an opposite pattern, more or less sharply defined. They were: Arkansas, Kentucky, Louisiana, and Mississippi. Florida and Oklahoma experienced slow but persistent declines over the whole period. South Carolina made fairly consistent gains throughout, but Alabama and Georgia had no significant changes.

For the period from 1939 to 1947, there are some interesting

[12] Throughout this section, comparisons will be made on the basis of the relative gains and losses of states rather than on absolute data.

differences in the behavior of the data for different states, arising partly out of differences in the composition of their industries. It was noted above that the tobacco group had a very low increase in value added while the textile group had an increase larger than average. Virginia has a large tobacco industry but comparatively few textile mills. In addition, from 1939 to 1947, Virginia had a below-average increase in production workers—44.7 per cent. As a result, Virginia had the smallest increase in value added of all the southern states— 180 per cent. North Carolina has a larger tobacco industry than does Virginia, but its textile industry is several times as large as its tobacco industry. But North Carolina had the smallest increase in production workers of all the southern states—only 30.1 per cent. This combination produced an increase in value added of only 203 per cent—the lowest except for Virginia and Tennessee (but tied with Florida). On the other hand, approximately two thirds of South Carolina's industry is in the textile group, and the state has virtually no tobacco industry. While that state also had a less-than-average increase in production workers (39.7 per cent), it had, by a considerable margin, the largest increase in value added of any state in the region—370 per cent. Thus the results in these three states depended to a considerable extent of the proportions in which textiles and tobacco were mixed in their industrial structures.

While the data on the point are not conclusive, they do suggest the hypothesis that between 1929 and 1939 there was a concentration of industry in the sense that those states which had most industry in 1929 experienced the greatest gains between 1929 and 1939, and vice versa. The data also suggest, although on this point they are still less conclusive, that that trend was stopped and even reversed after 1939. In 1929, five southern states—Georgia, North Carolina, Tennessee, Texas, and Virginia (the Big Five)—had 56.3 per cent of all production workers in the South. In 1939 they had 60.3 per cent and in 1947, 59.3 per cent. On the other hand the Little Five—Arkansas, Florida, Kentucky, Mississippi, and Oklahoma—had 20.3 per cent in 1929, 16.7 per cent in 1939, and 17.4 per cent in 1947. In terms of value added by manufacture, the Big Five had 57.2 per cent of the total in 1929, 63.0 per cent in 1939, and 59.4 per cent in 1947. In the same years the Little Five had, respectively, 22.0 per cent, 17.4 per cent, and 18.7 per cent. The continuing relative declines in Florida and Oklahoma offset somewhat the gains by the other three states in this category after 1939.

This tendency for rural and agricultural areas to experience a greater rate of industrial growth has been noted elsewhere. In a study of four southern states for years immediately after World War II, it was found that the rural counties had a considerably greater increase in industry than did the urban and industrial counties.[13]

SOME CHARACTERISTICS OF
SOUTHERN INDUSTRY

Power Equipment. In general, southern factories in 1939[14] had power equipment in keeping with the number of their employees and the value of their products. Installed horsepower per 100 workers was about the same in the South as elsewhere, although in the South somewhat more of the power was provided by prime movers and somewhat less by electric motors. Between 1929 and 1939, the total of installed horsepower increased about twice as much in the South as in the Non-South, but this was roughly comparable with the change in wage earners; the increase per 100 wage earners was slightly greater outside the South.

Electric energy purchased per wage earner was substantially greater in the South than in the Non-South in both 1929 and 1939; the increase over the decade was large in both regions. A part of the greater increase in the South may have been due to greater use of electricity in chemical processes which did not involve motive power. In so far as the difference was in motive power, it perhaps reflected the fact the southern products are typically heavier and coarser and thus require more power for their processing.

Electricity purchased per horsepower of installed motors was considerably more in the South and the difference increased between 1929 and 1939. In fact, in the Non-South the figure declined between these two years, reflecting the lower number of man-hours of employment. In part the higher southern figure undoubtedly is caused by the greater prevalence of double shifts of labor in the region. That

13 James M. Stepp, *Rural Industrial Development in Four Southern States Since World War II*, an unpublished study made for the NPA Committee of the South, June, 1948. The four states were Alabama, Arkansas, South Carolina, and Tennessee.
14 This analysis of power equipment is made as of 1939 because at this writing the 1947 data on this point are not available.

meant that southern manufacturers used their power equipment more intensively and thus spread the overhead over a larger volume of products.

Electric Generating Capacity. To meet the growing demand for electricity, generating capacity in the South has been increased greatly in the past 20 years. Between 1929 and 1946, public utilities in the South increased their total generating capacity by 91 per cent and their hydro capacity by 111 per cent. These were considerably larger increases than took place outside the South (see Table *XLVI*). In addition, in 1947, the TVA, the U. S. Army Engineers, and 32 privately owned utility companies had schedules calling for the installation of 5,383,000 kilowatts of new generating capacity, most of it by the end of 1951. This will increase the total as of 1946 by about 50 per cent and will be ". . . the greatest expansion in the history of the electric power industry of the South."[15] The cost was estimated at $2¼ billion, of which the private utilities were to provide $1½ billion, the Army Engineers $526 million, and the TVA the remainder. A large majority of the new installations planned by the privately-owned companies is to be steam powered.

TABLE *XLVI* ELECTRIC GENERATING CAPACITY OF UTILITIES IN THE SOUTH AND IN NON-SOUTH, 1929, 1939 AND 1946

(*Amounts in Thousands of Kilowatts*)

YEAR	SOUTH			NON-SOUTH	
	AMOUNT	% OF U. S.	% INCREASE OVER 1929	AMOUNT	% INCREASE OVER 1929
1929:					
Hydro	2,112	25.9	—	6,054	—
Total	5,460	17.3	—	26,163	—
1939					
Hydro	3,058	26.8	44.8	8,357	38.0
Total	7,200	17.9	31.9	33,118	26.6
1946:					
Hydro	4,455	30.0	110.9	10,394	71.7
Total	10,428	20.7	91.0	39,876	52.4

SOURCE: Computed from reports of the Federal Power Commission.

In 1946, Texas was first in total generating capacity with 1,494,-000 kilowatts, Tennessee second with 1,448,000, North Carolina

15 *The Daily News Record,* Nov. 22, 1947, p. 6.

third with 1,351,000, and Alabama fourth with 1,327,000. Mississippi was last with only 71,000 kilowatts. In hydro capacity, Tennessee was first with 1,023,000 kilowatts, Alabama second with 960,000, North Carolina third with 658,000, and South Carolina fourth with 651,000. Mississippi and Louisiana had no hydro power and Florida had only a nominal amount. South Carolina, with 82 per cent, had the highest proportion of hydro to total generating capacity.

Wages Paid and Value Added. By expressing the data for wages paid and value added by manufacture in terms of production workers, we can see some interesting trends within the South and make some significant interregional comparisons.[16] The computed figures are shown in Table *XLVII*. In 1929, both the average wage and average value added in the South were a little more than 63 per cent of the corresponding figure for the Non-South.

TABLE *XLVII* AVERAGE ANNUAL WAGE AND VALUE ADDED PER PRODUCTION WORKER IN MANUFACTURING IN THE SOUTH AND IN THE NON-SOUTH, 1929–1947

YEAR	AVERAGE ANNUAL WAGE PER WORKER					AVERAGE VALUE ADDED PER WORKER				
	SOUTH	PERCENTAGE CHANGE*	NON-SOUTH	PERCENTAGE CHANGE*	SOUTH AS PER-CENT-AGE OF NON-SOUTH	SOUTH	PERCENTAGE CHANGE*	NON-SOUTH	PERCENTAGE CHANGE*	SOUTH AS PER-CENT-AGE OF NON-SOUTH
1929	883	—	1,393	—	63.4	2,391	—	3,767	—	63.5
1931	770	−12.8	1,162	−16.6	66.3	2,188	−8.5	3,201	−15.0	68.4
1933	620	−19.5	920	−20.8	67.4	1,720	−21.4	2,541	−20.6	67.7
1935	715	+15.3	1,082	+17.6	66.1	1,858	+8.0	2,795	+10.0	66.5
1937	793	+10.9	1,254	+15.9	63.2	2,159	+16.2	3,087	+10.4	69.9
1939	791	−0.3	1,228	−2.1	64.4	2,314	+7.2	3,330	+6.9	70.1
1947	1,968	+149.1	2,655	+122.0	74.1	5,311	+129.0	6,429	+94.0	82.6

* Change from the last previous data; for 1947 the percentage changes are computed from revised 1939 data which are slightly different from those given here.
SOURCE: Computed from *Census of Manufactures.*

The average wage did not fall as much in the South as elsewhere between 1929 and 1933, nor did it rise as much between 1933 and 1937. Generally, the average southern wage between 1929 and 1939 fluctuated around levels slightly below two thirds of the non-southern

16 These figures are found by dividing the average number of production workers in the region into, respectively, the total of wages paid and the total value added by manufacture. The average annual wages thus found do not, of course, measure comparative wage rates between the South and the Non-South since the composition of jobs in the two regions varies widely.

wage with no consistent trend either up or down. In 1947, however, the southern wage was almost three fourths of the non-southern. Over the whole period, the average wage increased by 123 per cent in the South and by 91 per cent in the Non-South.

One striking aspect of the data for average wages is their behavior between 1935 and 1937. The federal minimum wage law went into effect in 1936. Because of the generally lower level of wages in the South, the obvious assumption would have been that this law would have raised southern wages more than non-southern and thus would have raised the South/Non-South ratio. Actually, that ratio dropped from 66.1 in 1935 to 63.2 per cent in 1937, thus wiping out the increases which had occurred after 1929. The reasons for such behavior are not apparent. One possible explanation[17] is that in the South where labor was not so strongly organized, there was a reduction in wage differentials between jobs and more wages were fixed at, or near, the minimum, whereas outside the South, where labor was more strongly organized, it was able to insist upon the differentials being maintained. An extensive and detailed study of wage rates would be required to determine the validity of that hypothesis.

In average value added per worker, the southern figure did not drop as much as the non-southern average between 1929 and 1933, and it rose somewhat more than the non-southern figure between 1933 and 1937. Generally, the southern figure tended to fluctuate slightly above two thirds of the non-southern figure, with a fairly distinct upward trend. Over the war period, the southern average increased considerably more than the non-southern and raised the ratio almost to 83 per cent. Over the whole period the southern average increased by 122 per cent, almost exactly the same as the increase in the average wage, while the non-southern average increased by 71 per cent in comparison with an increase of 91 per cent in the average wage.

From 1929 through 1935, the South/Non-South ratios for wages and for value added were almost identical. Then, between 1935 and 1937, the wage ratio dropped by almost three points and the value-added ratio rose by more than three points. In 1939, the value-added ratio was almost six points higher than the wage ratio and in 1947, more than eight points higher. Looked at in another way, between

[17] Suggested by our colleague, Dr. Frank T. deVyver.

1929 and 1947, almost half of the South/Non-South differential in value added per worker was wiped out but in the same period less than a third of the differential in annual wages was eliminated.

In the South, throughout this period the average wage and the value added per worker increased at about the same rate. In 1929, the average wage was equal to 36.6 per cent of the value added per worker; in 1947, it was equal to 37.1 per cent. In the Non-South, the average wage increased somewhat more than value added per worker. In 1929, the average wage was 37.0 per cent of the value added and by 1947 this figure had risen to 41.1 per cent.

SUMMARY

Since 1929, the South has realized substantial industrial growth in both absolute and relative terms. During the decade of the depression, the region just about held its own in absolute terms but made considerable gains in relation to the rest of the country. From 1939 to 1947, the South's industrial labor force increased by 50 per cent, which was slightly less than the increase in the rest of the nation. But in wages paid and in value added by manufacturing, the South had increases, respectively, of 274 per cent and 244 per cent, which were considerably greater than the corresponding increases in the Non-South.

The composition of the region's industrial structure was changed considerably by the fact that the textile group had by far the smallest rate of increase in production workers of any major group between 1939 and 1947, with the result that that group's proportion of total workers declined from 35 per cent to 27 per cent. Generally, the industry groups which employed most southern workers in 1939 (which were also low-wage groups) had low rates of increase in workers during the war period. Conversely, those industry groups which employed relatively few southern workers in 1939 and which generally paid high wages, had the highest percentage rates of increase in employment between 1939 and 1947. These changes tended to give the region a better balanced industrial structure with higher levels of wages. Geographically, North Carolina increased its lead as the first industrial state of the South between 1929 and 1939, but had that lead reduced substantially after 1939 as Texas made large gains; in certain respects, Texas now ranks first.

More than 19 per cent of all expenditures for new plant and equipment in the nation in 1947 were made in the South. For industry as a whole and for most of the major industry groups with substantial representation in the region, expenditures per production worker were greater in the South than in the Non-South. Expenditures were relatively high in the groups which pay high wages; the chemical group led with 22 per cent of the total. Among the states, Texas led with 26 per cent of the total, indicating a continuing expansion in that state.

VII SOME MAJOR SOUTHERN INDUSTRIES

The previous chapter has sketched the larger aspects of industrial development in the South in recent years. Now it may be proper and useful to consider in greater detail some of the particular industries or industry groups which are of major importance in the region. This chapter attempts to make such an examination, although necessarily in a very brief and general fashion. The lumber and timber group of industries, which has long ranked second in the South, and the paper and pulp group, which is of growing importance, are omitted here but are discussed in the chapter on Forest Resources and Policy.

THE COTTON TEXTILE INDUSTRY

The textile industry has been the heart of southern industry for more than a half a century. The textile industry, in turn, means mainly the cotton textile industry; for a long time the two were practically synonymous in the South. The cotton textile industry includes the spinning and processing of yarn and the weaving and finishing of cotton cloth, as contrasted with the fabrication of cloth into wearing apparel; this latter process falls into the apparel group. Activity in the cotton textile industry can be measured by the use of data on the number and activity of spindles and looms and the consumption of cotton. Adequate data are available on spindles and on cotton consumption, but statistics on looms and their output, especially by states or regions, are often difficult to find.

The Shift of Cotton Textiles. An overwhelming majority of the American cotton textile industry is located in two sections of the United States; the South and New England. Around 1900, New England had about 70 per cent of the industry's spindles, but the shift to the South began in earnest about that time. Total number of spindles in place increased from about 20 million in 1900 to nearly 38 million in 1924, the South getting the great bulk of the increase. The South surpassed New England in the number of active spindles in 1925 with 17.3 million and in the number of spindles in place in 1927 with

CHART *VII*   COTTON TEXTILE INDUSTRY: SPINDLE HOURS AND COTTON CONSUMED, SOUTH AND NEW ENGLAND AS PERCENTAGES OF UNITED STATES TOTALS, SELECTED YEARS, 1928–1948

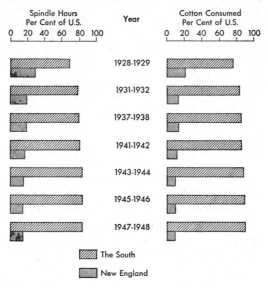

18.2 million. Several years before, the South had surpassed New England in the number of spindle hours and in the amount of cotton consumed, largely because of longer working hours and extra shifts of labor.[1] After 1925 the number of spindles in place in the industry declined steadily and fairly rapidly for more than 20 years, falling from almost 38 million to about 23 million. In New England the peak was reached in 1923 with almost 19 million; since then the decline

[1] The data in this section are taken largely from three principal sources: (1) *Cotton Textile Industry,* Senate Doc. 126, 74th Congress, 1st Sess., Washington, 1935 (The Cabinet Committee Report); (2) U. S. Tariff Commission, *Cotton Cloth,* Report No. 112, Second Series, Washington, 1936; and (3) the annual reports of the Bureau of the Census on *Cotton Production and Distribution.*

has been steady and rapid and the total now is less than five million. In the South, the number of spindles in place rose steadily to 18.6 million in 1930. Since then there has been a loss of about two million.

Table *XLVIII* shows, in percentages of U. S. totals, the figures on spindles in place, spindle hours, and cotton consumed in the South

TABLE *XLVIII* SPINDLES IN PLACE, SPINDLE HOURS, AND COTTON CONSUMED IN PERCENTAGES OF U. S. TOTALS FOR THE SOUTH AND FOR NEW ENGLAND FOR SELECTED YEARS, 1928–1948

| YEAR | SPINDLES IN PLACE | | SPINDLE HOURS | | COTTON CONSUMED | |
	SOUTH	NEW ENGLAND	SOUTH	NEW ENGLAND	SOUTH	NEW ENGLAND
1928–29	54.1	41.8	68.6	28.4	76.0	20.4
1931–32	60.4	35.9	78.0	19.3	82.9	13.9
1934–35	64.3	32.4	75.3	22.4	80.3	15.3
1937–38	71.3	25.7	79.7	18.3	84.9	12.3
1940–41	73.5	23.1	79.2	18.8	85.3	11.8
1941–42	74.8	22.3	80.1	17.8	85.3	11.8
1942–43	75.3	21.9	82.1	16.0	86.8	10.4
1943–44	75.9	21.4	83.6	14.7	87.9	9.6
1944–45	76.1	21.3	84.2	14.1	88.4	9.3
1945–46	76.0*	21.5*	83.9	14.5	88.1	9.3
1946–47	76.0*	21.6*	83.2	15.2	86.2	8.5
1947–48	77.1*	20.7*	83.7	15.0	87.0	8.5

* For these years the data are for cotton-*system* spindles in place. Some of the spindles in that system are used part of the time for spinning synthetic fibres or blends. For previous years, the data are for spindles used *solely* for spinning cotton.
SOURCE: Computed from reports of the Bureau of the Census.

and in New England since 1928. In 1928–29 the South had 54 per cent of the spindles in place, 69 per cent of the spindle hours operated, and accounted for 76 per cent of the cotton consumed. At present the South has something more than 77 per cent of the spindles in place, about 84 per cent of the spindle hours operated, and accounts for about 87 per cent of the cotton consumed. The principal reason for the larger proportion of spindle hours operated is the greater prevalence of two, and even three, shifts of labor operation in the South. The reasons for the larger proportion of cotton consumed are, in addition to the above: (1) principally, that the South produces, on average, coarser and heavier yarns; and (2) southern spindles are slightly larger and more efficient on the average.

The shift of the cotton textile industry to the South achieved its greatest momentum in the latter part of the 1920's and the early 1930's. Since then several factors have operated to slow down the movement. First, and perhaps most important, was the simple fact that a very large part of the industry was already in the South and hence the movement naturally had to taper off. Second, World War II created a demand which permitted all textile mills to operate at capacity for several years and at the same time made it difficult to build, move, or remodel mills. Even in the postwar years, construction costs were so high that new building was discouraged.

While the movement definitely slowed down considerably in recent years, it is not yet certain whether it has entirely stopped. For the textile industry group as a whole (which includes the woolen and synthetic industries as well as cotton), production workers in the South increased by 16.4 per cent between 1939 and 1947, while in the Non-South they declined by 2.0 per cent. In value added, the South had an increase of 276 per cent compared with an increase of 149 per cent elsewhere. The South's share of the national totals changed as follows:

	1939	1947
Production workers	44.0	48.3
Value Added	34.8	44.7

In this period the South's share of value added increased more than its share of production workers. This was probably due more to a relative price change in favor of the heavier goods produced in the South rather than to any change in the structure of the industry. Such a change in relative prices is typical of periods of scarcity and inflation.

As related more specifically to cotton and to the postwar years, the changes are not so clear. From 1946 to 1948, the number of cotton-system spindles in place increased by 1.3 per cent in the South and declined by 3.8 per cent in New England. But in both the number of spindle hours active on cotton and in cotton consumed, New England had increases in those years, and those increases were larger than those in the South. In spindle hours, the percentage increases were 17.5 in New England and 12.6 in the South; in cotton consumed, 6.3 and 2.3. These data indicate that in both regions the industry was turning toward the finer, lighter constructions. This was a normal development as shortages in the heavier and more basic types of cloth were made up after the war. New England has retained a larger proportion of the facilities for producing the finer goods, so that region naturally benefited more from this shift.

For these reasons it is not possible to say with certainty whether the shift of the industry southward was entirely halted in the postwar years. But in the nature of the case it is evident that the movement is largely completed. It may well be that the situation will soon become stabilized with New England retaining some 10 or 15 per cent of the industry, principally in specialties and the finer goods.

The general pattern of growth has been about the same for looms as for spindles, although a few years later in time. In 1904 the country had about 541,000 cotton looms. This increased to a peak of 715,000 in 1927, two years after spindles reached their peak. The number at present is probably about 450,000,[2] considerably below the 1904 figure. It is probable, however, that looms have been increased in size, speed, and general efficiency more than spindles. At any rate, annual cotton cloth production during World War II was the highest on record.

The shift of looms to the South has also followed the general pattern set by spindles. In 1904, the South had 180,000 looms, or 33.2 per cent of the national total. The proportion increased steadily until the region passed New England in 1927 with 342,000, or 47.8 per cent of the U. S. total. In 1931 the figures were 341,000 and 57.9 per cent. In 1942, the Bureau of the Census made a survey of cotton and rayon mill machinery combined. This gave the South 363,000 looms, or 69.6 per cent of the total, but there was no indication of the number being used for rayon.[3] A private trade manual lists 333,000 looms in the South as of July 1, 1947; this was 74.2 per cent of the total for the country.[4]

A very large proportion of all cotton cloth production is included in the Census subgroup "Cotton Broad Woven Fabrics." The South's share in this subgroup in 1947 is approximately indicated by the following figures for absolute amounts and percentages of the United States totals: production workers, 281,116 and 82.1; value added, $1,281 million and 82.0; expenditures for new plant and equipment, $68 million and 86.0.[5] These data would indicate that the South now

2 *Davison's Textile Blue Book*, 1947, p. 205.
3 Bureau of Census, *Cotton and Rayon Mill Machinery in the United States, 1942*, Washington, p. 25.
4 *Davison's Textile Blue Book*, 1947, p. 205.
5 These figures are for the "South and West" but they include only three establishments out of 409 which are not in the South as defined in this study, *Census of Manufactures, 1947*, "Cotton Manufactures: Rayon and Related Manufactures," (MC22A) p. 4.

has over 80 per cent of all cotton cloth production and that the proportion is increasing since the region is getting considerably more than 80 per cent of the expenditures for new plant and equipment.

The proportion of cloth produced in the South has consistently been higher than the proportion of looms in the region for the same reasons as given above for spindles; namely, longer hours of operation and heavier grades. Thus in 1927, when the South had 48 per cent of the looms, it produced 67.2 per cent of the cloth by area and 70.1 per cent by weight. In 1931, the figures were 74.8 per cent and 76.6 per cent. In 1933, the South was producing upwards of 90 per cent of all the coarser constructions such as drills, ducks, denims, osnaburgs, and print cloth, and over 80 per cent of the sheeting, shirting, and ginghams. The ascendancy of the South in this field continues at the present time.

Distribution by States. Six southern states have large interests in the cotton textile industry. On July 31, 1948, there were in the United States about 23.8 million spindles in the cotton textile system, of which 21.3 million, or 90 per cent, were active on cotton and 1.3 million, or 6 per cent, were active on other fibers. "North Carolina exceeds every other state in cotton-system spindles in place, having 5,927,000 or 25 per cent of the total for the United States in 1948; South Carolina is second with 5,642,000 or 24 per cent; and Georgia third with 3,217,000 or 13 per cent."[6]

As a major industry group (which includes synthetic and woolens as well as cotton), textiles ranked first, on the basis of production workers, in six southern states in 1947. Those states, together with the percentages which workers in textiles represented of all industrial workers, were: South Carolina, 67.8; North Carolina, 57.4; Georgia, 43.6; Alabama, 26.9; Tennessee, 17.5; and Virginia, 16.4. On the basis of value added, the textile group ranked first in the two Carolinas, Georgia, and Alabama, second in Virginia, and third in Tennessee.

Structural Changes. During the past ten years there have been several important changes in the structure and organization of the textile industry, most of them being some form of integration. Probably the most spectacular came as a result of price control by OPA. The war

6 Bureau of Census, *Cotton Production and Distribution, Season of 1947–48* (Bulletin 185), Washington, 1949, p. 44.

created an acute shortage of civilian textile goods and thus greatly reduced the marketing risks usually associated with such goods. When the OPA price schedules were set, they allowed generous, and probably even excessive, margins for the finishing, converting, and marketing processes. With most of the risks removed, manufacturers were reluctant to see those lucrative profits go to others and they began to take over those processes themselves. Finishers, converters, and sellers were then forced, in order to protect their sources of supply, to try to gain control of spinning and weaving capacity. This set off a fierce competitive struggle which drove up the prices of spindles and looms to fabulous levels in some cases. New producing capacity could not be built, so it was largely a process of buying and selling mills already in existence. Since most of the southern mills were small they could not for long hold out in this struggle nor resist the lure of the fantastically high prices, so many of them sold out. The net result of this movement was probably that a considerable amount of producing capacity passed from local control and became parts of large systems centered in New York or Philadelphia.

The same general conditions persisted for two or three years after the war, while the demand for cloth was being stimulated by a great export boom. Gradually it became possible to install new capacity, but, as we have seen, there has been no appreciable increase in the number of spindles and looms. There has been, however, a considerable increase in finishing capacity accompanied, in some cases, by the establishment of selling agencies by manufacturers to sell their own goods.

One part of this integration process—the absorption or consolidation of weaving capacity and the establishment of new finishing plants —is clearly revealed by census data. Between 1939 and 1947, the number of establishments producing cotton broad woven fabrics declined from 661 to 602; during the same time the number of establishments engaged in finishing textiles increased from 468 to 641.[7] The data do not show what part of these changes took place in the South, but in 1947 the region's share of the finishing business is indicated by the following data for amounts and percentages of United States totals: number of establishments, 68 and 10.6; number of production workers, 21,400 and 31.0; value added, $105.2 million

7 *Census of Manufactures, 1947,* "Cotton Manufactures: Rayon and Related Manufactures" (MC22A), p. 3.

and 29.3; expenditures for new plant and equipment, $11.3 million and 38.0.[8]

In some quarters there is concern that the process of integration and expansion may have gone too far. Some manufacturers have not only carried their integration through to the production of consumer goods, but have also set up retail and mail order stores.[9] While the risks in such integration are high, it is probably true that over the years the profits from finishing, converting, and selling are more dependable than the profits from spinning and weaving. By "integrating forward," southern textile producers are able to gain these profits and to reduce their dependence on converters and sellers in New York and Philadelphia. It is an example of the further processing of goods which is usually the more profitable and which the South needs.

Another type of integration, typified by the Burlington Mills, was going on before the war. It consists in assembling under one ownership a large number of mills producing diversified products, combined with "integration forward." In the case of the Burlington Mills, the products include both rayon and cotton goods. Considerable experimentation is under way in blending synthetic fibers with cotton and wool in various ways. The Burlington Mills have made an outstanding success, but whether it has been due to inherent principles of organization or to unusual managerial ability it is too early to say.

While there have been no significant increases in the number of spindles and looms, constant improvements are going on to increase their efficiency. Larger and faster machines and more automatic operations are being developed all the time. Recently one large North Carolina mill replaced 48,000 old spindles. In the space available they could put only 40,000 of the new, larger spindles, but from them they are getting about the same amount of yarn as from the old spindles. One recent study states that

Estimates of the present capacity of the cotton goods mills indicate that the maximum potential is about 30 per cent over the average pre-war output. New machinery and further improvement in techniques are expected to raise this potential considerably.[10]

Earnings and Profits. From 1921 through 1939, the cotton textile industry had, with the exception of two or three years, a very poor

[8] These figures include data for four plants out of the 68 which were not in the South. *Ibid,* p. 5.
[9] *Daily News Record,* Jan. 24, 1948, p. 6; Jan. 31, 1948, p. 7.
[10] *Ibid.,* Feb. 7, 1948, p. 5.

record of earnings. The experience for a large part of that period has been summarized as follows:

> Over the 14-year period, 1926–1939, during which the industry produced approximately $15 billion of cotton goods, the unbroken seepage of losses in prosperous and lean years alike reduced the net amount of income earned on this volume to approximately $10 million before federal income taxes. This was equivalent to one-fifteenth of a cent out of each dollar of sales. During these years the profitable companies paid $74 million in taxes—leaving the industry some $64 million in the red at its entrance into the war-stimulated decade of the Forties.[11]

From 1940 through 1948, however, and especially in the postwar years, the industry enjoyed handsome profits—probably the best in its history. During the war years, profits were restricted by two major factors—price control and taxes. The excess profits tax hit the industry especially hard because its earnings in the base period (1936–39) were low and because its invested capital is low in comparison with most manufacturing enterprises, partly because the turnover is comparatively high, especially in boom times. As a result, "including normal taxes, the industry paid out nearly 65% of its income to Federal tax collectors in 1942 and nearly 68% in 1943."[12]

During these years, one small sample of mills in the North showed an increase in net income from $0.6 million to $4.9 million; a similar sample in the South had an increase from $8.0 million to $13.8 million. As percentages of sales, the profits of the two groups were as follows:

	1939	1940	1941	1942	1943	1944
North	0.8	1.1	6.9	4.1	3.1	3.3[13]
South	4.7	6.1	5.8	3.6	3.3	3.4

These figures show that in the prewar, and supposedly more "normal," years the southern mills had a considerably larger margin of profits than the northern mills but that difference was quickly eliminated by a boom period, price control, and heavy taxes. If the data in these small samples for 1939 and 1940 are representative of the whole industry for normal years, they would indicate that the southern mills are considerably more profitable than the northern mills.

After the war, price controls were removed and the excess profits

11 Jules Bachman and M. R. Gainsbrugh, *Economics of the Cotton Textile Industry,* New York, National Industrial Conference Board, Inc., 1946, p. 142.
12 *Ibid.,* p. 151.   13 *Ibid.,* p. 215.

tax was repealed. Mill margins on cotton cloth almost trebled, rising from about 20 cents in 1945 to almost 60 cents in 1947. From 1939 to 1948, wholesale prices of cotton cloth trebled, a much greater increase than took place in the prices of other textile products (see Table *XLIX*). Although no satisfactory index of profits is available

TABLE *XLIX* WHOLESALE PRICE INDEXES FOR CERTAIN TEXTILE PRODUCTS 1939–1948

(1926 = 100)

YEAR	ALL WHOLESALE PRICES	ALL TEXTILE PRODUCTS	CLOTHING	COTTON GOODS	RAYON	WOOLEN AND WORSTED GOODS
1939	77.1	69.7	82.0	67.2	28.8	79.8
1940	78.6	73.8	85.2	71.4	29.5	46.8
1941	87.3	84.8	92.6	94.2	29.7	96.6
1942	98.8	96.9	106.9	112.4	30.3	110.4
1943	103.1	97.4	107.0	112.7	30.3	112.5
1944	104.1	98.4	107.1	115.7	30.2	112.7
1945	105.8	100.1	107.4	121.4	30.2	112.7
1946	121.1	116.3	119.3	150.5	30.7	115.7
1947	152.1	141.7	135.6	200.6	37.0	130.5
1948	165.0	148.6	147.5	207.1	41.2	147.7

SOURCE: Bureau of Labor Statistics, U. S. Department of Labor.

for this period, it is probable that, at least in the postwar years, the net earnings of cotton textile mills increased faster than margins or wholesale prices. The group of about 40 producers of cotton goods used by the National City Bank *Letter* showed a rate of earnings on net assets between 7 and 10 per cent from 1942 to 1945. In 1947 and 1948, that group topped the list of all industry groups in earnings with rates, respectively, of 34.8 and 31.5 per cent, compared with rates of 12.3 and 14.0 per cent for the whole sample of 3,262 corporations.[14]

Earnings were reduced sharply in the last few months of 1948 and the first half of 1949, but came back strong in the last half of 1949. One reason for the shortness of the "recession" period was that when demand weakened, production was cut back drastically and inventories were not allowed to accumulate. Consequently, it did not take long for supplies in the channels of distribution to become depleted and for demand to revive at the mill level. In former years it had been common practice to continue operations, perhaps at a reduced level,

[14] National City Bank of New York, *Monthly Letter on Economic Conditions, Government Finance, passim.*

and add the production to stock. The pressure of these enlarged inventories on the market then prevented any price recovery at the mill level for an indefinite period so long as operations continued. This was a situation typical of the industry between the two wars.

One factor responsible for the change of practice in 1948–49 was the relatively high level of wages in comparison with former years. This made it quite expensive to produce for stock and led most mills to curtail promptly when demand weakened. It was this fact that led one member of the industry to observe that high wages were proving to be the salvation of the industry because they helped to solve the perennial problem of surplus inventories. Perhaps the inflexibility of wages helped along the same line. In previous periods of slack demand, there were frequently wage reductions. These, coming in successive waves and alternating with price reductions on finished goods, made it difficult to determine when "bottom" had been reached. But in 1948–49, with only a very few minor exceptions, wages remained absolutely inflexible. Thus, when inventories had been reduced to normal by the sharp reductions in production, it was easy to see that a new bottom had been reached and the mills could start producing again without fear that some competitor might undercut them by reducing wages.[15]

Another factor which undoubtedly contributed to the quick recovery in 1949 was the reduction in the number of spindles. Following World War I there was a runaway expansion of the textile industry in the South. Excess capacity was created which, more than any other single factor, helped to cause chronic depression in the industry for more than 15 years. Leaders in the industry remember that episode and fear a repetition of it. In the Great Depression it was often stated that the industry had five million too many spindles, and there were proposals to seal off, destroy, or otherwise take them out of production.

Since that time, the industry has lost more than six million spindles

[15] Because of the organization of the textile industry, prices of finished goods declined considerably in most cases in 1948–49. In certain other industries where administered prices prevailed, these prices remained relatively unchanged in such a period. To an economist these considerations suggest an interesting thought: suppose that our economy generally develops into a situation in which prices and wages are as inflexible as the classical economists assumed production to be and in which production is as flexible as those same economists assumed prices and wages to be. That tendency can be observed in several fields, even (or especially) in agriculture when the government controls production. Under such conditions, how would our economic theory have to be recast?

while population has increased by more than 20 per cent and real income is much higher. True, the present spindles are larger and more efficient and more synthetics are being used. But many of the spindles can be used to spin synthetics and blends, and a considerable number are being so used. In fact, the spinning of blends of various kinds is one of the most significant developments now going on in the cotton textile business. Further, some of the spindles are even being used to spin wool in the "American System."[16] These factors, together with the rate of return realized on investment in the cotton textile industry in 1947 and 1948, would certainly indicate that the industry has worked off its excess capacity of spindles.

THE SYNTHETIC TEXTILES

The rapid increase in the use of rayon in recent years is too well known to be discussed here. From about 130 million pounds in 1927, consumption in the United States had risen to approximately 1,150 million pounds in 1948. Like the cotton textile industry, rayon is also predominantly a southern industry. As one writer expressed it, the South has achieved in rayon in 25 years what it took 100 years to achieve in cotton textiles—a substantial majority of the industry.[17]

Symbolic of the way in which modern industries are intertwined, the original process by which rayon is produced is a chemical process. Logically, therefore, it belongs with the chemical industries, but it will be discussed here for convenience. It is only when the staple fiber is spun or the yarn is woven that rayon enters the textile field proper.

Almost from the beginning, Tennessee and Virginia have been important centers of the rayon industry. In 1931, they had 45 per cent of the wage earners and turned out over 40 per cent of product by value. In 1947, the South had about 60 per cent of the capacity of the industry (about 75 per cent if West Virginia is included) and the proportion is likely to increase in the future since most of the large plants built after the war are located in the South. Virginia, with six large plants, is the leading state of the Union and in 1947 produced about a third of the nation's total. Tennessee is second in the country with four plants and Georgia, North Carolina and South Carolina have one or more plants each.

16 See below, p. 154 for an explanation of this system.
17 *Daily News Record*, Jan. 24, 1948, p. 4.

The initial phase of rayon production does not require a large number of workers. It was estimated that the total number employed in the South in 1947 was about 44,000; this was only about three or four times the number of employees 20 years earlier when production was only one-tenth as much. The investment required per worker was estimated at $10,000–$12,000, or more than twice the similar investment in cotton textiles.[18] Prevailing wages in the industry are high and there is practically no North/South differential.

Prices of cotton and rayon have behaved in strikingly different ways. From 1926 to 1939, prices of cotton goods declined by about a third while rayon prices declined by more than 70 per cent (see Table *XLIX*). The decline in rayon was due largely to the great technological advances made during the early stages of the development of the industry. From 1939 to 1948, cotton prices trebled while rayon prices rose by only a little more than 40 per cent. During the "recession" of 1948–49, cotton prices fell by 24 per cent while rayon prices fluctuated only about 4 or 5 per cent—first up and then down. This remarkable example illustrates both the difference between administered and competitive prices and the effects of great technological improvements in one field.

The requirements of the rayon industry made the South an almost inevitable choice for its location; there is probably no other industry which could find so many advantages in the South. One of the principal requirements is a large amount of pure water; it takes from 200 to 1,000 gallons of water to produce a pound of rayon, depending on the process. Other important requirements are proximity to acids, caustics, and other chemicals, and to coal fields (coal is used as a source of power and of steam for processing). Finally, large plant sites at some distances from heavily populated areas, a good labor supply and adequate transportation facilities are important. The southern Piedmont offered a better combination of these facilities than almost any other area.

Few data are available on the spinning and weaving capacity used to produce rayon. Cotton machinery can be used for these processes with only minor adjustments and in some cases the equipment is switched back and forth from one fiber to the other. When the Bureau of the Census made its survey of cotton and rayon mill machinery in February, 1942, it found a total of 27.6 million spindles

18 *Ibid*, Feb. 28, 1948, p. 7.

in place. At the same time about 24.1 million spindles were being used exclusively on cotton; that left 3.5 million spindles which were either idle, being used on rayon, on rayon and cotton jointly, or on blends. Since this was near the peak of the war boom for textiles, it is not likely that many were idle. Of the 3.5 million spindles, 2.9 million, or 82 per cent, were in the South. The data for the cotton system show that on July 31, 1948, 1,347,000 spindles in that system were active on synthetic fibres or blends. Of that number, 975,000, or 72.4 per cent were in the South. No data are available on the number of rayon spindles outside the cotton system.

While no data are available on the number of looms used for rayon, Census data provide some information of the characteristics and location of the rayon weaving industry. In 1947, the South had only 18 per cent of the plants producing rayon broad woven fabrics but the region had 44,230, or 48.5 per cent, of the production workers. This would indicate that the southern plants are much larger than those outside the South. The region produced $247.4 million, or 50.7 per cent, of the value added in the whole industry. This is one of the relatively few instances in which the South had a larger proportion of the value added than of production workers. In 1947, expenditures for new plant and equipment in the South amounted to $25.1 million, or 58.5 per cent of the total for the country. From this it would seem that expansion in 1947 was going ahead somewhat more rapidly in the South than elsewhere.

Very little information is available about the production of nylon. In 1947, about half of the country's production was in the South and the proportion was expected to increase. Since a great majority of the production was in the form of filament yarn and was used for hosiery, very few spindles or looms were involved in its processing.

THE WOOLEN AND WORSTED INDUSTRIES

The manufacture of woolen and worsted goods is of distinctly minor importance in the South at present, but there are indications that it may increase substantially. The value of southern production in 1929 was only 1.1 per cent of the national total, but in 1939 it was up to 5 per cent and in 1947 it was approximately 9 per cent. According to a private trade manual, the number of woolen and worsted spindles in the South and their proportion of national totals in recent years

were as follows: 1944, 159,000 and 4.1 per cent; 1946, 180,000 and
4.5 per cent; 1947, 234,000 and 5.8 per cent.[19] According to these
figures, the South in these years had an increase of 47.2 per cent,
while New England spindles increased by only 4.6 per cent and those
in other states declined by 6.1 per cent. This tendency is confirmed
by Census data. In 1947, the South had 12,712 production workers
in plants producing woolen and worsted fabrics or 10.4 per cent of
the national total, and produced 9.1 per cent of total value added,
but the region had 18.0 per cent of the expenditures for new plant
and equipment.[20] Those expenditures amounted to $301 per produc-
tion worker in New England and $557 in the South. These data leave
little doubt that a relative expansion is going on in the southern segment of the industry.

Some observers think that it is almost certain that a considerable
part of the woolen industry will shift to the South as did the cotton
industry. They cite the "deadly parallel" between the woolen industry
now and the cotton industry 40 or 50 years ago: several old and
indigenous firms in the South to provide a nucleus, an adequate supply
of labor in the South, and a New England industry with equipment
which is obsolete and badly worn after two decades of depression
and war.[21] In some cases even the old buildings are not suitable for
the new and modern machinery.

A special factor, the potentialities of which have not yet been fully
demonstrated, is the "American System" of spinning worsteds which
has been developed to a great extent in the South. It is a system in
which cotton-type spindles are substituted for the conventional equipment in spinning worsteds. Some mills are using it and its proponents
claim that it will produce better worsteds more cheaply than the older
conventional method.[22]

Since the war, at least seven woolen mills of considerable size have
been located in the South; three in South Carolina, two in Georgia,
and one each in North Carolina and Virginia. New England is aware
of this danger to one of its major industries and is fighting back, but
it would seem that there is a good chance for the South to make
considerable gains in this industry in the years ahead.

[19] *Davison's Textile Blue Book*, passim.
[20] Three of the 43 plants in the South by Census definition were not in the South
as here defined. *Census of Manufactures, 1947*, "Woolen and Worsted Manufactures," (MC22B), p. 3.
[21] *Daily News Record*, Jan. 24, 1948, p. 5.　　　[22] *Ibid*, Feb. 21, 1948, p. 7.

THE KNIT GOODS INDUSTRIES

The knit goods industries make up the last major segment of the textile group. Some of the knit goods industries, such as underwear and seamless hosiery, have been represented in the South for 40 years or more. In the past two decades those have expanded and there has also been a rapid growth of the full fashioned hosiery industry. In 1929, the South had about one fourth of the workers engaged in these three lines in the United States; in 1947, the region had more than half. The region has now about 80 per cent of the seamless hosiery, about 43 per cent of the full fashioned, and about a third of the knit underwear.

As a group, the knit goods industries employ about 94 thousand production workers in the South, a little less than a third of the national total. About half of the southern workers are in North Carolina. Tennessee, Georgia, and Virginia have most of the remainder. While the South had less than a third of the workers in these industries in 1947, approximately half of all expenditures for new plant and equipment were made within the region in that year.

THE APPAREL INDUSTRY GROUP

Closely associated with the textile group and a logical development from it is the apparel group of industries. This group has had a considerable expansion in the South in recent years and now ranks fourth among the major industry groups in number of production workers employed, with more than 130,000. It is, however, a low-wage industry which produces a low value of product per worker. In 1947, it ranked eighth in total value added and was the lowest of all the major groups in average annual wage per worker with $1,385. Production is fairly widely distributed in the South, the principal states, in the order of their importance being Georgia, Texas, Tennessee, North Carolina, and Virginia. North Carolina, with 140 per cent, had the greatest proportionate increase in workers between 1939 and 1947.

The South's production is concentrated principally in the field of men's cotton clothing, such as dress shirts, pajamas, work shirts and pants, overalls, wash suits, industrial garments, etc. In general these are the cheapest and simplest garments to manufacture. In the products named above, as a whole, the South has approximately a third of the nation's production. The region has very little production in the fields of women's apparel or men's woolen clothing.

FOOD AND RELATED PRODUCTS

The production of food and related products makes up the third largest industry group in the South, following textiles and lumber; in 1947 the group provided employment for 202,000 production workers. Since 1929 this group has had a fairly steady growth, both in absolute size and in relation to national totals. In 1929, the group had 105,000 workers, or 14 per cent of the national total, and produced goods worth about $1¼ billion, or 10 per cent of the total for the country. By 1939, the number of workers had increased by 20 per cent and value of products was up by 15 per cent, while outside the South workers were up by 8 per cent and value of product was lower by 15 per cent. From 1939 to 1947, workers in the group in the South increased by 60 per cent, giving the region 18.4 per cent of the national employment, while in the Non-South there was an increase of 32.5 per cent. The increase in value added in the South was 216 per cent compared with 150 per cent elsewhere. The South's proportion of total value added was 16.8 per cent. Kentucky was the only state which had an exceptionally large increase during the war years. In that state, workers increased by 107 per cent and value added by 555 per cent, reflecting large increases in both the prices and volume of whiskey produced.

Aside from the production of bakery products, ice, ice cream, and dairy products, which are fairly well distributed over the whole region, some of the more important forms of production are the processing and canning of citrus fruit products in Florida, the refining of cane sugar in Louisiana, and the making of whiskey in Kentucky. The processing and canning of fish and sea foods are important in Virginia, Florida, and Louisiana, while the canning of vegetables is significant in Virginia and several other states.

The production of oleomargarine is a growing southern business which is significant to both industry and agriculture. In 1932, approximately 215 million pounds of oleomargarine were produced in this country, of which three million pounds, or 1.4 per cent, were produced in the South. Coconut oil, at 128 million pounds, was the principal ingredient; 14 million pounds of cottonseed oil and four million pounds of peanut oil together made up 7.5 per cent of all ingredients. By 1939, national production was up to 333 million pounds, of which the South supplied 10 million, or 2.8 per cent.

The shortage of butter during the war gave a great impetus to oleomargarine production. Southern producers took advantage of that increase in demand, as well as sharp increases in 1947 and 1948. In 1948, total production was 890 million pounds, of which 121 million pounds, or 13.6 per cent, came from the South. The composition of the ingredients has changed drastically; in 1948 the use of coconut oil was down to 13 million pounds, while cottonseed oil, with 433 million pounds, and peanut oil with 15 million pounds, together made up 50 per cent of all ingredients.[23] Texas and Georgia are the leading producing states in the South. Production should be stimulated by the recent action of the Federal Government in repealing discriminatory taxes on the production and sale of oleomargarine.

TOBACCO MANUFACTURING

The manufacturing of tobacco is an old and well-established industry in the South. It is the one major industry group (as contrasted with subgroups or individual industries) in which the region has an absolute majority of the nation's employment and production. In 1947, the South had 60 per cent of the country's production workers in the group and 70 per cent of its value added. The group ranks low in employment afforded but fairly high in value of product and in value added, principally because of the high degree of mechanization of the principal field—the manufacture of cigarettes.[24]

The data for the group show an increase in workers of 51 per cent between 1939 and 1947, but this was due to a change in the coverage. In 1947, for the first time, the *Census of Manufactures* included data for tobacco stemming and redrying. Practically all of that activity is in the South, and the inclusion of that data accounted for all—and

23 *Annual Reports of the Commissioner of Internal Revenue, passim.*
24 In productivity, there is a very great difference between the production of cigarettes and the production of cigars. In 1947, the cigarette branch of the industry used 49.2 million man-hours of work in producing $368.4 million of value added—an average of $7.49 per man-hour. In the cigar branch, 84.0 million man-hours were used in producing $143.1 million of value added—an average of $1.70 per man-hour. Average wages for production workers did not differ nearly so much; they were $1.12 in cigarettes and $0.81 in cigars. *Census of Manufactures, 1947,* "Tobacco Manufactures" (MC21), p. 2.

more—of the increase in production workers for the group. In cigarettes, for example, the number of workers declined although the production of cigarettes more than doubled between 1939 and 1947.[25]

In value added, the group had an increase between 1939 and 1947 of only 89 per cent in the South—the smallest increase by far of any major group. As was noted in the previous chapter, the reason for this was the great increase in the price of leaf tobacco and in operating costs, while cigarette prices were held down first by price control and later by the situation within the industry.

TABLE L   TOBACCO MANUFACTURES IN THE SOUTH FOR SELECTED YEARS, 1929–1947

YEAR	MANUFACTURED TOBACCO*		CIGARS		CIGARETTES	
	MILLION POUNDS	% OF U. S.	MILLIONS	% OF U. S.	BILLIONS	% OF U. S.
1929	185	48.6	1,293	19.8	103	84.4
1931	199	53.6	1,094	20.5	107	91.5
1932	190	54.5	1,014	23.1	97	90.7
1933	194	56.7	1,135	26.4	106	92.2
1935	198	57.7	1,153	24.6	129	92.1
1937	197	57.8	1,554	29.3	154	90.6
1939	216	63.0	1,559	30.0	160	88.4
1941	225	65.8	1,687	30.1	196	89.9
1943	204	62.4	1,513	28.2	268	90.5
1945	205	62.0	1,482	28.1	302	91.0
1947	146	60.3	1,768	32.2	351	95.0

* Includes smoking and chewing tobacco and snuff.
SOURCE: Computed from Annual Reports of the Commissioner of Internal Revenue.

This group of industries is about as near depression-proof as any group in the American economy. While there was a noticeable drop in production in the single year 1932, it was quickly regained. With that one exception, cigarette production maintained a steady and rapid growth from 103 billion cigarettes in 1929 to 388 billion in 1948. Both manufactured tobacco and cigars reached a peak in 1941 and then declined during the war years. After the war, cigars rose again but the production of manufactured tobacco dropped sharply in both 1946 and 1947.

Table L shows production in the South for certain years since 1929 and the percentage of total national production in the region. The

25 It is not possible to give exact figures because in some instances the workers were not shown separately for cigarettes and manufactured tobacco in 1939.

South has increased its proportion in all three fields; in cigars, from about 20 per cent to over 30; in manufactured tobacco, from less than 50 per cent to over 60; and in cigarettes, from 84 per cent to 95. The concentration would seem to be increasing; in 1947, about 97 per cent of all expenditures for new plant and equipment in the cigarette branch were in the South, while for the group as a whole the proportion was over 80 per cent. On the average, the southern plants are considerably larger than plants outside the region. With about 10 per cent of the plants in the field, the South produces about 60 per cent of the manufactured tobacco; with 8 per cent of the cigar factories, it produces over 30 per cent of the cigars; and with about a third of the cigarette plants, it produces over 90 per cent of the cigarettes.

THE FURNITURE AND FIXTURES INDUSTRIES

The furniture group of industries showed a substantial growth in the South between 1929 and 1937;[26] the number of workers it employed rose from 35,000 to 40,000, representing an increase from 18.1 to 23.5 per cent of national totals. There was a corresponding relative gain in value of product, although the absolute figure was slightly below the 1929 figure. The larger group classification of "Furniture and Fixtures" employed 49,000 workers in the South in 1939.

Since this was one of the less essential industry groups during the war, its expansion was limited by shortages of manpower and materials. But by 1947 it had 75,000 workers in the South, which placed it sixth among southern industry groups. The rate of increase was 53 per cent—slightly more than the regional average. In relation to the whole country, the South now has about 26 per cent of the workers and produces about 21 per cent of the value added. In 1947, the region received 30 per cent of all expenditures for new plant and equipment. The industries in this group are heavily concentrated in North Carolina, which has about one third of the totals for the South. Virginia and Tennessee also have sizable shares of the totals.

THE CHEMICAL INDUSTRIES GROUP

The industries making up the chemical group have had a steady and substantial growth in the South in the past 20 years. They are basic

26 It is not possible to get comparable figures for 1939 because of a change of classification.

to most of the southern industries, especially the newer ones which have been growing rapidly. This group includes fissionable materials, explosives, industrial chemicals, synthetic rubber, rayon and nylon fibers, animal and vegetable oils, fertilizers, and other items. The great Oak Ridge Project in Tennessee represents the first category. In the field of industrial chemicals, the South has the large phosphate deposits of Florida and Tennessee and the sulfur deposits of Louisiana and Texas. The latter two states have practically all the reserves and production of sulfur in the nation. In certain other particular industries, such as cottonseed oil, gum and naval stores, and softwood distillation, the South also supplies nearly all of the national production. A large part of the synthetic rubber industry built up during the war is located in Kentucky, Louisiana, and Texas. As already mentioned, the production of rayon and nylon is of great and growing importance. Tennessee and Virginia have large segments of these industries, which were largely responsible for giving the chemical group second place in employment in each of those states. The fertilizer industry is one of long standing in the southern states and is of vital importance to southern agriculture because of the nature of the soils and of the crops raised. About 60 per cent of this industry is located in the South.

The various and diverse industries making up the chemical group are spread widely over the South. Three states, however, account for well over half of the total; they are Virginia, Tennessee, and Texas which together have about 56 per cent of the production workers in the region.

The number of production workers in the chemical group increased from 72,000 in 1939 to 120,000 in 1947—an increase of 67 per cent. In 1947, the group ranked fifth in the South in production workers and third in value added; in expenditures for new plant and equipment it ranked first, with over 22 per cent of the total for the region. Expenditures for plant and equipment per worker *for the one year* were $2,158—the largest for any group in the region and nearly four times the regional average. These would seem to indicate a considerable expansion under way.

In production workers, the South had approximately 26 per cent of the national total in the chemical group in 1947. On this point the region made no relative gain between 1939 and 1947—in fact, it lost ground slightly. But in value added it increased its share from 16.6 per cent to 20.2 per cent, indicating a considerable increase in productivity per worker. The region got 32 per cent of the expenditures for new plant and equipment made by the group in the nation. It is evident that the industry is preparing for a considerable expansion of its production and as increased emphasis is given to synthetics, plastics, and atomic energy, those preparations would seem to be justified. The South is in a good position to benefit from the expected growth of this industry group.

PETROLEUM REFINING

Petroleum refining is another industry which employs comparatively few people but produces large value added and turns out a large value of product. This is due, of course, to the fact that it requires large amounts of expensive equipment which are largely automatic in their operation. In 1929, the southern segment of this industry employed 33,000 workers, or 41 per cent of the U. S. total. During the next decade this number declined, although the volume of production increased. By 1947, the number of workers was up to 45,000 or about 40 per cent of the national total. In value added, the South also has about 40 per cent of the total. Since the region produces about 60 per cent of the country's crude oil, these figures would indicate that about a third of the crude is taken out for refining.

Over the past two decades, the South's share in this industry has not changed appreciably, although it has had a large absolute growth. In contrast with the conditions prevailing in most other industries, there were indications that in the postwar years the South was losing ground. The region received only about 26 per cent of the expenditures for new plant and equipment made in the industry in 1947. The amount per production worker was quite large at $2,039, but the amount outside the South was even larger at $2,487.

THE METALS, MACHINERY, AND EQUIPMENT GROUPS

Noticeably absent from the list of industries discussed above are the great metal-working industries. They are not at present important factors in the southern economy, although some of them did experience a considerable growth over the war period. At present they probably account, altogether, for less than 15 per cent of total industrial employment in the South.

During the war, employment in the southern iron and steel industries more than doubled but after the war it was cut back by about 50 per cent so that it was, relatively, less important than before the war. There is room for debate as to whether this was due to the reluctance of the big steel companies to expand capacity and shift production southward, to a lack of high-quality southern resources, or to other factors. In any event, there are no indications that the iron and steel industries in the South are increasing in relation either to total southern industry or to their own industries in the nation. Rather, there are some indications that they are not quite holding their own in these respects.

In machinery, the South is making progress both absolutely and relatively. Several textile equipment companies are now producing in the South and at least three of the agricultural machinery companies have located large plants in the region. Between 1939 and 1947, southern employment in the machinery industries increased from 21,000 to about 56,000, thus increasing the relative importance of these industries both in the southern economy and in the industries nationally. As the new, postwar plants came into operation, employment in the machinery industries was probably raised above the 2.8 per cent at which it stood in 1947.

The presence of bauxite in Arkansas, the port of Mobile, and cheap, abundant electricity provided by the TVA have given a big boost to the production of aluminum in the South. This, together with the location of a plant on the Gulf coast of Texas to recover magnesium from sea water, almost doubled the relative importance of employment in the nonferrous metal industries in the South between 1939 and 1946. In the latter year, that employment was 1.8 per cent of total southern employment and almost 10 per cent of national employment in the industry group. With the use of the "light metals" on the increase, these industries should be able to maintain their positions.

SECONDARY AND TERTIARY "INDUSTRIES"

The term "industry" as so far used in this and in the preceding chapter has really meant manufacturing. In a very real sense manufacturing, like agriculture, is generally the necessary and primal base upon which incomes earned in the supplementary "industries" such as trade and services, government, education, and the like are largely dependent. How much a given region can afford to spend upon services, government, education, and entertainment will, at least in part, depend upon how much the region can produce in agriculture and in manufacturing. Indeed, income attributed to trade and services may sometimes reflect, in part, inability of persons employed in this category to find more productive employment.

This is not true, of course, in the most rigid and limited sense. Expenditures on education, for example, will substantially affect productivity in agriculture and in manufacturing. Furthermore, services which one region furnishes to another operate to increase the income of the "exporting" region in much the same way in which goods produced by the region in agriculture or in manufacturing for export increases income. Income produced by "tourism" in Florida, for example, is just as useful to the state as income produced in orange groves and cigar factories.

A region must, however, either produce all the goods and services which it consumes or it must export enough to pay for those which it wishes to import. This is just like the members of a family which may do each others washing but must also do washing for others if the family must also buy groceries and pay rent. In just this way, the South largely depends upon the expansion of the productivity of its industry and agriculture and on its services sold to other regions to increase its expenditures and its income in the secondary and tertiary "industries."

One good illustration of this somewhat complex matter is afforded by income and expenditures in the field of education. Although suitable statistics are not available, it appears that the South was for years a net "importer" of educational services. That is, thousands of southern students went to northern colleges and universities and paid for these educational services out of income earned in the South. At the present time, thousands of northern students come South and purchase educational services from southern colleges and universities. No one can say with certainty on which side the balance now is, but there is certainly a greater degree of "offsetting" of income and expenditures in the educational field between regions than was formerly true.[27]

27 We are informed by President Van Leer, that approximately one half or about twenty-five hundred of the students of Georgia Institute of Technology are out-of-state students. He estimates an expenditure by these students of at least $1,500,000 per year for tuition, food, clothing, shelter, amusement, etc. So far as the state in which the Institute is located is concerned, this is roughly the equivalent of an

The opportunities for developing income sources other than in agriculture and in manufacturing in the South are very substantial and will become greater as productivity in agriculture and in manufacturing increase.[28] This can be seen the more plainly when it is realized that in 1948 agriculture and manufacturing together accounted for 31.6 per cent of income payments in the South, while government accounted for 16.5 per cent, trade and services for 26.1 per cent and "other" for 25.7 per cent.[29] Over the two decades from 1929 to 1948, the proportion of income derived from agriculture shrunk while the proportion derived from manufacturing increased by a roughly offsetting amount. The total proportion of income derived from all three other categories combined changed little during these same two decades, remaining not far from 68 per cent of all income.

One must conclude that while the economy of the South must always be firmly based upon agriculture and manufacture, the potentialities of other sources of income which account for twice the amount of income of both agriculture and manufacture taken together, are extremely important. With the substantial basis in agriculture and manufacture which already exists, trade and services, education, and other supplementary sources of income could and should be developed much beyond their present level. The opportunities which exist in this field have often been overlooked and inadequately exploited. As labor is released from agriculture through further mechanization we can expect almost two thirds of it to find employment in these categories. The opportunities for small enterprisers in this field during the coming years in the South are wide indeed.

---

export of commodities of like amount. Assuming the possibility of otherwise unemployed resources one might even apply a "multiplier" to this amount so that the effect upon the demand for the resources of the state might under some circumstances be double or even triple this amount.

28 Indeed, in some fields, as in the case of "tourism" increased potentialities depend even more upon national income than upon income in the South itself.

29 See Table *XXVII*, Chapter III.

VIII FINANCIAL RESOURCES

Previous chapters have shown that the South does not have a proportionate share of the nation's industry, that its farms are deficient in machinery and equipment, and that it has the lowest per capita income of any major region in the nation. If southern income is to be raised by developing the natural resources of the region, expanding industry, and increasing the efficiency of agriculture, large amounts of capital equipment will be required.[1] Thus we come, inevitably, to the crucial question which always arises in a discussion of the southern economy: how are investment funds to be provided to meet these requirements?

In so far as it must depend upon its own financial resources, the South faces the same problem faced by every low-income region: low income makes it difficult to accumulate investment funds, but such funds are necessary in order to raise income. The South suffers also from another handicap of low-income regions—poorly developed financial institutions for assembling and administering such savings as may be available. These handicaps are slowly being reduced but it will be many years before they are substantially overcome.

In respect to outside funds, the South has a pronounced advantage over most other low-income regions of the world. Within the same nation and with relatively few barriers intervening, there is the greatest capital funds market in the world. Also, the large industrial organizations of the North and Middle West can build new plants or relocate old ones in the South with no problems of tariffs, foreign exchange, blocked funds, quotas, or language.

[1] One group has estimated that from 1946 to 1965, cumulative investment requirements in the South for manufacturing and urban housing alone will be over $18 billion, or nearly a billion dollars per year. That estimate was on the basis of a price level much lower than now prevails and it did not contain any allowance for the service trades, roads, schools and other public buildings, agriculture, public utilities, and other important sources of demand for capital funds. *Economic Problems of the Cotton Belt*, pp. 622–23.

The purpose of this chapter is to make a rough survey of the financial resources available for the development of the South. For the most part, the data for such a survey are fragmentary and inadequate. Except for information on commercial banks, very few financial data are available on a state or regional basis.[2] In most cases, therefore, the approach will have to be indirect and the findings will be general and indicative rather than precise and demonstrable.

Just here it might be well to clarify our position on a few points respecting financial policies. We do not advocate subsidies to investment in the South in the form of artificially low interest rates or other specially favorable terms. Investments should be made in the South only if they are justified by sound economic considerations. Second, we do not believe that economic and financial policies should be designed, at all cost, to bring about an exact equality between income in the South and income in the remainder of the country. We are not advocating any "redistribution of the wealth" or "equalization of incomes." Rather, we feel that the region has great possibilities for economic development, to the benefit of both the South and the nation as a whole. If there are financial barriers or handicaps to that development, whether by southerners or outsiders, all reasonable efforts should be made to remove them.

COMMERCIAL BANKS

The commercial banking system is the nerve center of a modern economy and the chief source of short-term, working-capital funds. In the United States, however, commercial banks, especially in rural areas, frequently do a general banking business, including the making of long-term loans on real estate mortgages. In recent years there has been a significant growth of medium-term lending by commercial banks in the form of term loans to business units. Also, in the past 20 years commercial banks have greatly increased their loans to individuals and organizations to finance the purchase of consumer goods.

Short-term funds are usually scarce in a region undergoing industrialization. The South is no exception. Low incomes, with a consequent small volume of savings, is one reason. Another reason is the predominantly agricultural nature of the region, since ordinarily farm-

[2] In this connection see John B. McFerrin, "Resources for Financing Industry in the South," *The Southern Economic Journal,* July 1947, (Vol. XIV, No. 1). We have derived much help from this excellent pioneer study.

ers do not use commercial banks extensively. Finally, commercial banking tends especially to concentrate in large cities, of which there are relatively few in the South.

Banking Structure. Several characteristics distinguish the southern banking system. First, there are practically no savings banks in the region; the functions of such banks, to the extent that they are afforded at all, are performed by commercial banks, the postal savings system, and building and loan associations. Second, commercial banks in the South are typically smaller than those in the rest of the country. Table *LII* shows that in 1949 the South had approximately 29 per cent of the banks of the nation but only 16 per cent of total banking resources. The average southern bank had total resources of $6,087,-500 compared with $12,930,700 for the average non-southern bank.[3] Third, the South has a larger proportion of state banks, and especially of state banks which are not members of the Federal Reserve System, than does the remainder of the country. Approximately 60 per cent of southern banks are nonmembers compared with about 48 per cent in the Non-South. Fourth, the South has a large proportion of banks which do not clear their checks at par. About 47 per cent of all non-par banks in the country are located in the three southern Federal Reserve districts. Finally, branch banking is less developed in the South than elsewhere, although in three states—North Carolina, Tennessee, and Virginia—it is fairly well developed and in certain other areas there has been a growth of "chain" banking or other forms of interlocking ownership.[4] In brief, southern banks are characteristically small, independent unit banks, a majority of which are not affiliated with the Federal Reserve System.

Trends in Southern Banking. Banking in the South, as in the nation as a whole, has experienced momentous developments in the past 20

---

[3] Federal Deposit Insurance Corporation, *Assets and Liabilities, June 30, 1949, Operating Insured Commercial and Mutual Savings Banks.* One reason for the large difference is the existence of a few very large banks in New York and Chicago. Thus, if the states of New York and Illinois are left out, the non-southern average is reduced to $9,525,000. For cities and towns of the same size, the difference in size between southern and non-southern banks probably is not very great.

[4] In 1948, the South had about 29 per cent of all banks but only 22 per cent of the banks which operated branches and those banks had only 14 per cent of all branches in the country. Federal Deposit Insurance Corporation, *Annual Report for the Year Ended December 31, 1948,* pp. 74–81. The smaller number of branches is another reason for the smaller size of southern banks. In absence of branch banking, small communities must have their own independent unit bank if they are to have any banking facilities.

TABLE LI   BASIC DATA ON BANKING IN THE SOUTH FOR SELECTED YEARS, 1929–1949

(In Millions of Dollars)

	1929	1932	1934	1939	1944	1949
NUMBER OF BANKS	6210	4626	4100	3650	3661	3849
Assets:						
Due from F. R. Banks	325	209	414	607	1666	2438
Due from Other Banks	607	455	784	1502	2757	2517
U. S. Gov't Obligations	525	484	858	1071	7843	8848
Total Securities	1229	1162	1529	1767	8686	10355
Comm. and Ind. Loans	—	—	—	748	907	2502
Agricultural Loans	—	—	—	392	574	838
Real Estate Loans	230	273	342	409	441	1381
Total Loans and Discounts	4208	2399	1703	2810	3014	6628
Liabilities:						
Demand Deposits of						
Individuals, Etc.	2483	1455	1616	2820	8749	13541
U. S. Gov't Deposits	49	70	182	120	2227	248
Deposits of U. S. Banks	384	281	448	903	1940	1851
Total Demand Deposits	2892	1731	1946	4449	13910	17818
Total Time Deposits	1992	1383	1270	1587	2174	3965
Total Deposits	4994	3220	3883	6035	16090	21783
Capital Accounts	991	774	703	776	977	1528
Total Assets or Liabilities	6995	4692	4844	6843	17109	23431

Data are for June 30 of each year. For 1929, 1932, and 1934, the data cover all banks; for other years, they cover insured banks only.

SOURCES: Compiled from reports of: 1929–1934, Comptroller of the Currency; 1939–1949, Federal Deposit Insurance Corporation.

years. Table *LI* gives basic data on the assets and liabilities of southern banks for selected years since 1929 while Table *LII* expresses those data as percentages of U. S. totals. Table *LIII* shows the distribution of banking resources, the decline in resources from 1929 to 1934 by states and for the South as a whole, and the increase in resources from 1939 to 1949.[5]

Just before the stock market panic of 1929, the 13 southern states had seven billion dollars of banking resources, or about 10 per cent of the national total. During the next four or five years the deflation of banking assets in the South was somewhat more drastic than elsewhere, and as a result the South's proportion of the nation's banking resources declined. From 1929 to 1934, the decline in the South

[5] For 1929, 1932, and 1934, the data cover all banks; outside the South they include a number of savings banks. For 1939, 1944, and 1949, the data covers only insured banks, but those include over 92 per cent of all commercial banks by number and about 98 per cent by volume of resources. The data are for June 30 of each year.

June 30, 1934 was not the low point in banking resources; June 30, 1933 would have been preferable in many respects but on that date many banks had not reopened after the Banking Holiday and for that reason the data are not complete.

TABLE *LII* BASIC DATA ON BANKING IN THE SOUTH FOR SELECTED YEARS, 1929–1949; SOUTHERN TOTALS AS PERCENTAGES OF U. S. TOTALS

	1929	1932	1934	1939	1944	1949
NUMBER OF BANKS	24.6	24.2	25.9	26.9	27.6	28.7
Assets:						
Due from F. R. Banks	10.2	7.8	9.2	6.1	13.0	13.7
Due from Other Banks	17.2	15.7	18.1	24.5	31.4	32.2
U. S. Gov't Obligations	13.1	7.5	7.8	7.1	11.7	14.3
Total Securities	7.1	6.4	7.2	8.0	11.9	14.5
Comm. and Ind. Loans	N.A	N.A	N.A	14.3	12.2	15.4
Agricultural Loans	N.A	N.A	N.A	32.9	38.9	30.7
Real Estate Loans	2.2	2.8	3.7	10.3	10.1	12.7
Total Loans and Discounts	10.2	8.6	8.0	10.3	14.5	16.4
Liabilities:						
Demand Deposits of Individuals, Etc.	11.6	10.2	10.9	11.4	15.3	17.6
U. S. Gov't Deposits	17.3	16.5	10.5	16.2	11.8	10.8
Deposits of U. S. Banks	10.6	8.8	10.3	12.3	19.3	20.4
Total Demand Deposits	11.9	10.6	11.1	11.9	14.9	17.9
Total Time Deposits	6.9	5.6	5.7	10.5	10.3	11.0
Total Deposits	9.2	7.7	8.4	11.5	14.1	16.1
Capital Accounts	10.3	9.1	9.0	11.9	12.7	14.6
Total Assets or Liabilities	9.7	8.2	8.7	11.5	13.9	15.9

For notes and sources, see Table *LI*.

was nearly 31 per cent compared with 21 per cent in the Non-South (see Table *LIII*). The difference at the low point was probably somewhat greater than this, since by 1934 the South had made some relative recovery. Since the behavior of the banking system is a matter

TABLE *LIII* GROWTH AND DISTRIBUTION BY STATES OF TOTAL SOUTHERN BANKING RESOURCES, 1929–1949

STATE	PER CENT OF TOTALS			PER CENT DECLINE,	PER CENT OF TOTALS			PER CENT INCREASE,
	1929	1932	1934	1929–34	1939	1944	1949	1939–49
Alabama	5.4	5.1	5.1	35.0	5.1	5.5	5.3	257
Arkansas	3.9	3.1	2.8	49.4	2.9	3.1	3.3	288
Florida	6.0	5.1	5.2	39.5	6.3	8.2	7.7	317
Georgia	6.5	7.2	7.7	17.4	7.5	8.1	7.0	217
Kentucky	9.8	9.3	9.0	36.1	7.7	6.9	6.4	189
Louisiana	8.0	9.3	6.8	41.0	8.2	7.1	7.4	211
Mississippi	4.0	3.4	3.2	43.7	3.1	3.2	3.3	260
North Carolina	7.1	5.7	5.9	42.5	7.0	7.3	7.2	251
Oklahoma	7.8	7.6	8.6	23.4	7.5	6.6	7.0	219
South Carolina	3.2	2.5	2.2	52.4	2.2	2.4	2.8	338
Tennessee	8.3	8.5	7.6	36.1	8.6	8.5	8.3	231
Texas	20.7	21.7	24.9	16.5	23.9	24.3	26.2	276
Virginia	9.5	11.5	10.9	21.2	10.0	8.7	8.1	176
Total South	100.0	100.0	100.0	30.7	100.0	100.0	100.0	242
Non-South				21.3				135

of critical importance in a period of depression, it may be worth while to examine this development more closely to see, if possible, whether the cause was inherent in the southern banking structure.

Undoubtedly one cause of the greater decline of banking resources in the South was the large number of bank failures. Throughout the 1920's and the year 1930, the South's proportion of bank failures, measured by the number of banks or their deposits, was much greater than its proportion of banking resources. In 1928, 1929, and 1930, the proportion of failures was more than three times the proportion of resources.[6]

CHART *VIII*   TOTAL ASSETS OF COMMERCIAL BANKS IN THE SOUTH IN BILLIONS OF DOLLARS AND AS PERCENTAGES OF UNITED STATES TOTALS FOR SELECTED YEARS, 1929–1949

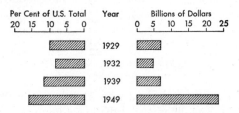

The causes of this disproportionate number of failures were many, but the chief ones were: too many small state banks; poor supervision and regulation, especially of the formation of new banks; lack of competent management; and a chronic agricultural depression.[7] After 1929, bank failures continued and increased in the South, but else-where they increased so rapidly that the South's proportion declined until it was only slightly greater than its proportion of resources. Since 1933 they have been insignificant in all sections of the country.

The larger number of bank failures was not the only cause of the greater banking deflation in the South. In a period of depression, the semicolonial nature of the South's industrial and financial systems encourages a drain of funds out of the region. Between 1929 and 1934, insurance companies in the United States increased their cash hold-ings by $434 million, but the South's share increased by only $8

6 Incidentally, this situation should be recognized as one of the South's major handicaps to economic progress in all lines in this period.
7 For a further discussion see, for example, Ray B. Westerfield, *Money, Credit and Banking* (Revised Edition), New York, The Ronald Press Company, 1947, pp. 846–57.

million (see Table *LIX*). During those years the total money supply was declining rapidly, so insurance companies were gaining cash from the rest of the economy. Some part of that cash came from the South; on the basis of insurance in the South, about 15 per cent, or $64 million. But cash holdings in the South increased by only $8 million, so there must have been a drain out of the region on the order of $50 million or more.[8] It is probable that the same movement was going on in large industrial companies, many of which have branches in the South. No specific data are at hand, but it is well known that in a period of depression the assets of large industrial and commercial companies become more liquid as inventories, receivables, etc., are reduced by conversion into cash.

It was only natural, especially in view of the weakness of southern banks, that such cash should be moved into larger, stronger depository banks nearer the home offices. It is known that during this period at least some of the larger insurance and railroad companies transferred ordinary working balances from small, local banks in the South to larger, stronger banks outside the region. Finally, financial operations of state and local governments caused a drain of funds out of the region. In the late 1920's many of them were borrowing heavily, bringing in funds from outside the region. They maintained considerable bank balances while those funds were being spent. But in the early 1930's borrowing stopped, the balances were exhausted, and the units had to begin remitting interest payments and installments of principal to bondholders outside the region. In some cases bankers complained that the reduction of public balances contributed directly to bank failures.[9]

The predominance of agriculture has contributed to banking instability in the South. In the past, the fluctuations of prices and incomes have been especially violent in agriculture; between 1929 and 1932, they fell even more sharply in the South than in the rest of the nation. Such violent fluctuations must inevitably have their effects upon the banking system.

The above factors are perhaps sufficient explanation for the greater banking deflation in the South between 1929 and 1934. Whether they will operate again in the event of another depression is uncertain.

[8] In this comparison, the South includes Delaware, Maryland, West Virginia, and the District of Columbia.
[9] See B. U. Ratchford, *American State Debts*, Durham, Duke University Press, 1941, pp. 554-55.

For the present, the problem of bank failures has been solved and there are good reasons for believing that for the long run it has been eliminated or greatly alleviated. Most of the excess banks, including the weaker ones, have been eliminated; the supervision and regulation of banking is much improved, especially that exercised by the Federal Deposit Insurance Corporation over small state banks; large holdings of U. S. Government bonds have improved the quality of bank assets; and, finally, deposit insurance greatly strengthens the whole banking system. Also, we have built up an elaborate system to protect against disastrous declines in agricultural prices and income. These factors should inspire more confidence in southern banks and remove or alleviate one of the major causes—fear—which has caused funds to be drained from the region in periods of stress in the past. However, until southern district and branch managers of large industrial and financial concerns have more autonomy than they now have, there will continue to be strong incentives for removing funds from the region in periods of declining business.

Between 1939 and 1949, banking assets in the South increased phenomenally, both absolutely and relatively. Total resources increased by 242 per cent, compared with an increase of 135 per cent in the Non-South. This relative gain is greater than we have found in any other major field of economic activity. Some part of it, perhaps, was due to the return of funds which had been taken out in the earlier period, but most of it was due to the operation of basic factors which brought funds into the region. As has been pointed out in a cogent analysis, the South was in a favorable position to gain funds in this period: prices of its principal agricultural products—cotton and tobacco—had unusually large increases; low-paid farm workers realized very large wage increases when they went into war plants and shipyards; and there were tremendous increases in federal payroll disbursements, civilian and military. Also for a part of the time, southerners could not make their normal purchases of durable goods such as automobiles, refrigerators, etc., which come from outside the region.[10]

Many observers felt that the South would lose funds when reconversion was completed and durable goods again became available. During the first four years after the war there was no evidence of such

[10] Malcolm Bryan, "The Supply of Funds In the South, 1946"; a speech before the Georgia Bankers Association, December 11, 1946.

a loss; on the contrary, the South increased its lead during those years. From 1944 to 1949, individual and corporate demand deposits in the South increased 55 per cent compared with 31 per cent in the Non-South. During the same years, commercial and industrial loans in the South increased by 176 per cent compared with 112 per cent elsewhere, and total loans and discounts increased by 120 per cent compared with 90 per cent.

Several factors may be cited as causes of the continued strength in southern banking in the postwar years. Among them are: a quicker reconversion in the South and less interruption by the steel, automobile, and coal strikes; a booming rayon industry; continued high prices for cotton and tobacco; and an exceptionally active and profitable cotton textile industry. Unusually large exports of cotton textiles were a part of the contribution of that industry. Also, it is likely that increased production of food, feed, and livestock in the South has had some effect in keeping down the outflow of funds. If and when a substantial business recession does come, the region will probably lose funds, as indicated above, but until that time the region seems to have a fair chance to keep the funds it has gained during the past ten years.

The South's proportion of banking resources is now about the same as its proportion of industry; it is somewhat lower than its proportion of income payments. While the South has made tremendous strides, it still has far to go to attain even approximate equality with the rest of the country in banking resources. In 1948, the region had 27 per cent of the country's population, about 19 per cent of income payments, but only 16 per cent of the commercial banking resources. Southern banking resources amounted to about $555 per person, while in the Non-South the figure was about $1,177. This contrast is made even sharper by the absence of savings banks in the South; in other parts of the country, principally the Northeast, such banks had total resources of some $17 billion.

In the distribution by states, Texas dominates the picture to an extent greater than in any other field. In 1949, that state accounted for more than a fourth of the total banking resources of the region; no other state has as much as 9 per cent. Between 1929 and 1934, Arkansas and South Carolina suffered especially severe declines, losing about half of their banking resources. But after 1939, both had higher rates of increase, as did Florida, also. It may be significant that every state which had 7 per cent or less of total banking resources in 1939 had a greater than average rate of growth in the years following, while every state which had more than 7 per cent of total resources in 1939 (except Texas) had a smaller rate of growth in the following years, and consequently declined in relative importance. The decline was especially marked in the case of Virginia. This would seem to indicate that there is no trend toward concentration in the financial resources of the region, but rather the opposite, except for Texas.

Characteristics of Southern Banking. In several respects banking in the South is different from banking in other parts of the country. This fact is demonstrated by a ratio analysis of bank assets and liabilities, such as is given in Table *LIV*.

TABLE *LIV*   CERTAIN BANKING RATIOS IN THE SOUTH AND THE NON-SOUTH 1939–1949

	1939		1944		1949	
	SOUTH	NON-SOUTH	SOUTH	NON-SOUTH	SOUTH	NON-SOUTH
ASSETS AS PERCENTAGES OF TOTAL ASSETS:						
Balances with F. R. Banks	8.9	17.9	9.7	10.6	10.4	12.4
Balances with Other Banks	21.9	8.8	16.1	5.7	10.7	4.3
U. S. Gov't Obligations	15.7	26.6	45.8	56.2	37.8	42.9
Total Securities	25.8	38.5	50.8	61.2	44.2	49.2
Comm. and Ind. Loans	10.9	8.5	5.3	6.2	10.7	11.1
Agricultural Loans	5.7	1.5	3.4	0.9	3.6	1.5
Real Estate Loans	6.0	6.8	2.6	3.7	5.9	7.1
Total Loans and Discounts	41.1	25.2	17.6	16.8	28.3	27.4
CERTAIN ITEMS AS PERCENTAGES OF TOTAL DEPOSITS:						
Individual Demand Deposits	46.7	47.4	54.4	49.6	62.2	55.9
U. S. Gov't Deposits	2.0	1.3	13.8	17.0	1.1	7.4
Total Demand Deposits	73.7	71.2	86.5	80.7	81.8	71.7
Capital Accounts	12.9	12.4	6.1	6.9	7.0	7.9
Total of Balances with F. R. Banks and with Other Banks	34.9	30.3	27.5	17.5	22.7	18.2

Bank reserves are a vital and significant part of bank assets. To a very great extent they govern the amount of credit banks can create by making loans or buying securities. They are nonearning assets; they do not bring in an income, and hence banks usually aim to keep them as low as is consistent with safety and convenience. They are usually in the form of deposits in the Federal Reserve banks or, in the case of nonmember banks, deposits in approved commercial banks, usually in larger cities. From Table *LIV* it will be seen that deposits of southern banks in Federal Reserve banks are comparatively low, while their deposits in other (commercial) banks are quite high. Further, the last line of that table shows that the total of balances with Federal Reserve banks and with other banks, expressed as a percentage of total deposits, is substantially higher in the South than in the Non-South. Why is this true?

Several facts contribute to the explanation. As noted above, many southern banks are small, nonmember, relatively isolated state banks. Such banks ordinarily carry larger proportionate reserves than banks in metropolitan areas. They must carry balances for clearing purposes with Federal Reserve banks or, more frequently, with correspondent banks in larger cities. Often they are not familiar with, nor in close touch with, facilities for keeping their funds invested up to the limit day by day. Further, the ½ per cent or 1 per cent which they can get on short-term investments may not appear worth while to them in comparison with the 6 or 8 per cent which they usually get on loans. It appears, too, that often the correspondent banks in the larger cities discourage the small banks from making investments; the larger banks would prefer to have the funds deposited with them so that they could make some profit by investing them and also to build up an "empire." Some would like to head "little Federal Reserve systems" in their particular areas. Finally, some small banks maintain deposits in large cities for purposes of prestige and convenience. "Some small bankers maintain balances in New York merely because when they make trips to New York they are entertained royally."[11]

The large net deposits of southern banks in banks outside the region further illustrates the semi-colonial, dependent nature of the southern financial system which characterized it in the past and still does so to some extent. Table *LI* shows that in 1949 southern banks had an excess of balances due from banks over what they owed other banks in the form of bank deposits of some $666 million. Undoubtedly a large part of this sum was necessarily kept on deposit in the large financial centers to insure the smooth functioning of the banking sys-

---

[11] Letter to one of the authors from a banking official who prefers to remain anonymous. It is possible that another reason why southern banks carry large balances with banks outside the region is the drain of funds out of the region in periods of severe depression as noted above. Experienced southern bankers may have experienced a situation in which no other asset protected their solvency quite so well as a substantial deposit in a New York or Chicago bank. Once the custom or practice of maintaining such deposits becomes established, it tends to persist and to become a tradition.

tem. But it is possible that some part of it—say two or three hundred million dollars—could have been brought home and used as reserves to support additional credit to the southern economy in the amount of a billion dollars or so.[12] In fact, it seems that in recent years they have been doing just that, at least in a relative sense. In 1929, southern banks had a net excess of balances due from banks over balances due to banks of $223 million, which was 3.2 per cent of their total resources. By 1939 the figures had risen to $599 million and 8.7 per cent. More recently the figures have been: 1944, $817 million and 4.8 per cent; 1947, $763 million and 3.4 per cent; 1949, $666 million and 2.8 per cent. From 1939 to 1949, balances due from banks declined from 21.9 per cent to 10.7 per cent of total assets.

Among the other assets, U. S. Government obligations have always ranked lower with southern than with non-southern banks, although this differential was reduced considerably during the recent war. The same is true of total securities, which are dominated by federal obligations. In view of the preponderance of agriculture in the region, it is somewhat surprising that southern banks have almost as large a proportion of their total assets in commercial and industrial loans as do non-southern banks; in 1939 they actually had a larger proportion. Agricultural loans naturally rank considerably higher in the South, but again it is noteworthy that southern banks have a lower proportion of real estate loans than do non-southern banks. In the past, small banks in rural areas have frequently taken on too many such loans. The higher ratio of non-southern banks now is probably explained by FHA insured loans, which have been placed mainly in urban communities.

In 1939, southern banks were using a substantially greater part of their funds to finance local and regional enterprise than were banks elsewhere. During the war this differential was greatly reduced by heavy purchases of U.S. Government bonds. In recent years the pre-war pattern has not been re-established. In fact, it would seem that the funds gained by bringing home balances held outside the region have been used to support the purchase of U.S. obligations rather than for making local loans. In 1949, the ratio of U.S. obligations among the assets of southern banks was considerably nearer the ratio prevailing in non-southern banks (37.8 per cent against 42.9 per cent) than it

---

[12] This assumes, of course, that the additional credit created would take the form of loans to industry, commerce, and agriculture. If it took the form of purchase of U. S. Government obligations it would have no effect.

was in 1939 (15.7 per cent against 26.6 per cent) or even in 1944 (45.8 per cent against 56.2 per cent). So, to a considerable extent, southern banks have substituted U.S. obligations for balances in banks outside the region.

The most striking feature of southern bank deposits is the high proportion of demand deposits and the corresponding low proportion of time deposits. To a large extent this was a development of the war period; in 1939, the South's proportion of the nation's time deposits was only slightly lower than its proportion of demand deposits, but during the war period the proportion of demand deposits increased by about 50 per cent while the proportion of time deposits hardly changed. Again, the significance of this fact is accentuated by the absence of savings banks in the South. During the war, personal savings in the South apparently went largely into Savings Bonds, but still it would seem that savings and time deposits are quite low in the region in comparison with other parts of the country. One further explanation may be that the rates which can be realized on loans, mortgages, etc., made by individuals are considerably higher in the South than in the Non-South while the rates offered by commercial banks on time deposits are about the same throughout the country.

In 1939, southern banks had a slightly higher ratio of capital accounts to deposits than did non-southern banks, and in both groups the ratios were above the rule-of-thumb minimum which required that capital equal at least 10 per cent of deposits. The large increases in deposits during the war were not matched by corresponding additions to capital, and the ratios declined everywhere, and more in the South. In 1949, the capital-deposits ratio in the South was 7.0 per cent compared with 7.9 per cent elsewhere. In southern banks, there was one dollar of capital for every $14.29 of deposits, compared with one dollar for every $12.66 of deposits in non-southern banks.

In recent years the Federal Reserve banks have made estimates, based on sample surveys, of the ownership of the demand deposits of individuals, partnerships, and corporations. A striking feature of the estimates for the South[13] is the small size of the deposits of manufacturing and mining companies. The region has from 13 to 17 per cent of the nation's manufacturing and mining activities, depending upon the basis of measurement. But in recent years southern banks have

13 The South here includes the Richmond, Atlanta and Dallas Federal Reserve Districts.

held only from 7 to 9 per cent of all the deposits of manufacturing and mining companies in the country. Two factors might explain such a result. One would be that southern companies conduct their business with smaller bank balances than non-southern companies. The other would be that much of the manufacturing in the South is carried on by branches of large national companies which carry locally only the deposits necessary for day-to-day business, while the principal balances are carried with banks at the home offices of the companies. Since the companies which operate branches in the South are large ones which often maintain accounts running into many millions of dollars, this is probably the more significant explanation.

Other deposits as estimated are in line with what might be expected. Deposits of financial organizations are comparatively low in the South and total business deposits are lower relatively than in the Non-South, as would be indicated by the smaller amount of industrialization. Personal deposits (including farmers') are higher in the South and have risen relatively in all parts of the country. The South has increased its proportion of the total deposits in keeping with its increased proportion of total banking resources.

One other phase of banking activity which is of significance to the southern economy is the rate of interest which commercial banks charge on the loans they make. Table *LV* presents some data on that

TABLE *LV*   CERTAIN EARNINGS AND PROFIT RATIOS OF MEMBER BANKS BY FEDERAL RESERVE DISTRICTS FOR SELECTED YEARS, 1937–1948

FEDERAL RESERVE DISTRICT	1937	1939	1941	1943	1944	1945	1946	1947	1948
Interest on Loans as Percentages of Loans									
Richmond	5.1	4.9	4.7	4.2	3.7	3.5	3.7	4.0	4.4
Atlanta	4.8	4.8	4.7	3.8	3.4	3.3	3.6	4.0	4.4
Dallas	6.1	5.7	5.5	4.2	3.8	3.5	3.9	4.4	4.6
All Districts	4.0	4.2	4.0	3.5	3.2	3.0	3.2	3.6	3.8
Net Profits as Percentages of Total Capital Accounts									
Richmond	7.2	6.9	7.7	8.0	10.0	10.2	10.7	9.1	7.6
Atlanta	7.9	8.5	8.9	9.4	11.2	13.4	12.2	9.7	8.0
Dallas	10.0	9.2	8.3	9.0	10.0	10.0	11.8	10.3	8.6
All Districts	6.3	6.3	6.7	8.8	9.7	10.9	9.6	7.9	7.2

All ratios computed from aggregate dollar amounts.
SOURCE: *Federal Reserve Bulletin.*

point. Those data show, first, that the rates of interest earned on loans in the southern districts were consistently and substantially higher than the national average. Second, in the early years there were considerable differences between the southern districts, and throughout the period, banks in the Atlanta District had the lowest rates. Third, all rates declined steadily until 1945; those districts with the highest rates in 1937 had the greatest declines, and differentials were thus reduced. By 1945, the three southern districts were much nearer to the national average than they were in 1937. As the rates rose slightly after 1945, however, there was a tendency for the differentials between the southern rates and the national average to increase. But over the whole period the general tendency was for southern banks to move closer to the national pattern.

The ratios in Table *LV* were computed from aggregate dollar amounts and thus were heavily influenced by the large loans made by the big banks at low rates. Actually, the regional differences in interest rates received on loans were caused more by differences in the size of loaning banks, variations in the size of loans, and differences in the characteristics of borrowers than by differences in regional schedules of interest rates. Based on 1946 data, a Federal Reserve study found that

> While for a given type of loan, rates in the Dallas and San Francisco Federal Reserve Districts were consistently above the national average, they were commonly much less than 1 percentage point higher. . . . Lowest rates were paid by borrowers in the New York, Richmond, and St. Louis Districts. . . . Customers in the Philadelphia, Atlanta, and Minneapolis Districts paid rates close to the national average. . . .
>
> In each district differences in rates paid by large and small borrowers were considerably larger than the variations shown between the highest- and the lowest-rate areas of the country.[14]

Thus the higher rates in the South are largely caused by the smaller size of banks and the smaller loans which they customarily make. This fact is probably accentuated by the fact that some of the larger and stronger southern business firms, which are able to borrow at the lowest rates, have the option of borrowing from the big banks in St. Louis, Chicago, or New York. There they can get larger loans and lower rates than most southern banks can offer. This helps to distort the statistical picture to the disadvantage of the South.

This situation, however, has not always prevailed; over the past 20 or 30 years there has been a considerable narrowing of the interest

[14] *Federal Reserve Bulletin*, July, 1947, p. 814.

rate differential between regions. The Federal Reserve study quoted above noted that

> During the past several decades several factors have worked to narrow regional differences in the price of bank credit, including the rapid economic growth and industrialization of many sections of the South and West, general improvement of methods of communication, the establishment of the Federal Reserve System and other financial institutions which tend to contribute to credit fluidity, and the extension by large banks of their lending activities on a wide scale throughout the country. A further factor of importance in recent years has been the rapid growth of deposits in all regions and the expansion of bank reserves and of bank assets that may be converted readily into reserves. As a result a large supply of loanable funds exists throughout the country.[15]

Despite these considerations, however, most southern borrowers do suffer a handicap in the form of higher interest rates. This is true because, typically, they obtain small loans from small banks. This disadvantage has been accentuated in recent years because interest rates on small loans have not declined as much as the rates on larger loans.[16] This is probably because there is little competition for such loans and most small bankers usually charge their traditional 6 or 8 per cent on loans, in the absence of competition.

Despite their smaller average size, southern member banks usually realize somewhat better earnings on their capital accounts. Over the past 12 years those earnings have usually been from 1 to 2 percentage points better than the national average. From 1941 through 1946, the banks in the Atlanta district had the best rate of earnings in the three southern districts; in 1937, 1939, 1947, and 1948, the banks in the Dallas district were first.

CURRENCY AND SAVINGS

Currency. The American people have retained a substantial portion of their savings of the past ten years in the form of currency. Between the end of 1937 and the end of 1948, currency in circulation in the United States increased from $6.6 billion to $28.2 billion—more than a fourfold increase. This was an increase greater than that shown by prices,

---

15 *Ibid.*
16 See, for example, the annual reports on "Trends in North Carolina Banking" prepared by the Research Committee of the North Carolina Bankers Association. These show that there was no significant change in the rate of earnings on loans by smaller banks from 1937 to 1944.

cost of living, income payments, or bank deposits. It is debatable whether some part of this large sum is in excess of current needs and might be available, under certain conditions, for investment. What parts of the total or of the excess, if any, are in the South is even more uncertain. Nevertheless, we have one clue which may afford some rough indication.

Federal Reserve notes now make up about 85 per cent of our currency in circulation. They are issued by the 12 Federal Reserve banks. While they circulate to a considerable extent outside the district of the bank which issues them, there is some tendency for them to stay in that district, since other Federal Reserve banks return them to the issuing bank when they come into those other Reserve banks in the normal course of business. Too, the circulation of the notes outside their own district is reciprocal and offsetting to a considerable extent. So, while it is only a rough indication and far from a precise measure of currency in circulation in the region, it may be worth while to examine the volume of Federal Reserve notes issued by the three south-

TABLE *LVI*   FEDERAL RESERVE NOTES ISSUED BY THE FEDERAL RESERVE BANKS OF RICHMOND, ATLANTA, AND DALLAS IN CIRCULATION AT SELECTED DATES, 1929–1948

DATE: END OF YEAR	AMOUNTS (IN $ MILLIONS) ISSUED BY				PERCENTAGE OF U. S. TOTAL
	RICHMOND BANK	ATLANTA BANK	DALLAS BANK	TOTAL	
1929	99	143	47	289	15.1
1932	102	97	39	238	8.7
1934	168	133	54	355	11.0
1939	230	163	84	477	9.6
1941	431	279	135	845	10.3
1942	787	547	252	1586	13.0
1943	1142	955	416	2513	14.9
1944	1488	1277	547	3312	15.2
1945	1738	1484	619	3841	15.6
1946	1782	1450	604	3836	15.4
1947	1742	1398	625	3765	15.2
1948	1658	1329	624	3611	14.9

SOURCE: Board of Governors of the Federal Reserve System.

ern Federal Reserve banks and see how it has behaved in comparison with the total of such notes. Table *LVI* makes such a comparison.

Over the period since 1929, the issues of the three banks have increased 13 fold. This rate of increase was characteristic of the total of Federal Reserve notes; it increased much more than total currency in circulation (which increased about sixfold) because of the retirement of the gold certificates and national bank notes. Between 1929 and 1932, total note issues of the three southern Reserve banks declined some 16 per cent, and their ratio to the national total fell drastically from 15.1 to 8.7 per cent. This tends to confirm the hypothesis that the money "squeeze" was much more severe in the South than elsewhere in the nation. Total currency in circulation increased by about a billion dollars between end of 1929 and end of 1932, but the South, according to this one indication, lost currency. If that did happen, it might be explained in this way: there was considerable hoarding of currency in 1931 and 1932, but in the South, with its low and falling income and small reserves of liquid savings, the people generally were not able to hoard. Rather the opposite; they were forced to spend their small cash holdings in order to live, and the currency they thus gave up was retired by the Federal Reserve banks.

The low ratio of southern note issues continued until World War II. By 1943 it was about back to the 1929 level. Since the high point was reached in 1945, it has declined slowly but steadily each year. But on all bases of comparison the ratio should be higher than it was in 1929. Southern wages, industrial production, and income payments were relatively higher than they were in the earlier year. Further, the region has a larger farm population and farm incomes have risen more than others. High farm incomes have always been thought to promote large currency holdings. On the other side of the picture, however, there is one development which may indicate part of the answer. The South has had an unusually large increase in demand deposits held by individuals. Perhaps more people in the South are using the facilities of the banks rather than holding (or hoarding) their liquid reserves in the form of currency.

Savings Bonds. Regarding Savings Bonds we have somewhat better data, although still far from precise. The Treasury publishes data on sales of such bonds by states; since October, 1944, state data on redemptions have also been published. Obviously, many of these bonds cross state lines after they are sold but, considering that some of those movements will offset each other, the figures should afford some rough indication of present holdings. Table *LVII* gives the absolute and relative figures on sales and redemptions and, for comparison, the South's share of the nation's income payments to individuals.

During the war years the South's purchases of Savings Bonds rose,

TABLE *LVII*   SALES AND REDEMPTIONS OF SAVINGS BONDS IN THE SOUTH
(*Amounts in Millions of Dollars*)

FISCAL YEAR	SALES AT ISSUE PRICES SERIES			PERCENTAGES OF U. S. SERIES			INCOME PAYMENTS IN SOUTH AS % OF U. S. (CALENDAR YEARS)
	E	F AND G	TOTAL	E	F AND G	TOTAL	
1942	534	276	810	15.1	11.2	13.5	18.3
1943	1,365	529	1,894	16.7	15.1	16.2	19.4
1944	2,046	538	2,584	17.3	16.2	17.1	19.8
1945	2,085	434	2,519	18.1	14.9	17.4	19.8
1946	1,237	376	1,613	18.4	13.1	16.8	19.2
1947	697	390	1,087	16.3	13.4	15.1	19.4
1948	614	298	912	15.3	13.5	14.2	19.2
1949	603	271	874	14.1	9.5	12.2	—
Total Through 6/30/49	9,181	3,112	12,293	16.8	13.3	15.8	

REDEMPTIONS AT REDEMPTION VALUES

	SERIES A THROUGH E	PER CENT OF U. S. TOTALS
1946	1,213	19.5
1947	919	18.9
1948	796	18.3
1949	750	18.7
Total 10/44 Through 6/30/49	4,279	18.8

SOURCE: Computed from *Treasury Bulletin.*

both absolutely and relatively, until they were fairly well in line with the region's proportion of income payments. Since 1945, however, while the region's share of income payments has remained about constant, purchase of Savings Bonds has declined faster than in the rest of the country; the proportion represented by southern purchases dropped steadily from 17.4 per cent in 1945 to 12.2 per cent in 1949. The proportion of redemptions was somewhat higher than the proportion of purchases in the South and remained quite steady from 1946 through 1949.

It might be estimated, very roughly, that in the latter part of 1949 there were outstanding in the South something like $4.5 billion of Series E bonds (including a few of Series C and D) and about $2.5 billion of F and G bonds, or a total of approximately $7.0 billion, computed at issue values. At maturity those bonds will have a total redemption value of about $9 billion. Clearly, a large part of those funds are not of the type which should be invested as equity capital, but even a minor fraction of this large sum would provide a considerable amount of investment funds in terms of southern needs. Considering the absence of savings banks, the small amount of time deposits in commercial banks, and the moderate amount of currency which apparently is in the region, the funds now invested in Savings Bonds represent the most promising source of indigenous individual investment funds in the immediate future.

Postal Savings Deposits. To a limited extent, the Postal Savings System takes the place of savings banks in the South. At one time the funds of the System were largely redeposited in commercial banks, but in recent years they have been invested in obligations of the federal government except for small working balances.

The South's proportion of Postal Savings deposits has been somewhat larger than its proportion of commercial banking assets. This is natural in view of the large number of bank failures and the absence of savings banks. The increase during the war, both absolutely and relatively, was quite pronounced, as shown by Table *LVIII*. It is

TABLE *LVIII*   POSTAL SAVINGS DEPOSITS IN THE SOUTH FOR SELECTED YEARS
(*Amounts in Millions of Dollars*)

	1929	1932	1934	1939	1944	1947
Total	24.3	128.2	179.0	193.1	375.0	683.9
Per Cent of U. S.	15.8	16.3	14.9	15.3	18.4	20.2
Index: 1929 = 100						
South	100	528	737	795	1543	2814
Non-South	100	508	788	827	1283	2095

Data are for June of each year.
SOURCE: Computed from Annual Reports of the Board of Trustees on Operations of The Postal Savings System.

probable that this was due to three factors: first, the greater increase in income in the region; second, the presence during the war of many individuals from outside the region who had no commercial banking connections; and, third, the continued decline in the rate of interest paid on savings deposits by commercial banks. The Postal System continued to pay 2 per cent while most commercial banks paid 1 per cent, or less. While these deposits have increased greatly on a percentage basis, they are still relatively small. Generally, they do not represent funds which could properly be invested in industry even if withdrawn, but they can perform the functions of a liquid reserve and in that way, perhaps, release other funds for investment.

Savings and Loan Associations. Another considerable pool of savings accumulates in savings and loan associations. Normally such funds are employed in financing local residential building, but during the war, when such building was halted, the accruing funds were invested in securities, principally U.S. Government obligations. By the end of the war, total security holdings of all associations in the United States amounted to over $2.5 billion, or more than a fourth of all assets. By the end of 1948, however, more than $1 billion of those had been liquidated and the proceeds invested in home mortgages.

Between 1929 and 1948, the number of savings and loan associations in the South fell from 1,309 to 982, but their ratio to the national total rose from 10.6 per cent to 16.3 per cent. The assets of those associations (in millions of dollars) and their percentages of national totals for selected years were as follows: 1929, 895 and 10.3; 1934, 614 and 9.5; 1939, 693 and 12.2; 1944, 1,028 and 13.8; 1948, 2,017 and 15.5.[17] By the end of 1948, the assets of such associations outside the South were 27 per cent higher than in 1929, but in the South they were up about 125 per cent.

LIFE INSURANCE COMPANY INVESTMENTS

In the United States, life insurance companies are the most important financial institutions assembling long-term investment funds. Each year they acquire several billion dollars of new investment funds. In earlier years those funds were invested principally in real estate mortgages and in seasoned securities. In recent years many insurance companies have been buying large issues of securities directly from issuing companies and making short- and medium-term loans to business firms.

Within the past few years some insurance companies have experimented with direct purchase of real estate, buying industrial and commercial properties and leasing them back to the original owners at rentals designed to amortize the capital outlay within a reasonable time. Virginia, in 1942, was the first state to permit this type of investment and now 39 states allow it. This type of financing is quite attractive to companies which do not wish to tie up a large amount of

17 Compiled from *Savings and Loan Annals* and the reports of the Federal Home Loan Bank Board and the Federal Savings and Loan Insurance Corporation.

funds in low-yielding real estate; it may be a significant form of financing in the future. It is reported that during 1948, insurance companies invested $277 million in real estate—an increase of about a third in one year in that type of investment.[18]

Southern Insurance Companies. A very large proportion of the life insurance business is highly concentrated in a few companies, no one of which is located in the South. In 1946, the ten largest companies had approximately two thirds of all insurance assets and of the insurance in force in this country; no southern company ranked higher than 31st in assets or 18th in insurance in force. There are a great many small southern companies—over 200 in 1949—but each of the four top companies in the country has more assets than all the southern companies combined.[19] In 1946, southern companies had about $2,124 million of admitted assets, which was 4.4 per cent of the total for the country; they had about $12,650 million of insurance in force, or 7.3 per cent of the national total. Total insurance in force in the South in 1946 was $29,128 million, or 17.1 per cent of the total for the country. Thus southern companies were carrying considerably less than half of the insurance in force in the region.

Although southern companies are relatively quite small, they had a considerably greater growth between 1929 and 1946 than did non-southern companies. Southern companies increased their admitted assets by 308 per cent against 172 per cent for non-southern companies; for insurance in force the figures were 153 per cent and 57 per cent; and for premium income, southern companies were ahead by 247 per cent to 57 per cent.[20] This faster growth was realized despite the fact that the insurance sold by the southern companies was more costly. Compared with other companies of comparable size outside the South, southern companies charged 3 to 4 per cent more for their policies, but compared with the five largest companies in the

[18] Mark Levy, "Lease-back Financing Expending," *Best's Insurance News, Life Edition,* June, 1949, L, pp. 37–38.

[19] *Best's Life Insurance Reports,* 1947, and *Best's Insurance News, Life Edition,* August 1, 1947, p. 11. In 1949, Texas was first in the country in number of companies with 104 and Louisiana was second with 63; these two states had about 28 per cent of all the companies in the United States. Levy, *op. cit.,* p. 37.

[20] *Best's Life Insurance Reports,* 1947. These figures are not exact because reports for a number of small companies are missing. These had no appreciable effects upon national totals but probably reduced the South's proportion slightly in both years.

country, their policies cost from a third to two thirds more.[21] The higher rates in the southern companies permitted higher commissions to agents and also allowed large cash dividends to stockholders.[22]

Investments of All Companies. While the assets of southern insurance companies are comparatively small, non-southern insurance com-

TABLE *LIX*   LIFE INSURANCE COMPANY INVESTMENTS* AND RESERVES IN THE SOUTH** AND THE NON-SOUTH, 1929, 1934, 1939, AND 1948

(*In Millions of Dollars*)

CLASS OF INVESTMENT	SOUTH				NON-SOUTH			
	1929	1934	1939	1948	1929	1934	1939	1948
Farm Mortgages	344	202	168	218	1586	979	617	614
Other Mortgages	855	680	732	2296	3895	3550	3539	5671
State and Municipal Bonds	253	300	455	245	288	715	1195	393
Railroad Bonds and Stocks	806	783	756	727	1971	2053	2080	2080
Public Utility Bonds and Stocks	240	311	569	1977	1159	1533	2985	6005
Other Bonds and Stocks	37	51	242	1636	209	314	624	3985
Policy Loans	469	612	545	333	1625	2617	2285	1403
Real Estate	7	232	213	58	292	1241	1669	870
Cash	7	15	27	47	102	528	798	708
Other Assets	3	9	—	4	26	12	20	6
Total	3021	3195	3707	7541	11153	13542	15812	21735
Reserves	2351	2478	3441	6546	13971	14662	19986	35978

* Investments in continental U. S. exclusive of U. S. Government bonds.
** In this table the South includes Delaware, Maryland, the District of Columbia, and West Virginia in addition to the usual 13 states. Data are for the end of the year.
SOURCE: Computed from reports of The Life Insurance Association of America.

panies have made large investments in the region. Each year the Life Insurance Association of America publishes data on the geographical

21 This is based upon a comparison of the net costs, over 10 and 20 year periods, of $1,000 of ordinary life (or endowment at 85) insurance written at age 25 in the five largest southern companies, in five companies of comparable size outside the South, and in the five largest companies in the country. The net costs were derived from the actual histories of policies written in 1927 and 1938. *1947 Flitcraft Compend.*
22 Most of the southern companies are stock companies and write only nonparticipating insurance. One of the larger southern companies has had an almost fantastic record of earnings. Counting cash dividends, stock dividends, surplus and contingency reserves it had, over a period of almost 40 years to the end of 1946, earned amounts equal, at simple interest, to more than 100 per cent *per year* on the capital paid into the business. Its record of stock dividends is as follows: 1922, 100%; 1926, 33⅓%; 1938, 100%; 1941, 100%; 1945, 150%. Cash dividends amounted to more than eleven times the original investment. For each company of this kind, however, there are scores of companies which start off with a few thousand dollars of capital, struggle along a few years, and then drop out of the picture.

distribution of the investments of its members, which account for about 90 per cent of the insurance business of the country. Figures are also given on reserves which the companies carry against policies outstanding in the different areas. These latter afford a fairly accurate indication of the amount of insurance in force in different geographical

CHART *IX*   INVESTMENTS AND RESERVES OF INSURANCE COMPANIES IN THE SOUTH, SELECTED YEARS, 1929–1948

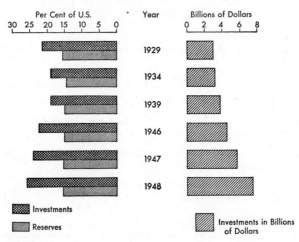

Investments

Reserves

Investments in Billions of Dollars

areas.[23] Tables *LIX, LX,* and *LXI* present and analyze data on these investments and reserves in the South as compared with the rest of the country.

In 1948, total investments in the South amounted to $7,539 million, or 26 per cent of the total for the country. The increase from 1929 to

[23] These reports appear, before 1943, in the annual *Proceedings of the Association of Life Insurance Presidents;* for 1943 and later years, in the *Proceedings* of annual meetings of the Life Insurance Association of America. They are also available as separate pamphlets. The breakdown is according to census districts and not by states. Hence for this discussion the South includes, in addition to the usual 13 states, Delaware, Maryland, District of Columbia, and West Virginia. A breakdown by states for the year 1938 indicates that the 13 states had about 82 per cent of the investments and 77 per cent of the reserves for these three census districts. This is offset in part by the fact that the Association data include only about 90 per cent of total insurance company investments. It is likely that the proportion of the assets of southern insurance company assets not covered is somewhat larger.

In its totals, the Association includes obligations of the Federal Government, which are allocated on the basis of population. For the purpose of this study it seems best to leave those out; in recent years they have made up a large part of total investments. Securities of railroad, public utility, and industrial companies are allocated on the basis of the location of physical property.

TABLE *LX* PATTERNS OF LIFE INSURANCE COMPANY INVESTMENTS IN THE SOUTH** AND THE NON-SOUTH FOR SELECTED YEARS: INVESTMENTS BY CLASSES AS PERCENTAGES OF TOTALS

CLASS OF INVESTMENT	SOUTH				NON-SOUTH			
	1929	1934	1939	1948	1929	1934	1939	1948
Farm Mortgages	11.2	6.3	4.5	2.9	14.2	7.2	3.9	2.8
Other Mortgages	27.9	21.3	19.7	30.4	34.9	26.2	22.4	26.1
State and Municipal Bonds	8.3	9.4	12.3	3.2	2.6	5.3	7.6	1.8
Railroad Bonds and Stocks	26.3	24.5	20.4	9.6	17.7	15.2	13.2	9.6
Public Utility Bonds and Stocks	7.8	9.7	15.4	26.2	10.4	11.3	18.9	27.7
Other Bonds and Stocks	1.2	1.6	6.5	21.7	1.9	2.3	3.9	18.4
Policy Loans	15.3	19.2	14.7	4.4	14.6	19.3	14.5	6.5
Real Estate	1.5	7.3	5.7	0.8	2.6	9.2	10.6	4.0
Cash	0.2	0.5	0.8	0.6	0.9	3.9	5.0	3.0
Other Assets	0.1	0.3	—	0.1	0.2	0.1	0.1	—
Total	100.0	100.0	100.0	100.0	100.0	100.0	100.0	100.0
Investments* in Region as Per Cent of Reserves Required in Region	152	129	108	95	80	92	79	54

* Investments in U. S. Government obligations excluded from both regions.
** See definition of South in Table *LIX*.
SOURCE: See Table *LIX*.

TABLE *LXI* SOME RATIOS OF LIFE INSURANCE COMPANY INVESTMENTS IN THE SOUTH* AND THE NON-SOUTH FOR SELECTED YEARS

| CLASS OF INVESTMENT | SOUTH AS PER CENT OF U. S. | | | | PER CENT CHANGE | | | |
					SOUTH		NON-SOUTH	
	1929	1934	1939	1948	1929–48	1946–48	1929–48	1946–48
Farm Mortgages	17.8	17.1	21.4	26.2	−36.6	+41.6	−61.3	+18.8
Other Mortgages	18.0	16.1	17.1	28.8	+168.5	+96.6	+45.6	+38.2
State and Municipal Bonds	46.8	29.6	27.6	38.4	−3.2	+46.7	+36.5	+35.1
Railroad Bonds and Stocks	29.0	27.6	26.7	25.9	−9.8	+8.7	+5.5	+4.9
Public Utility Bonds and Stocks	17.2	16.9	16.0	24.8	+723.8	+66.3	+418.1	+51.8
Other Bonds and Stocks	15.0	14.0	27.9	29.1	+4321.6	+113.6	+1806.7	+92.2
Policy Loans	22.4	19.0	19.3	19.2	−29.0	+8.8	+13.7	+8.7
Real Estate	13.9	15.7	11.3	6.3	+23.4	+41.5	+197.9	+41.9
Cash	6.0	2.8	3.3	6.6	+571.4	+34.3	+548.0	+33.3
Other Assets	10.3	42.9	—	40.0	+33.3	−33.3	−61.5	−23.1
Total	21.5	19.1	19.0	25.8	+146.3	+67.5	+94.5	+41.4
Reserves	15.1	14.5	14.7	15.4	+178.5	+16.1	+157.5	+14.0

* For definition of the South as used here, see Table *LIX*.
SOURCE: See Table *LIX*.

1948 was 146 per cent compared with an increase of 95 per cent in the Non-South. The changes from 1946 to 1948 were particularly striking; investments in the South increased by $3,038 million, or 68 per cent, while in the Non-South the increase was $6,353 million, or 41 per cent. For the single year of 1948, the increase was 30 per cent for the South and 19 per cent for the Non-South.[24]

Among the specific types of investment, farm mortgages, railroad securities, and state and municipal bonds declined over the whole period, although the latter category was increasing before the war. Real estate holdings increased greatly during the depression as properties were taken over on defaulted mortgages, declined sharply during the war, and then rose again after the war as insurance companies bought industrial and commercial properties as noted above.[25] Cash holdings in the South increased by fivefold but still were insignificant in relation to holdings outside the region. There was also a substantial increase in "other" mortgages, reflecting an improved urban real estate market and the guarantee of federal agencies.

The largest increases, however, were in the fields which are most significant for increased industrialization in the South; that is, in the securities of public utility and other companies, the "other" being principally industrials. Between 1929 and 1948, holdings of public utility securities increased by more than sixfold, while holdings of "others" multiplied more than 40 times. Holdings of these types of securities were increasing in other parts of the country but the growth was faster in the South as is shown by the fact that the South's proportion of national totals in these two categories increased from 17.2 to 24.8 per cent and from 15.0 to 29.1 per cent, respectively. Since 1929, the insurance companies have increased their investment in these two sectors of the southern economy by about $3.3 billion, which was about 75 per cent of the net increase in their total investment in the region. This was an average of nearly $167 million per year for the whole period, but actually the increase was concentrated in a few years during which it undoubtedly was a major source of investment funds for these two fields.

Since such a large part of the insurance business of the South is done by companies located outside the region, it is often asked whether the net effect of this business is to drain funds out of the region. While it is not possible to give a definite answer to this question, some light is thrown on it by some computations made for the TNEC covering

24 It should be remembered that obligations of the U. S. Government are omitted from this analysis. The large increases in both regions in 1947 and 1948 represented partly the liquidation of federal obligations and the reinvestment of their proceeds in private investments.   25 See above p. 185.

the year 1939.[26] Those show premium income and disbursements including benefits to policyholders, taxes, fees, commissions, and all other expenses. In 1938 there was, in the three census districts under consideration, an excess of premium income over all disbursements of about $48 million. This included both southern and non-southern companies. If cash dividend payments to stockholders of the southern companies were included, this excess would be reduced. On the other hand, if the figures were expanded to cover companies not included in this group, it would probably be increased. But we may take $50 million as indicating roughly the order of magnitude of the excess of premium income over expenses in the region. As we have seen, new investments specifically allocable to the region have been considerably in excess of this figure. In addition, there were the investment funds returned to the region indirectly through the purchase of U.S. obligations by the insurance companies.

Another phase of the problem is the income on insurance company investments in the region. If we apply the rate earned on all insurance investments in 1938—approximately 3.6 per cent—to the investments specifically allocable to the region, we get a figure of about $128 million. Since all disbursements have been offset against premium income, this would be a net addition to the excess stated above and would give a total excess of between $175 and $180 million. In some years, investments specifically allocable to the South have exceeded this figure by a considerable margin, while in others it has fallen far below it and has even been negative. For example, for the years from 1932 through 1938, new investments were negative in four years, negligible in two years, and in the other year,—1937—were a positive $327 million. Over the years, it would seem that the region has received its full share of insurance company investments—and more—because in 1948 the region had 25.8 per cent of total investments in the United States while reserves against policies outstanding in the region amounted to only 15.4 per cent of the national total (see Table LXI).

Apparently the situation may be described in this way: since the large companies which do most of the business of the region are located outside the region, the natural drift of funds is outward. It requires a positive act of investment by the insurance companies to

26 *TNEC Hearings*, Part 28, pp. 15, 590–93. It is not so stated, but presumably these figures cover only the 29 companies affiliated with the Association of Life Insurance Presidents.

return the funds to the region. In years when investment opportunities are scarce or when insurance company executives are not favorably impressed by southern prospects, there is a net outflow which is either invested elsewhere or remains idle. As noted earlier, this is especially true of cash in depression years, when cash has an importance greater than is indicated by its dollar amount. The net effect of the above factors would seem to be in the direction of increasing the swings of the business cycle in the southern region.

The life insurance business deserves more attention than it has received in the South. First, we should have some thorough studies of the formation, supervision, operation, profits, and failures of insurance companies in various southern states; graduate students in southern universities might find suitable topics for Ph.D. dissertations here. Second, we need a few large companies which can offer effective competition to the large northeastern companies. Undoubtedly, we have too many small, weak companies in the South now. Their rates are necessarily high because their costs are high. Their high rates plus their financial instability mean that they cannot sell much insurance to those who buy insurance on a competitive basis. The few companies which do overcome all obstacles and attain considerable size no doubt are tempted to keep their rates up in order to pay large dividends to stockholders.

There would seem to be no highly specialized locational requirements for life insurance; development is probably dependent largely upon an early start and tradition. Higher incomes in the South now offer a promising market for life insurance. Southern insurance companies have made large relative gains during the past 20 years despite their handicaps. The way is open for such larger gains if they can offer rates which can compete with the rates of the biggest companies in the country.

LOCAL VERSUS OUTSIDE CAPITAL

Ownership of Southern Industry. The question is often raised as to how much of southern industry is locally owned and how much is owned by outside capital. It is doubtful that even an approximate answer could be given to this question except by a detailed, company-by-company analysis of a fairly large sample of southern industry. Such an undertaking is not feasible for this study. Some state tax departments show the assessment of industrial property according to domestic and foreign corporations, but such a classification indicates only whether the companies were incorporated in the particular state; it tells nothing about their ownership. We know that most, if not all, the large southern plants in such fields as tobacco, rayon, paper and pulp, and petroleum are owned by large national companies which have their headquarters outside the region. The same is true of the railroads and often of the public utilities. We do not know what proportion of the stocks of such companies are owned by southerners, although in most cases we would be safe in assuming that it was quite a small minority.

In so far as the receipt of cash dividends is indicative of stock ownership, we have one rough measure of stock ownership in the analysis of income reported on individual tax returns to the Federal Government.[27] In 1929, dividends on stock of domestic corporations reported in tax returns filed in the 13 southern states amounted to $372 million, or 7.8 per cent of the $4,786 million reported on all returns. In 1942, the southern figure was $367 million, but this was 13.0 per cent of a much smaller total of $2,833 reported on all returns.[28] The same source shows that in 1942 interest on deposits, notes, mortgages, and bonds on southern returns was $95 million, or 11.0 per cent of the total reported on all returns. These fragmentary data would indicate a fairly high proportion of southern ownership in relation to the proportion of industry located in the region, but they are much too vague and incomplete to have any weight.

Significance of Ownership. It may be asked whether it makes any real difference whether southern industry is owned by southerners or outsiders. There are many aspects to the problem and the answer is by no means a foregone conclusion. If we may assume, as is usually true, that outside capital enters the region in the form of branch plants of large national companies, it affords the region numerous advantages in comparison with the development of local companies financed by

[27] These are found in *Statistics of Income,* prepared by the Bureau of Internal Revenue.

[28] In its studies of national income, the Department of Commerce has estimated corporate dividends in the United States at $5,944 in 1929 and $4,299 million in 1942. The total reported on all income tax returns in 1929 was 80.5 per cent of the estimated total; in 1942, it was 65.9 per cent. With much smaller personal exemptions in the income tax in 1942, it would be logical to expect an increase in the coverage. This behavior is an additional reason for treating these figures with the greatest reserve.

indigenous capital. The large companies can raise larger amounts of capital on more favorable terms by selling stock, retaining earnings, or borrowing. The southern branches have access to all the advantages of large-scale production enjoyed by the large company, such as improved techniques, research facilities, large-scale purchasing, use of by-products, etc.[29]

On the other hand, there are disadvantages attached to outside capital. Profits made by exploiting southern resources may be taken out and invested elsewhere. As we have seen, there is a tendency for large companies to drain cash funds from the region in depression periods. Company policies which are uniform for the whole country may in some cases be inappropriate for one region. Large companies have their disadvantages; they tend to become cumbersome and inflexible. Frequently they are the special target for government regulation, labor demands, and public hostility. Their formal, impersonal methods may not secure the cooperation of green southern labor.

It should be said in passing that when indigenous southern companies become big and profitable, they may acquire most of the above characteristics and their control may, nominally or actually, fall into other hands. They establish an office, or even the principal office, in New York City. They borrow from New York banks. Their advertising is planned and carried out by New York advertising firms. Prominent industrialists from other parts of the country are placed on their boards of directors, partly for "window-dressing" purposes. Non-southerners buy large blocks of their stock. They may reincorporate in a state with more lenient corporation laws. Thus they may become "strangers in their own home." Some of the tobacco companies went through such a transition.

CONCLUSION

One prominent economist and banker in the South has said that, regardless of any difficulties which other parts of the United States might have in absorbing and using available savings in the future, "it does not appear at all probable that the South will have any difficulty in absorbing into an expanding Southern economy—or in absorbing, if in no other way, simply by repaying our interregional indebtedness—every dollar that southern individuals and institutions can save for a

[29] See Chapters IV and XV for further discussion of this point.

good long time."[30] That conclusion would seem to be warranted by the developments of the past and the prospects of the future. Even more, it would seem that for a considerable time interregional indebtedness must be increased by the use of outside funds. If the South is to attain anything approaching equality with the rest of the country in income and use of resources, it must have something like a fourth of the capital investment of the country; in agriculture, in industry, in the services, and throughout the economy. Indications are that at present it has between 15 and 18 per cent of that investment. If that is to be brought up to 25 per cent or more in the next 15 or 20 years, it will require considerably more than 25 per cent of the new investment funds of the country.

In the business sector, southern business probably could not, at best, save and reinvest more than about 20 per cent of all business savings. As for personal savings, the South receives only about 19 per cent of the income payments of the country and per capita incomes in the region are about a third below the national average. That, together with the ratios of savings given above in this chapter, would indicate that not more than about 14 or 15 per cent of total personal savings are likely to be found in the South. So, if the South is to realize its goal in the foreseeable future, it must obtain between 30 and 40 per cent of the nation's investment funds; from its own resources it will be able to provide somewhat less than 20 per cent of the national total.

30 Bryan, *op. cit.*, p. 13.

IX TRENDS IN PUBLIC FINANCE

During the past 20 years the scope of governmental activities in the United States has greatly increased. The way in which governments collect and spend a large proportion of the nation's total income affects every phase of the economy. The purpose of this chapter is to outline the larger movements of public revenues, expenditures, and debts in the South since 1929.

REVENUES

The Background. In public, as in private finances, the year 1929 was the culmination of several years of rapid expansion. In the years immediately preceding, state and local governments had embarked upon ambitious programs of road and school building and betterments of various kinds. That movement was accentuated in the South. In North Carolina, which probably had the greatest expansion next to Florida, total state and local tax levies increased by 195 per cent between 1920 and 1929.[1]

Between 1922 and 1927, revenues of southern states increased by 83 per cent; in non-southern states, by 44 per cent.[2] In addition to the increased revenues, state and local governments were spending heavily of borrowed funds. Between 1922 and 1932, per capita gross debts of state and local governments in the South increased by 111 per cent compared with an increase of 65 per cent outside the South.[3]

Revenues from highway taxes showed the greatest increase. Motor fuel taxes, which did not exist before 1919, produced some $129

[1] Clarence Heer, "The North Carolina Tax Situation," in *Taxation in North Carolina,* University of North Carolina Extension Bulletin, Vol. XII, No. 4, 1932, p. 6.
[2] James W. Martin, *Southern State and Local Finance Trends and the War,* Bulletin of the Bureau of Business Research, No. 10, Lexington, 1945, p. 86.
[3] *Ibid,* p. 99.

million for southern states in 1929, or about a third of all their revenues. Revenues from the motor vehicle license tax also increased rapidly because of a rapidly growing registration and higher rates. In 1929, these two taxes produced slightly more than half of all revenue received by southern states; outside the South they produced about 40 per cent of state revenues (see Table *LXIV*). During this period five southern states adopted the income tax in addition to three which were already using it, while six states levied taxes upon tobacco products for the first time. These taxes did not produce large amounts of revenue at the time, but since then they have become important sources of revenue. In the tobacco taxes, southern states were leading the way since in 1929 only five non-southern states were using such taxes.

Local government revenues in the South during the 1920's were boosted sharply by the last great increase in revenue from the property tax. This tax was pushed to the limit of its productivity in these years; revenues fell off sharply in the Great Depression and did not regain the levels of 1929–30 until after World War II.

Highlights of the Period. Major developments affecting public revenues in the South between 1929 and 1948 may be listed as follows: (1) State revenue increased by almost fivefold while local government revenues (other than fiscal aid received from the states) increased only slightly until after World War II. (2) Revenues from the property tax showed no gain in absolute amount until after the war, and declined sharply in relative importance. (3) Revenues from motor fuel taxes increased about 225 per cent (slightly more than the increase in non-southern states) but motor vehicle revenues showed only a modest gain; combined revenues from the two taxes declined steadily in relative importance after 1932. (4) New taxes on general sales and alcoholic beverages have become major sources of revenue, while tobacco taxes have been growing steadily in use and in yield. (5) Income taxes are now levied by every southern state except Florida and Texas; the revenue which they produce, while still small, has increased more than sixteen fold since 1932. (6) Severance taxes have grown steadily in importance and are now producing substantial amounts of revenue in three states: Louisiana, Oklahoma, and Texas. (7) Unemployment compensation taxes have become a major producer of special-purpose revenue; they are substantially less important in the South than in the Non-South because of differences in the degree of industrialization.

State-Local Relations and the Property Tax. Table *LXII* summarizes total public revenues in the South for 1932 and 1942. These two years when the decennial census of governments was taken are the only ones during this period for which complete data are available.[4] Because the finances of the two levels of government are closely interrelated, such a consolidated statement is necessary to give a complete statement of total revenues. Among other things, this table shows the great change in the position of property taxes and a great shift in the fiscal importance of the two levels of government.

TABLE *LXII*   GENERAL REVENUES (EXCLUDING FISCAL AID) OF COMBINED STATE AND LOCAL GOVERNMENTS IN THE SOUTH AND THE NON-SOUTH, 1932 AND 1942

REVENUE SOURCE AND YEAR	SOUTH					NON-SOUTH				
	STATE	LOCAL	TOTAL	PER CENT DISTRIBU- TION	PER CAPITA	STATE	LOCAL	TOTAL	PER CENT DISTRIBU- TION	PER CAPITA
	($ *Millions*)					($ *Millions*)				
1932										
Property Taxes	87	546	633	56.5	$18.78	241	3807	4048	66.8	$46.53
Other Taxes	305	38	343	30.6	10.18	1257	77	1334	22.0	15.33
Total Taxes	392	584	976	87.1	28.96	1498	3884	5382	88.8	61.86
Charges and Misc.	75	70	145	12.9	4.30	124	552	676	11.2	7.77
Total Revenues	467	654	1121	100.0	33.26	1622	4436	6058	100.0	69.63
1942										
Property Taxes	68	543	611	33.9	15.95	203	3730	3933	45.1	41.18
Other Taxes	942	56	998	55.4	26.06	3802	267	4069	46.7	42.61
Total Taxes	1010	599	1609	89.2	42.01	4005	3997	8002	91.8	83.79
Charges and Misc.	70	124	194	10.8	5.07	224	489	713	8.2	7.47
Total Revenues	1080	723	1803	100.0	47.08	4229	4486	8715	100.0	91.26
Per Cent Increase, 1932–42	131	11	61			161	1	44		

SOURCE: Computed from Governments Division, Bureau of the Census

In absolute terms, property tax revenues declined very slightly between 1932 and 1942 in both the South and the Non-South. Relatively, they fell from 56.5 per cent of total revenues in 1932 to 33.9 per cent in 1942 in the South; in the Non-South the decline was from 66.8 to 45.1 per cent. Many causes have been cited for the decline; Martin enumerates nine major ones.[5] The most important ones stem, directly or indirectly, from the depression of the 1930's. Collections

[4] These data were compiled principally from two publications of the Governments Division of the Bureau of the Census, both dated 1948. They are: *Revised Summary of State and Local Government Finances 1942*, and *Historical Review of State and Local Government Finance*. To avoid duplication, all state aid to local governments was omitted. Also, to get a more exact measure of the financial effort of the region, federal aid to states was omitted. Local shares of state-collected, locally shared taxes are included in state collections but not in local revenues.
[5] See Martin, *op. cit.*, pp. 7–8 and works cited there.

dropped off sharply and delinquencies piled up. With thousands of mortgages in default, it was not feasible to sell real property for taxes. Property owners had a strong case for tax relief and governmental units had to turn to other sources for revenues. The result was that many states assumed local government functions or increased fiscal aid to local units, adopted sales taxes or other substitute sources of revenue, exempted homesteads from the property tax,[6] set limits to property tax rates, and in various other ways tried to lighten the load of property taxes. Further, in some states or communities there was a definite purpose to keep tax rates low as an inducement to industry.

In 1932, the division of revenues between states and local governments in the South was 42 per cent to states and 58 per cent to the localities; in 1942, it was almost reversed—60 per cent to states and 40 per cent to local units. In the Non-South, states increased their share from 27 per cent in 1932 to 49 per cent in 1942. These are large changes indeed for one decade and indicate the rate at which local governments are becoming financially subordinate to, and dependent upon, the states.

Although state revenues had a greater percentage increase in the Non-South than in the South, total southern revenues increased by 61 per cent compared with 44 per cent for non-southern. This was true for two reasons; in the South, state revenues weighed more heavily at the beginning and local revenues increased by 11 per cent compared with a 1 per cent increase outside the South.

Highway Taxes. After their spectacular rise in the 1920's, revenues from highway taxes showed a much slower rate of growth after 1930. While motor fuel revenues continued upward at a reduced rate, motor vehicle revenues dropped sharply during the depression and did not regain their 1929 level until after 1942. During the depression, many states made drastic reductions in motor vehicle license fees, partly out of consideration for the motorists and partly with the thought that motor fuel revenues would be raised by allowing more cars to operate. In Georgia and Mississippi, fees were reduced to nominal amounts for passenger cars and have remained there. The sharp increase in motor vehicle revenues between 1942 and 1946 is a reflection partly of increased registration but perhaps more of the adoption of mileage taxes

[6] In 1942, eight of the 13 states which exempted or gave preferential treatment to homesteads were in the South. *Tax Systems,* Ninth Ed., Chicago, Commerce Clearing House, Inc., p. 169.

on common carriers. North Carolina, with a 6 per cent tax on gross receipts, has one of the highest taxes of this kind in the nation. Several other southern states have similar taxes with rates of 2 or 3 per cent.

During the 1930's, and again after World War II, southern states pushed up the rates on their motor fuel taxes ahead of the rest of the country. In 1949, the rates prevailing in the South and the Non-South were as follows:

Cents per Gallon	2	3	4	4½	5	5½	6	6½	7	9
Number of States levying:										
South	0	0	1	0	0	0	5	2	4	1
Non-South	1	4	12	1	8	1	7	1	1	0

These figures show that the typical or average tax in the southern states is about two cents per gallon more than in the rest of the country. Because of the lighter traffic in the South, the higher rate is necessary to provide anything approaching equality in road facilities.

World War II did not reduce motor fuel tax revenues as much as was expected. In the fiscal year 1942, revenues were slightly above 1941. In 1943, they dropped by 19 per cent in the South compared with 17 per cent elsewhere.[7] In 1948, they were about 38 per cent

TABLE *LXIII*   GENERAL REVENUES* OF STATE GOVERNMENTS IN THE SOUTH AND THE NON-SOUTH FOR SELECTED YEARS, 1929–1948

(Dollar Amounts Except Per Capita in Millions)

SOURCE OF REVENUE	SOUTH					NON-SOUTH				
	1929	1932	1937	1942	1948	1929	1932	1937	1942	1948
Taxes	402	392	674	1010	1753	1419	1498	2686	4005	6038
Grants from U. S.	28	56	132	182	412	91	172	433	627	987
Charges and Misc.	64	75	57	76	208	155	124	219	241	628
Total	494	523	863	1268	2373	1665	1794	3338	4873	7653
Indexes (1929 = 100):										
Taxes	100	98	168	251	436	100	106	189	282	426
Total Revenues	100	106	175	257	480	100	108	200	293	460
PERCENTAGE DISTRIBUTION										
Taxes	81.4	75.0	78.1	79.7	73.9	85.2	83.5	80.5	82.2	78.9
Grants from U. S.	5.7	10.7	15.3	14.4	17.4	5.5	9.6	13.0	12.9	12.9
Charges and Misc.	12.9	14.3	6.6	6.0	8.7	9.3	6.9	6.5	4.9	8.2
Total	100.0	100.0	100.0	100.0	100.0	100.0	100.0	100.0	100.0	100.0
PER CAPITA AMOUNTS										
Taxes	11.93	11.30	18.57	26.37	44.19	16.31	16.58	29.23	41.94	56.73
Total Revenues	14.66	15.07	23.77	33.10	59.81	19.14	19.87	36.32	51.04	71.89

* Include local shares of state-collected, locally shared taxes, but do not include earnings of trust and sinking funds.
SOURCE: Computed from reports of the Governments Division, Bureau of the Census.

[7] Martin, *op. cit.,* p. 12.

above the 1942 level in the South and about 31 per cent above that figure in the Non-South.

Sales Taxes. Mississippi's successful experiment with the general sales tax in 1930–32 provided the spark which touched off a wave of adoptions in the years immediately following. Despite that fact, however, southern states do not depend on that tax as heavily as do the other states. In 1948, it produced 11.5 per cent of total southern state revenues and almost twice that proportion of non-southern revenues. Heavy collections in the three big states of California, Illinois, and Michigan largely account for the difference.

The southern states have chosen to rely more heavily on special commodity or luxury taxes, especially those on soft drinks, tobacco products (mainly cigarettes) and alcoholic beverages. The cigarette tax has proven to be a steady and lucrative source of revenue and is fairly easily administered. Its use has spread steadily until now all southern states except the tobacco-producing states of North Carolina and Virginia employ it, together with 29 non-southern states. As with the motor fuel tax, the tendency has been to push up the rates as the tax demonstrated its ability to produce revenue. The typical rate now is probably three cents per package of 20, although several states have

TABLE *LXIV* PERCENTAGE DISTRIBUTION OF STATE TAX COLLECTIONS* IN THE SOUTH AND THE NON-SOUTH FOR SELECTED YEARS, 1929–1948

TAX SOURCE	SOUTH					NON-SOUTH				
	1929	1932	1937	1942	1948	1929	1932	1937	1942	1948
General Sales and Use	—	0.8	6.2	5.6	11.5	—	0.3	14.6	14.4	21.1
Motor Fuels	32.1	38.8	32.6	29.9	23.8	21.3	25.0	18.7	16.0	13.9
Alcoholic Beverages	—	—	3.6	5.6	6.8	—	0.1	5.6	5.0	5.1
Tobacco Products	(a)	3.3	4.2	4.1	5.9	(a)	0.4	2.0	2.2	3.9
Other Sales	(a)	6.4	4.7	5.6	6.9	(a)	10.4	5.1	5.0	7.0
Total Sales	(a)	49.3	51.3	50.8	54.9	(a)	36.2	46.0	42.6	51.0
Motor Vehicle Licenses	19.4	13.8	7.9	6.6	7.0	19.0	18.8	11.0	7.8	7.8
Other Licenses and Priv.	(a)	(a)	5.6	6.1	4.8	(a)	(a)	5.4	6.1	5.0
Individual Income	(a)	4.1	2.5	3.5	5.4	(a)	9.1	6.8	5.4	6.7
Corporation Income	(a)	(b)	3.7	5.5	7.5	(a)	(b)	4.9	5.4	7.5
Property	24.4	22.2	11.0	6.7	4.1	25.4	16.1	8.1	5.1	3.4
Death and Gift	1.7	1.3	1.5	1.1	1.0	10.0	9.5	3.9	2.5	2.7
Severance	(a)	3.1	5.9	4.6	6.4	(a)	0.5	0.3	0.4	0.3
Unemployment Compensation	—	—	8.2	13.1	8.3	—	—	10.9	23.6	15.1
Other Taxes	22.4	6.4	2.4	1.9	0.6	24.3	9.8	2.6	1.1	0.4
Total	100.0	100.0	100.0	100.0	100.0	100.0	100.0	100.0	100.0	100.0

* Includes local shares of state-collected, locally shared taxes.
(a) Included in "Other Taxes."
(b) Included in "Individual Income."
SOURCE: For 1932, computed from *Tax Yields, 1940*, published by Tax Institute, Inc.; for other years, computed from reports of Governments Division, Bureau of the Census.

a rate of four cents. Arkansas levies a tax of six cents and Louisiana leads the country with an eight-cent rate.

Revenues from the sale tax on alcoholic beverages have had a very rapid growth in the South. Despite lower incomes and the fact that many areas still have prohibition, per capita collections from this tax in the South (plus profits from state liquor monopolies in Alabama and Virginia) were almost equal to similar per capita figures in the rest of the nation; the figures for 1946 were $3.55 for the South and $3.78 for the Non-South. Florida, with $9.52, had a figure almost three times the national average while Virginia was second in the South with $6.69. Higher rates in the South are the principal explanation.

Despite the decline in the importance of the motor fuels tax, total sales taxes continue to produce well over half of all tax revenues for southern states. With non-southern states, the average is only slightly lower; it was 51 per cent in 1948.

Income Taxes. Southern states were fairly early to adopt the income tax. By 1929, eight of them were using it and since then three more have levied it, leaving only Florida and Texas, the two states which usually have highest per capita incomes, without it. Contrasted with 11 out of 13 southern states, only 23 of 35 non-southern states levy the tax.

The individual income taxes levied by southern states are not much different from those levied by other states. Personal exemptions are somewhat higher in the South. For example, in 1942 no southern state had an exemption for a single person of less than $1,000, but seven non-southern states had exemptions below that figure.[8] Six southern and six non-southern states had exemptions of more than $2,000 for heads of families. In 1947, Arkansas raised its exemptions, already well above the federal exemptions, to $2,500 for single persons and $3,500 for heads of families. Exemptions for dependents were continued at $400.[9] For a state with low incomes, that is going a long way toward repealing the income tax.[10] Rates on the income tax are about

8 Roy G. Blakey and Violet Johnson, *State Income Taxes,* Chicago, Commerce Clearing House, Inc., 1942, p. 35.
9 Wm. G. Herzel, "State Tax Legislation in 1947," *National Tax Journal,* Vol. I (March, 1948), p. 83.
10 As a result, in 1948 Arkansas collected only $2.6 million from its personal income tax—less than any other southern state which levies a general tax of this kind. South Carolina, with about the same population and only slightly more total income, collected $9.3 millions.

the same in southern as in non-southern states. On one point the southern states are less liberal with the taxpayer; five of the 11 states do not allow the deduction of federal income taxes in computing the state tax, while only six of the 23 non-southern states have such a feature. This has been a matter of considerable importance under the high federal tax rates of recent years. Some idea of the effect of the provision is afforded by a comparison of income tax revenues in Georgia, which allows deductions, and North Carolina, which does not. Between 1942 and 1946, personal income tax revenues in North Carolina increased by 160 per cent; in Georgia, by 52 per cent. There were no significant changes in rates or exemptions in either state.

Professor Blakey has computed the amount of income tax due on certain hypothetical incomes in various states in 1940.[11] For example, a married man with two dependent children and an income before exemptions and federal tax of $3,000 would have paid an income tax in only four southern states. The taxes would have ranged from $7.00 to $18.00 and would have averaged $12.50. The same man would have paid a tax in 20 non-southern states, ranging from $1.00 to $34.00 and averaging $13.19. For this same man with different amounts of income (before personal exemptions and federal tax), the average tax and the range would have been as follows:

		AVERAGE TAX	RANGE
$ 5,000	South	$ 46	$ 16–$ 84
	Non-South	56	17– 117
10,000	South	248	100– 416
	Non-South	235	67– 457
50,000	South	2,332	1,373– 3,445
	Non-South	2,101	819– 4,780
100,000	South	4,598	2,812– 7,436
	Non-South	4,079	1,652– 8,774

On smaller incomes, the average tax was lower in the South, probably due to the slightly higher personal exemptions. There are no substantial differences between the average rates until incomes get over $10,000, and the difference there was due in large part to the fact that half of the southern states did not allow the deduction of federal income taxes.

On an income of $100,000, the average tax in non-southern states was about 13 per cent higher. In all cases the range was greater in

11 Roy G. Blakey and Violet Johnson, *op. cit.,* pp. 39–41.

the non-southern states. In most states, progression stops before income reaches $50,000. In the above example, there was no progression between $50,000 and $100,000; in fact, in both regions the tax on the second $50,000 was slightly less than on the first $50,000. Again, this was due to the large number of states which allowed the deduction of federal taxes.

Rates on corporate income taxes are slightly higher in the South; the median rate among southern states is 4 per cent, while among the non-southern states it is 3 per cent. In both regions, revenues from the corporate tax amounted to 7.5 per cent of the total, but 11 of the 13 southern states use it while only 22 of the 35 non-southern states levy it. Such important industrial states as Illinois, Michigan, New Jersey, and Ohio do not use the tax.

Between 1932 and 1948, income tax revenues (personal and corporate) in the South rose from $16 million to $225, or by more than sixteenfold. In the Non-South the increase was from $136 million to $859 million, or more than sixfold. Personal income and death taxes are the two forms of taxation in which progressive rates can be applied. In the South they account for about 6 per cent of total revenues; in the Non-South, for about 10 per cent.

Other Taxes. Severance taxes are important sources of revenue in Louisana, Oklahoma, and Texas and are applied principally to oil, natural gas, and sulfur. These taxes are spreading slowly to other states. They can well be applied in several fields, especially to coal and timber lands as a substitute for the property tax. They are an essential part of a sound conservation program.

Distinctly business taxes, such as corporate franchise taxes and business privilege taxes, have not increased as fast as total revenues. Despite the South's reputation for using taxes of this kind, they do not contribute as large a proportion of total revenues to southern as to non-southern states.

Total Tax Revenues. Between 1929 and 1932, total tax revenues declined by 2 per cent in the South while they increased by 6 per cent elsewhere. This again indicates the greater severity of the depression in the South in the early years. By 1942, they were 151 per cent above the 1929 level in the South and up by 182 per cent in the Non-South. The gap was closed during the war years, and by 1948 the increase was 336 per cent for the South and 326 per cent for the Non-South.

EXPENDITURES

The Background. The decade of the 1920's was one of rapidly mount-
ing expenditures as well as revenues, both in the South and in the
nation as a whole. In fact, expenditures grew more rapidly than revenues, for in those booming years state and local governments added
almost a billion dollars a year to their debts. The increased borrowing
was especially pronounced in the South. The functions which were expanded most were those closely related to the capital outlays which
were financed by the borrowing; that is, highways, public schools, and
educational institutions.

The increase in highway expenditures was especially great. Between 1920 and 1929, expenditures for construction of state-administered highway systems in the South increased by 157 per cent, compared with an increase of 123 per cent outside the South. In the
same period, expenditures for maintenance multiplied more than 11
times in the South while they increased by 134 per cent in the Non-
South.[12]

While expenditures for other purposes did not keep pace with those
for highways, they were still quite large. Heer found that in North
Carolina, expenditures of tax funds by both state and local governments for educational institutions increased by 214 per cent between
1920 and 1929; for public schools, the increase was 141 per cent.[13]
In both cases the increases would have been larger if borrowed funds
had been included. Even the Civil War figured as a cause of increased
expenditures; most southern states increased their pensions to Confederate veterans and their dependents. Such payments reached a peak
around 1928 or 1929 at more than $19 million.[14]

Major Developments. The major developments affecting public expenditures of state and local governments in the South during the past
20 years are listed below. Most of these will be discussed in greater
details in following pages. (1) Total expenditures of states, except for
debt retirement, increased by 316 per cent between 1929 and 1948,
somewhat less than the increase outside the region. (2) There was
no significant change in local government expenditures between 1932
and 1942, either in the South or elsewhere. (3) In the South, state

[12] Public Roads Administration, *Highway Statistics; Summary to 1945*, pp. 44–47.
[13] Heer, *op. cit.*, p. 6.
[14] See B. U. Ratchford and K. C. Heise, "Confederate Pensions," *The Southern
Economic Journal*, Vol. V (Oct. 1938), p. 208.

expenditures for operations and aid to local governments increased
in about the same proportion; outside the South, aid to local governments increased much more. (4) After a dip in the early 1930's, state
expenditures for operations in the South rose substantially in relative
importance; outside the region, the dip came in the late 1930's and
early 1940's and by 1948 the ratio between the regions was the
same as in 1929. (5) Expenditures for interest have been relatively
more important in the South, but have declined in importance in both
regions. (6) State expenditures for highways have consistently been
of greater relative importance in the South but have steadily declined
in importance in both regions. (7) Southern state expenditures for
schools increased by more than fivefold and retained their relative
size while outside the region they increased by 240 per cent but
declined in relative importance. (8) In both regions, state expenditures for public welfare experienced the greatest increase, both absolutely and relatively. In the South the increase continued during the
war, while elsewhere it was reversed. (9) State contributions to trust
funds are relatively less important in the South both because of smaller
collections of the unemployment compensation tax and because southern states make smaller payments to retirement funds for employees.
(10) In 1948, the three functions of highways, schools, and public
welfare accounted (directly, through aid to local governments, and in
capital outlays) for about 71 per cent of the total expenditures of
southern states; for non-southern states, the ratio was approximately
52 per cent.

State and Local Relations. Southern states have tended to take over
certain governmental functions directly rather than to subsidize them
through aid to local governments. This tendency is strikingly illustrated by the action of North Carolina and Virginia in taking over
financial responsibility for all rural highways and North Carolina's
assumption of the responsibility for the basic public school program.
In the field of public welfare, too, especially with old-age assistance,
most southern states administer the program directly.[15] This tendency
accounts in large measure for the higher proportion of operating
expenditures and lower proportion of aid to local governments found
in the South.

15 In 1948, southern states spent $309 million, or 90.4 per cent, of their welfare
funds directly and gave $33 million as aid to local governments. Non-Southern
states spent $647 million, or 56.7 per cent, directly and granted $495 million to
local government.

Just why this tendency should obtain is not entirely clear. Two considerations may help to explain it. In the early 1930's, local governments in several southern states were in acute financial distress and heavily burdened with debt; the states had to do a very large rescue job in order to prevent serious deterioration of important governmental functions. With public welfare, it is probable that in most southern states there did not exist local administrative machinery adequate to meet federal standards and it was probably decided that a system of direct state administration could be established more quickly and more efficiently than the local system could be built up.

Since local expenditures remained approximately constant between 1932 and 1942 while state expenditures were increasing substantially, the latter increased greatly in relative importance. In the South, state expenditures (excluding aid to local governments) were about 54 per cent of total local expenditures; in 1942, the ratio was 111 per cent. For the Non-South, the figures were 27 per cent for 1932 and 59 per cent for 1942.[16]

TABLE *LXV* GENERAL EXPENDITURES OF STATE GOVERNMENTS IN THE SOUTH AND THE NON-SOUTH FOR SELECTED YEARS, 1929–1948

(*Dollar Amounts in Millions*)

TYPE OF EXPENDITURE	SOUTH					NON-SOUTH				
	1929	1932	1937	1942	1948	1929	1932	1937	1942	1948
Operations	210	217	343	465	1020	643	841	1131	1451	3331
Aid to Local Gov'ts.	131	153	203	305	641	417	611	1166	1485	2526
Capital Outlays	190	219	195	177	448	464	556	517	438	977
Interest	24	38	34	36	22	70	76	88	75	50
Contributions to Trust Funds and Pub. Serv. Enterprises	(a)	1	55	140	180	18	22	334	986	1027
Total Exc.Debt Retirement	555	628	830	1123	2311	1612	2106	3236	4435	7911
Indexes (1929 = 100):										
Operations	100	103	163	221	486	100	131	176	226	518
Aid to Local Gov'ts.	100	117	155	233	489	100	147	280	356	606
Total Exc. Debt Retirement	100	113	150	203	416	100	131	201	275	491
Per Capita Amounts (Dollars) Operations	6.23	6.25	9.45	10.81	25.71	7.39	9.31	12.30	15.19	31.29
Aid to Local Gov'ts.	3.89	4.41	5.59	7.96	16.16	4.79	6.77	12.68	15.55	23.73
Total Exc. Debt Retirement	16.47	18.10	22.87	29.35	58.22	18.52	23.32	35.21	46.44	74.32

(a) Less than $500,000.

SOURCE: Computed from reports of Governments Division, Bureau of the Census.

[16] Total local government expenditures were: South—1932, $882 million; 1942, $887 million; Non-South—1932, $5619 million; 1942, $5429 million. The 1932 figures are partly estimated and it is not possible to give an accurate breakdown of them.

Capital Outlays. Capital outlays have accounted for a higher proportion of total expenditures with southern than with non-southern states.
Several factors account for this. The functions which the states have
been taking over from local governments are those which involve
heavy capital outlays. Highways are an outstanding example. Further,
the South, during much of this period, has been striving to "catch-up"
—frequently with the aid of borrowing—on its governmental services
and this nearly always requires heavy outlays for physical plant.
Finally, it is probably true that there is a larger differential between salaries paid to governmental employees in southern and non-
southern states than there is between construction costs in the two
regions.

Highways. While operating expenditures for highways by southern
states increased from $54 million in 1929 to $147 million in 1946,

TABLE *LXVI*   PATTERNS OF STATE GOVERNMENT EXPENDITURES IN THE SOUTH
AND THE NON-SOUTH FOR SELECTED YEARS, 1929–1946

TYPE OF EXPENDITURE	PERCENTAGE DISTRIBUTION				
	1929	1932	1937	1942	1948
SOUTH					
Operations	37.8	34.6	41.3	41.4	44.2
Aid to Local Governments	23.6	24.4	24.5	27.1	27.7
Capital Outlays	34.2	34.9	23.5	15.7	19.4
Interest	4.3	6.3	4.1	3.2	0.9
Contributions Trust Funds	(a)	(a)	6.6	12.5	7.8
Total Exc. Debt Ret.	100.0	100.0	100.0	100.0	100.0
NON-SOUTH					
Operations	39.9	39.9	35.0	32.7	42.1
Aid to Local Governments	25.9	29.0	36.0	33.5	31.9
Capital Outlays	28.8	26.4	16.0	9.9	12.3
Interest	4.3	3.6	2.7	1.7	0.6
Contributions Trust Funds	1.1	1.0	10.3	22.2	13.0
Total Exc. Debt Ret.	100.0	100.0	100.0	100.0	100.0

(a) Less than 0.1 per cent.
SOURCE: Computed from reports of Governments Division, Bureau of the Census.

they did not keep pace with total expenditures and hence declined in
relative importance. The same trend existed in non-southern states,
although with them highway costs were never so important relatively.
One reason for the relative decline was that, as noted above, revenues
from the highway taxes did not keep pace with total revenues. Further,
in many states a substantial part of those revenues must go to service

debt incurred when the road system was being constructed. A larger reason, perhaps, is that once the basic network of highways is completed, the cost of maintaining it does not grow as fast as do the costs of other governmental functions; per unit operating costs should decrease rapidly as traffic increases.

The Bureau of Public Roads of the Federal Government has compiled construction and maintenance costs for state-administered highway systems by states for a number of years.[17] These data show that from 1922 through 1946, southern states spent $3.3 billion for construction, and $1.3 billion for maintenance of their highways. These figures were, respectively 28.9 and 28.0 per cent of the national totals. These ratios are remarkably close to the ratios of the land area of the country contained within the southern states.

At the end of 1946, the 13 southern states had 116,093 miles of surfaced highways in their primary systems of rural state highways. This was 36.5 per cent of the total for the country. The South's proportion of surfaced mileage is thus somewhat higher than its proportion of funds spent for construction. One reason for that is that southern states have a higher proportion of the narrower roads (less than 27 feet) and of the lower types of surfacing.[18]

Education. The great bulk of public expenditures for education is for the public schools, and these are shared in varying proportions between state and local governments. This discussion is based on data supplied by the U.S. Office of Education which combine state and local expenditures.[19] From 1927–28 to 1945–46, the South (state and local governments) increased current expenditures for public schools from $283 million to $555 million, or by 96 per cent. Outside the region, the increase was from $1,515 million to $2,152 million, or 42 per cent. Per pupil enrolled, the increase was from $34.29 per year to $72.21 per year in the South, or 110 per cent, and from $89.31 to $137.87 per year outside the South, or 54 per cent. All of these figures have risen considerably in the later postwar years, but complete data on them are not yet available. As noted elsewhere, total southern

17 See Note 12 above.
18 Southern states had 37.5 per cent of the roads less than 27 feet in width, but only 18 per cent of those 27 to 36 feet wide and 25 per cent of those over 36 feet wide.
19 See "Statistics of State School Systems" in the *Biennial Survey of Education in the United States.*

expenditures were equal to 1.78 per cent of income payments in the region, compared with a ratio of 1.71 per cent outside the region.

The expanded southern expenditures have brought improvements in a number of ways, some of which are difficult to measure quantitatively and others of which would require too much space for presentation here. As one example, the length of the school term has been increased substantially. In 1927–28, the average number of days attended by each pupil in the South was 112 (median of state averages), or 80 per cent of the national average. By 1945–46, it had risen to 144, or 96 per cent of the average for the whole country. Also, a larger proportion of the children of school age are now enrolled in the South.

Despite the progress which has been made, education is still far from adequate in the South. In 1945–46, total annual expenditures per pupil in average daily attendance varied from a low of $47.49 in Mississippi to a high of $134.41 in Texas, compared with a national average of $144.02. Only four southern states—Florida, Louisiana, Oklahoma, and Texas—had expenditures of more than $100. The crux of the problem is that the South has about a third of the nation's children of school age but slightly less than a fifth of the nation's payments out of which to pay for their education.

Public Welfare. State and local expenditures for public welfare have increased phenomenally in all parts of the United States during the past 20 years. In 1929, southern states made almost no payments for this purpose except for Confederate Pensions, which accounted for more than $19 million of the $21 million listed under this heading. In 1948, they spent $309 million, which was 30 per cent of all operating expenditures. This was a larger amount than was spent for any other purpose and a larger proportion than was spent by non-southern state.[20]

---

[20] Because of the erratic way in which expenditures for public welfare are divided between state and local governments from state to state, this does not tell the whole story. Two other measures are available. In 1942, as is shown in Table LXVIII, 8.8 per cent of *all* (not merely operating) expenditures of state and local governments in the South were for public welfare, compared with 12.9 per cent in the Non-South. For 1948, we can get a more accurate measure by combining state operating expenditures and aid to local governments. Of this combined total, 20.6 per cent went for public welfare in the South, compared with 39.0 per cent for schools and 14.6 per cent for highways. In the Non-South the ratios were 19.5 per cent for public welfare, 25.5 for schools, and 12.4 for highways.

Several aspects of public welfare expenditures are worthy of note. In the first place, a large part of the southern expenditures is concentrated in Oklahoma and Texas. In 1948, out of a total for the South of $342 million (direct state expenditures plus aid to local governments), those two states had $142 million, or 42 per cent. Over $115 million of the $142 million was for old-age assistance.

In the second place, public welfare expenditures continued to increase both absolutely and relatively in the South during the war. In the Non-South, there was some absolute increase but a relative decline. The reason was that before the war general assistance or relief payments were quite large outside the South. During the war those payments declined sharply. All states continued to increase their appropriations for other parts of the program in order to qualify for federal funds. Outside the South, that increase was largely offset by the decline in relief payments.

TABLE *LXVII*   EXPENDITURES FOR PUBLIC ASSISTANCE* IN THE SOUTH AND THE NON-SOUTH BY SOURCES OF FUNDS FOR SELECTED YEARS

(Amounts in Millions of Dollars)

	SOUTH			NON-SOUTH	
	AMOUNT	PER CENT DISTRI-BUTION	PER CENT OF U. S.	AMOUNT	PER CENT DISTRI-BUTION
*1937–38***					
Federal Funds	31	41.8	15.4	170	20.6
State Funds	43	58.2	6.1	658	79.4
Local Funds	—	—	—	—	—
Total Funds	74	100.0	21.5	828	100.0
1942					
Federal Funds	73	47.1	18.9	314	37.2
State Funds	72	46.4	16.7	359	42.6
Local Funds	10	6.5	5.6	170	20.2
Total Funds	155	100.0	41.2	843	100.0
1946					
Federal Funds	125	50.6	24.6	383	37.5
State Funds	109	44.2	18.0	496	48.5
Local Funds	13	5.2	8.3	143	14.0
Total Funds	247	100.0	50.9	1,022	100.0

* Includes old-age assistance, assistance to dependent children and the blind, and relief payments or general assistance.
** Includes only net disbursements to recipients; does not include any administrative costs. Includes only general assistance payments for Virginia; other assistance plans in that state had not been approved for federal participation in that year.
SOURCE: Computed from *Social Security Bulletin* and *Social Security Year Book.*

Total expenditures for four principal elements of the public welfare program, with the sources of the funds, are shown in Table *LXVII*. Several aspects are significant. Total expenditures in the South increased from 8.2 per cent of the national total in 1937–38, to 19.5 per cent in 1946. The latter proportion is about the same as the proportion of income payments in the South. The proportion of funds contributed by local governments has been very low throughout, while the proportion of federal funds has been high. The total of state and local funds in the South almost trebled, between 1937–38 and 1946, while elsewhere there was a small decline. This again reflects the great reduction in relief payments outside the South.

While the southern states have made large gains in public welfare expenditures, both absolutely and relatively, average payments are still low in relation to other states. In December, 1948, average monthly payments under four programs were as follows:[21]

PROGRAM	SOUTH	NON-SOUTH	U. S. AVERAGE
Old Age Assistance	$31.43	$48.53	$42.02
Aid to Children	17.76	33.65	28.11
Aid to Blind	33.40	49.20	43.54
General Assistance	22.65	51.87	47.37

Oklahoma and Louisiana showed payments above the national average in old-age assistance, and Oklahoma in aid to the blind. Otherwise, all states were below the national average in all categories. The differential was greatest in general relief, which does not receive federal funds. This, as well as the great increases made by the southern states, reflects the pressure to match federal grants.

While average payments were lower, participation rates in the southern states were higher than the national rate under each program except that for general assistance, where it was only about half as great. For example, under the old-age assistance program, the national participation rate in December, 1948 was 228 per 1,000 population aged 65 and over. Every southern state except Virginia (with 94) had a higher rate than that. The median rate in the South was 439. Louisiana was at the top with 791, while Georgia and Oklahoma had rates above 500. Outside the South, Colorado was the high state with a rate of 440, approximately equal to the median rate for the South, and only three other non-southern states had rates above 300.

[21] *Social Security Bulletin,* Feb., 1949, pp. 33–35.

The higher participation rate in the South almost offset the effect of the lower payments. For the month of December, 1948, expenditures per capita of total population for the four programs in the South amounted to $1.01 compared with $1.14 outside the South. For old-age assistance alone, the southern figure was higher by $0.76 to $0.70. Undoubtedly the need is considerably greater in the South and the coverage of the Old-Age Annuity and Insurance program is not as great in the region, but nevertheless it may be questioned, in the light of the above facts, whether the programs have been designed and administered with as much discrimination in southern as in non-southern states, and whether the southern states, with their limited means, should undertake such broad programs.

The above discussion of average payments was not meant to imply that average payments in the South should be as large as those in the Non-South. Considering prevailing levels of income, southern payments would be "at par" if they were about two-thirds as large as those in Non-South. Except for general relief, the South has a higher ratio in all of the welfare payments than it has in educational expenditures. With a limited amount of funds, it is difficult to decide between taking care of the aged, the poor, and the afflicted on one hand and training the children on the other; between succoring the weak and ineffective members of society at present and preparing the producers of the future.

Major State Expenditures by Functions. To get a more comprehensive view of the purposes for which states spend their funds, it is well to combine by functions the expenditures for operations, aid to local governments, and capital outlays. On this basis, three functions dominated all state expenditures in 1948, more so in the South than in the Non-South. The figures (in millions of dollars) and the percentages of total expenditures were:

	HIGHWAYS	SCHOOLS	PUBLIC WELFARE	TOTAL OF THREE FUNCTIONS
South	555	710	343	1641
Per Cent of Total	25.5	30.7	14.8	71.0
Non-South	1401	1603	1148	4152
Per Cent of Total	17.7	20.3	14.5	52.5

Combined State and Local Expenditures. Table *LXVIII* is a consolidation of state and local expenditures, excluding state aid to local gov-

TABLE *LXVIII* GENERAL EXPENDITURES OF COMBINED STATE AND LOCAL
GOVERNMENTS IN THE SOUTH AND THE NON-SOUTH, 1942

PURPOSE	AMOUNTS ($ MILLIONS)		PER CENT DISTRIBUTION		PER CAPITA IN DOLLARS	
	SOUTH	NON-SOUTH	SOUTH	NON-SOUTH	SOUTH	NON-SOUTH
General Control	124	544	7.1	6.6	3.24	5.70
Public Safety	103	654	5.9	7.9	2.69	6.85
Highways	168	639	9.7	7.7	4.39	6.69
Sanitation	24	167	1.4	2.0	0.63	1.75
Health and Hospitals	90	482	5.2	5.8	2.35	5.05
Public Welfare	153	1073	8.8	12.9	3.99	11.23
Schools	445	1920	25.7	23.1	11.62	20.10
Miscellaneous	100	529	5.8	6.4	2.61	5.54
Total Operations	1207	6009	69.6	72.4	31.51	62.91
Capital Outlay	244	773	14.1	9.3	6.37	8.09
Interest	138	378	7.9	4.6	3.60	3.96
Contributions to Trust Funds and Public Service Enterprises	145	1140	8.4	13.7	3.79	11.93
Total Excluding Debt Retirement	1734	8299	100.0	100.0	45.28	86.89

SOURCE: Computed from Revised data published by Governments Division, Bureau of
the Census.

ernments, for 1942. The distinctive features discussed above are
present here but usually they are not so pronounced as they are with
state expenditures alone. The great increases in state spending in
recent years have been largely concentrated in a few fields to meet
needs which have developed or expanded greatly in the past two or
three decades. Local expenditures, especially in the South, still have
much the same pattern as they had 20 years ago. When the two are
combined the sharp differences produced by the past 20 years are
reduced and interregional differentials less well defined.

Relation of Expenditures to Revenues. A comparison of Tables *LXIII*
and *LXV* shows that general expenditures (except debt retirement)
of southern states exceeded their general revenues by considerable
margins in 1929 and 1932. The 1929 over-all deficit was probably
due to the fact that many states were borrowing heavily for capital
improvement programs, while the 1932 deficit was principally due to
current operating deficits which were general throughout the region.
Non-southern states as a group had a deficit only in 1932. In 1937,
revenues and expenditures were fairly well balanced, but in 1942 and
1946, revenues exceeded expenditures by wide margins. The surpluses,

caused to a considerable extent by the enforced reduction of capital outlays, were used to pay off debt, build up sinking funds, and to establish postwar reserve funds. In 1948, southern state revenues exceeded expenditures by a small margin, but outside the region there was a deficit of over $250 million.

TABLE *LXIX*   STATE AND LOCAL GOVERNMENT EMPLOYMENT AND PAYROLLS IN THE SOUTH AND THE NON-SOUTH, 1941, 1944, AND 1947

	JANUARY 1941	APRIL 1944	JANUARY 1947
Employment (in thousands):			
South	738	742	837
Per Cent of U. S.	22.8	23.3	23.3
Non-South	2,504	2,444	2,758
Monthly Payrolls (in millions of dollars):			
South	63	73	115
Per Cent of U. S.	16.5	17.7	19.0
Non-South	318	339	489
Average Monthly Salary Per Employee:			
South	$ 83.37	$ 98.38	$137.40
Non-South	$127.00	$138.71	$177.30

Number of State and Local Employees per 1,000 Inhabitants, January, 1947

	SCHOOL EMPLOYEES	NONSCHOOL EMPLOYEES	TOTAL EMPLOYEES
United States Average	11.5	16.7	28.2
South—Median of State Averages	11.6	10.9	22.2

SOURCE: Computed from Bureau of the Census, *Government Employment.*

Government Employment. Since 1941 the Bureau of the Census has compiled data on the employees and payrolls of state and local governments. The South has about 23 per cent of the total of such employment for the country, a ratio somewhat less than the region's ratio of population (see Table *LXIX*). This difference is even more pronounced among nonschool employees. In January, 1947, the South had about the same number of school employees per 1,000 population as the country as a whole. (Per 1,000 school children, however, the ratio in the South would be somewhat lower.) But in nonschool employees, the region had only about two-thirds as many governmental employees per 1,000 population as the nation as a whole. On this point, Florida was the only state with a figure above the national average, and its figure was twice the median for the region.

In 1941, the average monthly salary of southern employees was not quite two-thirds the average salary of non-southern employees.[22] By January, 1947, the average salary in the South had risen by $54, or about 65 per cent, while in the Non-South the increase was about $50, or 40 per cent. This is an additional indication of two trends in wages and salaries during the war period; namely, the tendency for the lower wages and salaries to rise more proportionately than higher ones and the tendency for interregional differentials to decline.

DEBTS

Background. For several decades before 1912, state and local debts in the South had been in line with the region's wealth and income.[23] In the two decades which followed, however, southern units borrowed much more rapidly than the rest of the country and accumulated a debt load out of proportion to their wealth and resources. The figures for the debts (gross debts less sinking funds assets) of state and local governments combined on three dates for the South and Non-South were, in millions of dollars, as follows:

	1922	1932	1942
SOUTH	1603	3890	3590
NON-SOUTH	7087	13687	13730

Between 1922 and 1932, debts in the South increased by 143 per cent while elsewhere the increase was only 93 per cent. In 1932, the South had about 22 per cent of total state and local debts but the region was receiving only about 15 per cent of the nation's income payments. This was to spell trouble.

Debt Changes. In 1929, the period of heavy borrowing was drawing to a close and the South was facing, unknown to it at the time, the most troublesome period with its debts since Reconstruction days. Borrowing by local governments came to a sudden halt and was not resumed on any considerable scale until after 1945. Between 1932

---

22 Computed by dividing number of employees at the end of the month into the pay roll for the month. This understates the average salary in both regions slightly because of part-time workers, but this discrepancy is not material.
23 For a general discussion of debts in the South for the period immediately preceding 1936, see B. U. Ratchford, "Public Debts in the South," *The Southern Economic Journal,* Vol. II (Jan., 1936), pp. 13–25.

and 1942, combined state and local debts in the South declined by $300 million or 7.7 per cent; outside the South there was practically no change.

State governments continued to borrow, in the early 1930's partly to cover operating deficits, until 1940. For southern states, total debts in 1942 were just about twice the amount outstanding in 1929 (see Table *LXX*). After 1940, state debts declined, slowly at first and then quite rapidly during the war as revenues mounted and capital outlays were sharply curtailed. From 1932 to 1946, per capita debts were substantially higher in the South than in the Non-South.

TABLE *LXX* NET LONG-TERM DEBTS OF STATES IN THE SOUTH AND THE NON-SOUTH FOR SELECTED YEARS, 1929–1947

	SOUTH			NON-SOUTH	
YEAR	AMOUNT IN $ MILLIONS	PER CAPITA	PER CENT OF U. S.	AMOUNT IN $ MILLIONS	PER CAPITA
1929	433	$12.86	28.4	1,095	$12.58
1932	687	19.80	31.9	1,466	16.24
1937	834	22.96	33.3	1,668	18.13
1942	873	22.80	33.3	1,747	18.29
1944	695	18.30	33.1	1,405	14.86
1946	579	15.15	33.3	1,159	11.40
1947	601	15.51	27.1	1,690	16.15
1948	601	15.15	23.1	1,996	18.75

SOURCE: Computed from reports of Bureau of the Census.

The fiscal year 1947 marked a sharp reversal of trend and gave the South a slightly lower per capita figure. Debts of non-southern states jumped by $531 million, or 46 per cent, while the increase in southern states was only $22 million or less than 4 per cent. The explanation was heavy borrowing by a few non-southern states in order to pay veterans' bonuses. The new trend continued in 1948.

More than half (58.2 per cent) of the debts of southern states outstanding in 1942 had been incurred for highways, 7.7 per cent for schools, and the remainder for a variety of purposes and for refunding. The distribution for non-southern states was not essentially different.

Forms of Borrowing. During the past 25 or 30 years, governmental units, especially states, have developed a number of new ways of borrowing funds. These usually involve the issue of revenue bonds by some department, agency, or institution of the state, based on some source of revenue but not carrying the pledge of the state. The purpose is usually to avoid constitutional debt limitations.[24]

Several of these forms pertain to highways. Several states, such as Florida and Texas, have indirectly assumed local highway debts by allocating a part of the proceeds from the motor fuels tax to local units, with varying directions that it be used for debt service. Other states, such as Georgia, Arkansas, and Tennessee, have directly assumed local highway debts. The Georgia assumption was by constitutional amendment, but some courts have held that such an increase in the state debt is not covered by constitutional prohibitions. In other states, such as Alabama and Kentucky, state highway departments or specially-constituted authorities have issued revenue bonds to build bridges, the debts to be serviced from tolls.

In a number of states, including 11 southern states, educational institutions have issued revenue bonds to build dormitories, dining halls, etc., the bonds to be serviced by rentals or profits. In 1940, the total of such debts in southern states amounted to $40.9 million out of a total for the nation of $74.6.[25]

The total of indirect, revenue obligations of states and state agencies in 1940 was about $1,120 million, of which some $700 million were serviced directly from the funds of states or state agencies. About $300 million, or 43 per cent of this $700 million, were in the South.

The latest form of revenue obligations is illustrated by an issue of $15 million sold by New Orleans in April, 1948. The city sold tax-exempt bonds and reloaned the proceeds to finance the construction of a union station and the elimination of grade crossings. The bonds are to be serviced from rentals paid by the participating railroads.[26] This may represent the beginning of a new method of financing.

Defaults. By far the most significant development affecting debts in this period was the wave of defaults which reached epidemic proportions in the early 1930's, subsided somewhat during the latter part of the decade, and dropped sharply during the war. The movement had its beginning in Florida following the collapse of the wild land

---

[24] For a fuller discussion see B. U. Ratchford, "New Forms of State Debts," *The Southern Economic Journal,* Vol. VIII (Apr., 1942), pp. 459–78.
[25] *Ibid,* p. 469.
[26] *The New York Times,* April 25, 1948, Sec. 3, p. 1.

boom in 1926, and that state has led throughout in the number and extent of defaults. With the onset of the Great Depression, it spread rapidly to other states, especially those in which local government units had borrowed most heavily, such as Arkansas, Louisiana, North Carolina, and Texas. The South, with only about 16 per cent of the nation's governmental units (24,522 units out of 155,116 in 1942), had a large majority of the defaulting units throughout the period. On January 1, 1936, when the number of defaults was near its peak, the South had 1,950; the Non-South, 1,209. On January 1, 1942, the figures were, respectively, 552 and 336. By January 1, 1948, the figures were down to 160 and 81.[27]

In 1935, the four states of Arkansas, Florida, Louisiana, and North Carolina had about 45 per cent of all defaults in the United States. In 1932, these four states had 9.5 per cent of all state and local debts in the country, but only 3.7 per cent of the estimated wealth, 3.7 per cent of income payments, and 4.4 per cent of retail sales.[28] In comparison with the country as a whole, their debt was more than twice as great as their resources for carrying it.

A comprehensive discussion of the causes of such widespread defaults would require a volume. Below are listed some of them. Overborrowing for rural highways, irrigation and drainage districts, and urban improvements was the most obvious cause. This, in turn, had been brought about by the growing number of automobiles and rapid urbanization. The "New Era" philosophy of the 1920's, which did not recognize the possibility of a future depression, had its effects on both the borrowing and lending sides. Wild real estate speculation in Florida, western North Carolina, and some other places added its contribution. Then came the drastic deflation of the early 1930's; prices of farm commodities went down and down, land values collapsed, tax delinquencies mounted, real estate mortgages were defaulted by the thousands and local governments were hard pressed to meet their most essential operating expenses.

To facilitate the readjustment of defaulted debts, the Federal Government enacted a Municipal Bankruptcy Act. The first law, passed in 1934, was held unconstitutional and a second act was passed in

[27] These figures are from a series compiled and published by *The Bond Buyer*. See annual volumes titled *Municipal Bond Sales*.
[28] See work cited in note 23.

1937. This act was upheld by the Supreme Court in 1938 and it probably was responsible in large measure for the large number of units which adjusted their debts and came off the default list in 1939.

In passing, it should be noted that some local units benefited substantially by defaulting. A large majority of municipal bonds are non-callable and had been issued during the 1920's at comparatively high rates of interest. When interest rates declined in the 1930's, most units could not take advantage of the low rates. But if a unit was badly in arrears on its debt service, the whole debt, or a large part of it, was frequently refunded. Callable bonds were often used in such refunding. After a year or two, many of the units got back into good financial condition and were able to call their bonds and refund them at lower rates of interest. Thus today many units which defaulted are enjoying lower interest rates than their neighboring units which have regularly met their obligations.

Only two states are listed as having defaulted during the 1930's— both of them in the South. South Carolina was in technical default for a time, but later made all payments in full without any adjustment. Arkansas defaulted in August, 1932. The state attempted to push through a refunding plan which would have imposed considerable sacrifices on bondholders. This was successfully resisted and a second refunding act was passed in 1934. This was accepted by the bondholders and the state came out of default in 1935. Bondholders suffered no loss in principal but took some reduction in interest.[29]

Debt Management. The large number of defaults by local units naturally directed attention toward the controls and limitations which all states impose on local borrowing. North Carolina was one of the few states to initiate a thorough reform on this point. It set up a Local Government Commission which has considerable discretionary power to supervise all aspects of local debts. The Commission must examine and approve all bond and note issues of local units (in certain cases its decisions can be reversed by a popular vote); it advertises and sells the obligations and transmits the funds to the local units; it supervises the levying of taxes and the collection and transmission of funds for debt service. It gave substantial aid and advice to defaulting units in working out readjustments of their debts. This reform has

---

[29] For details, see B. U. Ratchford, *American State Debts,* Durham, Duke University Press, 1941, Chap. XV.

been recognized as one of the outstanding contributions to the technique of state control of local borrowing in recent years.[30]

In the management of their own debts, the states suffered heavily from their lack of foresight during the 1920's. Most of the bonds had been issued with comparatively high interest rates and were noncallable. During the 1930's, federal income tax rates rose sharply and interest rates declined greatly. By 1936, good state bonds could be sold at interest rates no more than half those which prevailed during the 1920's. But the states could not take advantage of this situation by refunding their bonds, as most private debtors could and did. Further, the noncallable bonds made the debts inflexible so that they could not be adjusted to meet other changing conditions. For example, on occasions Tennessee had funds accumulated sufficient to pay off considerable amounts of its debts, parts of which bore 6 per cent interest, but the bonds could not be redeemed; the state had to continue to pay 6 per cent on its obligations and invest the accumulated funds at 1 per cent. In 1945, North Carolina had a surplus in its General Fund sufficient to pay off its entire General Fund Debt— more than $50 million. The funds had to be invested in federal obligations to yield from 1 to 1.5 per cent while the state continued to pay from 4 to 5 per cent on much of its debt.[31] There are no indications that the states have profited from this costly lesson in debt management.

TAX AND DEBT LOADS

The burden represented by debts and taxes is greatly affected by ability to pay. Dr. Wylie Kilpatrick, formerly of the Bureau of the Census, has computed for the different states some indexes which indicate the relative burden of debts, debt service, and general revenues of state and local governments combined in 1942. He did this by first computing index numbers representing ability to pay based upon per

[30] For further discussion see B. U. Ratchford, "The Work of the North Carolina Local Government Commission," *National Municipal Review,* Vol. XV (June, 1936), pp. 323–27; and J. W. Fesler, "North Carolina's Local Government Commission," *Ibid.,* Vol. XXX (June, 1941), pp. 330 ff.

[31] In 1944, North Carolina 5 per cent bonds were selling in the market as high as 150. If an individual had bought $100,000 of such bonds at par when they were issued in the 1920's, he would have had a tax-exempt income of $5,000 per year for the whole period, would have paid no taxes from it to help finance the war, and would have had a paper profit of 50 per cent in 1944.

capita income payments in the years 1929, 1935, 1940, and 1942, with the United States average as 100. Thus, if in State A, average per capita income payments were three fourths of the average for the whole country, the index of ability to pay for that state would be 75. Similar per capita indexes were computed for general long-termed debt, for general debt service, and for general revenue. The indexes of burden were then computed by dividing the index of ability into the indexes for debt, debt service and for general revenues and multiplying the results by 100. Thus, for example, if State A had per capita state and local debts equal to twice the national average, its debt index would be 200. Its index of debt burden would then be 200 divided by its index of ability (75), times 100, or 267 (200 ÷ 75 × 100). Average burdens for the South and the Non-South (medians of state figures) were as follows:

	GENERAL LONG-TERM DEBT	GENERAL DEBT SERVICE	GENERAL REVENUES
South	150	137	102
Non-South	77	84	103

According to these figures, the burden of state and local debts, in relation to income, was almost twice as heavy in the South as in the Non-South. Five states in the whole country had index numbers of 200 or more; they were Florida (269), Arkansas (242), Louisiana (212), Tennessee (202), and Mississippi (200). Three other southern states and three non-southern states had index numbers between 150 and 200. Only four southern states had burdens below the average for the country: Georgia (54), Kentucky (65), Virginia (81), and Oklahoma (88).

In almost every case, southern states had lower index numbers for debt service than for debts. Since they did not enjoy lower interest rates on their debts, that must mean that they were making less provision for debt retirement.

There was no appreciable difference in the burden of general revenues between southern and non-southern states. In other words, revenues were in about the same proportion as income payments in the two regions. But since a substantially greater proportion of those revenues had to go for debt service in the southern states, those governments had a smaller part of them left to meet current needs. Finally, in terms of the real or "psychic" burden, general revenues which represented the same proportion of income payments may well have been somewhat more burdensome to southern taxpayers with their substantially lower level of incomes.

THE IMPACT OF FEDERAL FINANCES

The previous pages have dealt with the finances of the state and local governments. But today federal finances overshadow state and local finances in most respects. This brief survey would not be complete without some attention to the South's share in the nation's finances.

Tax Collections. Although data are available by states on federal collections of internal revenue taxes, they do not accurately measure the burden of federal taxes. First, many of the large southern industrial plants are owned by companies which have their headquarters and pay their taxes outside the region. Second, a large part of the collections in the South are excise taxes on tobacco which are shifted to the consumers throughout the country.[32] But as they stand, these data show that in 1940, federal tax collections in the South amounted to $1,104 million, or 20.7 per cent of the national total. This proportion declined steadily until 1945, when it reached 13.7 per cent; it then rose to 14.8 per cent in 1946 and 16.0 per cent in 1948, when collections amounted to $6,700 million. Two factors which help to account for the rise in recent years are the repeal of the excess profit tax, of which the South never had any large part, and a greater increase in collections from the individual income tax in the South than in the Non-South.

With the statistics now available, individual income tax collections provide the best measure of the federal tax burden of a region. Those taxes are usually paid where the income is earned, there is little if any shifting, and this tax now accounts for more than half of all federal tax revenue. Between 1940 and 1948, individual income taxes paid in the South rose from $115 million to $2,828 million, for an increase of 2,459 per cent compared with an increase of 2,096 per cent outside the South. From 1945 to 1948, the increase was 17.6 per cent in the South and 9.3 per cent in the Non-South. As percentages of national totals, the rise was from 11.7 in 1940 to 12.6 in 1945 to 13.5 in 1948.

The drastic reduction in personal exemptions under the income tax

[32] It is true that these are offset partly or entirely by excise taxes on manufactured goods bought by southerners from outside the region.

during the war made the tax one of general application in the South for the first time. Before that time the tax had been paid by only 3 or 4 per cent of the population. Since the war, most of the changes in federal tax laws have benefited the South less than the rest of the country. The repeal of the excess profits tax helped the South relatively little because of the low level of industry in the region; the income-splitting and estate-splitting provisions of the Revenue Act of 1948 were of relatively little significance because of the low levels of income and estates and because three southern states already enjoyed those features through community property laws. The increase of personal exemptions from $500 to $600 in 1948 was of real help to the South. At the present time, there are valid reasons, on a national basis, for raising personal exemptions to the point where they will be equal in purchasing power to the levels prevailing during the war. Such a change would have special significance in the South; it would increase the consumer's purchasing power and would enable the low income of the region to support a slightly higher standard of living.

Although it is a very rough estimate, we may hazard the guess that the South now pays about 15 to 18 per cent of all federal taxes in the country.

Federal Expenditures in the South. Data indicating total federal expenditures in the South are no better than those indicating total tax payments. Payments in the nature of grants-in-aid and benefits to individuals are usually distributed geographically roughly in proportion to population and other physical factors. Of such payments, the South usually receives around 30 per cent. In 1948, the Secretary of the Treasury listed the distribution by states of some $5½ billion of such payments; southern states received 31.3 per cent of the total.[33] On the other hand, the South probably did not receive more than 15 per cent of the interest payments on the federal debt. The region's share of the federal funds spent for manufactured goods would also be low. The ratio would be somewhat higher with military expenditures for installation and pay of personnel.

Again, as a very rough estimate, federal expenditures in the South may be put at from 20 to 25 per cent of the total, or from 5 to 8

[33] *Annual Report of the Secretary of the Treasury,* 1948, pp. 614–22.

percentage points above the ratio of tax collections in the region. With a federal budget in the area of $40 billion, this would indicate that the region gains from $2 billion to $3 billion per year from the financial operations of the Federal Government.

Grants-in-Aid. In the fiscal year 1948, state and local governments in the South received approximately $475 million in grants from the Federal Government. Of these, $156 million were for old-age assistance and $105 million for highways—a total of $261 million, or 55 per cent of the total. Of the old-age assistance grants, three states— Florida, Oklahoma, and Texas—received $85.6 million, or 55 per cent of the total. Those states had about 30 per cent of the southern population and usually have the highest per capita incomes, but they received over half of the federal grants for this purpose.

This fact calls attention to the dilemma which many southern states face in respect to federal grants. Roughly half (on the basis of expenditures) of the federal grants are for alleviative or humanitarian purposes—designed to provide aid for the unfortunate and, usually, nonproductive members of society. This is a commendable purpose and southern states would like to take full advantage of all federal funds available. But, as was indicated above, at some point they must make the hard choice between more funds for this group and more funds for educating and training the young. The fact that their "humanitarian" dollars will be accompanied by federal funds and will thus go farther puts pressure on the legislators to spend more money in that direction; very few federal funds are available for resources development and public school education generally. The effects of this pressure are also evident in the low level of spending in the South for general relief, for which no federal funds are available.

Poorer states have been helped by a 1946 amendment to the Social Security Act which provided that for old-age assistance and aid to the blind, the federal share would be two thirds (instead of one half) of the first $15 of monthly payments and one half of the balance of matchable expenditures. For aid to dependent children, it was two thirds of the first $9 plus one half of the balance. In view of the change in prices since that time, it would seem that it might be appropriate to double those figures now, making the federal share two thirds of the first $30 and $18, respectively, and one half of the balance of matchable expenditures. This would provide a minimum national standard which would certainly not be too high for any region, would require the states to contribute something towards that minimum, and would encourage them to go beyond that level.

Federal Aid to Education. The area in which the South most needs assistance is that of public school education. The case for federal aid in that field may be stated briefly as follows: with a third of the nation's children, the region has only a fifth of the nation's income. Although the region is making as great an effort as the rest of the country in relation to income, facilities are still far from adequate. Further, the nation as a whole has a special interest in education in the South because of the heavy tide of migration which normally flows out of the region and into the rest of the country. These are valid and important considerations; in the absence of strong counter arguments they would be decisive.

The case against federal aid rests primarily on two points. First, political considerations will require that the total amount of aid be larger than that required for equalization purposes alone. It will have to be large enough to provide some payment for every state. Once aid is begun, there will be an inevitable tendency for it to grow over the years until it becomes a major portion of all school funds. A huge school fund distributed from Washington will invite pressure-group tactics and manipulation and may eventually put public school organizations into federal politics.

Second, substantial federal aid will inevitably bring federal control of educational policy. Despite all assurances to the contrary, when federal aid is firmly established, that system will be used to improve the educational practices of "backward" areas by bringing to them the most "progressive and enlightened" methods, texts, and doctrines. The South will be especially affected by one change which, it can confidently be predicted, will be proposed and perhaps adopted—to require the abolition of racial segregation in order to qualify for federal aid. One such amendment was proposed but defeated during the debate on the Education Aid Bill in the Senate early in May, 1949.[34] Even if such a requirement is not written into the law, there is always the chance that it will be proclaimed and enforced by administrative action, as was done in the case of federal aid to housing in the fall of 1949. Southern states will not accept such a condition now nor for many year to come, if ever. If a bitter fight should develop over such

34 *The New York Times,* May 4, 1949, p. 22.

an issue as this and if federal aid to public schools should be cut off as a result, it would be far worse than if no such aid had ever been provided.

There is urgent need for federal aid to public education in the South. If and when such aid is provided, every possible precaution should be taken to prevent the amount from growing to enormous size and to prevent the system from being used as an instrument of social reform by any group which can capture enough votes in Congress or influence administrative decisions. Congress should prescribe the formula to govern the distribution of the funds, require the Treasury Department to make the allocations, strictly limit the personnel and pay of the unit making the allocations, and carefully limit the imposition of any requirements in order to qualify for the funds.

X NATURAL RESOURCES AND POLICY

In a region such as the South, which suffers from low income, the utilization of natural resources is of special importance. In other chapters of this book we discuss the South's agricultural and forest resources and suggest policies for their most effective use. In this chapter we shall be concerned with the water and mineral resources of the region.

WATER RESOURCES

Water resources take a variety of forms and are put to many different uses. In form they may appear as the ocean water surrounding the area, inland lakes (natural or artificial), streams, or subsurface water. They may be used as a highway for commerce, as a site for recreation, as a source of food, as a source of power, as a raw material for industry and agriculture, and, last but by no means least, as a most basic and essential household commodity. Like most other basic and powerful forces, they are not an unmixed blessing. They may appear as a destructive force when they erode the soil, cause flood damage, or cover fertile soils to produce swamps and marshes.

In one short section of a chapter it is not possible to deal with all phases of water resources. Elsewhere we touch upon the problem of soil erosion. Flood control is a major problem in some areas and affects nearly all uses of water resources; we touch upon it elsewhere and give some attention to it here, but will not deal with it as a separate question. The problems of water supplies for irrigation and the maintenance of the ground water level are especially important problems in Oklahoma and Texas but they cannot be discussed separately here. The possibilities of more intensive use of water resources for recreation purposes and the potentialities of commercial fisheries and the production of seafood are topics worthy of special studies but cannot be explored at this point. The region's facilities for the use of intercoastal and ocean shipping are equally attractive as a subject of investigation but it does not seem feasible to consider them here. Rather, we have limited our discussion to three major phases of the problem of water resources: water power, inland navigation facilities, and the supply of water for industrial and residential purposes.

The pattern or framework of the water resources for most of the region is set by the topographical "backbone" which is the southern Appalachian Mountains. These mountains extend down through Virginia, Kentucky, Tennessee, North Carolina, and into northern Georgia and Alabama. This mountainous area has a heavy rainfall, amounting in some places to more than 80 inches per year. As this large volume of water flows down to the Atlantic Ocean and the Gulf of Mexico it creates a great power potential and provides abundant supplies of water for industrial and municipal purposes, but it also erodes the soil and often causes floods and limits the possibilities of navigation.

Water Power. For more than 30 years the South has been aggressively developing and using its water power potential. For example, in the eight years between November, 1921, and January, 1930, installed hydroelectric generating capacity in the South increased by 156 per cent, compared with an increase of 58 per cent in the Non-South.[1] In other words, the rate of increase in the South was almost three times the rate in the rest of the country. During those years the region's portion of the national total rose from one sixth to almost one fourth. Table *XLVI* shows that from 1929 to 1946 the growth continued, both absolutely and relatively, although at a considerably reduced rate. In those 17 years hydroelectric generating capacity in the South increased by 111 per cent compared with an increase of 72 per cent in the Non-South, giving the region 30 per cent of the nation's capacity in 1946. At the present time the South is probably using a larger proportion of its potential water power than any other large section of the country.

This large-scale development of water power has produced tangible benefits in the form of abundant supplies of electric energy and lower rates, and has been a significant factor in the rapid industrial de-

1 Bureau of Census, *Statistical Abstract of the United States*, 1930, p. 374.

velopment of the region. In 1947, manufacturing plants in the South purchased electric energy at an average cost of 0.72 cents per kilowatt-hour compared with an average of 0.99 cents in the Non-South.[2] The influence of TVA policy has undoubtedly been an important, but not the only, factor in producing the low rates in the South.

Two sets of circumstances—one technological and the other political—make difficult the formulation of any state or regional policy in relation to water power resources. Among the technological considerations there is the fact that quite likely the best and most accessible sites have already been developed. Proposals for developing remaining sites will have to be screened carefully to see that power can be produced economically, that the distance to markets is not too great, and so on. On the other hand, there is the fact that in some cases new products and new techniques of production in recent years have given industries more latitude in their choice of locations. It may now be feasible to locate large plants close to water power which heretofore could not be developed economically. Water power resources should be restudied periodically in the light of changing techniques of production.

In the political field, there is much confusion and overlapping of federal, state, and private interests in water power. Just now the Federal Government exercises the dominant authority in respect to many sources of water power.

Private utility companies are virtually precluded from developing new sites in major portions of the nation because of Federal competition. The Federal Power Commission has demonstrated a reluctance to issue license for private companies to build at sites where Federal agencies are contemplating construction, and private capital has demonstrated a reluctance to make heavy investments in areas where the Federal Government may establish a competitive project.

Present plans for federally operated transmission systems indicate a tendency to duplicate and compete with those operated by private companies.[3]

---

[2] *Census of Manufactures*, 1947, "Fuels and Electric Energy Consumed" (Preliminary Report, November 18, 1949), pp. 4–5. The southern figure was affected considerably by the very low averages of Tennessee and Alabama; if these two states are eliminated, the average for the South becomes 0.87 cents per KWH. Only two states in the South had averages above one cent per KWH—Arkansas with 1.01 and Virginia with 1.02. In the four leading industrial states of Illinois, Michigan, Ohio, and Pennsylvania, the averages varied from 1.00 cents to 1.15 cents per KWH.
[3] The Commission on Organization of the Executive Branch of the Government, *Task Force Report on Water Resources Projects* (Appendix K), Washington, 1948, p. 8.

Obviously a situation of this kind does not encourage the rapid development of water power. It would be helpful if the Federal Government would indicate the extent of its interests and intentions in the matter of water power development and give states, municipalities, and private interests free access to the remaining resources.

Inland Navigation. Ready access to good water transportation is an important economic advantage to any region. Water transportation is slower, but considerably cheaper, than land transportation. So the heavy, staple, and relatively cheap commodities, with which speed is not essential, are likely to move by water when facilities are available. As was noted earlier, the South has over 60 per cent of the nation's navigable waterways. These have been of considerable advantage to the region in moving such commodities as cotton, lumber, crude oils, coal, and ores. Where water shipping facilities can be extended or improved without undue cost it may be advantageous to do so. For example, it is sometimes possible to improve navigation facilities at moderate cost in connection with water power or flood control projects.

There are, however, many misconceptions and illusions about water transportation. Modern industry demands speed and flexibility in its transportation facilities and water transport cannot provide these. Some of the newer industries are not so closely tied down by transportation requirements; they range farther afield to find their locations and so are not so likely to be situated where they can use water transportation. This is especially true of those industries which produce the relatively lighter, more highly processed, and more valuable commodities which the South needs to produce—and which it is producing more and more.

But perhaps the greatest illusion respecting water transportation has to do with its cost. There is one line of reasoning which implies that water transportation is more economical under any and all circumstances, regardless of the cost which might be required to construct and maintain the waterways; in other words, that there is something magical about water transportation. The reason is fairly obvious; the cost of building and maintaining the waterways is nearly always borne by governmental bodies, while the benefits of the low cost of actually moving the goods accrue to the advantage of private companies. Unless a given project will result in a substantially lower *total* cost (public and private) of transportation for a large area of the public, there is no more reason to subsidize water transportation than there is to subsidize any other form of transportation.

The Tennessee Valley Authority estimated that in 1947 the users of its navigation channel realized freight savings of "about $3,000,000, or about a third those foreseen when traffic reaches full development on the new channel." During the fiscal year 1947, the Authority listed "Net expense of navigation operations" amounting to $2,955,989.[4] This left nothing as a return on the approximately $140 million of cost which had been allocated to the construction of navigation facilities. If the ultimate goal of $9 million of savings is realized, it is probable that that sum will be approximated, if not equaled, by annual cost, including operating expenses and a fair return on costs allocated to construction. In addition, there is a larger aspect. We must maintain a network of railroads in any event. If considerable traffic is diverted to water transportation, unit costs will be higher for the railroads and somebody will have to pay the bill.

Water for Industrial and Municipal Purposes. One major aspect of the problem of water resources which has been generally neglected until quite recently is that of providing adequate supplies of water for industrial and municipal uses. Within the past few years a critical situation has developed in many areas, for several reasons. One is urbanization, which has brought great increases in the demand for water, especially for air conditioning. More important has been the development of new techniques of production in industry which in some cases require enormous—almost incredible—amounts of water.[5] This has been especially pronounced in the chemical and paper fields but is also important in the petroleum refining, food processing, and textile finishing fields, and several others. Competition for sites with adequate amounts of usable water has increased sharply and the whole problem has been aggravated by growing stream pollution as industrial plants return waste matter to the streams.

The plight of New York City during the past year has dramatized this aspect of the water problem and stirred up public interest. The following quotation is from a comprehensive survey made by *The New York Times:*

4 *Annual Report of the Tennessee Valley Authority,* 1948, pp. 1, A12.
5 For example, in a typical paper-making process, about one hundred pounds of water are used in making one pound of paper. *The New York Times,* Jan. 16, 1950, p. 29.

The United States faces heavy economic losses in the foreseeable future because of unplanned, excessive increases in the use of its most precious mineral resource—water.

In recent years, overdevelopment of ground water resources by industry, more widespread use of air conditioning, overdevelopment for irrigation fostered by high farm prices and the growth and shift of population all have combined to create specific area shortages of a magnitude and variety that will proscribe economic development.

The chemical industry, which uses water as one of its principal raw materials, has been sharply affected in terms of plant expansion by the decreasing availability of adequate supplies of cool water.

. . . while there are abundant underground and surface supplies of water, all areas of the country do not share equally in this asset.

It is this lopsided distribution . . . that nourishes the basic problem of an adequate supply where it is needed, when it is needed, and of the desired quality.

Likewise, it is overdevelopment of supplies in short areas . . . that will force some communities, unable to augment their sources, to stand by idly while a part of their industry and population is liquidated.

Of perhaps even greater significance in resolving the paradox of a famine in the midst of plenty are the serious gap in the nation's basic data on water resources, in the opinion of the United States Geological Survey. . . .

The deficiencies, it is contended, have their roots in the absence of a comprehensive national plan of developing water resources. The development of a plan has been stymied in part by the number of federal agencies involved in the total water problem, the multiple sources that finance investigations, widely divergent concepts of water development, and by the Government's passive attitude.

Staff members of the Interior Department admit freely that there are few, if any, problems that could not have been solved to facilitate total development of the nation's economic potential if the basic data on local and area conditions had been available prior to the present critical stage.

The nation now uses about 700 gallons a day for each person, and even greater use can be expected in the next generation, with the ultimate extent of demand not yet in sight.

A vital and significant step toward meeting the demands and avoiding shortages, the nation's scientists say, can be taken by adequate evaluations of supplies in areas of present and potential development.

Much has already been done in scattered areas, but more remains to be done. The nation's water scientists contend that with their present knowledge of hydrology, the development of superior engineering and pumping apparatus, there should be no excuse in the future for haphazard development, serious overdevelopment and waste of water resources.

. . .   .

In some areas, the problem of over-consumption and under-supply are being met with a variety of ingenious remedies. In others, relief is being achieved through legislative controls, the expenditure of vast sums for remedial projects, and recognized scientific techniques.

Basic to every technique, however, are knowledge of present supply and the geology of the surrounding terrain, and whether the technique has economic and engineering feasibility.

. . .   .

The water resources of the South are good. Generally speaking, the yield of ground water (wells and springs) and surface water (streams and rivers) is plentiful. There are coastal areas with a threat of salt water intrusion due to overdrawing of ground water supplies, and in some highly industrialized sections there is a decline of water tables because of heavy pumpage and use of ground water.

However, the growing industrialization of the South has not yet seriously affected the water resources in a broad regional sense.

. . .   .

In southwestern Louisiana there is a serious ground water shortage. This results from the irrigation practices of rice growers. Years ago rice was irrigated by surface water, but now half of it is irrigated by ground water. The ground water levels have been drawn down by the heavy demand and there is salt water intrusion from the Gulf of Mexico. This situation has also developed in spots on the Florida and Georgia coasts.

The water tables in North Carolina, site of the textile industry, are at high levels. Only at New Bern, Kinston, and Elizabeth City has increased pumpage lowered the levels. In Georgia water levels are high except for industrial and municipal pumpage lowering them in the Savannah and Brunswick areas. Water levels are normal in Alabama except for critical localities around Montgomery, Selma and Dothan with industrial pumpage. This general picture prevails throughout the South.

Progress, slow but definite, has been made in the region toward legislation for pollution control.[6]

Undoubtedly the South's adequate supply of water has been an important factor in attracting industry to the region, especially in recent years. Many of the industries which have developed or expanded in the South recently are heavy users of water. A recent survey of the factors affecting plant location in the South, although it did not make

6 *The New York Times,* Nov. 21, 1949, pp. 1, 18. Quoted by permission.

a separate analysis of water as a locational factor, did mention seven specific cases in which water was an important, if not a decisive, factor in the location decision. These included plants in the tire, synthetic fiber, pulp and paper, food processing, petroleum refining, and textile industries.[7] Undoubtedly water was a significant factor in many other cases covered in that survey, including those of four other paper and pulp plants.

The South has rather suddenly reached a position in which it is not able to say that it has plenty of water for all users at all times and under any circumstances. It is faced with the necessity of taking early and comprehensive action to conserve its industrial water supplies. True, the region is blessed with more adequate water resources than any other in the country. The region has plenty of water in the aggregate, but its availability is limited by two developments. The first is the concentration of demand in certain areas, causing critical local shortages. Industrial plants are not able to tap the aggregate water supply; they must use particular supplies. Other locational factors may prohibit them from locating at places where there is plenty of suitable water and force their concentration in a few areas where they compete for a limited supply. For example, in one case which recently came to our attention, an industrial plant which would use large amounts of water had about decided to locate at a certain place in North Carolina. The water supply was adequate there, but further investigation showed that the chosen site was subject to flooding about once every ten years, and so the site was rejected. The development of industry in an area is likely to stimulate the growth of cities and towns, thus raising the municipal demand for water and increasing the danger of shortages.

The second development limiting availability is the growing pollution of streams. As industrial plants return waste matter to streams, they prohibit or limit the use of water from that stream for miles downstream and increase the cost of purification for any who use it. If that cost is great, it may make water economically unusable for industry.

The measures needed for the proper conservation and protection of water supplies are fairly clearly indicated. As the above quotation stated, the first and primary need is for thorough and continuing hydrologic surveys to provide the basic data on the extent and character-

7 Glen E. McLaughlin and Stefan Robock, *Why Industry Moves South* (NPA Committee of the South Report No. 3), Washington, 1949, pp. 42, 54, 60, 64, 66, 81.

istics of the water supply. These data can be used by state agencies in informing and advising industrial companies on the proper location of plants. Also, it could be used in controlling the water level of reservoirs. No intelligent action on any major aspect of the problem is possible until such basic data are available.

The second measure needed is comprehensive legislation for the control of stream pollution. In most cases stream pollution can be greatly reduced if industrial plants process their waste before releasing it into the stream. Great strides have been made in this branch of chemical engineering in recent years and some plants have found that the processing is not necessarily a burden; it can even be a source of profit. Wood pulp companies are now extracting valuable products from waste matter which they formerly dumped into streams.[8] Companies which can grapefruit juice have had a serious problem in disposing of the grapefruit pulp. Now it is reported that they are able to process the pulp and produce an excellent feed for cattle. But in any event it is important that limits be placed on the extent to which one company may pollute the water of a stream and thus prevent its use by other companies—or raise the cost of purification to prohibitive levels.

THE TENNESSEE VALLEY AUTHORITY AS A CASE STUDY IN THE MANAGEMENT OF WATER RESOURCES

The Tennessee Valley Authority represents the most ambitious and far-reaching attempt the Federal Government has ever made to bring about the coordinated, integrated, long-range conservation and development of the natural resources of a large area. For that reason it may be well to note the progress it has made and the effects it has had upon the region.

---

8 "Disposal of waste cooking 'liquor,' the residue of pulp-making which many states and communities no longer permit to be dumped into streams, is a . . . water problem, but one that most mills are solving successfully and even profitably . . .

"By-products of this waste, in addition to the wood fiber that can be recovered from it, include alcohol, yeast and vanillin. Four large mills . . . are now converting their waste, one producing a high-grade alcohol usable for gin-making. In reclaiming this liquid, known as vat liquor, it is also possible to evaporate it down to a solid that makes a good fuel . . .

"Should the price of coal go much higher . . . pulp mills might begin producing a substitute fuel.

"The average sulphite pulp-producing mill . . . has 1,700 gallons of recoverable waste liquor for each ton of pulp produced." *The New York Times*, Jan. 16, 1950, p. 29. Quoted by permission.

Up to June 30, 1948, the Federal Government had made a net investment of approximately $807,000,000 in TVA. This sum was derived as follows:

Appropriations and property transferred to TVA	$777,329,978
TVA Bonds held by U. S. Treasury	54,000,000
Total	831,329,978
Less: Repayments by TVA into U. S. General Fund	23,059,000
NET INVESTMENT	$808,270,978

This total does not include any allowance for interest on the appropriated funds nor for the interest subsidy on the TVA bonds held by the Treasury, which bear only 1 per cent interest. Neither does it include several million dollars to cover the cost of properties transferred to TVA, which that body did not consider as useful or profitable to its operations. Expenditures from appropriations were $27 million in 1949, and estimates for 1950 and 1951 are, respectively, $52 million and $96 million. At this rate, the federal investment in the project will soon reach a billion dollars.

The Water Power Program of TVA. In the fiscal year 1948, net income from power operations was $16,617,811, bringing the accumulated total from this source to about $109 million. The net loss on other operations in 1948 was $12,187,784, giving a total net income for the year on all operation of about $4.6 million. Net power income for 1949 and 1950 was estimated at $19.7 million and $15.8 million, respectively. According to TVA accounting, the net operating revenue from power operations in 1948, which was $17,176,448 (net income of $16,617,811 plus interest paid of $558,637), was equal to about 4¼ per cent on the average investment allocated to power operations in that year, namely, $405 million.

Many questions have been raised concerning TVA accounting methods; no attempt is made here to pass judgment on that problem as a whole.[9] Certainly, however, one major item of power costs is definitely understated in comparison with private utility operations. In 1946, major private electric power companies in the United States paid taxes equal to 18.7 per cent on their operating revenues.[10] In 1948, TVA made payments in lieu of taxes amounting to $2,005,000,

[9] For some of those questions see "TVA's First Audit by GAO Points Way to Businesslike Evaluation," *Journal of Accountancy,* Vol. 83, June, 1947, pp. 507–510. For a reply see E. L. Kohler, "The TVA and Its Power-Accounting Problem," *The Accounting Review,* Vol. 23, Jan., 1948, pp. 44–62.
[10] *Statistical Abstract of the United States,* 1948, p. 497.

or about 4 per cent of operating revenues. If TVA had paid taxes or their equivalent at the same rate as private electric companies, it would have paid about $9,125,000 and its net income from power operations would have been reduced to $8,050,000, or about 2 per cent on power investment.[11] Again, the Federal Power Commission has adopted ". . . for the use of its staff in determining the cost and value of power, allowances of 1.4 per cent of the Federal hydroelectric power investment . . . for payments in lieu of property taxes to reimburse State and local governmental units for taxes lost as a direct result of the construction of the project."[12] Use of this formula would have required TVA to pay to state and local governments about $5.7 million and would have reduced net income from power to $12.9 million. If a federal income tax of 38 per cent had been paid on this remainder, it would have left net income after taxes of about $7.4 million, or a return of about 1.8 per cent on power investment. This would have been about $4,750,000 short of 3 per cent return on the property, the usual goal in projects of this kind. To produce the additional $4,750,000 net after federal taxes would require earnings before taxes of about $7,660,000.

The importance of tax exemption and low interest costs is indicated by a cost analysis of TVA power and privately-generated power.[13] In the fiscal year 1947, TVA and its governmental and cooperative affiliates paid taxes and tax equivalents equal to 0.4 mills per KWH on the power they sold; class A and B private companies paid 3.1 mills. The difference (2.7 mills) was almost exactly equal to the net profit (2.8 mills) which the TVA group showed on each KWH of power sold and was 67.5 per cent of the total expense (4.0 mills) of

11 A representative of TVA contends that this is not a valid comparison since TVA deals in wholesale power, while private power companies "obtain most of their revenues from much more lucrative retail sales." In respect to property taxes, it would be logical to expect wholesale power companies, and especially hydroelectric companies, to have a higher ratio of taxes to revenue than other companies, because of the large investment in submerged lands, dams, generating plants, and transmission lines. TVA does not pay to governments as much as privately owned companies would pay in taxes if they owned the same property, hence some adjustment must be made before a valid comparison can be drawn.

Income taxes depend on earnings. If the wholesale business is not profitable, then income tax liabilities would be low. If the TVA statement of net earning from power operations in 1948 is a valid statement of net income for income tax purposes it would have carried, for a private company a federal income tax liability of some $6.3 million. This, of course, would have been lower if more property taxes had been paid.

12 Task Force Report on Water Resources Projects, op. cit., p. 38.

13 The following data are from Kohler, op. cit., p. 58.

the TVA group.[14] The TVA group also had a low interest cost, due to the fact that most of the funds it spent were federal appropriations. (Ordinarily the interest cost is greater for hydroelectric companies than for other power companies because of the heavy capital investment required). The interest cost for the TVA group was 0.2 mills per KWH sold, contrasted with 1.0 mills for the private companies. This difference (0.8 mills) added to the 2.7 mills difference on taxes makes a total difference on these two items of 3.5 mills, which is 0.7 mills per KWH more than the net profit per KWH shown by the TVA group and is equal to 87.5 per cent of the total TVA expense per KWH.

Total electric generating capacity in the TVA territory has more than trebled since 1933, rising from about 800,000 KW to almost 2,-600,000 KW. Electric power actually generated in 1948 was almost 15 billion KWH—nearly ten times the amount generated in 1933. This great increase in generating capacity and the accompanying low rates have been an important factor in stimulating industrial growth. Lower rates and abundant power have also brought about an enormous increase in residential use of electricity. This is summarized in two brief statements:

In 1933, the average annual use by residential consumers in the United States was 600 kilowatt hours and the average cost per kilowatt hour was about 5½ cents. In the present TVA service area, average use was practically at the same level and average rates were slightly higher . . .

. . . Average residential use of electricity per consumer (in 1948) was 2,520 kilowatt hours at an average cost of 1.57 cents per kilowatt hour, as compared with national averages of 1,505 kilowatt hours and 3.06 cents. Average residential use was more than four times greater than in 1933.[15]

---

[14] The result of this *cost* analysis is quite close to the result obtained from an analysis of the *charges* made by public and by private power companies. The Task Force on Water Resources Projects of the Hoover Commission analyzed "typical residential and commercial bills" in several areas (including the TVA area) "supplied by publicly owned and privately owned utilities."

"In general, this analysis shows that the differential between public power bills and those for privately owned power companies is roughly equal to the tax component." *Task Force Report, op. cit.,* p. 39.

[15] *Annual Report of the Tennessee Valley Authority, 1948,* Washington, 1948, pp. 1–2, 94. Some part of the difference in cost per KWH—probably one fourth—was due to the difference in the average amounts of current used. One of the authors of this report pays, for current supplied by a privately-owned electric company, about 1.56 cents per KWH—on an average annual consumption of about 10,000 KWH.

Two factors are pertinent in this connection. Since the War, all of the increase in power sales has been in sales to municipalities and co-operatives; sales to "federal agencies, industries, and other utility systems totalled about the same in 1948 as in 1945." The great increase was in residential consumption (through sales to municipalities and cooperatives), which doubled between 1945 and 1948. Second, the Authority is pointing to a serious shortage of power in the years immediately ahead and is asking for authority to build more steam generating capacity.

This raises a major question of policy; how far is the Authority to go in developing residential and commercial uses of current and supplying it with steam power? There can be little question that the TVA has been a most important factor in bringing about a sharp reduction in power rates, not only in its own area, but throughout the nation. That has been a great and significant contribution by the Authority. The two important questions which remain are: how much farther is it to be carried, and are present rates covering all true costs? If the rates are not covering all costs, then there is an element of subsidy in them, and the Federal Government is helping householders of the Valley to pay their utility bills.

For operations outside the power program, it is difficult to measure results accurately. For 1948, the Authority estimated that flood damage averted amounted to $14.6 million. It estimated that direct annual benefits from flood control for the future, based on past records, will average about $11 million.[16]

In the field of navigation, a minimum nine-foot channel is now available up the river as far as Knoxville. A number of terminals have been established along the river, and several communities have enjoyed a substantial economic growth as a result of the river traffic and the savings in freight which it has brought. At Chattanooga, some 150,000 tons of freight were handled in 1948 compared with 40,000 tons in 1945; at Knoxville, some 250,000 tons compared with 7,500. On the river as a whole, the "ton-mile traffic for 1947 was over five times that for 1945 and nine times that of 1926."[17] As noted above, the Authority estimated freight savings in 1947 at $3 million and ultimate annual savings at about $9 million.

[16] *Ibid*, p. 1.
[17] "Transportation on the Tennessee," *Monthly Review*, Federal Reserve Bank of Atlanta, Feb. 28, 1949, pp. 13–19.

Total estimated savings or benefits from navigation and flood control in 1947 were thus $17.6 million. Operating expenditures allocated to those two functions in the fiscal year 1947 were approximately $5.4 million. Total investment outlays allocated to those two functions were in the neighborhood of $300 million. A 3 per cent return on this sum would have been about $9 million. Total costs were thus something more than $14 million in comparison with estimated benefits of $17.6 million.

TVA's Other Resources Development Program. In addition to the above activities, the TVA is carrying on a broad program of resources development.

Agriculture receives the greatest attention. The Authority cooperates with state and federal agencies to encourage soil conservation by promoting terracing and the growing of cover crops; it conducts test and experiment farms; it produces and promotes the use of fertilizers; it carries on research for the development of new and more efficient farm equipment; it encourages the development of pastures and the raising of livestock; and, finally, it promotes rural electrification and better marketing methods. The cost of the agricultural program was $4.1 million in 1947 and $2.6 million in 1948.

In forestry, the Authority helps to extend protection against forest fires; promotes reforestation by distributing million of seedlings; and encourages better methods of forest management. Other phases of the resources program include the development of mineral and recreational resources; studies of stream sanitation and public health; research and advisory work in the fields of transportation, industry, and public finance; and topographic mapping. The total cost of all developmental activities was $7.5 million in 1947 and $5.0 million in 1948.

The peculiar contribution of TVA has been the unique pattern of governmental activity which it has established in the field of resources development. It has coordinated many activities of federal, state, and local governments and has eliminated overlapping. It has brought about an integrated development of resources which would not have been possible under any other arrangement. In this respect it has largely accomplished the purpose for which it was created.

General Appraisal of TVA. After 17 years, how has the TVA program affected the economic life of the area? It is hazardous to attempt to pass judgment after such a hasty survey, especially since many of the activities have not yet exerted their full effects.

TABLE *LXXI* PERCENTAGE INCREASES IN SELECTED SERIES FOR THE TVA AREA AND FOR OTHER AREAS FOR SPECIFIED YEARS

AREA

SERIES AND PERIOD COVERED	TENNESSEE	EAST SOUTH CENT. STATES*	NINE OTHER SO. STATES	UNITED STATES
Population, 1930–1948	21.5	11.8	19.8	18.3
Income Payments to Individuals, 1929–1948	236	205	224	149
Cash Receipts from Farming, 1929–1948	196	165	155	170
Manufacturing, 1929–1947:				
Number of Production Workers	49.8	47.7	52.5	34.8
Wages Paid	219	214	240	160
Value Added by Manufacture	197	211	202	133
Assets of Commercial Banks, 1939–1949	231	227	247	148

* Alabama, Kentucky, Mississippi, and Tennessee.
SOURCES: Computed from publications of the U. S. Department of Agriculture, U. S. Department of Commerce, and the Federal Deposit Insurance Corporation.

In Table *LXXI* we have computed the changes in certain significant economic series in an attempt to measure the effects of TVA activities. These computations were made first for the state of Tennessee, site of the principal activities of the Authority, on the assumption that that state would feel the most pronounced effects of those activities. Computations were made next for the East South Central states which include, in addition to Tennessee, Alabama, Kentucky, and Mississippi. Most of the activities of the Authority outside of Tennessee have been in those three states. For comparative purposes, computations were then made for the other nine southern states and for the United States as a whole.

In general, these data do not show, in comparisons between Tennessee, the TVA states, and other southern states, any pattern of substantial and consistent variations such as would be required to indicate that the Authority has been a dominant force in the economy of the area. In most cases the variations between TVA and the other southern states were no larger than might have been expected for the areas and time periods under consideration. The largest comparative gain by the TVA area was in cash receipts from farming; in that series Tennessee had a substantially larger gain than surrounding states and all of the East South Central states had somewhat larger gains than other southern states. In the manufacturing series and in the assets of commercial banks, there were only small differences, but such advantage as there was rested with the southern states outside the TVA area.

Data on expenditures for new plant and equipment by manufacturing plants in 1947 indicate that the rate of expansion going on in the TVA area in that year was no greater, but rather less, than in other areas. Expenditures per production worker were approximately as follows: Tennessee, $434; East South Central states, $458; other nine southern states, $616; the United States, $504.

These data indicate that, while the TVA has accomplished much, it has not been the dominant factor in southern economic development. It has contributed materially to the economic development of the South, but it has not determined, nor substantially changed, the pattern of that development.

On the other hand, the TVA has been of real significance and value to the area affected and, to a less extent, to other areas. In the first place, the water power of the Valley has been harnessed, and electric generating capacity has probably been expanded beyond what would have been done under private enterprise. Not only has this been an important factor in stimulating industrial development, but it was an invaluable asset during World War II. It made possible a great expansion of aluminum production when that metal was desperately needed, and it provided the power for the atomic project at Oak Ridge. It might be said that in those two respects alone the project justified itself. Further, the power operations of TVA has been instrumental in lowering power rates in many parts of the country.

The TVA has made other important contributions. It has promoted industry where it was needed most, and it has raised incomes where they were lowest. It has facilitated a balanced economic development of the area. It has put natural resources to work and helped to conserve and improve soil and forest resources. In all of these respects, it has been a successful experiment.

MINERAL RESOURCES AND POLICY

Mineral resources are exhaustible. They cannot be replaced; once they are used they are gone forever. "Cost of production" does not have the same meaning, nor the same effect on supply as it does in connection with reproducible goods. Because of these simple facts, the economic laws governing the production and use of minerals are different from those applying to goods which can be reproduced freely. Also, there is a greater public interest in mineral resources since the welfare and even the security of future generations may be involved in the development of mineral resources.

Need for More Information. The first requirement for any intelligent policy-making with respect to minerals is more data—much more data —than we now have on our resources. True, there have been innumerable surveys of mineral resources in almost all the states. But most of those surveys have been by geologists who were interested primarily in the physical phenomena. Quite often they have shown the presence of a long list of minerals from asbestos, diamonds, and gold to zinc and zirconium. Such reports often stir up in the public mind a false optimism and enthusiasm about the possibilities of mining and industrial developments.

For example, a few years ago an important commission was created to study a major governmental function in one of the southern states. The commission recommended a great increase in appropriations for that function and pointed to the state's resources as proof that the state could afford them.

"(State Blank) contains a wide variety of mineral resources, both metallic and non-metallic, with more than 300 kinds of minerals and rocks known to occur in the state.

. . .   .

"For more than 60 years, (State Blank) has been recognized as an important state for the production of non-metallic minerals . . . The wide range of such minerals in the state indicates that this status can be maintained indefinitely.

"The mineral industry has made important advances in (State Blank) during recent years, but the progress to date is only a fraction of what should be accomplished in the future.

Of course, the mere fact that certain minerals or "rocks" happen to be present in the state has no economic significance in itself. Any meaningful evaluation of mineral deposits must be based upon full data concerning their quantity and quality, their chemical and physical properties, their accessibility, the demand of industry for those minerals, the present state of techniques for treating and processing the ores, and many other facts. There is urgent need for more analysis of southern mineral resources by engineers, chemists, and economists to appraise the technical possibilities of the minerals which exist in the region. Admittedly, this would be a vast undertaking, but if it were properly carried out it would be more valuable than all the mineral surveys which have been made up to the present. Until such information is available, it is almost impossible to formulate any intelligent, long-range program for the development of the mineral resources of the South.

Since such information is not now available, it is not possible to delineate the sharp outlines of a policy to deal with mineral resources. Most of the minerals present no special problems and hence require no special policy. A few present problems which are technical, complex, and highly controversial. Below selected aspects of a few major minerals are discussed.

Iron Ore. Currently, the South produces only about 8 per cent of the nation's iron ore, although it has some billion and a half tons of "measured and indicated" ore; this is about 38 per cent of that class of ores in the United States (see Tables *III* and *V*). Of "potential ores" the South has almost none, while the rest of the country is estimated to have some 63 billion tons. The southern ores are not of the best quality and most of them come from underground mines, while in some parts of the country most, or all, of the ores are from open-pit mines. Open-pit mining is usually more economical and also permits of a more rapid expansion of production in times of emergency or greatly increased demand.

The best ores of the United States are being exhausted and the large steel companies are actively searching for better and more economical methods of treating the lower-grade ores. It is perhaps natural that this research is concentrated in the areas near the great steel centers where the facilities for conducting the research, handling the ores, and making the steel are available. It is also natural that the research should be concentrated on the problems of dealing with the ores present in those areas, which may differ in their characteristics from southern ores. "The present trend indicates continued development of the major districts and the probable increase in treatment of the lower-grade and impure ores in them."[18]

[18] *Mineral Position of the United States, op. cit.,* p. 253.

If the South is to benefit from the enforced attention being concentrated upon low-grade ores, some agency or group is going to have to spend considerable money and effort on the specific problem of southern ores and how to treat them economically and in large quantities. For the reasons noted above, the steel companies are likely to concentrate their efforts elsewhere. This may well be a problem large enough to require the joint efforts of several states together with private industry. It is a special regional problem because, "The grade of iron ore mined depends in large degree upon local conditions, both as to source and technology, and in some districts significant quantities of material are mined that would be considered subgrade elsewhere."[19] This might be the strategic time for the investment of a few million dollars in the best talent and facilities for intensive research on this problem.

Recently there have been important discoveries of iron ore reserves abroad and several steel companies are actively preparing to utilize them. Southern steel mills may benefit from the importation of foreign ores because of their favorable location in relation to transportation facilities and because it is not possible to send the ores into the Great Lakes from the Atlantic without transshipment. One company is definitely planning to bring ore from Liberia, probably for use in the South.

A very recent discovery of ore in Venezuela has been heralded as the most important in history. One authority estimates that within a few years the U. S. Steel Corporation will be importing some 15 million tons of ore per year from this deposit. "The first 2 million annual tons of Venezuelan ore should certainly go to Mobile and up the Warrior River to T. C. I., where blast furnaces are now literally a-gasping for such ore. Production may rise there as much as 15 per cent with the same furnaces."[20]

Whether from the use of lower-grade ores or of foreign ores, it seems likely that the South will, in the future, be in a somewhat better competitive position in respect to supplies of iron ore.

Coal. The South has a little more than one fifth of the nation's current coal production and coal reserves. The United States has about half of the known coal reserves of the world and those reserves are estimated

19 *Ibid.*
20 T. W. Lippert, "Cerro Bolivar; Saga of an Iron Crisis Averted," p. 16. Reprinted from *Journal of Metals and Mining Engineering,* Feb. 1950.

to be adequate to meet the nation's needs for 3,000 years or more. Despite increasing energy requirements, coal production has dropped sharply in recent years. From an all-time high of 631 million tons in 1947, it dropped to 600 million tons in 1948 and to an estimated 435 million tons in 1949.[21]

At one time coal provided about 90 per cent of the nation's energy requirements. In 1920 the figure was 78 per cent, and in 1940, 53 per cent. As late as 1947 it was about 50 per cent, but then it fell to 46.5 per cent in 1948 and to an estimated 38.5 per cent in 1949. The consumption of coal by railroads, one of the most stable consumers, fell from 109 million tons in 1947 to less than 70 million tons in 1949, a decline of about 37 per cent.[22] The reason for this decline in the use of coal was, of course, widespread conversion to the use of oil and gas as fuels. That conversion, in turn, while it was caused partly by technological and price considerations, was greatly stimulated by a growing uncertainty in regard to the supply of coal. That uncertainty grew largely out of the whims and caprices of one man; a man with no observable regard for the public welfare.

There is no regional problem in regard to coal. There is an acute problem, but it lies in the field of national politics. National political leaders have not mustered the ingenuity and the political courage necessary to deal with it successfully.

Oil and Gas. The two minerals which present acute problems and for which there is urgent need for an intelligent, long-range public policy are petroleum and natural gas. Production and consumption of both of these have more than doubled in the past 15 years. The production of crude oil rose from about one billion barrels in 1935 to about two billions in 1948. The production of natural gas rose from less than 2½ trillion cubic feet in 1935 to over 6 trillion in 1948. Production and consumption of natural gas would have increased considerably more in the postwar years if adequate transmission facilities had been available. Thirty years ago we derived about 20 per cent of our energy requirements from gas and oil; as late as 1943, the figure was less than 40 per cent. But by 1949 it has risen to an estimated 56.5 per cent.

Despite the heavy increase in production, estimated proved reserves have risen steadily and now stand at the highest figures on record. The latest estimates stand at around 25 billion barrels of crude oil and about 175 trillion cubic feet of gas. About 70 per cent of the oil re-

[21] *The New York Times,* Jan. 26, 1950, p. 18.   [22] *Ibid.*

serves and 80 per cent of the gas reserves are in the South. Although these are large figures, the reserves of oil and gas each represent only 0.2 per cent of the estimated total reserves of mineral fuels in the United States.[23] Thus we are currently obtaining more than half of our fuel from two sources, which, combined, represent less than 0.5 per cent of our total fuel reserves. Even if the estimates of oil and gas reserves were doubled or trebled, that would represent a dangerous trend in the long run.

There are many reasons for the rapid increase in the use of oil and gas. Because of their convenience and cleanliness, both are "luxury" fuels and their demand normally rises disproportionately in periods of high incomes. Further, many of the new production techniques in industry require liquid or gas fuels. Favorable relative prices constituted another powerful stimulant to the use of oil and gas. During the war, prices of both were rigidly controlled while the price of coal rose steadily. After the war, oil prices rose considerably but gas prices advanced very little and in 1947 remained well below their 1932 levels.[24] The uncertainty about coal supplies caused by the coal strikes was still another important factor increasing the demand for oil and gas. Together, these forces caused a tremendous increase in the demand for oil, and particularly for natural gas, in the postwar years. The Big Inch and the Little Inch pipe lines were converted from oil to gas and "within a very few days, over 100 million cubic feet of gas daily were being delivered from these lines for distribution to consumers."[25] The Federal Power Commission was beseiged with applications to construct new pipe lines from the Southwest to the Middle West and Northeast. The stimulus to pipe-line construction was increased not only by the increased demand for gas but also by improved technological methods and by the fact that proved reserves now assured a supply of gas for a number of years, which had not always been true before the war.

Some idea of this "gas rush" may be gained from the situation in Texas. On January 1, 1947, installed pipe-line capacity in that state was 1,754 million cubic feet of gas per day. By June 1, 1948, installed

23 Keith W. Johnson, "Natural Gas Industry of the Southwest and Its Significance to Industrial Development," Federal Reserve Bank of Dallas, *Monthly Review*, March 1, 1949, p. 34.

24 "For a group of (electric) utilities using coal, fuel costs per thousand kilowatt-hours rose 71 per cent from 1939 to 1947, while unit fuel costs decreased 9 per cent for a group of utilities using natural gas." *Ibid*, p. 36.

25 U. S. Bureau of Mines, *Minerals Yearbook*, 1946, p. 808.

capacity plus authorized construction amounted to 3,600 million cubic feet per day and applications for additional capacity of 1,803 million cubic feet per day were pending.[26] It was reported that steel companies had as many orders for pipe as they could fill through the year 1952. It is doubtful that we have ever before seen such a rapid increase in the exploitation of one of our major natural resources.

In recent years Texas has had a great industrial growth. That industry is largely dependent upon oil and gas, both as fuels and as raw materials. The whole area has very little coal and almost no water power; if oil and gas are ever exhausted, industry would be most seriously handicapped. The whole nation is affected, for, unless adequate substitutes were developed, the exhaustion of oil and gas would paralyze our economy and menace our national security. But every year Texas and surrounding states are pumping out trillions of cubic feet of gas and hundreds of millions of barrels of oil to serve as fuels in states which have almost inexhaustible supplies of coal. The effects of the great expansion of pipe-line capacity on industrial and residential use of gas in the Southwest are not delayed until supplies of gas are nearing exhaustion; they may be almost immediate. This is true because of the practice of the Federal Power Commission which requires companies applying for permission to build pipe lines to have contracts for supplies of gas for several years in the future. Sound business practice would require the same thing before the lines could be financed. The effect of this requirement is to tie up immediately large portions of gas reserves for export out of the area and pre-empt them from local use. Thus local industries may be denied gas long before supplies are exhausted.

Some deny that there is a serious problem here and point to the fact that reserves have been rising steadily in the face of large increases in consumption. While different estimates vary somewhat, it is true that all of them show that at present reserves are greater than ever before and much larger than ten years ago; in the case of gas, more than twice as large. One reason for this is that improved methods of exploring and drilling have added deeper-lying and formerly inaccessible deposits to the total of proved and usable reserves. Another reason may well be that companies have a strong incentive *not* to

26 From a brief submitted by Mr. David Heath to the Senate Oil, Gas and Conservation Committee of the Texas Legislature in support of the Chambers Resolution, 1949.

prove and add to their reserve deposits which they strongly suspect to be present until near the time they are to be used. In many states they are taxed on the value of their holdings and any increase in their proved reserves would increase their taxes. Both of these considerations are in keeping with a recent statement of the Bureau of Mines and the Geological Survey:

Recent studies have shown that 80 per cent of the additions to reserves during the 10 years from 1937 to 1946 were due to extensions and revisions of previously discovered fields. The remaining 20 per cent of the additions to reserves during this period were credited to discoveries of new fields.

This study also reveals the fact that nearly 60 per cent of the present remaining proved reserves are due to gains in reserves before 1932.[27]

It is true that large new discoveries of oil and gas, such as the oil field now being developed in Canada, or the development of synthetic fuels, or the distillation of oil products from shale, or the use of atomic power for industrial purposes may solve the problem of fuel supply. In that connection, however, two points are pertinent. First, new discoveries elsewhere may not help the Southwest or even the United States; the states of the Southwest may suffer from industrial blight even if oil is plentiful in other parts of the world. Second, we have no assurance that atomic power will ever be feasible on a commercial basis; until we do have such assurance it would be prudent to conserve the most valuable reserves of fuels we now have.

It is not possible here to specify in detail what steps should be taken to further conservation. Much is already being done; better methods of extraction are utilizing deposits which were formerly wasted; new and better processing techniques are yielding more products from the gas and oil which are taken out; better transmission facilities are bringing to market much gas which formerly went to waste. But apparently nothing is being done to retard the wholesale conversion from coal to gas and oil. In 1942 Louisiana, by statute, prohibited the export of gas to states well supplied with other fuels, but the law was repealed in 1947.[28]

In any event, there may be doubt about the legal authority of a state to prohibit a company from exporting gas once that company has obtained permission from the Federal Power Commission to operate.

[27] *Mineral Position of the United States, op. cit.*, p. 206.
[28] U. S. Bureau of Mines, *Minerals Yearbook*, 1946, p. 808.

There can, however, be no question of the legal authority of a state to levy a substantial severance tax on the production of oil and gas. Such a tax could be adjusted so as to slow up the increase in the consumption of oil and gas by restoring something approaching the prewar balance in prices. If desired, the funds produced by the tax could be treated as a trust fund to alleviate the transition if and when oil and gas are exhausted. The best measure of all would be the solution of the coal problem as discussed above, so that we could use our coal resources in a rational and efficient manner.

XI FOREST RESOURCES AND POLICY

In Chapter I there was a very brief description of southern forest resources. It is the purpose of this chapter to indicate the place of forest
resources in our economy, to describe more fully the forest resources
of the region as they exist at present, to state a reasonable goal for
forestry policy, to outline a program for attaining that goal, and to
suggest some means for implementing that program.

THE PLACE OF FORESTS IN OUR ECONOMY

Forests probably affect our economy in more ways than any other
natural resource or raw material. Those effects may be separated into
two broad groups: those associated with timber products harvested
from forests and those exerted by growing forests.

Timber Products. The principal timber products are lumber, fuelwood,
pulpwood, furniture stocks, veneer logs for plywood and veneer products, and a host of minor products such as shingles, railroad crossties,
poles, piles, tool handles, cooperage, etc.

Lumber is by far the most important timber product and accounts
for nearly half of all timber used. Although we live in an "age of
steel," lumber remains of commanding importance in hundreds of
uses. It is the most widely used building material, it is the unrivaled
material for many shipping purposes, and it enters into thousands of
fabricated products. Housing is one of the major perennial problems
of our economy and the cost of building materials is an important element of that problem. Since 1926, the wholesale price index for building materials has risen more than the index for any other major group
of commodities, not excluding foods and farm products. Wholesale

252

lumber prices, in turn, have risen far more than the prices of any other group of building materials. Table *LXXII* gives the data for selected years. There are indications that this rise in lumber prices has been caused by declining stocks of saw timber, poorer quality, and reduced accessibility.

TABLE *LXXII*   INDEXES OF WHOLESALE PRICES OF LUMBER, BUILDING MATERIALS, AND ALL COMMODITIES IN THE UNITED STATES FOR SELECTED YEARS, 1926–1948
(*1926 = 100*)

YEAR	ALL COMMODITIES	BUILDING MATERIALS	LUMBER
1926	100	100	100
1929	95	95	94
1932	65	71	59
1935	80	85	82
1938	79	90	87
1940	79	95	103
1942	99	110	133
1944	104	115	153
1946	121	133	178
1947	152	180	277
1948	165	199	311

SOURCE: Bureau of Labor Statistics.

Fuel is the second most important use of timber. In millions of homes on farms, in rural communities, and in small towns it is the sole material used for space heating and cooking. Without it, the drain upon coal and petroleum resources would be greatly increased and living costs would be raised substantially for many low-income families.

In recent years, steadily increasing per capita consumption of paper and paperboard products of all kinds and of synthetic fibres has brought a corresponding increase in the amount of timber used as pulp wood. This is now the third most important use of timber and is likely to grow in relative significance. For many years the United States has been dependent on imports for a considerable part of its wood pulp and paper products and consequently has been affected by the worldwide shortage in these fields.

There are dozens of minor uses of timber. No one of them accounts for a large volume, either in terms of value or of physical amount, but in several cases the wood used occupies a strategic position. Examples would be railroad crossties and telephone and telegraph poles;

in neither case has any satisfactory substitute for wood been developed.

In addition to present uses, research and experimentation are opening up new ways to use wood and wood products. New and different ways of treating and/or processing wood yield products which are resistant to fire, decay, and insect damage. Density and hardness can be varied and, within limits, products can be made to meet desired specifications. Also, there are distinct possibilities of developing, partly from inferior trees and from the large amount of wood now wasted, many new products such as ethyl alcohol, insulation, protein food for cattle, and many others.[1] In all these cases, future possibilities will depend largely upon the extent to which costs can be reduced.

In addition to the economic importance of the specific uses of timber, many important industries, employing hundreds of thousands of workers, are entirely dependent upon forests resources for their raw materials. In 1947 the three industry groups which were most closely related to timber supplies—lumber, furniture, and paper—employed 1,271,000 production workers in the United States and 440,000 in the South.[2] Further, an adequate supply of timber and well-organized industries for processing it are essential to our national security. Both World Wars demonstrated that fact beyond doubt.

Economic Functions of Growing Forests. In addition to the timber which they produce, growing forests make other contributions to our economy.

(1) Peculiar to the South are the naval stores—turpentine and rosin—produced from pine trees, principally in southern Georgia and northern Florida. These goods are essential materials for a large number of industries. Value of annual production has varied widely from about $20 million to nearly $50 million in recent years. The United States produces about half of the world supply, and half of the American production is normally exported. Recent developments have reduced the dependence of the industry on standing timber by making possible the utilization of pine stumps and certain by-products of pulp

---

[1] Cf. Forest Service, USDA, *Forests and National Prosperity,* Washington, 1947, pp. 65–67.

[2] Cf. in 1939, "about one out of every three manufacturing workers in . . . Alabama, Florida, Georgia, Louisiana, Mississippi, and Tennessee, was employed in a forest industry" and "20 per cent of the total value of manufactured products in the (Sixth Federal Reserve) District was contributed by the forest industries." Federal Reserve Bank of Atlanta, *Monthly Review,* May, 1946, p. 42.

manufacture. In 1943, production from these new sources accounted for over 40 per cent of the total.[3]

(2) Forests retard or prevent soil erosion. Millions of acres of hilly land, particularly in the South, are not suitable for either crop land or pasture. An adequate stand of trees is the best, if not the only, method of preventing serious erosion.

(3) Closely related to the above, forests retard the runoff of rain water, maintain the water level in the ground, and regulate stream flow. These matters are important for agricultural crops and for the whole problem of water supplies of municipalities and industrial plants,[4] for power dams, and for navigation. A quick runoff means destructive floods and a reduced water supply later; it means heavy erosion and the rapid silting up of water supply reservoirs and power dams. A well-forested watershed is the best protection against these hazards.

(4) Forests are important as wildlife refuges. Without forests, game animals would practically disappear. This aspect is important primarily for the sport it provides but it also provides considerable quantities of food, especially for low-income rural families. In 1942, forest game supplied an estimated 104 million pounds of dressed meat and some 200 million pounds of fish, together with some furs and hides, all valued at about $150 million.[5]

(5) Forests are useful as recreation sites. Every year millions of people visit forests for hunting, fishing, picnicking, and sightseeing. As incomes rise and paid vacations become general, the number should continue to increase.

(6) Finally, forests are used as ranges for livestock. The grazing of forests, particularly of hardwoods, must be done with great care to avoid damage. But pine forests, such as those in the South, afford a limited amount of grazing for several months of the year. It is estimated that some 142 million acres of southern forest land, about three fourths of the total, are so used.[6]

---

[3] C. F. Korstian and Lee M. James, "Forestry in the South," Richmond, Monograph I, Southern Association of Science and Industry, 1948, p. 53.

[4] "Better cutting practices on industrial and municipal watersheds in the Southeast are essential if these areas are to continue to supply usable water at reasonable cost." *Biennial Report of the Southeastern Forest Experiment Station*, 1947-1948, p. 30.

[5] *Forests and National Prosperity, op. cit.*, p. 76.

[6] *Ibid*, p. 71. See also H. H. Biswell, J. E. Foster, and B. L. Southwell, "Grazing in Cutover Pine Forests of the Southeast," *Journal of Forestry*, Vol. 42, March, 1944, p. 195.

SOME ECONOMIC ASPECTS OF FORESTRY

The considerations noted above show that forests provide a great many services and commodities to our economy. Obviously, a resource which covers so much land area and affects the economy at so many points presents a most difficult subject for economic analysis. For one thing, it presents a problem of joint costs compounded many times. The matter is further complicated by the fact that most of the forest *commodities* are subject to private ownership and can be exploited for private gain, while most of the *services* fall within the public domain and are matters of special public concern. Neither time nor space would permit an attempt at an extended analysis even if we felt competent to undertake it. We can only point out a few economic aspects which are peculiar to forestry and consider their implications.

Forests as a Public Utility. Forests are a matter of public concern for two reasons. On the one hand, as we have seen above, the public has a substantial interest in the maintenance and improvement of our forest lands. On the other hand, owners of forest lands are dependent upon governmental services, especially in the case of fire protection, and to a less extent for technical advice and assistance in growing, harvesting, and marketing forest products. It is also clear, as will be developed more fully below, that free enterprise and competition have not produced satisfactory results in the management of our forest resources. In some other fields, that combination of circumstances has led the state to declare the industry or activity a public utility and to subject it to public regulation. We are not justified, however, in jumping to the conclusion that that is the proper solution in this case. In most public utilities there are only a few operators, the activity is subject to the economic law of decreasing costs, and each operator has a monopoly in his own area. In forestry there are millions of operators, the activity is an extractive one and hence subject to the law of increasing costs, and holdings are scattered and far-flung and are closely intertwined with the daily lives of the owners. The effective administration of an extensive system of regulation under these conditions would require something like a police state.

The economic characteristics of forests and the present supply situation would seem to justify and require a status for forests approaching that of a quasi-public utility. In the past, that fact has been partly recognized by the establishment of national, state, and county forests.

A few states have enacted forest legislation which indicates that the legislators have been groping toward a new concept of property rights in forest lands.[7] Thus far, however, there has been no satisfactory reconciliation of private and public interests in this field.

In the meanwhile, the situation is not improving and time is running out. Recently the Council of Economic Advisers stated:

> The depletion of our remaining supply (of saw timber), especially in small, privately owned forest properties, is proceeding so rapidly that immediate consideration should be given to legislation for regulation of forest practices. Unless much more rapid progress is made along the lines of improved private practices or State legislation for the control of cutting practices, national interest and security will require Federal-State action.[8]

It would be desirable to have more experimentation by states and groups of timber owners to see if the problem can be solved without federal interference and with a minimum of public compulsion. Considerable progress has already been made in this direction but much remains to be done.

Production Principles. Forestry authorities point out that we may regard our forests either as a mine to be exploited without hope of renewal or as a crop to be grown and harvested regularly. In the eastern United States we have passed the "mining" stage because we have cut practically all our virgin timber. Yet we are not on a crop basis, for relatively little of our forest land is on a sustained-yield basis and much of it is not managed at all in any true sense of the word. Further, it is

---

[7] The state of Washington requires that before any owner or operator of forest land starts logging operations he must secure a permit from a state agency. To get the permit, he must agree either to leave a minimum number of trees for reseeding purposes or to restock the area unless the land is being cleared for *bona fide* agricultural, mining, industrial, or residential purposes. *Laws,* 1945, Chap. 193; 1947, Chap. 218. This legislation has been upheld by the Supreme Court of the State of Washington (*Dexter v. Washington,* 202 P2d 906) and by the Supreme Court of the United States in a *per curiam opinion* (338 *U.S.* 863 (Nov. 7, 1949)).

[8] Council of Economic Advisers, *The Annual Economic Review: January, 1949,* Washington, 1949, p. 68. Cf. ". . . since the course of action which yields maximum returns in the near future may not be that which will yield maximum returns in the far future, there may be a conflict between the interests of individuals and those of society at large so long as the two groups discount the future of (at?) different rates. This conflict is additional to that which may arise through differences in the degree of rationality of the two groups. It follows that in any society in which the interests of the people at large are considered in policy formulation, such policy will call for some measure of control by the public over the business of timber production." William A. Duerr, *The Economic Problems of Forestry in the Appalachian Region,* Cambridge, Harvard University Press, 1949, p. 129. Copyright 1949 by the President and Fellows of Harvard College.

always possible to change policies abruptly and to consider the forest resources existing at any given time as a mine and exploit them fully. For any successful solution of the problem, however, we will have to treat our forests as a crop and manage them carefully.

There are major differences between forests and agricultural crops and, indeed, between forests and all other kinds of production carried on by private enterprise. These differences are such as to raise questions concerning the applicability of ordinary principles of production to forests; for example, whether market prices can be expected to function successfully as a regulator of production. For one thing, the production cycle is longer than in any other type of private activity. In most cases the individual who starts a crop can hardly expect to harvest it—or at least not until his old age. Outlays for production are in the nature of investment rather than current expense. A long period of waiting is required and heavy carrying charges accumulate. Further, forest activities are nearly always a sideline; rarely does an individual devote full time to them. Some owners regard these investments built up on the side as an emergency reserve to be used in time of distress or old age. Under such conditions, is it reasonable to expect market price to function successfully as a guide to production? For example, high prices during a boom period might well stimulate premature cutting and cause a shortage in succeeding years.[9] Or low prices now are no reliable indication that the timber supply will be abundant 30 or 40 years from now, when seedlings of the present will be ready for harvest. Some of these problems would be solved if forest lands were on a sustained-yield basis. Then current outlays would be covered by current revenues, and would not require a steady input of investment funds. Within limits, cutting could be adjusted to demand and market price could regulate the flow of timber. But it is doubtful whether millions of small holders can be taught to understand what a sustained-yield basis is and whether they can be persuaded to do the investing and the waiting necessary to attain that state. Finally, the lure of quick profits will always induce some holders to liquidate holdings even after they have developed a good current income.

9 "The theory that farmers, through obtaining larger income from timber sales, would take greater interest in their woodlands and automatically give them greater care has not been demonstrated in practice. More commonly, the better prices have stimulated overcutting and liquidation of resources." Forest Service, USDA, "Forest Cooperatives in the United States" (Report 6 from *A Reappraisal of the Forest Situation*), Washington, 1947, p. 3.

PRESENT STATUS OF SOUTHERN FOREST
RESOURCES AND USE

Table *LXXIII* summarizes the principal data on southern forest resources and use as of 1944 and 1945. In this table, and throughout this chapter, the definition of the South is that used by the U. S. Forest

TABLE *LXXIII* BASIC DATA ON SOUTHERN* FOREST RESOURCES AND USE 1944–45

ITEM	UNIT		SOUTH	SOUTH AS % OF U. S.
Total Forest Land	Mil Acres		187	30.0
By Type: Commercial	"	"	183	39.7
Noncommercial	"	"	4	2.5
By Ownership (Commercial Only):				
Private	"	"	167	48.4
Farm	"	"	69	49.6
Industrial and other	"	"	98	47.6
Public	"	"	16	13.8
National Forests	"	"	10	13.5
Other Federal	"	"	4	26.7
State and Local	"	"	2	7.4
Volume of Standing Timber:				
Saw Timber	Bil. bd. ft.		338	21.1
Softwood	"	" "	194	15.0
Hardwood	"	" "	144	47.4
All Timber	Bil. cu. ft.		131	27.9
Softwood	"	" "	59	18.4
Hardwood	"	" "	72	48.0
Ownership of Saw Timber:				
Public	Bil. bd. ft.		21	3.1
Private	"	" "	317	34.7
Current Annual Timber Growth:				
Saw Timber	"	" "	19.9	56.4
Softwood	"	" "	12.9	59.2
Hardwood	"	" "	7.0	52.2
All Timber	Bil. cu. ft.		6.4	47.8
Softwood	"	" "	3.5	51.5
Hardwood	"	" "	2.9	43.9
Current Annual Timber Drain:				
Saw Timber	Bil. bd. ft.		24.9	46.2
Softwood	"	" "	15.6	40.4
Hardwood	"	" "	9.3	60.4
All Timber	Bil. cu. ft.		6.5	47.4
Softwood	"	" "	3.7	45.7
Hardwood	"	" "	2.8	50.9
Drain Ratio: Saw Timber			125	
All Timber			102	

* See text for definition of South used in this table.
SOURCE: Computed from Forest Service, USDA, *Forests and National Prosperity*.

Service, which excludes Kentucky and all of Oklahoma and Texas except the eastern counties.[10]

Characteristics of Forest Lands. In 1945, the South, as defined above, had 30 per cent of the nation's forest lands, 40 per cent of its commercial forest lands, and almost half of its privately owned commercial forests. This is due in part to the fact that much of the forest land in the Rocky Mountain region, to a considerable extent federally owned, is so remote and inaccessible that it is presently classified as noncommercial, whereas most southern forests are readily accessible. The proportion of forest lands in the South which is publicly owned is small— only about one-seventh. This means that the problem of improving forest conditions in the South is largely a problem of improving the conditions of *private* forests, and that must be done by working with and through the private owners. This problem is accentuated by the fact that about 40 per cent of southern forests are on farms. On the average, southern farms are considerably smaller than non-southern farms, many of them are operated by tenants, and both owners and tenants typically have low incomes, a very limited amount of equipment and little knowledge of forest management. Under such conditions the task of improving forest practices is a most difficult and complex one.

Volume, Growth, and Drain of Timber. The South has a smaller proportion of the nation's standing timber than it has of the nation's forest lands; about 28 per cent of all timber and 21 per cent of the saw timber. The principal reason is that nearly all of the region's virgin timber has been cut and the present stand is second growth. The proportion of hardwoods is considerably higher because there are still sizeable areas of virgin bottomland hardwood and because hardwoods have been allowed to take over many softwood areas after they were cut over.

One significant reason for the South's low volume of growing timber is found in thin or inadequate stocking; that is, forest lands do not have an adequate crop of trees. In 1945, the Forest Service estimated that 46 per cent of the commercial forest area of the South was denuded

10 The data are from the Forest Service's *Reappraisal of the Forest Situation* which was based upon resources as of 1945 and use as of 1944. The eastern counties of Oklahoma and Texas include practically all of the forest lands of those states.

or poorly stocked, compared with 35 per cent in the North and 18 per cent in the West.[11]

The figures on annual growth give a striking demonstration of the South's natural advantages in forestry. With only 30 per cent of the nation's forest lands and 28 per cent of the growing stand, the South provides almost half of the country's annual timber growth. With saw timber the comparison is even more striking—21 per cent of the growing stand and 56 per cent of the annual growth. The explanation lies largely in the South's longer growing season and abundant rainfall. The Forest Service sums up the situation in these words:

> In the South, where growth is generally rapid and an appreciable part of the harvest may be taken from thinnings or other intermediate cuttings, only 16 to 18 board feet should be needed as growing stock for each board foot of annual drain. At the other extreme, in the Rocky Mountain region, because of slow growth and less favorable markets for small trees, the saw-timber growing stock will need to be 50 times the annual drain.[12]

These facts have important effects upon the relative costs of producing timber in the South. In order to produce a given amount of timber, the southern producer has to maintain a much smaller number of growing trees than his non-southern competitor. This means smaller amounts invested, lower carrying charges (principally interest and taxes), and a smaller investment exposed to the hazards of fire, storm, insects, and disease.

Great as is the South's annual timber growth, it is exceeded by the annual drain. In 1944, when lumber production was considerably below the 1942 peak, but when drain was approximately normal despite the war, drain was about 2 per cent greater than growth. In saw timber the excess of drain was 25 per cent. The principal elements of the drain as estimated by the Forest Service were as follows:

	LUMBER	FUEL WOOD	PULP WOOD	OTHER COMMOD- ITIES	FIRE	INSECTS, DISEASE, ETC.
Amount (Million cu. ft.)	2,837	1,169	575	1,004	280	595
Per Cent of U. S.	42.3	53.1	44.0	51.2	60.9	58.4

With less than 30 per cent of the nation's standing timber, the South

[11] Forest Service, USDA, *Gaging the Timber Stand of the United States,* Washington, 1946, p. 22.
[12] *Forests and National Prosperity, op. cit.,* p. 40.

had approximately 60 per cent of the country's loss from fire, insects, and disease.

The large net drain on saw timber is the most disturbing aspect of the picture. If it continues into the immediate future it will seriously deplete the region's timber resources. The Forest Service describes the possible result in these words:

For the South as a whole, a continuation of the 1944 cut and prevailing forest practices for 20 years would mean a decline of 117 billion board feet, or one-third of the present saw-timber volume. Obviously such a decline in saw-timber volume would mean curtailment of the forest industries and drastic readjustment in independent communities. Such economic and social losses would be serious for the South, which needs additional industral development to offset the displacement of labor by reduction of the acreage in cotton and by mechanization of its cultivation and harvesting.

. . .   .

If this 20 year projection (for the Nation as a whole) were to become a reality, it would impair the chances for full employment, increase the burden of taxation on other forms of property, and affect our national security.[13]

This is rather a gloomy picture but, even so, the aggregate figures on growth and drain do not tell the whole story. Quite naturally, production in the past has been concentrated on the most accessible timber. As a result, "local shortages of timber suitable for the established industries are critical. They are not fully revealed by regional data on timber volume and growth."[14] In the same way, lumbermen in the past used the best trees of the more desirable species.

Exploitation of favored species in the past aggravates the raw material problem now. The removal of the best trees of the choice species often leaves the land in possession of a poor quality stand dominated by low-value species. Such conditions are unfavorable for a new crop of the more valuable species. Thus poor-quality hardwoods have taken over large expanses of eastern forests that formerly supplied valuable mixed timbers.[15]

The southern picture is not improved when we consider how existing forests are being managed. The Forest Service has worked out a system of grading forest land according to the quality of its management, the principal factors being cutting practices, fire control, and the extent to which it is being operated for sustained yield. The per-

13 *Forests and National Prosperity, op. cit.,* p. 32.
14 *Ibid,* p. 59.   15 *Ibid.*

centages of forests lands falling in the different categories of management in 1945 were as follows:

	INTENSIVE	EXTENSIVE	WITHOUT	NON-OPERATING
North	2.0	33.7	53.7	10.6
South	2.9	18.7	68.5	9.9
West	0.9	58.1	20.5	20.5
All Regions	2.1	33.4	51.9	12.6[16]

Only about 22 per cent of southern forest land is under management, compared with 36 per cent in the North and 59 per cent in the West. This is the heart of the forest problem. There are some signs of improvement: "Lands owned by pulp companies now show indications of good management; more than two thirds of the acreage in their holdings is under intensive and extensive management" and lumber companies are managing about one third of their lands. The rub comes with small private holdings, where only 18 per cent of the land is receiving any form of management.

TABLE *LXXIV*   MANUFACTURING DATA FOR THREE FOREST-RELATED INDUSTRY GROUPS IN THE SOUTH, 1939 AND 1947

(*Lumber, Furniture, and Paper*)

	AMOUNTS		PER CENT OF U. S.	
	1939	1947	1939	1947
Number of Establishments	6,947	15,476	32.1	40.6
Production Workers (Thousands)	289	440	32.8	34.6
Value Added by Mfg. ($ Mil.)	459	1,724	22.3	25.5

SOURCE: Compiled from the *Census of Manufactures*, 1947.

Industries Dependent on Forests. At this point it may not be amiss to mention briefly those industries of the South which are most closely connected with the forests and most dependent upon forest resources for raw materials. Table *LXXIV* gives certain data for three industry groups (Lumber and Products, Furniture and Fixtures, and Paper and Allied Products, all as defined by the Bureau of the Census), for the years 1939 and 1947. Table *LXXV* gives data on two specific timber products (Lumber and Wood Pulp) for selected years.

The manufacturing data show that between 1939 and 1947 these three forest-related industries in the South made considerable progress,

[16] Forest Service, USDA, *The Management Status of Forest Lands in the United States,* Washington, 1946, Table 15.

both absolutely and relatively. The large increase in number of establishments is due in part to increased coverage of small sawmills and other lumber plants in the 1947 Census. The 440,000 workers in these three industry groups comprised about 22 per cent of all wage earners in manufacturing in the South in 1947. The increase over 1939 was 52 per cent compared with an increase of 40 per cent in those groups in the Non-South and an increase of 50 per cent in all southern wage earners. In value added by manufacture, these three industry groups contributed about 16 per cent of the South's total in 1947; the increase over 1939 was 273 per cent compared with an increase of 215 per cent in the Non-South and an increase of 244 per cent for southern industry as a whole. One encouraging aspect is that the greatest increases occurred in the paper group where value added per worker is highest; that group showed an increase of over 75 per cent in workers and about 340 per cent in value added.[17]

The figures on lumber production show a large absolute, and a somewhat smaller relative, decline over the past 40 years. Even the strong demand during World War II did not raise production to the levels of 30 and 40 years ago. That resulted partly from a shortage of manpower and partly from the depletion of southern forests. In wood pulp, however, the trend was quite different; there absolute production increased about sevenfold between 1929 and 1947 and the South's proportion of the nation's production approximately trebled. The expansion of pulp and paper production in the South was largely due to the develoment of methods for using southern pine in the production of kraft paper and, later, of newsprint. The expansion has continued steadily since the war and this increase should continue, even though, perhaps, at a slower rate.

[17] The Census of Manufactures data for 1947 permit one very interesting, although very rough, comparison of average wages in these three industry groups and in the South and the Non-South. For each industry group a rough average annual wage was computed by dividing the average number of production workers into the total of wages paid. This was done for both the South and the Non-South. The results are as follows:

	LUMBER	FURNITURE	PAPER
South	$1,438	$1,787	$2,455
Non-South	2,527	2,500	2,628
South as Per Cent of Non-South	56.9	71.5	93.4

It would be interesting and enlightening to compare the extent to which variation in the interregional wage differential in these industry groups varies with (1) the amount of equipment used per worker; and (2) the extent to which workers are organized.

TABLE *LXXV* PRODUCTION OF LUMBER AND WOOD PULP IN THE SOUTH FOR SELECTED YEARS, 1909 TO 1948

| YEAR | LUMBER | | WOOD PULP | |
	AMOUNT IN MILLION BD. FT.	PER CENT OF U. S.	AMOUNT IN THOUSANDS OF TONS	PER CENT OF U. S.
1909	22,058	49.6	—	—
1919	17,382	50.3	—	—
1924	19,769	50.0	—	—
1928	—	—	601*	13.3
1929	17,555	45.3	759	16.4
1934	8,390	44.6	—	—
1939	12,477	43.4	—	—
1940	13,762	44.2	3,600	40.7
1941	16,038	43.9	—	—
1942	16,084	44.3	4,800*	45.1
1943	14,874	43.4	4,400*	46.6
1944	13,069	39.7	4,700*	47.3
1945	11,924	42.4	4,800*	47.2
1946	15,339	42.1	5,000*	46.9
1947	14,078	39.8	5,700*	48.2

* Partly estimated.
SOURCE: Compiled from reports of the Bureau of the Census.

FORESTRY GOALS FOR THE SOUTH

As part of its reappraisal of forest resources in the United States, the Forest Service has made an extensive study of future timber requirements. It attempted "to estimate the quantity of timber products that might be used by consumers afforded reasonable latitude in choice of readily available materials, including timber products, in a national economy functioning at a high level of employment and output."[18] It studied in considerable detail every important use of timber and estimated future requirements in the light of past trends, and probable future developments, in national income, construction, railroad mileage, wood pulp consumption, and other activities affecting timber consumption. It arrived at the conclusion that as a long-range goal "the United States should aim to grow 18 to 20 billion cubic feet of timber annually, including 65 to 72 billion board feet of saw timber."[19] This estimate contains a margin for unpredictable losses, for "ineffective growth," for a national security reserve, and, perhaps in the later stages, for export.

To achieve this goal it will be necessary to increase the growth of

[18] Forest Service, USDA, *Potential Requirements for Timber Products in the United States,* Washington, 1946, p. 1.
[19] *Forests and National Prosperity, op. cit.,* p. 33.

all timber by 50 per cent and to double the growth of saw timber. The Forest Service has worked out the allocation of these increases by regions. Under that plan, the South would increase the annual growth of all timber by 60 per cent, or from 6.39 billion cubic feet to 10.14 billion cubic feet. In saw timber it would approximately double the annual growth, raising it from 19.9 billion board feet to 37.4 billion.[20]

This would seem to be a thoroughly sound goal, at least for the beginning. The ultimate goal cannot be realized for 70 or 80 years; in the meantime, the important thing is to raise annual growth as fast as is feasible. If the ultimate goal later proves to be too high there will be ample time to alter the program. As the Forest Service concludes, "certainly we need not fear timber surplus. The goals would not be vitiated if demand should fall below annual growth in periods of depression. The resulting increase in growing stock would simply put the country in position to achieve the goals sooner."[21] Such a goal as that outlined above would be in keeping with the findings and recommendations of the group which made the studies for the Pace Subcommittee on Cotton. That group emphasized especially the need for a more intensive development of the land now nominally in forests.[22]

The attainment of this goal of timber production would automatically take us a long way toward realizing desirable goals for other forest services. The forest practices necessary to produce the timber would do much to control floods and soil erosion, provide recreation sites and wildlife refuges, etc.

A PROGRAM FOR ACHIEVING THE GOAL

The goal is fairly easily and simply stated. Further, there should be little difficulty in securing agreement on it in principle. There can be no reasonable doubt that we need a substantial improvement in the present situation. There may be some doubts as to whether that improvement should amount to 50 per cent, or 100 per cent of the goal stated above. But such differences need not cause any disagreement over a program of action. In any case the program would be essentially the same for the next 30 or 40 years; the only difference would be in the time required to reach the goal.

What Needs to Be Done. What needs to be done to accomplish the goal is fairly clear. The Forest Service and many others have pointed

[20] *Ibid*, p. 39.   [21] *Ibid*.
[22] See *Economic Problems of the Cotton Belt*, p. 42.

it out and elaborated on it many times. It may be well to point out first that the problem is not primarily one of increasing the acreage of forest lands. In general, the present acreage is sufficient. It is true that in some localities there may be considerable land that should be withdrawn from crops and placed in forests. On the other hand, there may be limited areas of forest land that could profitably be cleared and used as crop land or pasture. But the total land affected by such shifts would be comparatively small.

Basically, what needs to be accomplished can be stated very briefly as follows: (1) We need to get more growing trees on existing forest land; that is, improve the stand. (2) We must give those trees better protection against fire, insects, and disease. (3) The level of forest management must be raised substantially. That means better thinning and cutting practices, and more planning and effort to put forests on a sustained-yield basis. (4) Forest waste should be reduced sharply— waste in the harvesting, processing, and marketing of timber products. (5) Finally, and partly as an inducement to the accomplishment of the above objectives, there must be better facilities for marketing forest products. The remainder of this chapter will be devoted to a discussion of how these objectives may be realized.

Classes of Owners. There are several classes of owners of forest land that will have to be dealt with in accomplishing this program. First, there are public owners—the federal, state, and local governments. Publicly owned lands are comparatively small in the South, amounting to less than one seventh of the total. Generally, too, these lands are already being fairly well managed for the purpose of accomplishing the above objectives. Second, there are the medium and large private owners—those owning over 5,000 acres. There are about 2,500 of these in the South and they hold nearly one fourth of all forest land. These include mining, railroad, lumber, and paper companies as well as individuals. Finally, there are about 1,650,000 small owners, mostly farmers, who own about two thirds of the total. The average amount owned is 74 acres. These are the owners which, in every sense, present the greatest problems. There are more of them, they own most of the land, they are harder to reach, individually they have little at stake, and they have very limited equipment and money to work with.

Possible Ways of Implementing Program. There are at least three general methods of trying to achieve the stated objectives. One would be to try to bring a great deal of additional forest land under public ownership and accomplish the objectives by direct government action. While there is considerable room for an increase in state and county forests, this method does not hold out much hope as a general solution of the problem. The cost would be too great, much of the land in the larger holdings probably would not be available for purchase, and purchases of small holdings would be too scattered and disconnected for effective administration. Too, a large part of the forest land is on farms and it would not be feasible to separate such land from the rest of the farm. In one respect, however, this method deserves serious consideration. Where large areas of land have been forfeited for taxes and where they have been chronically tax-delinquent, the state or county might well take advantage of the situation to create public forests. In such a case there would be no cash outlay and the tax authorities would be giving up only a highly uncertain source of revenue.[23]

Another method would be for the states or the Federal Government to enact a comprehensive regulatory program for private owners. As was indicated above under the discussion of the public utility concept, it would be most difficult to administer such a system effectively. It it doubtful that public sentiment in this country is ready for such action yet and it is doubtful that we can get efficient forest practices by compulsion. It may be necessary to use legislation to correct some of the worst abuses, but beyond that its use is questionable at the present stage.

Since the possibilities of the first two methods seem to be distinctively limited, the principal reliance will probably have to be placed on the third method, which is to secure the voluntary cooperation of private owners of forest lands. This should be done through a combination of inducements plus a minimum of compulsion. Owners must be persuaded to plan for better forest practices. This is the first and most vital step in achieving the stated objectives, for unless it is realized none of the others can be attained. Such persuasion would seem to require action on two broad fronts. First, there must be a campaign of information, publicity, and education. This should be directed first at the general public to create a favorable public sentiment and to show the taxpayers the necessity of spending the public funds required. It should be directed next at the large private owners to impress them

23 Cf. William A. Duerr, *op. cit.,* pp. 115–17.

with public responsibility in managing forests and to show them, if they are not already convinced, that good forestry can be made to pay good dividends. Finally and especially, it will have to be directed at the large number of small private owners—mostly farmers. Here the emphasis will have to be largely on possibilities of profit. Use should be made of all existing media such as agricultural schools, the Extension Service, and county agents. In addition, test and demonstration forests should be established in as many farm communities as possible.

In addition to publicity and education, facilities must be provided to aid small owners in managing their forests profitably. Substance must be provided to back up the argument that good forestry pays. Suggestions are given below for providing such facilities.

Reducing Risks and Carrying Charges. As noted above, the first big step in getting better forest practices is to prevail on private owners to make the decision and to plan for better forest management. Because of the long production cycle, two of the big deterrents are the risks involved and the carrying charges which accumulate. The possibility of loss by fire, especially in the South, is one of the chief risks, while interest and taxes make up most of the carrying charges. Each of these factors has long been recognized as a problem and proposals have been advanced for governmental help in solving each. It is now proposed that, in an effort to overcome the initial "hump" of owner resistance, they be attacked as a group. The solution proposed is a coordinated, integrated, four-pronged program which would be put into effect as a unit. It would include adequate fire protection facilities, forest insurance, low-interest loans, and assurance of moderate taxation for the duration of the program. The arrangement would be tied together so that the owner would have to carry insurance and cooperate in fire protection in order to qualify for a loan or for tax benefits. Taken together these provisions should go far to assure owners that their risks would be definitely limited and that carrying charges would not be excessive. Each provision is discussed in detail below.

Fire Protection. Forestry authorities have long decried the great losses from forest fires in this country and have urged better fire-protection facilities. This has been especially true of the South, which has poorer protection and more fires, proportionately, than the rest of the country. Table *LXXVI* shows that fire losses in the South are proportionately more than ten times as great as in the Non-South. The "burning off" of forest land to provide better grazing for cattle is widespread in many sections of the South and is responsible for many of the fires. For a long time the Forest Service and other forestry authorities condemned this practice unconditionally, but recently they have come to the conclusion that there are certain advantages in it and are recommending prescribed burning under certain conditions and with careful control.

The estimated damage by fire on unprotected lands in the South in 1946–47 was almost 32 cents per acre, or more than the property taxes in most southern states. Experience has shown that fire losses can be sharply curtailed if adequate facilities are provided and that the savings will far exceed the cost.

TABLE *LXXVI*   PER CENT OF FOREST AREA BURNED IN DIFFERENT REGIONS OF THE UNITED STATES, 1946–1947 AVERAGES

REGION	PROTECTED LANDS	UNPROTECTED LANDS	TOTAL FOREST LAND AREA
South	1.6	21.8	10.5
North Central	0.3	5.6	1.1
East	0.4	3.5	0.6
Pacific	0.3	—	0.3
Rocky Mountain	0.1	0.4	0.2

SOURCE: *Biennial Report of the Southeastern Forest Experiment Station*, 1947–1948, p. 6.

The Federal Government makes available to state and local governments, on a matching basis, a fund of $9 million for forest fire protection. In 1947 total expenditures by all agencies, public and private, were about $22 million. The Forest Service estimates that adequate protection would cost about $40 million per year.[24] A reasonable minimum program for fire protection would be for the Federal Government to make available as its share $20 million and for state and local governments to strive to match that sum as quickly as possible. In recent years, southern states have sharply increased their appropriations for this purpose. In the Sixth Federal Reserve District,

From 1944 to 1947, state and county expenditures for fire protection have doubled. For the 1947 fiscal year total expenditures for this purpose in the District states amounted to 3.3 million dollars, of which the Federal

24 *Forests and National Prosperity, op. cit.*, p. 84.

Government contributed 1.3 million, state and county governments 1.4 million, and private agencies and individuals 0.6 million.[25]

With the help of these funds, more fire-fighting units are being organized and more forest lands are being brought under protection, with substantial reductions in the area burned each year. In Florida, 32.3 per cent of unprotected forest land was burned over in 1947, while only 1.6 per cent of protected land was burned.[26]

In addition to more funds, two other things are needed to reduce fire losses; better state laws for fire-prevention, and a little intelligent effort by small owners, especially farmers. The laws should regulate intentional burning, prescribe penalties for damages resulting from careless burning, require brush-burning permits, and regulate slash disposal, campfires, and provide for restricted use of forests during hazardous periods. Small owners could construct fire breaks, dispose of slash properly, and suppress small fires before they get beyond control. "On most farms only a few pieces of inexpensive equipment are needed for this work."[27]

Forest Insurance. When fire losses have been reduced as much as possible there will still be a substantial risk of loss from natural causes. There should be insurance against such losses.

Risks from fire, insects, disease, and other destructive agents are not only reducible but also insurable. Forest insurance is well established in several European countries. But in this country, although commercial companies have given considerable attention to the possibilities and have written some policies at high rates, forest insurance has been slow to catch on. Studies in the Pacific Northwest and the Northeast indicate that commercial insurance is practicable at reasonable rates if it avoids poor risks and is based on good protection, reasonably good forest practices, and broad coverage.[28]

The way is open and the need is urgent for some state, as an example, to develop a sound system of forest insurance. That state should first provide adequate funds for fire protection. Systems of low-interest loans and a preferential tax system for forest lands should then be provided, as discussed below. An insurance system could then be set up, with rates based on estimated losses under favorable condi-

---

[25] Federal Reserve Bank of Atlanta, *Monthly Review,* June, 1949, p. 56.
[26] *Ibid,* Aug., 1948, p. 82.   [27] *Ibid.*
[28] *Forests and National Prosperity, op. cit.,* p. 97.

tions, the state agreeing to underwrite the plan for, say, ten years.

In order to qualify for the loans or the preferential tax, owners would have to carry insurance; to get the insurance, they would have to agree to cooperate in fire prevention and to observe a certain minimum level of forest management. If no state takes the initiative, the Federal Government might well establish both the loan system and the insurance plan. There would be ample justification and precedent for subsidizing the insurance plan in the early years. If soundly conceived and managed, it might well develop into a self-supporting and mutual organization after the fashion of the Federal Deposit Insurance Corporation.

Long-Term Credit. Because of the very long production cycle, the rate of interest which must be paid for capital is a factor of major importance in determining the cost of producing timber.

> . . . the rate of interest is a major determinant of the best course to pursue with respect to products to be produced, species to be favored, length of rotation, cutting-diameter limits, frequency and intensity of cutting, quantity and character of growing stock to be maintained, and other types of management alternatives. The rate of interest is a major factor, also, in deciding the basic question, whether forestry, or some other use, or some combination of uses is most economical in a given case.
>
> . . .   .
>
> Of all the variable factors affecting the choice of alternatives, in forest management, the rate of interest is frequently found to be the most influential. That is to say, a change in this factor amounting to a given proportion of its reasonable range will produce a larger shift in the result than a comparable change in any other factor.[29]

The sharp declines in interest rates generally in the past 20 years should have, and probably have, induced considerable investment in forestry, but those low rates have not been made available generally to owners of forest lands in the form needed.

> Forest owners and operators generally lack sources of satisfactory credit —long-term or intermediate—adapted to their special needs. Today, when specialized credit facilities for farming and for industry have been developed to a high state of efficiency, forestry is the outstanding category where credit needs remain neglected.[30]

[29] William A. Duerr, *op. cit.*, p. 130. Copyright 1949 by the President and Fellows of Harvard College.
[30] *Forests and National Prosperity, op. cit.*, p. 97.

The basic problem is to make long-term, low-interest loans available to small owners. This problem is especially important and especially difficult during the transition period until most of the forests can be put on a profitable, sustained-yield basis. Once that transition has been made, it probably will not be difficult to obtain the necessary financing on a commercial basis. In some cases it may be feasible for privately owned institutions to make loans at sufficiently low rates now, but is doubtful that they can be made available to small owners generally.

As suggested above, a desirable arrangement would be to have a publicly financed or a publicly guaranteed loan system tied in with the fire-control, insurance, and tax systems. Loans would be made for periods up to 50 years at interest rates of 3 to 4 per cent. Borrowers would be required to cooperate in fire control, carry forest insurance, and observe a minimum level of forest management. Under such a system it should be possible to make loans at not more than 3½ per cent. The Federal Government could supply or guarantee the funds without any element of subsidy at 2½ per cent, leaving a margin of 1 per cent to cover operating expenses. If it should be considered desirable to subsidize operations as a further encouragement, loan rates might be reduced to 3 per cent.

A precedent and a possible pattern for a loan system of this kind might be found in the Federal Farm Loan System. That system was instrumental in reducing interest rates for farmers and has been successful generally except for heavy losses during the worst years of the depression. The system, in fact, might have been used as a means of extending forest loans except that in the beginning its powers were rather narrowly restricted to making loans closely related to agricultural purposes. Consequently its policies and practices have developed in such a way that it could not easily be adapted to forest loans at this time even if its powers were changed.

Taxing Forest Lands. It has long been recognized that high property taxes promote uneconomical and wasteful cutting of timber and discourage reforestation. The reason is fairly clear; heavy annual taxes require steady inputs of investment funds, thus raising interest charges and putting more funds at risk. Other complaints against the property tax are: poor assessment techniques, the almost universal practice of over-assessing small properties in relation to large properties, and the competitive disadvantage of investment in forest lands, which can be neither moved nor concealed, in relation to investment in intangibles which can be moved or concealed.

For a long time property taxes were regarded as a major obstacle to better forest management and much effort was exerted in trying to work out some modification more favorable to forests. Recently, however, there has been a change of attitude; now the Forest Service states: ". . . the effect of property taxes as a deterrent to forestry has generally been exaggerated . . . Less than half the private land is likely to be influenced in its management by property taxes, and only a fraction of this is probably appreciable affected."[31] The principal reason for that change has been a great reduction in the importance of property taxes; 40 years ago they produced almost half of all tax revenues in this country, while today they produce only about 10 per cent. In the past 20 years, prices and nearly all other taxes have been increased greatly while property taxes have increased very little and in some cases have declined.[32] For those who pay income taxes, the importance of property taxes has been reduced further by the fact that they can be deducted in computing income tax liability. For all these reasons, property taxes are no longer the urgent problem they were a few years ago.

Income taxes, which have increased most in recent years, probably do not have any detrimental effect on forest practices. In fact, ". . . the high (income) tax rates of recent years may have encouraged concerns with high income to spend more for forestry."[33] One reason for this is that the Federal Income Tax Law permits the receipts from the sale of timber to be treated as a capital gain. For all income taxpayers

[31] *Forests and National Prosperity, op. cit.,* p. 97.
[32] No data are immediately available on property taxes paid on forest lands as such but taxes paid on farm real estate are probably a good indication of the taxes paid on small holdings of forest lands. For certain recent years tax levies on farm real estate in cents per acre have been as follows in selected states:

STATE	1920	1930	1935	1940	1943	1946
Alabama	19	25	21	20	21	22
Arkansas	33	32	28	29	31	31
Georgia	28	30	23	14	15	24
Louisiana	55	57	45	32	33	35
North Carolina	34	59	32	37	38	41
South Carolina	35	40	30	30	25	23
Virginia	23	34	25	26	26	28
United States	51	57	37	38	37	46

Agricultural Statistics, 1946, p. 600; 1947, pp. 564–65.

[33] *Forests and National Prosperity, op. cit.,* p. 98.

this cuts taxable income in half and for those with large incomes it sets a maximum tax rate of 25 per cent on the gain.

Although the problem has declined in urgency, it still is desirable to give the owner of forest land some assurance that in the future he will not be saddled with heavy property taxes. Various methods have been proposed to accomplish this. One widely discussed method some years ago was to substitute a yield tax for the property tax but this has been disappointing in practice and is no longer recommended.[34] Other proposals are too elaborate and complex for practical use. Perhaps the simplest and most feasible plan for use in southern states is the differential timber tax. This plan

> leaves the land subject to the ordinary property tax but classifies the timber for differential assessment . . . A fixed percentage, definitely stated in the law, would be deducted from the assessed value of the timber, determined in the ordinary way, in order to obtain the taxable value to which the regularly determined tax rates would be applied.[35]

The Fairchild group, which made the most extensive study of forest taxation ever attempted in this country, believed that the use of this plan ". . . would cause no immediate loss of local tax revenues that would be serious, and its ultimate effect on tax revenues in forest districts should be favorable."[36]

Another possibility would be a "modernized" yield tax of the type recently adopted by New Hampshire. That law

> . . . removed the old property tax from standing timber and substitutes a 10 per cent stumpage tax when the wood actually is cut.
>
> Where the New Hampshire law goes one step farther is in a provision that permits owners and operators to obtain an abatement of 3 per cent if the Forestry Board finds that the cutting complied with a program of orderly cutting procedures and forest conservation as outlined in the legislation.
>
> The new law further provides for reimbursement of lost property-tax revenues to towns through a $300,000 bond issue. This, in turn, is to be amortized by allocating $25,000 annually from the forestry-recreation fund.[37]

[34] Alabama has an optional yield tax and Mississippi has a general compulsory yield tax adopted in 1940.
[35] F. R. Fairchild et al., *Forest Taxation in the United States*, Washington, Forest Taxation Inquiry, Misc. Pub. No. 218, 1935, p. 603.
[36] *Ibid*, p. 608.
[37] *The New York Times*, July 31, 1949, Sec. 1, p. 37. Quoted by permission.

Getting Trees Planted. Once facilities have been provided to aid land owners in starting a forestry program, the next important step is to get trees planted—billions of them—on the millions of acres of poorly stocked and denuded lands of the South. Most of the states have, with federal aid, established state nurseries to supply seedlings to forest owners free or at a nominal cost. These should be expanded. Federal aid helps to make available technical aid and advice to forest owners. The Production and Marketing Administration makes conservation payments to farmers to plant trees and improve their forests. These aids should be developed and publicized. These things can be done at a small cost and offer the best promise of large returns.

Several southern states are already making extensive efforts along this line. In 1946, southern farmers planted 19,692,000 trees on their farms, the bulk of them in the four states of Florida, Georgia, Mississippi, and South Carolina. Total costs were $165,000, of which the states provided $131,000.[38] In Louisiana in 1948 it was reported that,

The demand for tree seedlings to replant idle lands exceeds fifteen or twenty times the number of tree seedlings the Commission is now producing. The backlog of orders for seedlings approximates 100,000,000 trees.

Tree planting machines are being purchased in large numbers by landowners. Such machines will set out 10–15,000 trees per day. Banks and Chambers of Commerce have bought these machines for loan to landowners in their areas.[39]

From another source it is reported that

State tree nurseries in the five Southeastern states (from Virginia through Florida) produced over 50 million seedlings for distribution in 1948. Even so, supplies fell far short of demands. In many states the demands this year are double or treble what they were last year. Production goals for Southeastern state nurseries in 1949 total 98½ million seedlings, and even this will not satisfy requests.[40]

Farmers and other small landowners can restock their idle acres at a very small expenditure of time and money. Every effort should be made to inform them of this fact and get the trees growing. Policies for the forest insurance and contracts for the low-cost loans described above should require a specified minimum number of growing trees

[38] *Agricultural Statistics,* 1947, p. 651.
[39] Louisiana Forestry Commission, *The Louisiana Forestry Plan, Explanatory Notes,* Baton Rouge, 1948, p. 3.
[40] *Biennial Report of the Southeastern Forest Experiment Station, 1947–1948,* p. 13.

per acre. The differential tax plan should contain a similar provision. These practices, plus the natural reseeding which goes on all the time, could bring about a great change in the southern landscape in a relatively few years.

More Trained Personnel. The program here outlined would require for its effective administration a great increase in the number of trained foresters. Arrangements would have to be made to recruit those men and make them available in the most effective way. Provisions would also have to be made for training more men. The ultimate success of the program would depend heavily on the calibre of the technicians obtained to administer it.

Providing Harvesting Aids and Facilities. The program as outlined thus far would, if successful, get a forest program launched, get the trees planted, and provide a satisfactory minimum level of forest management. The final steps, and often the most crucial ones profit-wise, are to get the timber products successfully harvested and marketed. In these steps the small owner will need considerable advice and assistance.

In harvesting he will need advice and, in the beginning, probably actual assistance in choosing what trees to cut and when. He must decide whether to sell the timber on the stump or to cut and deliver it himself. With pulp wood he could do the harvesting himself with the aid of equipment usually available on the average farm, but for the saw timber he may need expensive equipment which he could not afford to buy for a few days use per year. In the latter case, he might be able to rent it or form a cooperative group with his neighbors to buy it.

If the small owner is to make a profit from forestry operations he must do so by using them to provide employment in slack seasons. Cotton and tobacco farming provides several weeks, if not months, of very low employment each year.[41] The harvesting of timber offers an almost ideal opportunity for the use of labor during such periods since it is readily adaptable to the time available. Further, harvesting may offer a greater return than any other phase of forestry; for a few days of work in harvesting an acre of timber, an owner may derive a

41 For example, charts of the labor requirements in man-hours on farms in the tobacco belt of North Carolina show that for any feasible combination of crops (excluding dairying and poultry and cattle raising) the labor requirements for the months of January, February, and December are very low or nil.

greater return than he obtains from 30 or 40 years of tree growth.[42]
It is another application of the general principle that larger profits
are to be made from the further processing of the raw materials.

Providing Better Marketing Facilities. Marketing facilities have probably received less attention than any other phase of forestry operations.
Here the small owner is at great disadvantage, especially in selling
saw timber. The market is poorly organized, poorly financed, and
widely scattered geographically so that there is usually little competition between buyers at any given place. The small seller usually makes
only a few sales during a lifetime and so is unfamiliar with every
phase of the operation, while buyers usually specialize in that operation. The usual practice is to sell all the timber on a given tract of
land for a lump sum. The seller usually has no way of knowing how
much timber he is selling, what its quality is, or what the current market price is.[43] He may be under financial pressure to sell and, in any
case, the lump sum offered, even though it be unreasonably small,
may appear large to him. Obviously, much needs to be done in educating and assisting the small owner in selling his saw-timber. The
Department of Agriculture has spent, and is spending, large amounts
of money for research, study and promotion of the sale of agricultural
crops. The expenditures of small amounts on the marketing of forest
products would seem to offer the promise of a great improvement.

With pulp wood the principal needs are to provide sellers with
market information, establish points to which they may deliver their
wood, and provide facilities for assembling small lots into lots large
enough for shipment. Also, some agency must negotiate the best price
possible and arrange for prompt payment to sellers.

---

[42] "One study concerning pine timber indicates that on the average a tree 15 inches
in diameter with standing timber at $5 per thousand board feet would be worth
$0.80 on the stump, but cut and delivered to the mill would be worth $2.40. Similarly, with pulpwood worth $1 per cord in standing timber, a 10 inch tree would
be worth $0.13, but cut and delivered would be worth $0.72.

In a hardwood operation, timber worth $5 on the stump is estimated as worth
$20 delivered as logs to the mill. A profit of 31 per cent is figured, on the average,
for cutting and delivering. Thus, if a farmer would perform these operations himself, he could earn $8.80 for his labor in cutting, skidding, and hauling (providing
he could do the work as efficiently as the operators), and also take a $6.20 profit."
Federal Reserve Bank of St. Louis, *Monthly Review*, June 1, 1948, p. 78.

[43] "When stumpage is sold not by measure but simply by the boundary for a lump
sum, obviously there is no standard of comparison between transactions and the
concept of a market price disappears altogether." William A. Duerr, *op. cit.*, p. 188.
Duerr devotes almost half of his book to a comprehensive and detailed discussion
of marketing problems.

The problems here are many and difficult. Some attempts are being made to establish services which will supply price and market information. The Department of Forestry at Purdue University publishes about four times a year a timber marketing bulletin.

Timber owners contemplating selling can send details on the amount and kind of stumpage for sale. These listings are assembled and sent out to veneer mills, sawmills, mines, basket companies and other wood users. Such users are able to travel farther than they ordinarily would to bid on a particular tract of timber fulfilling their requirements. Thus an individual farmer may be brought in contact with several buyers who ordinarily might not have been contacted.[44]

In Georgia, the Extension Forester, in cooperation with the Georgia Crop Reporting Service and the Southeastern Forest Experiment Station, is trying out a price-reporting service for forest products, but it is still in the experimental stage.[45]

Other attempts have been made to deal with the problem through cooperatives. There have been cooperative associations and groups in forestry for many years, but their success has been no better than mediocre at best.[46] The small-scale, side-line nature of the forest activities of small owners and the spasmodic nature of the returns do not provide the owners with much incentive to join cooperatives. Some attempts have been made to have regular farm groups and cooperatives help with marketing forest products. In one southeastern Illinois county, a branch of the local county Farm Bureau handles pulp wood and saw-timber.[47] In 1946 The Farmers Mutual, Inc. of Durham, N. C. embarked on an experimental project to market pulp wood. One study covering the first two years of the operation of this project found that it had been fairly successful.

Its financial success has stimulated interest by the officials of The Farmers Mutual, and to the patrons it has given an outlet for their forest products, an added cash return for labor already on the farm, and a cash return on farm machinery that would otherwise be idle.[48]

[44] Federal Reserve Bank of St. Louis, *Monthly Review*, June 1, 1948, p. 78-79.
[45] Letter from James W. Cruikshank, Chief, Division of Forest Economics, Southeastern Forest Experimental Station.
[46] See Forest Service, USDA, *Forest Cooperatives in the United States,* Washington, 1947.
[47] Federal Reserve Bank of St. Louis, *Monthly Review*, June 1, 1948, p. 79.
[48] J. Norman Worsham, "Financial Operations of Cooperative Marketing of Forest Products by the Farmers Mutual, Inc. in the Vicinity of Durham, North Carolina," (Unpublished thesis in the Duke University Library), p. 43.

There is a challenging problem in marketing here, and it will become more acute as more farmers and other small owners come into the market with timber products. We need more research and experimentation to indicate the best arrangement. It is possible that different arrangements will be needed to meet varying conditions in different parts of the country.

Marketing Facilities for Naval Stores. Naval stores are the only forest products for which there is a well-organized market. This is probably due mainly to the fact that there are only a comparatively small number of producers and most of the production is concentrated in rather a small area. There are adequate facilities for assembling, processing, and distributing the principal products—turpentine and rosin—and those commodities are regularly bought and sold in several markets. Price quotations are published regularly in several newspapers and in at least one trade journal.

In addition, prices of gum naval stores are supported by the Commodity Credit Corporation, operating through a producers' cooperative association. In 1949, the loan rate was 80 per cent of parity (reduced from a previous 90 per cent). In 1948, about 80 per cent of the rosin and 20 per cent of the turpentine went into loan. In June, 1949, the government was holding, from 1948 and earlier loans, some 7,500,000 gallons of turpentine valued at $3,750,000 and 133,143 tons of rosin worth $22,164,315. These figures represented, for turpentine, about 61 per cent, and for rosin, about 133 per cent, of normal annual consumption.[49]

Profits in Forestry. Although the return is long delayed, good forestry can be profitable, even to small owners. Records from the Norris-Doxey farm forestry projects show that

In 1947, the net return (stumpage value) on 13,531 farms representing a million and a half acres of timber was $4.05 per acre, or $472 per farm. This cut represented more than one year's growth on most of the farms, but in most instances cuts were made according to accepted practices and young stock was left to mature.

Another study of 89 midwestern farm woods in the hardwood areas for the ten years, 1935–44, indicates that annual net profits of $3.42 per acre were made after paying labor, taxes and interest on the investment.[50]

49 Letter from Mr. Carl E. Ostrom, Officer in Charge, Southeastern Experiment Station, Lake City, Fla.
50 Federal Reserve Bank of St. Louis, *Monthly Review,* June 1, 1948, p. 79.

In the South with its favorable growing conditions and usually low land values, good forest management should produce even better results.

One of the most widely accepted . . . general estimates is that timberland suited to the growing of pines can be made to yield a net income of $2.00 to $4.00 an acre (per year). Although no satisfactory data are available on forest land prices, this would mean a rate of return of at least 10 per cent on the capital investment.[51]

The above computations are on the basis of total costs. In many cases, however, there are idle acres which are producing little or nothing but which could produce timber. Interest and taxes must be paid on the land whether it is used or not. On such land the marginal cost of producing a crop of timber will be only a few dollars and a few days labor. On that marginal investment the rate of return might be large indeed.

[51] Federal Reserve Bank of Atlanta, *Monthly Review,* June 30, 1949, pp. 57–58. Elsewhere in the South it was reported that, "Offseason work by farmers with normal farm equipment netted about $1.00 per hour in wages in two studies over a four- to five-year period. This was labor profit only. At Bent Creek the gross return per hour varied from $0.81 for fuel wood to $2.50 for black locust posts." *Biennial Report of the Southeastern Forest Experiment Station,* 1947–1948, p. 17.

XII AGRICULTURAL POLICY

CAUSES OF LOW INCOME IN SOUTHERN AGRICULTURE

Low per capita income in the South has been rooted in the kind of agriculture carried on in the South and in the kind of market in which the products of this agriculture have had to be sold. Cotton culture constituted an inheritance from the economic conditions of pre-Civil War Negro slavery. This crop remained the mainstay of the South after the Civil War because it continued to fulfull the needs of an economy which was changed only by the freeing of the slaves and the widespread destruction of capital.

Under post-Civil War conditions the production of cotton, with the use of the simplest agricultural implements and with the system of sharecropping cutting down to a minimum the necessity for capital by the man actually working the soil, afforded a means for embodying a large volume of labor in a staple product. This embodied labor could always be sold at some price without the necessity for the use of great ingenuity in developing demand or catering to it or in developing an intricate market mechanism.

The poor terms of trade which this situation made inevitable were worsened by the existence of a protective tariff levied on imports of consumer goods in the interests of a vigorously expanding industry which was called "domestic" but which was scarcely domestic at all as far as the South was concerned. The protective tariff facilitated the job of insuring that the South should sell its labor cheap and buy dear the products of the labor of other countries and of other sections of this country. As large scale industry characterized by administered prices and monopolistic competition developed in the North, few of the advantages of technological progress in industry could accrue to the southern farmer, who had to market his product under the rigorous conditions of nearly "pure and perfect competition."

Apart from the disadvantageous terms of trade, the high ratio of labor to land and capital likewise condemned the southern population to low per capita returns as long as their incomes were dependent upon this type of agriculture. As long as one man in the South could tend no more than fifteen or twenty acres of cotton he could not hope to have the income of a midwestern farmer who with the use even of horse-drawn machinery could produce in the mixed farming which characterized his area, perhaps forty to sixty acres of corn, plus a substantial acreage of oats and hay which was largely turned into high-value animal products before they were marketed.

An agricultural policy for the South which affords the hope of per capita income at the national average must consequently operate to overcome these two causes of low income; namely, poor "terms of trade" and the even more basic factor of high ratio of labor to land and capital.

Great efforts have been made to overcome both these causes of low income and a substantial degree of success has been achieved. Greater attention has, however, been devoted during the last decade and a half to overcoming the poor terms of trade by the direct use of the powers of the state than to improving the poor ratio of capital and land to labor. Following the further worsening in the terms of trade for southern agriculture occasioned by the depression which began in 1929, the direct powers of government were invoked to this end. The whole galaxy of New Deal measures to improve the purchasing power of farmers, including acreage limitation, marketing quotas, governmental loans, outright purchases by government, together with benefit payments to farmers, was placed at the service of American farmers, including those of the South.

How much of the improvement in farm income which took place during the period of the "New Deal," the War period and the period of the Truman "Fair Deal," was due to these direct aids to agriculture and how much was due to improved domestic and international purchasing power, first accompanying the recovery from depression and then accompanying the war, it is impossible to say. The votes of the farmers of the nation, including those of the South, seem to offer abundant proof that they are convinced that direct governmental aid to agriculture was effective and that they desire it to continue.

The very popularity among farmers of the South of governmental agricultural price support programs has obscured the possibilities of improving the terms of trade of southern agriculture other than by governmental intervention and by measures which would improve income through a better ratio of land and capital to labor. Fortunately, almost unnoticed in the excitement of the controversy over governmental intervention to raise agricultural prices, a trend has been going forward which affords the opportunity to southern agriculture to produce greater results in increasing per capita income than anything which government is likely to be able to do by direct action in raising the price of agricultural commodities.[1]

The way toward higher value product per worker has been marked out by the trend of the last two decades in southern agriculture. The trend has been in the direction of: somewhat larger farm units, greater yields per acre, fewer persons employed in agriculture, greater mechanization on the farm, a shift away from the production of cotton alone and toward a system of mixed farming, combining cotton raising with the production of other crops not so dependent upon cheap labor and with dairying and the raising of poultry and beef cattle. In mixed farming, the return per worker is usually substantially above that which is obtainable from the production of cotton by traditional methods, so long as the price of cotton is not supported by the government at prices much above recent comparable levels for other farm products.[2]

The changes which have taken place are reflected in statistics com-

[1] It is questionable, of course, whether there is any limit to what could be done by government through a combination of price supports and outright payments from the U. S. Treasury of various sorts.

[2] It is obvious, of course, that the production of dairy products and mixed farming does not in all cases result in a higher value product per worker than in the case of cotton. In many circumstances the reverse would be true, depending upon the character of the soil and many other factors. If the current trend is not obstructed, cotton production will tend to be concentrated primarily in the areas where level land and high yields would facilitate mechanization.

It should be noted also that the trend towards larger farms does not reflect a trend towards the large, plantation type of farm. It reflects primarily a trend towards a moderate-sized unit which is large enough to make the purchase of a tractor economical and to permit some reasonably efficient degree of crop diversification. In many cases in eastern North Carolina, for example, farmers who owned sixty acres of crop land have rented forty more in order to have an economic, efficient-sized one-man farm.

paring acreage, physical production, and cash receipts from southern agriculture during the years 1929, 1939 and 1948 shown in Tables *XXIX, XXX,* and *XXXIV* in Chapter V.

The most striking change is shown in the lessened importance of cotton. The percentage of cotton in harvested acreage of major crops shrank from 39.6 per cent of acreage in 1929 to only 22.0 per cent in 1948. In spite of a substantial improvement in yield per acre, cotton was the only crop of importance which had a lower total physical production in 1948 than in 1929. During the same period other crops increased in volume of output, from corn which increased by only 5.4 per cent, through wheat, which increased 79.3 per cent, to soybeans which increased 554.4 per cent. More significantly, during the period cattle and cattle products increased the share which they contributed to cash receipts from farm marketing from 8.1 per cent to 15.1 per cent.

Along with the trend towards larger farm units, fewer persons employed in agriculture, and the mechanization of agriculture, has gone the trend towards soil improvement of all kinds. Improved practices in the use of fertilizer, erosion control through terracing and the like, the increased use of soil-improving legumes and grasses, such as lespedeza, ladino clover, and orchard grass, have contributed greatly to increased value productivity per worker. Immense room for improvement remains, however.

The role of the Federal Government in this field is well known. Research carried on in agricultural colleges and in experiment stations has had substantial support by the Federal Government. Erosion control and soil conservation have been facilitated by numerous federal agencies. The Cooperative Federal-State Extension Service, through county agents, has served to make available to literally millions of farmers the results of research in agriculture and given guidance in developing the most profitable types of agriculture and of agricultural practice. All the activities of the Federal Government which have stimulated soil improvement and improved methods of production— even though their administration sometimes may have been overlapping and not always highly efficient—have been of inestimable value to the farmers of the South. State governments have supported similar activities.

The activities of the Federal Government in agriculture have been described in countless governmental publications. Through the aid and guidance given by federal and other governmental agencies, increased physical output per capita in agriculture is likely to be facilitated in the future as it has been in the past. There has already been developed such a backlog of knowledge that increased physical output per capita in southern agriculture is already taking place and can be tremendously expanded upon the basis of existing knowledge.

Substantial stimulation of the trend towards greater productivity in agriculture would be afforded by the more general extension of loans for soil improvement and for similar purposes by local banks at reasonable rates. While this is primarily a matter of local policy, some of the Federal Reserve banks, notably that in St. Louis, have worked out a comprehensive program for the guidance and encouragement of local banks in making such loans.

The role of the Farmers' Home Administration in making loans available—primarily to share croppers and tenant farmers who wish to improve their productive efficiency and economic status through the purchase of fertilizer, workstock, machinery, and the like—has been one of the most important types of assistance to southern agriculture by the Federal Government. Assistance given through loans by this agency has been of substantial service in enabling tenant farmers to become land owners. Since other economic forces were favorable also, the number of farms operated by tenants in the South has been reduced from 1,762,000, or 57 per cent of the total, in 1929, to 1,140,000 or 42 per cent of the total, in 1944. This statistical change probably does not, however, reflect purely an improvement of the status of tenants. In some cases persons who were formerly tenants became day laborers and in other cases left the farm altogether.

RELATION OF FARM PRICES TO PRODUCTIVITY
AND FULL EMPLOYMENT

Increased physical productivity of southern agriculture would be of little avail if the domestic and international market could not absorb the larger crops which resulted. Nor would the southern farmer benefit from producing larger crops if these crops had to be sold at prices so low that his real income would not be improved by the larger output.

In a full laissez-faire economy, characterized by full competition, if the southern farmer produced larger crops which would bring lower prices, he could expect that the prices of goods which he bought would decrease likewise, since the production of goods which he bought from industry would also be expanding with resulting lower prices. Under these circumstances, lower money prices for his products would have been no disadvantage to the farmer. This process depended, however, not merely upon the operation of competition, but upon a considerable degree of freedom in international exchange of goods and upon a high level of industrial activity and employment. Farmers, however, have learned that they could not count upon the preconditions which would allow them to produce as much as possible without having to worry about the price relationship between the products they sold and the goods they bought. They discovered that during depressions agricultural production was maintained while prices fell. Industrial prices could be and were maintained because production could be and was curtailed when necessary to accomplish this end. Consequently, farmers have demanded, and have obtained since 1933, the intervention of the Federal Government in the setting of prices of farm products at levels favorable to farmers.

The South has, of course, been primarily concerned with the prices of cotton and tobacco, although there is an important interest in the prices of many other agricultural products. There has been an increasing tendency to work out a separate program for raising the price of each farm product. There can, however, be little justification from the national viewpoint for the natural tendency of growers to try to use the powers of government simply to get the prices which give the highest total profit to the growers of each of the different commodities.

PROBLEMS IN THE USE OF GOVERNMENTAL
POWER TO RAISE FARM INCOMES

The experience of both tobacco and cotton growers with governmental intervention and control up to now has demonstrated that—on the assumption that the same growers are to continue to produce these crops and that the entrance of new producers into the field is limited—they can obtain through government programs sufficient control of production, price supports, general and special subsidies, various types of benefit payments and the like, to raise their per capita income substantially over what it otherwise would be. It is not very convincing to point out to cotton growers, that even doubling the price of cotton through governmental action, for example, would not raise per capita farm income in the South to the level of the Iowa farmer. Doubling the price of cotton would of course diminish sharply the amount which could be sold without subsidy. But even if this were not so, doubling the price of an average sized crop of cotton above that which would exist without government intervention would still not overcome the basic disadvantages of the typical southern producer of cotton which is low productivity per worker. The southern farmer is likely to retort that in the absence of price supports by government his income would be a still smaller fraction of that of the middle western farmer.

The farmer is coming more and more to be unwilling to depend merely upon the highest price which can be obtained through production control. He has learned that there are such things as governmental subsidies which may be obtained in amounts running into hundreds of millions or even billions of dollars beyond what he receives in the form of market prices of the commodities he sells. The farmer is inclined, like other citizens, to be more interested in the size of his income than in the workings of the economic machinery which determine his income. It is difficult to explain to him that too high price supports may result in controls which would substantially hamper the development of a more profitable type of agriculture in the South.

The popularity of "governmental farm programs" is not a cause for wonder. Cash receipts from farming in the United States increased from a low of $4,743,000,000 in 1933 to $30,500,000,000 in 1947, more than a sixfold increase. The farmers' share of the consumer's dollar, which naturally tends to increase with the increase of farm prices relative to others, increased during the period from 32 cents in 1933 to 54 cents in 1947.[3]

Even though prices paid by farmers for commodities increased from 122 in 1930–34 to 246 in 1947 (1910–1914 = 100) it can be seen that this virtual doubling of prices paid by farmers for commodities purchased still left them three times as well off in terms of the real value of cash receipts in 1947 compared with their position in the depths of the depression of the thirties. This phenomenal improve-

[3] Data from *Agricultural Statistics*, 1948, and from *The Agricultural Situation*, U. S. Dept. of Agriculture.

ment reflected both an increase in prices and an increase in production.

The increase in cash receipts during the latter part of the period, namely from 1939 to 1947, is striking also. The increase for this period was from $8,168,000,000 to $30,500,000,000. This represents a doubling of real income. The increase for the South during substantially the same period was of a similar order of magnitude.[4] During substantially the whole war and postwar periods the so-called parity ratio of farm prices was above 100. It reached 121 in 1947. It has now (Jan. 1950) fallen somewhat below 100, however. Skeptics might question how much of this unprecedented improvement in the real income of farmers during the period of governmental farm programs was due to these programs but farmers were inclined to reason *post hoc, propter hoc,* even though they did not do it in Latin.

The question no longer is whether the per capita incomes of the producers of the staple crops of the South can be increased by governmental action—certainly, if the U. S. Treasury can always be relied upon substantially without limit. Experience has proved that this can be done. The pertinent question is—what are the criteria by which the success of such a program is to be judged?

In developing a program of federal aid to support the prices of agricultural products in the South, three criteria are essential: First, such a program should be generally consistent with national agricultural policy. Second, such a program should not obstruct, but on the contrary wherever possible should actually accelerate, the trend towards higher production per capita in southern agriculture which is already under way. Finally, a program for agricultural price supports must take into account the interests of both farmer-consumers and non-farmer-consumers as well as those of farmers who produce one particular farm product. It is obviously extremely difficult to propose a specific program of agricultural price supports by the Federal Government which would be satisfactory to the farmers of the South while meeting these three criteria.

The maintenance of parity prices on some historical base raises the problem of how the consumer is to obtain any advantage from the great improvements in technique and increases in volume of production which are taking place in agriculture. Assuredly a large part of

4 See Chapter V, Table *XXXIV*.

the net advantage of the mechanization of cotton production, for example, should accrue to the farmer. Is the consumer, however, to have none of the advantage in the form of lower prices?

The answer, in terms of justice, likely depends upon the future nature of our systems of pricing and distribution. If improvements and inventions in industry could be expected to result in lower prices to the consumer for the products of industry, then attempts to retain for the farmer all the advantage of technical improvements in production in his field seem definitely unfair. If improvements in industrial technique do not result in lower prices to consumers, but are instead embodied in higher wages and dividends through collective bargaining and administered prices, then the farmer can hardly be expected to allow the consumer to have the advantage of technical progress in the form of lower farm prices either.

The problem of the use of political power to accomplish economic purposes is not primarily one in relation to agriculture, but applies as well to the profits of corporations and to the wages which can be obtained by labor unions through collective bargaining facilitated by the use of governmental power. It raises with great force the question of whether a body which represents the interests of the whole country rather than those of separate regions or economic groups is not needed to consider the general welfare when decisions which affect that welfare are being made. The need is crucial for such a body to carry on economic analysis, to explore economic issues, and to stimulate industrial, agricultural, and labor groups to apply objective economic criteria to the solution of conflicts of interest.

Governmental intervention in the cotton and tobacco economies— while undoubtedly beneficial to the growers who have a historical base —has demonstrated serious shortcomings in respect to the most economically advantageous allocation of resources. The support of cotton and tobacco prices has probably helped to "freeze" production patterns in these commodities and limit desirable adjustments towards better agricultural production practices.[5]

The perpetuation of support prices for staple crops as high relative to other prices as those now current (1950) would probably necessitate much more rigid controls than those so far used. It would not be, in

---

5 It is arguable, nevertheless, that considering the whole period of governmental control, crop production is more diversified than if no control program had been in effect.

all likelihood, simply a question of limiting the acreage which could be planted to cotton and tobacco. Measures would almost certainly be taken to prevent the expansion of the production of corn, soybeans and other crops in the South, lest they compete with the production of those crops in the areas of "commercial production" (largely in the Middle West) where acreage limitations would be in effect.

Furthermore, the use of allotments in tobacco and cotton, together with the relatively higher prices brought about by controls, has made it possible for uneconomically small farms to continue in existence. This perpetuates the present unsatisfactory level of per capita productivity on southern farms which is so low compared with that of midwestern farms, for example. Finally, governmental intervention through export subsidies—either outright or virtual—on cotton, wheat and tobacco, has caused substantial difficulties in carrying out our national policy in international trade.

It has been pointed out above that there is one condition which is of the greatest possible importance in the maintenance of agricultural prices but which, paradoxically enough, agricultural price support legislation cannot by itself hope to achieve. A strong and steady demand for the products of both industry and agriculture is the most desirable of all conditions in order that satisfactory prices may be obtained for farm products. If this strong and steady generalized demand were always in existence, it would be difficult to argue in favor of governmental price supports, or any other forms of governmental control for agricultural products, except such as might be useful in preventing temporary sharp fluctuations in prices. During a period of generally strong demand for all products in the whole national economy, agriculture would not ordinarily need governmental measures to raise prices on farm products since the possibility of employment outside agriculture would eventually enable both farm operators and farm labor to command appropriate compensation for their services.

The desirability of intervention by the Federal Government in advisory "planning" of the acreage of various crops would still exist. "Forward pricing" by the Federal Government so that farmers would have some guarantee against fluctuations in prices might still be desirable. *In the absence of depression conditions, however, these guaranteed forward prices would not constitute a means of raising farm prices substantially above the average which would otherwise exist over a period of years. Such price supports would be justified only if prices were truly minimum floor prices.*

Somewhat paradoxically, however, although the failure of demand for goods in general which occurs during a depression is the principal reason why governmental farm price supports combined with production controls are demanded, it is perfectly hopeless to try to "cure" a general economic depression by action in the field of agricultural policy alone. This means that an agricultural program which may be necessitated by a depression cannot be counted upon primarily to cure it, and that the cure must be sought largely in measures outside the agricultural field.

The utilization of the powers of the Federal Government in dealing with falling agricultural prices during a general economic depression can indeed be counted upon to exert a supporting effect through the placing of the familiar "floor" under farm income. Support levels for farm income, just as in the case of support of incomes anywhere in the economy, can be of great use in stopping a cumulative fall in producer incomes which, if allowed to happen in any large and crucial sector of the economy, may initiate or at least seriously aggravate an economic depression. Furthermore, these income supports serve to a degree the same purpose as do minimum relief payments to the unemployed. They do help to maintain consumer purchasing power if during a depression the government has to borrow funds to support farm income and thus causes expansion in bank deposits. They may help to maintain consumer purchasing power also if funds for the support of farm income are obtained from taxes on the higher income brackets.

Appropriate limitations would need to be set on the use of such governmental price supports. These "forward prices" should not be set high enough by the Federal Government to encourage the expansion of production beyond the quantities which could normally be marketed. It is likewise important, however, that prices which are supported by governmental action should not primarily be used as an inducement for over-all curtailment of agricultural production. The Federal Government should not have to be in the position of saying to the growers of any farm product, "The height of the price which the government will support depends entirely upon how strictly you, the growers, will agree to restrict production. The more you will restrict production, the higher the support price which the government will allow you to have." This is an undesirable policy since, in effect, it is simply using the powers of the Federal Government to enforce a monopolistic price and to curtail production.

It is obvious, for example, that the Federal Government should not continue to support the price of potatoes when each year an almost incredible number of millions of dollars have to be spent to dispose of surplus potatoes, unless acreage reduction is carried out by the growers. However, what is basically wrong with the potato price support program is that guaranteed prices have been set too high by the government. The payment of millions of dollars by the Federal Government to dispose of surplus potatoes can be avoided most effectively, not by production control, but by lower prices. The lower the price, the less the difficulty in preventing abnormal expansion of production of any particular crop.

COMPENSATORY PAYMENTS AS SUPPORTS FOR FARM INCOME

On the assumption that there is to be some sort of governmental support of farmers' income, "compensatory payments" to farmers which would have the same effect as support prices in supporting farmers' incomes but which would allow prices of farm products themselves to move freely would seem to afford substantial advantages. Under such a plan the Federal Government might announce its intention of guaranteeing to the producer of farm products, say, 85 or 90 per cent of normal market price. This "normal market price" would be the price which, under conditions of a high level of consumer demand and reasonably full employment, might be expected to induce the production of neither a surplus nor a deficit in the quantity of the product needed to meet the estimated domestic and foreign demand. This "normal market price" could be expected to be substantially lower than parity price as it has been computed in past agricultural legislation. It would also afford a monetary return per unit produced substantially lower than under the formula of the Brannan Plan. If abnormally large surpluses were produced after "normal market prices" had been computed for a given year, the "normal market price" for subsequent years would be reduced.

If, during a depression, the price of a farm product fell below 85 or 90 per cent of the calculated "normal market price," farmers would be paid out of the United States Treasury an amount sufficient to make up the difference between the actual market price and 85 or 90 per cent of the "normal market price."

This scheme[6] would have the advantage of allowing prices to fall in a depression with the consequent encouragement to consumption, without diminishing incomes of farmers below the minimum set by 85 or 90 per cent of "normal market price." United States citizens would meet the cost of these compensatory payments through taxes instead of by paying higher prices for farm products. There would be the further advantage that the farmers who received compensatory payments would realize that they were receiving an outright subsidy from the United States Treasury and hence from the taxpayer. Under a system of price supports the farmer is not likely to realize that the size of his income depends upon government action just as truly as when the government hands him a subsidy check. Financed out of general revenues of the government, the compensatory payments system would be less "regressive" in its effects than would be the payment of higher prices by consumers—which would be the result of government price support. Furthermore, if firmly adhered to, such a program would prevent the accumulation of "crop surpluses" since farm products would keep moving onto the market at whatever price was necessary to move them. Above all, consumers would actually be getting the goods in larger volume instead of our allowing them to spoil or our having to dump them on the foreign market through gifts or export subsidies.[7]

The grower of cotton, tobacco, potatoes, or any other farm product is naturally likely to accept this doctrine of the limited functions of a governmental program to support farm income with extreme reluctance. He is likely to reason: "The purpose of farm programs by the

6 Somewhat along the lines of that proposed by Professor Theodore W. Schultz in his *Agriculture in an Unstable Economy,* New York, McGraw-Hill Book Company, Inc., 1945. The mechanics of our proposal are similar to those outlined for perishable crops in the Brannan Plan except that the compensatory payments would apply to staple as well as perishable crops. Payments to farmers out of the U. S. Treasury would also be far lower than under the Brannan Plan.

7 If crop restrictions were imposed as a condition for the maintenance of farm income through compensatory payments, it is highly desirable that specific soil conservation and soil-improving practices should be required as a condition for receiving benefits under such a program. It would also be desirable that a top limit, of say $25,000.00, should be placed upon the amount of compensatory payments which any one farmer could receive from the government.

Federal Government is to raise the price of farm products to levels higher than they would be if there were no such programs. If so-called normal prices are to be lowered as production increases the growers would have no advantage at all. God knows we have no trouble in getting lower prices when we increase production. We do not need the government to help us to do that!"

The answer to this is, in the first place, that the guarantee of compensatory payments based upon a percentage of normal price is bound to prevent farm incomes from going as low as they otherwise might during a time of depression or of temporary glut of the market. This function is the principal one that such payments can legitimately be expected to perform.

Farmers have a right to look to the Federal Government to prevent the catastrophic falls in prices of agricultural products in general which accompany economic depressions. Appropriate action by the Federal Government can go a long way toward "curing" depressions and even preventing them. If it can be demonstrated that depressions can be prevented without governmental intervention in agriculture, almost the whole case for governmental regulation disappears. Preventing economic depressions and facilitating the international exchange of goods and services must be relied upon as the principal means by which the Federal Government prevents general declines in farm prices below reasonable levels. Appropriate action by the Federal Government on the national and international level to maintain a general high level of demand for goods involves, however, fundamental measures in addition to those involved in governmental farm programs.

This is not the proper place to attempt to set forth in any comprehensive way the kind of federal policy which would be required to insure high levels of employment or to eliminate excess unemployment if it were actually to occur. It is almost self-evident, however, that our economy is momentarily dependent to a critical extent upon the demand engendered by our export surplus, financed through the Marshall Plan, and by our program of military rearmament. If the situation were to change so fortunately that either or both of these sources of national expense could be eliminated or greatly curtailed, we should have to substitute at once some combination of public works expenditures, extension of social security payments, federal aid to education, reduction in taxes—particularly in the lower income brackets—and the like on a large scale, if we were to avoid a catastrophic fall in demand.[8]

It does not follow that an economic system must always have a very high rate of expenditures by government to avoid a depression. In the current conjuncture, however, given the present state of development and organization of the American economy, it appears that the Federal Government must stand ready to support the level of demand essential to a high level of employment should the occasion demand it. Just when "the occasion demands it" calls for a high order of judgment indeed upon the part of Congress and the officials of the executive branch of the Federal Government.

INCREASED PRODUCTIVITY ESSENTIAL FOR INCREASE IN SOUTHERN FARM INCOMES

If governmental control and price supports are not by themselves a satisfactory program for southern agriculture, what are the additional elements of an adequate policy? As pointed out above, the control programs for cotton and tobacco have demonstrated that the incomes of the growers of these southern staple crops can be improved by such programs.[9] Nevertheless, it is certain that the most effective source of increased farm income per capita is increased productivity per person employed in agriculture. It has been pointed out that increased income obtained simply by raising the price of cotton and tobacco has two serious shortcomings. Raising the price will lower the amount that can be sold without subsidy, even though the elasticity of demand for both raw cotton and tobacco on the domestic market is relatively low. There is a decided limit upon the extent to which total income can be increased simply through raising the price of agricultural products. It is even more important that gains in the income to growers through price increases are likely to be at the

8 We could thus construct more hospitals, school buildings, bridges, and have larger social security payments and aids to education for ourselves instead of having either to furnish goods without charge to the citizens of other countries or to provide airplanes, tanks, artillery and atomic bombs for our own military forces. Consumers in the lower income brackets could buy more cotton shirts and sheets, more meat and more cigarettes as a result of the lower taxes.

9 Cotton and tobacco are chosen as examples of the application of this policy because these crops are peculiarly important to the South. Its applicability to other crops would, of course, be important to the South also. For an account of the applicability of one particular system to cotton, see Chapter XIII. For tobacco, see Chapter XIV.

expense of consumers. Increases in income that are the result of increases in output per man-hour, on the contrary, result in advantages which are likely to accrue to the consumer as well as to the producer.

MEANS FOR INCREASING PER CAPITA PRODUCTIVITY IN AGRICULTURE

It probably is not feasible to count upon a satisfactory rate of increase in the per capita income of persons employed in agriculture in the South if the number of people engaged in farming remains as high as it is now. The increase of productivity per man-hour to a satisfactory level must depend upon mechanization of agriculture as well as upon other changes in the type and methods of production in agriculture which combine to reduce the need for manpower while lowering cost of production.

If the number of workers on the farm remained unchanged, income per capita could be increased with difficulty, wages would remain low, and mechanization and the reduction of costs of production would be slowed up. A high ratio of population to crop land has been the basic factor in low per capita income in southern agriculture. In 1940, harvested crop land per capita of the farm population in eight southern states (Alabama, Arkansas, Georgia, Louisiana, Mississippi, North Carolina, South Carolina, and Tennessee) averaged 5.0 acres as compared with 15.2 acres in four midwestern states (Illinois, Indiana, Iowa, and Ohio) and 10.5 acres for the country as a whole.

To a considerable degree, low per capita income in southern agriculture reflects also the failure to develop labor-saving methods in the production of cotton and tobacco at the rate which has characterized development of such methods in the production of other crops. During the past century the amount of man-labor required to produce a unit of wheat was reduced by four fifths, corn by seven tenths and cotton by slightly more than one half. In 1880, a farmer could produce 200 bushels of wheat with the same amount of labor required to produce a bale of cotton, while at the present time he can produce over 400 bushels with the amount of labor required to produce a bale of cotton. The trend toward different types of production during the last decade has been in the direction which is essential if per capita income in southern agriculture is to reach much higher levels—levels which are assuredly attainable.

Acreage in cotton between 1929 and 1948 shrank by more than half, although it has increased again from the lowest point. Almost one fourth of the farms which had previously produced cotton ceased entirely to do so during this period. The average yield of cotton per acre in the South increased from 151 pounds in 1929 to an estimated 291 pounds per acre in 1948. While this reduction in cotton acreage was taking place, the acreage of open pastures increased by some 40 per cent. Acreage in hay, soybeans, small grains, and other crops also increased. Dairy cattle increased some 35 per cent in number, roughly, during the same period. All other cattle increased by some 75 per cent. Chickens on farms increased somewhat also. Livestock and livestock products accounted for 28 per cent of total cash farm marketing in 1929 and 39 per cent in 1948.[10]

This shift in type of production was definitely in the direction of greater value of output per capita. While this shift in the type of agriculture was going on, a reduction in the labor force employed on farms was also taking place.[11] Even though the mechanization of cotton has been greatly hampered by inability of the agricultural machinery industry to meet the demand for mechanical pickers and strippers during the war and immediate postwar periods, substantial progress has taken place. The number of tractors on farms has increased from 1940 to 1947 by well over 300 per cent.

The possibilities for further mechanization of cotton production are very great. One study made at the Delta Branch Experiment Station at Stoneville, Mississippi, showed 160 man-hours required to produce and harvest an acre of cotton under standard nonmechanized methods. Using mechanical methods thus far developed, an acre of cotton yielding nearly a bale of cotton was produced and harvested with 21½ man-hours of labor. A later study[12] indicates that both the mechanical picker and the stripper still suffer from substantial limitations. Only where a relatively large acreage of cotton is to be picked is mechanical picking cheaper than hand picking. The actual advan-

10 See Tables in Chapter V, Recent Developments in Agriculture.
11 Between 1935 and 1945 the average number of persons employed in agriculture in the South declined from about six million to about five million. One year later, however, there had been an increase of about one hundred thousand persons. B.A.E., U. S. Dept. of Agriculture, Farm Wage Rates, *Farm Employment and Related Data,* pp. 162–164, 1943; *Agricultural Statistics,* 1947, p. 503, U. S. Dept. of Agriculture, Washington, 1948.
12 J. Gwyn Southerland and H. Brooks James, *Mechanical Harvesting of Cotton in North Carolina,* Information Series No. 22, N. C. State College, Dept. of Agricultural Economics, Jan. 1950.

tage of fully mechanized methods depends upon the particular set of conditions on the farm producing the cotton, and upon the level of wages paid to agricultural labor. In some cases the financial advantages of mechanization are substantial. In other cases—where the land is not level, where the acreage to be harvested is small, and for other reasons—mechanized methods of production are not economical. Yet there can be little doubt that mechanization of cotton production is well under way and will continue to progress, with a consequent diminution in the amount of labor required.

The progress of mechanization obviously depends upon the availability of labor and the rate of wages. High wages in industry attract laborers away from the farm and raise the wages of those who remain. This process increases the cost advantage of mechanized methods of crop production and stimulates the rate of substitution of machines for men. Depression conditions in industry consequently could be expected to retard the rate of mechanization of agriculture. However, it is extremely unlikely that the government would allow wage levels to decline substantially even during a depression. Consequently, even if a depression did occur, mechanization would be delayed more by an increased availability of labor and a shortage of capital for the purchase of farm machinery than by any shift in the ratio of labor cost to machine cost.

A further change which would represent economic progress is a shift towards the type of agriculture which permits more continuous use of the labor supply on the farm and avoids the underemployment which has characterized southern agriculture. Thus in Mississippi in 1944, farmers worked 567 per cent more during the month in which they were busiest than in the month in which they worked least. In Iowa the figure was only 167 per cent.[13]

The substitution of other types of farming for cotton and tobacco tends to correct this uneconomical labor requirement during the "peak load" season. This trend toward other types of farming is already well under way. It has been estimated that the development of more efficient agriculture in the South would be accompanied by a reduction of about one third in the farm population directly dependent upon farming as a major source of income.

[13] A considerable portion of the data dealing with southern agriculture has been taken from speeches and articles by Dr. Frank Welch, and particularly from his unpublished speech on Jan. 29, 1949, referred to earlier, *Adjustments in Southern Agriculture and Farm Labor Requirements.*

EMPLOYMENT OF DISPLACED AGRICULTURAL
LABOR DEPENDS UPON INDUSTRIAL EXPANSION

It is obvious that a program for southern agriculture, which assumes a great increase in production per capita together with a lowering of the cost of production through mechanization and a shift in type of agricultural production, could be of advantage to the South and to the nation only if the labor no longer needed in agriculture could find productive employment in manufacturing, in commerce, and in the service industries. Improvements in the efficiency of agriculture, which would permit increased production while dispensing with the need for employment on the farm of one third of the existing population, might appear to raise the spectre of mass unemployment. As has been pointed out, however, the re-employment of manpower released from the armed forces and from war industries demonstrates conclusively that under favorable economic conjuncture no unemployment need arise. The trend away from agriculture as a source of income and towards industry has been pronounced during the past two decades. In 1929 income from agriculture in the South was about 65 per cent greater than from manufacturing. In 1948 it was only 10 per cent greater.

The absorption of workers displaced by the development of greater efficiency and productivity in agriculture could be counted upon, however, only if the demand for consumer goods and the expansion of industry were to remain at a tempo not greatly below that of the period immediately following the war. If a considerable volume of industrial unemployment were to occur, it would be absolutely essential that both emergency and long-term measures to deal with it should be undertaken by the Federal Government. Public works programs and other emergency measures, coupled with more basic measures designed to encourage the expansion of employment in industry, would be required if desirable adjustments in agriculture were to have a chance to be accepted as socially desirable.

ALTERNATIVE TYPES OF AGRICULTURE

Aside from governmental control measures, and even apart from more basic developments to increase the mechanization of agriculture and to reduce the number of uneconomically small farms and in general to improve the ratio of land and capital investment per worker, there are other alternatives for southern agriculture which cannot be stated in general terms but which may offer opportunities just as great. The measures outlined above would have the effect of increasing the incomes of southern farmers by making southern agriculture more like that of the Middle West. There are other alternatives which in their effect would make southern agriculture resemble somewhat more the agricultural organization which characterizes California.

The possibilities for using in the South some of the techniques of production and marketing which characterize the state of California can be perhaps visualized by suggesting a fantastic hypothesis. Suppose, an actual impossibility, that a tract of land of, say, fifty thousand acres, now located in North Carolina, valued at, say, fifty dollars per acre, with all its geological and climatic features intact could be transported and set down in one of the fruit- or vegetable-producing areas or in some other area in California producing a high value per acre. Such a fifty thousand acre tract in North Carolina might include some land which had been producing corn and cotton. A substantial portion would be somewhat eroded and covered with brush or with a mixture of second-growth pine and hardwood. What could happen to this land if it could be transported complete with its climate, including its annual rainfall, to one of the California areas mentioned? One could be quite sure that a considerable capital investment would at once take place. The timber and brush would be cleared away. It is quite possible that even with an annual rainfall as high as that in North Carolina, some irrigation facilities would be provided by the California proprietors of the mythical, transported land to insure that the water would be available during the period of sporadic deficiency. Heavy expenditures for fertilizer would be made.

The capital investment entailed might well be one hundred dollars per acre, or even double this amount. The land would quite possibly, however, now be able to produce crops such that its worth would be say, a thousand dollars per acre. Instead of producing one crop and letting the land lie idle the rest of the year, the Californians would plant as many successive crops as the season (remember by hypothesis, the North Carolina season) would permit. Planting, cultivation, and harvesting would be as fully mechanized as possible. If carrots were raised, for example, they would be sent to market in huge trucks, perhaps with trailers attached. The carrots would have been washed, sorted, and graded and a time schedule would have been carefully worked out so that the quality of the carrots would not have been damaged by the time spent in each particular stage of their transport. Instead of each small-scale producer selling his crop individually for what someone offered him, the Californians would probably have developed a highly organized marketing system.

The Californians, indeed, might seize the opportunity to start producing and marketing some exotic fruit or vegetable, hitherto uncommon or unknown on the American dinner table. They might, on the other hand, even decide to raise cotton. If this decision were made, however, one could be pretty sure that the yield per acre would be much higher than it is in North Carolina and that the land would have to bear other crops in addition to cotton after the cotton was picked and before the land had to be planted in cotton for the next season.

All this is not to support the doctrine that Californians are supermen. It is simply that a differently organized type of agricultural society developed in California. There are no basic barriers to developing in the South somewhat the same kind of agricultural production and marketing system which has characterized California, however. In this direction the possibilities are very great.

There is reason to believe that the development of irrigation in some areas of the South would result in substantial gains in productivity. This is particularly true with respect to the possibilities of "sprinkle irrigation." Because it is possible to produce crops without irrigation, neither agricultural experiment stations in the South, nor farmers themselves have adequately considered whether irrigation during periods of deficiency in rainfall would not more than pay for its costs.

In general, most of the South is blessed with plentiful rainfall. Nevertheless, there are periods of several months in many areas of the South, when a supplementary crop could be raised were it not for insufficient rainfall during a few critical weeks. Often the land would bear another crop if water were provided for these weeks of insufficient rainfall, even though annual rainfall is more than adequate. Often the growth of pastures and of other crops is severely cut because of sporadic deficiency in rainfall. Yet in these areas, water in creeks and rivers is often only a few hundred yards distant. The development of light-weight, flexible pipes which can be readily moved from place to place by the use of light tractors further accentuates the possibilities of sprinkle irrigation for a number of areas in the South.

It has been pointed out that substantial progress has been made in the direction of a type of agriculture which through mechanization, and the development of meat, poultry, and dairy production makes possible the more continuous and efficient utilization of land, equipment, and labor. Progress which has taken place in North Carolina, for example, through the use of new types of legumes and grasses is making possible what the South has so badly needed, really productive pastures. This gives promise of what might be called a minor agricultural revolution. The importance of this development in making use of one of the South's great advantages, a long growing season, can hardly be over estimated. Similar developments are taking place in the agriculture of other southern states.

Closely associated with this type of development are the potentialities which are inherent in the truly vast amount of land in the South which is not now in production but which could be brought into use by relatively modest capital investment. Much of this land has been farmed in the recent past but has been abandoned, as its fertility was exhausted and as erosion set in. Of course, much of this land had better be used for reforestation rather than reclaimed for agricultural uses. The trouble is that so much of it is "neither fish, flesh, nor fowl." It is often allowed to grow up in brush or in timber of little or no commercial value. There is usually inadequate fire protection. Such land is of no use for agriculture and may never be of much value for purposes of forestry either.

A number of recent developments have made the prospects for agricultural uses of such land a good deal brighter. The development of more efficient bulldozers and other earth-moving equipment has helped. The development of new types of legumes and grasses particularly adapted to the South has been mentioned. It is reported that the use of chemicals of the weed killer type in eliminating underbrush has substantial possibilities in the direction of cheapening the process of clearing the land. Finally the more effective utilization of fertilizers also is of importance in this connection.

What is needed is greater imagination and a series of leaders who will in effect act as catalytic agents to get the process started. Often land is not put to far more profitable uses simply because initiative is "stymied" by the thought of spending perhaps as much on the amelioration of a tract of land as its present worth in its unimproved state. This may often be true, even though the total investment may not be very great and even though the value of such land might be tripled or quadrupled by the additional investment. Less spectacular additional investment devoted to increasing the productivity of land which is already in cultivation would often yield substantial returns. There has been encouraging experience in the results of making loans on land for such purposes by banks in agricultural areas of the South but only a beginning has been made.

There can be little doubt that the marketing of specialty crops which could be produced in the South has not been developed to any substantial fraction of its possibilities. For example, the possibilities of marketing hams from peanut-fed hogs, cured "country style," have been developed only to a very limited extent. Rarely outside the South is it possible to purchase real southern yams (of the so-called Puerto Rican type), at least in tolerable condition. In consequence, the average non-southerner has no conception of the gustatory possibilities of sweet potatoes. It is perfectly true that yams bruise easily in shipment and that they are ruined by exposure to freezing weather. Yet it would be ridiculous to argue that their relative perishability need be an effective bar to their profitable marketing in the North. Far more perishable products are marketed without serious difficulty. The list could be further expanded but these will serve as illustrations of what the failure to organize the marketing end of agriculture has cost the South.

There have also been notable instances of the development of specialized types of agriculture which indicate that there is no reason why California should have a near-monopoly on this type of development. In one of the mountainous counties of western North Carolina, a large fraction of the population was on relief during the depression. Most farms ranged in size from five to thirty acres. It seemed almost hopeless to try to achieve self-support for these people under such circumstances. A conference of governmental agencies concerned was called. Production plans for farms of five, fifteen, and thirty acres were worked out. In the main, reliance was placed upon the development of poultry-raising to improve per capita income in the county and farmers were encouraged and aided in building up large flocks of chickens. The almost phenomenal improvement in per capita income which practically transformed the county did depend in some degree on the success which was attained in marketing these eggs for hatching purposes at premium prices due to the lower degree of fertility of eggs produced in areas further South.

This one small illustration points up substantial possibilities of what can be done when imagination, initiative and persistence are actually operative. As the generally improved level of education, and the progress made by the agricultural colleges and experiment stations in the South begin to show substantial results, there is reason to believe that the great lag in per capita income in southern agriculture compared with that in other regions can be overcome. Consequently the importance of avoiding interference with progress due to the introduction of rigidities through too restrictive governmental control programs is once more emphasized.

XIII THE COTTON PROBLEM

ACREAGE, PRODUCTION, CONSUMPTION, AND EXPORTS

Since the 1920's the general trend of cotton production in the United States has been downward in number of acres planted and upward in yields per acre.[1] Cotton acreage in 1945 was not far different from what it had been in 1890. In the meantime it had doubled, only to decline again. The ten most important cotton producing states of the South reduced their acreage planted to cotton to less than one half, from 42 million acres in 1929 to 18 million acres in 1944. Total acreage in cotton in the United States declined somewhat less, for acreage outside the South was expanding during the period. For the United States as a whole, the reduction in acreage during this period of decline was over 40 per cent.

However, apparently an upward trend has once more begun. Acreage harvested in 1948, amounting to 23.3 million acres, represented an increase of almost 10 per cent over the previous year reaching an amount slightly above one half of the acreage in 1929. In 1949 cotton acreage expanded again, reaching a total of 25.9 million acres.

Yield per acre which had declined up to the early part of the 1920's as a result of boll weevil damage, thereafter began to increase and the trend has continued unevenly to the present time. At the beginning

[1] See Miscellaneous Publication No. 584, United States Department of Agriculture, issued December, 1945, "Looking Ahead With Cotton," for a brief survey of trends in cotton production and consumption up to 1945. One of the best current source of information about cotton is *The Cotton Situation,* published by the Bureau of Agricultural Economics of the Department of Agriculture. This chapter draws heavily on this valuable source. An immensely useful compendium of information on cotton is to be found in the Hearings of the Special Subcommittee on Cotton of the Committee on Agriculture, Eightieth Congress, first session, commonly known as the Pace Report.

TABLE *LXXVII*   COTTON ACREAGE, PRODUCTION, AND YIELDS

	ACREAGE HARVESTED			PRODUCTION (500 POUND GROSS WEIGHT BALES)			LINT YIELD PER HARVESTED ACRE		
STATE	AVERAGE 1937–46	1947	1948	AVERAGE 1937–46	1947	1948	AVERAGE 1937–46	1947	1948
	Thousand Acres			*Thousand Bales*			*Pounds*		
Mo.	388	431	526	365	311	505	451	345	459
Va.	35	23	24	24	18	24	342	369	480
N. C.	789	647	718	582	452	680	355	335	454
S. C.	1,182	1,050	1,130	753	651	890	308	298	377
Ga.	1,747	1,270	1,308	864	651	760	238	246	279
Fla.	55	24	26	17	11	13	159	213	239
Tenn.	708	700	750	537	520	650	366	356	416
Ala.	1,810	1,500	1,620	971	931	1,200	261	298	356
Miss.	2,504	2,350	2,540	1,700	1,569	2,350	324	320	444
Ark.	1,990	2,050	2,340	1,392	1,276	2,000	337	298	410
La.	1,042	830	933	588	505	760	265	292	392
Okla.	1,616	1,120	1,030	566	330	370	165	141	172
Tex.	8,061	8,350	8,750	2,894	3,437	3,200	170	198	176
N. Mex.	116	151	213	118	179	240	489	570	540
Ariz.	208	225	274	182	234	320	424	497	559
Cal.	361	534	804	444	772	960	589	693	572
All Other[1]	20	14	17	17	10	15	414	350	423
U. S.	22,631	21,269	23,003	12,014	11,857	14,937	254.2	267.3	311.5
Amer. Egypt.[2]	65.4	1.5	3.4	30.6	1.2	3.0	266	395	426

[1] Illinois, Kansas, and Kentucky.
[2] Included in State and United States totals. Grown principally in Arizona, New Mexico, and Texas.
SOURCE: *Crop Production, Annual Summary*, Crop Reporting Board, BAE, U. S. Dept. of Agriculture. Dec. 1948.

of crop control under the AAA, the average yield of cotton for the immediately preceding five year period, 1928–32, had been 174 pounds per acre. In 1948, an all-time record yield of 311.5 pounds per acre was attained following an almost continuous upward trend. Improved methods of production and improved boll weevil control had accounted for part of the increase in production. Government crop control, through acreage restriction, had also encouraged the use of the "best acres" for cotton production after 1933. Despite the tendency of acreage allotments and marketing quotas, during the years when these were in force, to keep cotton production on the farms which were entitled to such historically based allotments and quotas, during the years when production controls were relaxed or discontinued, cotton production kept moving westward where yields were higher on irrigated land and costs of production were lower on the high plains of Texas and Oklahoma, even with low yields per acre (see Table *LXXVII*). *By 1949, 52 per cent of the entire crop production of that year was produced in Oklahoma, Texas, New Mexico, Arizona, and California.* Some 60 per cent of the crop was grown west of the Mississippi. The pre-eminence of the Southeast as the major cotton producing area of the United States was disappearing.

During the first decade of the present century almost two thirds of all cotton produced in the United States was exported and only about one third consumed by domestic mills. Until the acreage control program of the New Deal got under way, exports were usually greater

TABLE *LXXVIII*   COTTON: EXPORTS FROM THE UNITED STATES, 1920–1949

SEASON BEGINNING AUGUST	TOTAL[1] 1,000 RUNNING BALES
1920	5,744.7
1921	6,184.1
1922	4,822.6
1923	5,655.9
1924	8,005.2
1925	8,051.5
1926	10,926.6
1927	7,542.4
1928	8,043.6
1929	6,689.8
1930	6,759.9
1931	8,707.5
1932	8,419.4
1933	7,534.4
1934	4,798.5
1935	5,972.6
1936	5,440.0
1937	5,598.4
1938	3,326.8
1939	6,162.9
1940	1,111.9
1941	1,125.1
1942	1,480.3
1943	1,138.1
1944	1,924.4[2]
1945	3,552.7[2]
1946	3,544.0
1947	1,968.0
1948[3]	4,747.6
1949[3]	5,770.6

[1] Compiled from reports of the Bureau of Foreign and Domestic Commerce and the Bureau of Census.
[2] Excludes shipments made by the War Department.
[3] Preliminary.
SOURCE: *The Cotton Situation.* Bureau of Agricultural Economics, Oct. 1949.

than domestic mill consumption (see Tables *LXXVIII* and *LXXIX*). Thereafter, exports never exceeded one half of total production and were generally far below this proportion.[2]

As exports declined, there was a general trend towards increased domestic mill consumption of cotton in spite of the competitive inroads of other fibers. During the war and the immediate postwar period, domestic mill consumption of raw cotton was at the rate of ten million bales or more per annum. Indeed, in one crop year, 1945–46, domestic mill consumption, at somewhat over nine million bales, was in excess of total production in that year when only about eight and one half million bales of cotton were raised on American farms. This increase in domestic consumption was due to population growth and particularly to the general higher level of industrial production, reflected in full employment which characterized the war and immediately postwar period.[3] Exports of cotton cloth fell off in 1948, accompanied by a drop in domestic mill consumption of cotton to nine million bales. An annual rate of domestic mill consumption of somewhat less than nine million bales, assuming that after the abnormally large exports of the immediately postwar period have diminished, we export about one-half billion square yards of cotton cloth, would appear about "normal" for a high level of industrial activity accompanied by full employment.

While acreage was declining, yield per acre increasing and total production of cotton fluctuating with no very pronounced trend, the relative importance of cotton to the South was steadily diminishing. For the ten chief cotton producing states of the South, the percentage of total cash farm income derived from cotton and cottonseed was 55 per cent, in the five-year period 1925–29, 39 per cent in 1935–39 and 33 per cent in 1940–44.[4] By 1948 the percentage was down to 27.2. Even more important was the rise of industry in the South during the period, which diminished the importance of the production of raw cotton in contributing to total income in the South. Thus cash

[2] Financed largely by Marshall Plan funds, exports of the 1948–49 season were around four and three-quarter million bales.

[3] It should be noted that so-called domestic consumption includes production of textiles for export, which in 1947 was at the abnormally high rate of almost one and one-half billion square yards, or the equivalent of almost one and one-half million bales. During the war years domestic consumption included consumption for military purposes.

[4] Data from a paper presented by Frank J. Welch to the National Cotton Research Council at Dallas, Texas, July 18, 1947.

TABLE *LXXIX* COMMERCIAL COTTON, ALL GROWTHS: WORLD SUPPLY AND CONSUMPTION, 1920–49

	SUPPLY					MILL CONSUMPTION[1]		
	Carry-over Aug. 1							
YEAR BEGINNING AUG.	UNITED STATES	FOREIGN COUNTRIES	WORLD TOTAL CARRY-OVER	WORLD PRODUC-TION	WORLD TOTAL SUPPLY	UNITED STATES	FOREIGN COUNTRIES	WORLD TOTAL CONSUMP-TION
	1,000 bales[2]	*1,000 bales*[2]	*1,000 bales*[2]	*1,000 bales*[2]	*1,000 bales*[2]	*1,000 bales*[2]	*1,000 bales*[2]	*1,000 bales*[2]
1920	3,563	8,189	11,752	20,628	32,380	4,893	12,258	17,151
1921	6,534	8,635	15,169	15,173	30,342	5,910	13,868	19,778
1922	2,832	7,662	10,494	18,451	28,945	6,666	14,671	21,337
1923	2,325	5,246	7,571	19,090	26,661	5,681	14,346	20,027
1924	1,556	5,058	6,614	24,094	30,708	6,193	16,541	22,734
1925	1,610	6,338	7,948	26,743	34,691	6,456	17,712	24,168
1926	3,543	6,932	10,473	27,930	38,403	7,190	18,489	25,679
1927	3,762	8,892	12,654	23,343	35,997	6,834	18,608	25,442
1928	2,536	7,999	10,535	25,802	36,337	7,091	18,687	25,778
1929	2,312	8,229	10,541	26,251	36,792	6,106	18,769	24,875
1930	4,530	7,362	11,892	25,376	37,268	5,263	17,169	22,432
1931	6,370	8,438	14,808	26,479	41,287	4,866	18,023	22,889
1932	9,678	8,658	18,336	23,461	41,797	6,137	18,514	24,651
1933	8,165	8,951	17,116	26,066	43,182	5,700	19,902	25,602
1934	7,744	9,796	17,540	23,042	40,582	5,361	20,119	25,480
1935	7,208	7,864	15,072	26,141	41,213	6,351	21,178	27,529
1936	5,409	8,240	13,649	30,729	44,378	7,950	22,688	30,638
1937	4,499	9,196	13,695	36,745	50,440	5,748	21,825	27,573
1938	11,533	11,169	22,702	27,509	50,211	6,858	21,649	28,507
1939	13,032	8,606	21,638	27,326	48,964	7,784	20,724	28,508
Average 1935–39	8,337	9,015	17,352	29,690	47,042	6,938	21,613	28,551
1940	10,564	9,698	20,262	28,720	48,982	9,722	16,923	26,645
1941	12,166	10,001	22,167	25,616	47,783	11,170	13,913	25,083
1942	10,640	11,945	22,585	25,582	48,167	11,100	13,273	24,373
1943	10,657	12,913	23,570	24,521	48,091	9,943	12,641	22,584
1944	10,744	14,660	25,404	23,631	49,035	9,568	12,668	22,236
1945	11,164	15,434	26,598	19,890	46,488	9,163	13,974	23,137
1946	7,326	15,715	23,041	20,154	43,195	10,025	15,927	25,952
1947	2,530	14,567	17,097	23,332	40,429	9,354	17,052	26,406
1948[3]	3,080	10,823	13,903	27,315	41,218	7,798	18,502	26,300
1949[3]	5,283	9,485	14,768					

[1] Excludes estimates for quantity destroyed and quantity used as adjustment items.

[2] American in running bales (counting round bales as half bales); foreign in bales of equivalent 500 pound bales.

[3] Preliminary.

Data on carry-over and consumption in United States from reports of the Bureau of the Census. Other data estimated by the Department of Agriculture or compiled from reports of the New York Cotton Exchange Service.

SOURCE: *The Cotton Situation*. Bureau of Agricultural Economics. Oct. 1949.

receipts from cotton including cottonseed, were 11.5 per cent of total income payments in the South in 1929 but had fallen to 6 per cent in 1948.[5]

While cotton production in the United States fluctuated during the last thirty years from a low of around 8 million bales to a high of around 19 million bales, a "normal" year's production might be taken

CHART X   UNITED STATES PRODUCTION, CONSUMPTION, AND EXPORTS OF COTTON AND YIELDS PER ACRE, 1929–1948

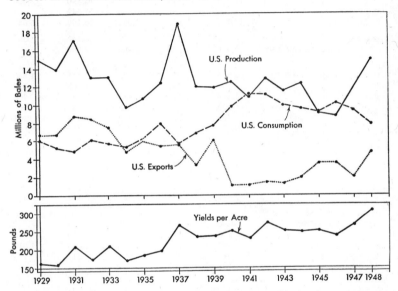

to be around 13 million bales (see Table LXXX).[6] During the New Deal, and during the war and postwar years when one could not speak of a pronounced trend either upward or downward in production in the United States, foreign production, with the exception of the war years, was expanding. In 1920 total foreign production was around

5 If cash receipts were reduced to net income the percentages would be in the neighborhood of 8 per cent and 4 per cent. See Chapter III, p. 63.

See also Chapter XVII, International Trade Policy, for an analysis of the diminishing importance of cotton exports in the economy of the South. See "The Stake of the Cotton South in International Trade" by John Van Sickle, University of California Press, 1945, for a statement of the point of view which still sees the future of the South vitally dependent upon its cotton exports.

6 This concept of "normal" is a hybrid one, meaning a sort of average of annual production since New Deal agricultural policy has been in effect.

TABLE *LXXX* PRODUCTION OF COTTON IN SPECIFIED COUNTRIES, AVERAGE 1935–39—ANNUAL 1946–49

	YEAR BEGINNING AUGUST 1				
LOCATION	AVERAGE 1935–39	1946–47	1947–48	1948–49[1]	1949–50[1]
	1,000 bales[2]	*1,000 bales*[2]	*1,000 bales*[2]	*1,000 bales*[2]	*1,000 bales*[2]
North America					
Mexico	334	460	484	570	815
United States	12,783	8,517	11,552	14,580	15,800
All other	40	36	45	49	67
Total	13,157	9,013	12,081	15,199	16,682
Europe	147	118	135	166	207
U. S. S. R. (Europe and Asia)	3,430	2,240	2,400	2,600	—
Asia					
China and Manchuria	2,855	1,925	2,136	2,115	1,860
India		2,341	2,510	1,960	2,400
Pakistan	5,348	1,157	925	826	900
Turkey	249	204	218	308	367
All other	568	229	259	303	321
Total	9,020	5,856	6,048	5,512	5,848
South America					
Argentina	289	334	423	446	—
Brazil	1,956	1,350	1,260	1,500	—
Peru	384	299	282	264	—
All other	87	97	78	104	—
Total	2,716	2,080	2,043	2,314	2,445
African and Oceania					
Anglo-Egyptian Sudan	248	235	215	256	—
Belgian Congo	172	172	184	220	—
Egypt	1,893	1,252	1,314	1,836	1,616
Uganda	281	193	141	317	275
All other	246	308	349	392	—
Total	2,840	2,160	2,203	3,021	2,772
Total Foreign Countries:	18,527	12,950	13,358	14,232	14,954
World Total (Agricultural)	31,310	21,467	24,910	28,812	30,754

Office Foreign Agricultural Relations except for United States which are from reports of Crop Reporting Board.
[1] Preliminary.
[2] American in running bales; foreign in bales of 478 pounds net in 1935–39 averages, other years in bales of 480 pounds net weight.
SOURCE: *The Cotton Situation.* Bureau of Agricultural Economics, Oct. 1949.

7 million bales. In 1936, three years before the outbreak of the war, it had reached more than 18 million bales. Foreign production was set. back during the war but is rapidly recovering.[7] During the six

[7] In the 1949–50 season, foreign production of cotton is expected to be about 15½ million bales. *The Cotton Situation,* October 1949.

years prior to World War II consumption of American growths abroad declined almost 50 per cent while consumption of foreign grown cotton expanded almost 70 per cent.

COTTON VS. SYNTHETIC FIBERS

Cotton had to meet not only the competition of foreign grown cotton but it had also to meet the competition of synthetic fibers, production and consumption of which were increasing phenomenally during this same period. In 1920 United States production of rayon was the equivalent of about 23,000 bales of cotton. World production was

CHART *XI*   PRICE COMPETITION, COTTON VS. RAYON: PRICES PER POUND OF RAYON FILAMENT YARN AND COTTON YARN, 1930–1948

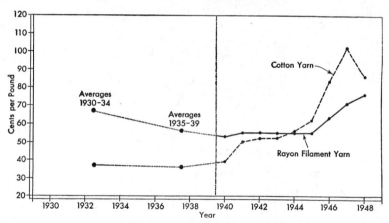

the equivalent of 78,000 bales. By 1944 United States production had reached the equivalent of 1.7 million bales. World production in 1942 had reached the equivalent of 8.2 million bales. By 1948 production of rayon in the United States had reached 2.6 million bales. By 1950 expected plant capacity in the United States will be the equivalent of nearly 3 million bales of cotton. By the same year foreign operable plant capacity is expected to be the equivalent of 6.5 million bales. Thus total world rayon producing capacity will by 1950 be the equivalent of twice the volume of our exports of raw cotton, even when these exports have been sustained by the Marshall Plan, and about equal to total domestic consumption.

The proportion of rayon in the total consumption of fine fibers in the United States increased about 6½ times in the twenty years prior to 1948, from 2.5 per cent of consumption to 16 per cent. Since 1942 the proportion of cotton in the total consumption of fine fibers has decreased every year.

At first the price of rayon was so high that it could not compete with cotton on a price basis at all. In 1920 filament rayon prices were over seven times higher than cotton yarn prices. By 1947 prices of filament yarn had dropped to only 70 per cent of prices of comparable cotton yarns. Even after the decline of cotton from peak prices, prices of rayon yarn were, in August 1949, only 92 per cent of those of cotton yarn. The competitive position of cotton was even more sharply

TABLE *LXXXI* COTTON AND RAYON: ACTUAL PRICES OF YARN AND EQUIVALENT PRICES OF RAW FIBER, UNITED STATES, 1930–34, 1935–39, AND 1940–1949

YEAR BEGIN-NING AUGUST	ACTUAL PRICES PER POUND		EQUIVALENT PRICES PER LB. OF USABLE FIBER			RATIOS		
				COTTON[4]		RAYON YARN TO COTTON YARN	RAYON STAPLE FIBER TO MID. 15/16″	RAYON STAPLE FIBER TO S. M. 1 1/16″
	RAYON FILAMENT YARN[1]	COTTON YARN[2]	RAYON STAPLE FIBER[3]	MIDDLING 15/16″	S. M. 1 1/16″			
	Cents	Cents	Cents	Cents	Cents	Per cent	Per cent	Per cent
Average 1930–34	67	37	46.83	11.68	13.54	186	436	369
Average 1935–39	56	36	28.56	13.37	14.95	155	215	193
1940	53	39	26.25	13.71	15.34	136	191	171
1941	55	50	26.25	22.33	25.01	110	118	105
1942	55	52	26.25	24.55	27.45	107	107	96
1943	55	52	25.20	25.07	27.97	107	101	90
1944	55	56	26.25	26.47	28.97	98	99	91
1945	55	62	26.25	31.26	33.15	89	84	79
1946	63	83	30.58	41.83	43.44	76	73	70
1947	71	102	36.33	41.39	44.87	70	88	81
1948	76	86	38.40	38.90	41.58	88	99	92
1949 August	71	77	36.75	38.17	40.54	92	96	91

Compiled from data from Bureau of Labor Statistics and Cotton Branch, Production and Marketing Administration.
[1] Wholesale price of Viscose on skeins first quality yarn, 150 denier until June 1947 since July 1947 "on cones."
[2] Wholesale price of Single 40's carded until July 1946, since August 1946, twisted carded.
[3] Wholesale price of Viscose, 1½ denier. Assumes net waste multiplier of 1.05.
[4] Price of Memphis Territory growths, landed Group B mill points and assuming net waste multiplier of 1.15.
SOURCE: *The Cotton Situation*. Bureau of Agricultural Economics, Oct. 1949.

threatened by the competition of rayon staple fiber which was introduced on the market in 1927. Rayon staple fiber in August, 1949 was only 91 per cent as high in price as Strict Middling 1-1/16″ cotton.

At this same date, raw cotton prices were almost three times as high as in 1935–39. Cotton yarn prices were over twice as high. Prices of rayon, both filament yarn and staple fiber, were only about ¼ higher than prewar. Cotton now had become the underdog in the price war with rayon (see Table *LXXXI*[8]). The future of cotton will be fundamentally determined by the degree to which it can meet price competition both of foreign growths and of synthetic fibers. So far, among the synthetic fibers only rayon is a serious competitor. Other synthetic fibers, such as nylon, are constantly being developed. They also may eventually become really competitive with cotton on a price basis although this has not yet happened. So far their use has not displaced statistically significant quantities of cotton.

MECHANIZATION OF COTTON PRODUCTION

In this connection the possibilities of mechanization in lowering costs of production of cotton are of first importance. Experiments conducted in an area favorable for mechanization have shown that the number of man-hours required to produce and harvest an acre yielding nearly a bale of cotton can be reduced by mechanical methods to not more than one eighth of the number of man-hours required under standard nonmechanized methods.[9] It is more difficult to transmute these man-hour data into comparable monetary costs.

Mechanizing the harvesting of cotton has limited effects in lowering costs if the planting and cultivating cannot also be mechanized, since it is difficult to obtain labor for only one or more operations when much less labor is used at another season. The development of the flame cultivator and check-row planting offer partial solutions for this problem. Much remains to be done, however, before a reasonably balanced seasonal demand for labor will facilitate mechanization.

The use of the mechanical picker, and to some extent the use of

8 *The Cotton Situation,* October, 1949.
9 See Chapter XII for a further discussion of mechanization of southern agriculture. A recent study indicates that both the mechanical picker and the stripper still suffer from substantial limitations. Only where a relatively large acreage of cotton is to be picked is mechanical picking cheaper than hand picking. See *Mechanical Harvesting of Cotton in North Carolina,* by J. Gwyn Southerland and H. Brooks James. Information Series No. 22, N. C. State College, Dept. of Agricultural Economics, Jan. 1950.

the stripper, is limited both by the levelness of the ground and variety of cotton. In addition cotton must be defoliated either by frost or by mechanical means for satisfactory harvesting by mechanical pickers and strippers. The grade of cotton is reduced when the stripper is used.

Nevertheless all these shortcomings are being steadily reduced. Excessively tall and "bushy" varieties of cotton are less easily handled by the mechanical picker. New varieties of cotton are being developed, the bolls of which tend to grow further from the ground and are more easily handled by the mechanical picker and are being adopted to fit the needs of mechanization. Ridging of the cotton rows during cultivation must be avoided if the picker is to operate to best advantage.

The rate at which mechanization will go forward will be greatly effected by the wages and relative scarcity of labor. If a depression were to occur mechanization would probably be seriously delayed.[10] With the continuation of relatively full employment in our economy it now appears certain that mechanization would go forward steadily. Progress was delayed during the war and immediately postwar periods on account of the inability of the agricultural machinery industry to deliver as many pickers and strippers as were wanted. This shortage is in the course of disappearing. The reduction in cost which mechanization promises must be the main reliance of cotton in maintaining its position as an important source of income in the South. Reliance upon governmental price supports to the exclusion of reductions in cost of production could eventually be ruinous for cotton producers.

GOVERNMENT CONTROLS

Until the depression of the thirties, the production and pricing of cotton in the United States was carried on almost entirely without governmental intervention and in very nearly complete harmony with the principles of a capitalistic laissez-faire economy. The South, indeed, had felt a deep-seated sense of injury over a period of a century at the one significant element of governmental intervention in the economy of cotton. The protective tariff forced on the South by the rest of the country could be credited with worsening the terms of trade under which the South had to market its great staple commodity.

[10] It must not be supposed, however, that wages of labor would be allowed to fall to anything like the relative levels of the depression of the thirties. Governmental relief payments, make-work programs and minimum wage legislation would prevent this even if a depression occurred.

Possessed of a large and growing population in relation to its supply of fertile soil and capital equipment, the South had to place its reliance for employing its masses of labor on the production and sale of a commodity which paid very poorly in compensation per man-hour. Cotton did indeed absorb large amounts of labor which could not easily have found other employment. This offset somewhat the low rates of compensation which could be earned in its production. It was natural that the South should feel embittered at the effect of the tariff in reducing the means by which other countries could pay for cotton raised in the South. In this way the already low real rates of compensation for growing cotton were made lower still.

New Deal Cotton Program. The feeling of resentment against governmental subsidies to manufacturers through the protective tariff played some role in developing southern support for the "Agricultural Adjustment" policy of the New Deal. This represented a major step in the direction of governmental direction and control of the economy of cotton. In the main, however, it was the fall in the price of cotton during the Depression of the Thirties which brought about the fundamental transformation in the direction and control over the production and price of cotton. When fixed charges of farmers, for interest, taxes, and the like remained an unrelieved burden, when the prices of manufactured goods which farmers had to purchase did not decline in proportion to the fall in prices of farm commodities, the old system had become intolerable. A year's production of cotton at five cents per pound did not absorb, during a growing and harvesting season, enough of a man's labor to pay for the annual cost of the necessities of life. If more had been produced the total return would have been even less. Cotton growers joined corn, wheat, and tobacco growers in demanding that somehow the government give them a price for their products which would enable them to buy the products of industry.

It is doubtful whether the cotton farmers, any more than the farmers who produced other staple crops in the United States, wished permanently to change their economic system. Certainly the curative legislation which was enacted reflected the hope that control of production and support of price would be temporary. Furthermore, at this early date the new legislation reflected not primarily the intention to obtain by its means the highest possible total return to growers of cotton but the firm intention to obtain a "balanced position" within the American economy.

The farmers and administrators of this Agricultural Adjustment Act at first clung firmly to the belief that farmers would require special governmental action in their behalf only so long as manufacturers could and did maintain the prices of the goods which they sold to farmers by means of reducing production in their factories. Farm organizations demanded that legislation be written which would give farmers the power to do what the corporate organization of industry had enabled manufacturers to do. Farmers thus felt the need to rationalize and justify their reducing production in order to raise prices by, in effect, tying their own action in this respect to the previous actions of manufacturers.

The first Agricultural Adjustment Act reflected this feeling. The goal to be attained for prices of agricultural products was designated as "parity prices," defined as the prices for products produced by farmers which would given them the same purchasing power with reference to commodities purchased by farmers which had existed immediately prior to World War I. In order to attain the goal of higher prices, production of cotton and other commodities was to be reduced by means of benefit payments made to farmers for taking an agreed-upon percentage of acreage out of production.

Funds for benefit payments to farmers were to be obtained through processing taxes placed upon the sale of the commodities, the production of which was to be reduced. These regressive taxes which bore with especial weight upon lower income classes were justified by a vague belief that in this way each commodity was somehow paying its own way.

There was written into the Agricultural Adjustment Act a so-called consumer protection clause, which stipulated that the proportion of the consumer's dollar going to the farmer for processed farm commodities should not be greater than it had been during the base period, 1909–1914. This "consumer protection" clause was, however, confused in purpose and largely ineffective.

In the case of cotton, as well as of the other staple farm commodities, the original program of attaining parity prices by means of restriction of production through benefit payments to growers financed through processing taxes proved inadequate for the purpose. In addition, other measures were instituted. These included the Bankhead Act (soon declared unconstitutional) which placed a penalty upon "over-planting," the purchase of cotton to be used in relief distribution, and a system of price supports through government loans without recourse to growers, who could "put their cotton in the loan" without risk of loss through subsequent decline in price. Gradually events were thus moving towards a policy by which both the original and basic justifications and means of carrying out governmental control of production and support of prices of farm products were in practice to be abandoned, without, however, a clear realization that any fundamental change in policy had taken place.

The *Hoosac Mills Case,* in which the Supreme Court declared the Agricultural Adjustment Act unconstitutional, actually facilitated this movement away from the old concepts upon which "Agricultural Adjustment" had been based. As a result of this decision it became impracticable to finance the program any longer out of processing taxes levied upon the commodities the production of which was being restricted. From the standpoint of social justice this was to be welcomed. There was certainly little justification for financing the restriction of production of goods by making the consumers of these goods pay for the process of restriction. If production control in agriculture was to be a function of government, there was every reason why it should be financed by the most advantageous and least regressive kinds of taxes. In other words, financing the agricultural adjustment program out of general revenues of the government, which was what actually came about as the result of the decision of the Supreme Court, was clearly a net gain, not only to cotton growers but to the purchasers of cotton goods as well.

Nevertheless, the elimination of processing taxes was an important further step in the emasculation of the old doctrine of historical parity price as a goal and in the development of the new doctrine that the type of acreage control and price support which was most desirable was simply that which would maximize the total receipts of producers of particular commodities. As is explained in Chapter XIV, this policy of maximizing returns to growers without any particular concern for historical price relationships could be carried out even more directly in the case of tobacco than in the case of cotton.[11]

11 A substantial proportion of the increased returns received by tobacco growers as the result of an acreage control and price support policy which resulted in tobacco prices around 50 per cent above parity if it had been computed the same as for the other farm commodities, apparently represented a deduction from huge profits which would have otherwise gone to a few large tobacco companies. Moreover, tobacco was not an essential commodity in the sense which was true of cotton and the other agricultural commodities. Finally any increase in retail price which the

Cotton growers were not so fortunate. The demand for cotton abroad was much more dependent upon price. Furthermore the production outside the United States expanded to a greater extent in the case of cotton than in the case of tobacco. Finally, domestic consumption of cotton did not expand as much as did that of tobacco. This did not, however, prevent the cotton program from being shaped more and more towards a policy of highest practicable total returns to growers.

The original formula which was based upon the idea that agricultural adjustment was necessary because industry would not maintain full employment and that agricultural prices should maintain a fixed relation to the prices of manufactured goods was being rapidly left behind. When the prices of American-produced cotton on the international market became "out of line" with that of Brazilian and other growths, a subsidy was paid in order to maintain the price of cotton to the American grower to avoid losing the foreign market.[12] Thus the returns to growers became affected by a complex of governmental measures, ranging from outright purchases, loans, and subsidies of various sorts, to benefit payments and payments for proper soil conservation practices.

Postwar Cotton Programs. In form, the parity concept has been tenaciously adhered to for all farm products, but the parity formula has been altered whenever it appeared that the returns to growers might be lowered by too meagre a definition of parity. It seems probable that the parity formula for cotton would have been altered even more than it was if that would have increased materially the returns to cotton growers.

Conservative economists had criticized the original base period chosen for parity on the grounds that the period 1909 to 1914 was a period in which price ratios were unduly favorable to the producers of agricultural commodities. Developments of recent years, in which the original parity formula has been varied in order to obtain higher returns to growers, show that the leaders of cotton growers, like most farm leaders, now that the device of governmental intervention and

---

program might cause was not likely to produce a marked decline in demand with consequent diminution in total returns to growers. In actual fact, the consumption of tobacco continued to expand so that tobacco growers benefited not only from much higher prices but from increased sales as well.

[12] This took place during the war years and during the years immediately after the war when Brazilian cotton sold for a time at lower prices than United States growths.

regulation has been made available to them, push their own economic interests with no more restraint than labor union leaders show in their pursuit of higher wages or corporate executives show in their pursuit of profits. The problem of what happens when there is no coordination in this complicated process of collective bargaining for shares in the national income remains not only unsolved but almost unstudied.

When the cotton crop of 1947 was just beginning to come on the market, surplus stocks of American grown cotton had been entirely eliminated. A succession of small crops, combined with heavy domestic mill consumption during the war, had reduced the carry-over of cotton to barely normal proportions. Even the somewhat increased crop which was harvested in 1947 was not much more than sufficient to provide for domestic mill consumption plus exports of cotton financed in large part by Marshall Plan funds.

Now, if ever, it seemed that governmental control of production and support of the price might be abandoned in favor of a return to laissez faire. The price of cotton was above parity. Industry was operating at full blast. Cotton growers could purchase in larger amounts than ever before the products of industry on relatively more favorable terms than in the base period, 1909–1914, which had been established as the goal to be attained by the original Agricultural Adjustment Act.

Cotton farmers having tasted the delights of 35 cents a pound cotton were, however, not disposed to rely upon the so-called automatic forces of a laissez-faire economy to guarantee them their "share" of the national income. They feared that unrestricted production without price supports might once again produce "five cent cotton." The producers of other farm crops apparently felt the same way.

There was, indeed, an attempt to "taper off" on price support. The Agricultural Act of 1948 was passed which reduced price supports on some crops under certain circumstances to a figure as low as 60 per cent of parity. The level of price support was made dependent upon the willingness of producers to restrict, if necessary, the size of the crop. The larger the supply, the lower the per cent of parity at which price support by government would take effect. In this way it was hoped that there would be some "negative incentive" which would automatically help to reduce production of crops in surplus.

With a crop of some 15 million bales produced during the 1948 growing season and a crop of even larger size in 1949, we were, however, once more confronted with the problem of "surplus" cotton. The re-election of President Truman in 1948 by an electorate in which the "farm vote" constituted a heavy fraction of his support meant that legislation in the economic interests of the farmer, including the cotton grower, was bound to have a high priority. While the die has apparently been cast for the continuance of production control and price supports, at perhaps even higher levels than those provided by the Agricultural Act of 1948, it is useful to compare the probable advantages to the cotton grower of the two alternative policies, control vs. no control.[13]

These alternatives have usually been represented as: (1) the continuance of high governmental support prices for cotton accompanied by production controls, with the result of almost no export of raw cotton, and (2) the removal of governmental controls, support prices and subsidies, and the marketing of cotton under circumstances which would enable us to sell a substantial proportion of our cotton crop abroad at competitive prices. Actually these two alternatives break down into almost countless others. Under the first alternative, one question would be at what level support prices would be set and under what circumstances controls would be used. Under the second alternative, there would be subsidiary questions of foreign trade policy which would produce not one but a number of alternative combinations of policies.

Above all, either policy, governmental intervention or completely free production and marketing, would produce far different results under conditions of economic depression as compared with conditions of full employment. In order to compress the analysis into manageable proportions, full employment in the United States might be assumed for both alternative policies. Let us then first examine the alternative of removing controls and support prices and selling our cotton abroad at whatever price it would bring.

First Alternative: No Governmental Intervention. We can begin the analysis of this alternative by asking how much cotton would be produced under these circumstances and at what price it could be

[13] For a useful analysis of the problem of cotton production and consumption in relation to price, see *Cotton's Way Forward* by M. K. Horne, Jr., Bureau of Business Research, Oxford, University of Mississippi, 1949.

sold. This problem has usually been attacked by trying to estimate how much American grown cotton could be sold abroad under these circumstances. The price and quantity produced and sold under the circumstances assumed, however, would of course be mutually interdependent. The amount produced by American growers would be dependent upon the price which they expected to receive, while the price received for American grown cotton on the international market would at the same time depend in part upon the amount grown in the United States and marketed abroad.[14]

If there were no subsidies on American exports of cotton, either general or through special American aid such as that provided under the Marshall Plan, the British Loan, and the like, it seems reasonable to surmise that American grown cotton would sell on the international market at so low a price that growers would not produce more than a million or so bales of cotton in excess of the amount of cotton that would be consumed domestically, say a total of some ten million bales.

It should be pointed out at once that this is violently in contrast with the customary assumptions which have been made. It has been almost universally assumed that without controls the amount of cotton produced would be greatly in excess of what it would be with government price supports and controls. It has been generally believed that it would be at least four or five million bales in excess of domestic consumption. If at a time when cotton was selling at six and one half cents per pound, as it was in 1932, and if exports in that year were at a level of over eight million bales, it might, indeed, seem a fair inference that at least four or five million bales above domestic re-

[14] It is quite impossible to forecast with any precision in terms of dollars and cents what any given quantity of American grown cotton sold abroad would bring per pound. It would be difficult to do so if the whole world were on the old style gold standard and if substantial freedom of trade existed. Under present circumstances it is an almost impossible problem to reduce prices in francs, lira, marks, and pounds sterling to dollar equivalents. Price levels in the United States may move in the same direction or in opposite directions from those in other countries. It is even difficult to determine when the movements of prices are in the same or opposite directions when currencies are wholly or imperfectly convertible, much less compute the difference in rates of movement. There are other difficulties but space precludes even the briefest analysis. It is thus impracticable to set up a demand schedule for American cotton, which might be used, along with a cost schedule, to forecast the probable price for American grown cotton under the assumption of a free market and no control. In all the discussion which follows, specific cotton prices on either the domestic or international markets are used only for illustrative purposes and do not represent forecasts of actual dollar and cents prices even under the assumed circumstances. The Korean crisis has already made the monetary prices assumed in the text obsolete. It is believed that the *relation* between the assumed prices, quantities and costs still retains validity.

quirements would be produced and exported at any figure at which cotton is likely to sell on the international market under present circumstances. But two things must be remembered in this connection. In 1932 the general price level was less than half that of 1949. Furthermore, in 1932 we were at the bottom of the depression. Domestic consumption of cotton was running at less than five million bales. With huge unemployment in the United States and with other crops selling at unprecedentedly low prices, cotton growers during the depression had no alternative employment for themselves, their labor, and their land and capital. What could not be sold domestically had to go into export regardless of how low the price was.

If, on the contrary, we assume full employment in the United States and if we further assume the general level of prices of 1949 except for agricultural commodities, (which by hypothesis would be much lower in price since they would not be controlled in production nor their price supported) it seems possible that if cotton could not be sold for more than say, twelve cents per pound on the domestic and international market without any type of governmental price supports, gifts, or loans to foreign countries, domestic production would not be much above the ten million bales, annual rate. Total dollar receipts from cotton would thus be about 600 million dollars. It might be possible to export as much as one million bales of cotton without general or special subsidy, while at the assumed price the domestic market would probably take the remaining nine million bales.

Under these assumptions of a production of cotton of some ten million bales selling at twelve cents per pound, we could reasonably expect that cotton production would be carried on largely by mechanized methods of production on soil best adapted for cotton production.[15] The labor force required to produce ten million bales of cotton under these circumstances might be nearly cut in half. The surplus labor would be released for the production of other crops and, above all, for employment in industry, commerce, and the service trades. A substantial acreage taken out of cotton production would be available for planting to other crops which yield a higher return per worker than does cotton as now produced.

It might at once be objected that such a "surplus" of labor and land

[15] For a discussion of the mechanization of cotton production see also the chapter on Agricultural Policy. It should be pointed out that under the assumed conditions the women and children now employed in cotton production would be largely withdrawn from the labor market instead of being in any real sense unemployed labor.

would be catastrophic. But it should be pointed out that even if as many as a million persons were released from cotton production it would not be a large number in comparison with the number absorbed in our economy following the demobilization of our armed forces and war industries at the end of the war. It would indeed be necessary that vigorous national economic policies should be followed in order to maintain full employment. There is no fundamental reason to suppose, if these economic policies were followed, that the shift of labor out of cotton production to other employment under such circumstances would need to cause a substantial general problem of unemployment. There would arise special problems, of course, since labor previously employed in cotton production might not be immediately adaptable to other employment. This would not seem, however, to offer insuperable difficulties.

It should be remembered that the land, labor, and capital so released could be used to produce commodities and services which we cannot now enjoy so long as these resources are employed in producing cotton under conditions in which real additions to national income per man-hour of employment are so low. Furthermore, under the assumption of no controls, no support prices and no export subsidies, either general or specific, as well as no benefit payments, the saving of funds to the United States Treasury would be very great and taxes substantially lower. Likewise prices of cotton goods to consumers would be lower as well.

It should be pointed out also, that under the circumstances assumed the loss of our export markets for raw cotton is not an actual loss. One of the most difficult and basic problems which has to be faced by the whole world at the present time is the difficulty which the rest of the world faces in paying for imports from the United States. Our cotton exports are not needed in order for us to be able to meet any potential deficit in our balance of payments. In one very real sense, we have not actually been receiving payment for at least a major fraction of the cotton which we have been exporting in recent years. We have, in effect, been exporting this cotton while the United States Treasury provided funds to foreign purchasers to buy the cotton. Thus we have not, in essence, been receiving real goods and services in exchange for a large part of our cotton but have been "giving it away."

Fundamentally, it would make much more sense if we were to have a balance between exports and imports so that we did receive real values for our exports. It is to be seriously questioned whether cotton produced by hand methods is a commodity which we should be exporting on any considerable scale for consumption abroad. A substantial case could be made for the proposition that American labor is too valuable to be so used. The expansion of cotton production abroad to meet foreign consumption needs would in part mean that dollars which formerly had to be provided by the United States Treasury to enable foreigners to purchase our cotton could instead be left in the pockets of American tax payers to pay for an increased standard of living. These dollars formerly taken away from taxpayers would be available to purchase additional goods produced by labor, land, and capital formerly used in the production of cotton exported abroad.

Second Alternative: No Controls or Price Supports but Removal of International Trade Barriers Plus Foreign Aid. The case for doing away with all forms of governmental price supports and production controls for cotton can be made to look much better if we assume the most favorable circumstances in international economic affairs from the standpoint of maximizing our exports. If we were to remove crop controls and price supports could we hope that a similar removal of controls in other countries would take place? Could we assume that a sweeping reduction in barriers to world trade would also take place? Could we assume that the vexatious deficit in the balance of trade of almost all other countries of the world with the United States would somehow disappear? If a substantial part of the deficit had not disappeared, would the United States still continue to provide funds to meet the deficit by some new successor to Lend-Lease, UNRRA, the British Loan, the Export-Import Bank and International Bank Loans, or the Marshall Plan? These circumstances, be it noted, might or might not exist either with or without governmental controls over cotton.

Let us examine the possibilities of working out the elements of a "no-crop-control situation" under the assumption of the widest possible international approach to free trade and the most favorable set of expectations with respect to foreign markets for our cotton.[16]

16 Yet "the widest possible international approach to free trade" is unlikely to result in the near future in anything very closely resembling the economic assumptions upon which economists developed the principles of international trade prior to World War I. In addition to control of foreign trade by governments and apart from barriers to trade erected by these same governments, we have, paradoxically enough, the type of "interference" with international trade previously referred to through the financing of our exports abroad by the United States government at a rate

Under these assumed circumstances one might suppose that without crop control or a special cotton export subsidy, but with the continuance of a general subsidy on our exports plus a considerable relaxation of trade restraints, a crop of, say, 13 million bales would on the average be produced and could be sold on the home market and abroad for, at a guess, 17 cents per pound. Of this amount we might expect, after allowance for additional imports of cotton cloth into the United States of perhaps as much as the equivalent of one million bales of raw cotton, eight million bales to be consumed at home and five million bales to be sold abroad. The total dollar income thus received, if 13 million bales were produced and sold at 17 cents per pound, would be $1,125,000,000.[17] Thus, under the highly favorable assumptions stated, total returns from cotton would be almost double those under the assumptions of no general or special subsidies and without any particular change in the institutions and policies of international trade.

Third Alternative: Governmental Controls and Price Support with Production Limited to Domestic Consumption. Now let us consider the alternative of continuing support prices plus controls by government. Under this assumption let us assume that a support price of 30 cents per pound would be set (see Table *LXXXII*).[18] What would be the consumption of cotton in the United States under these conditions? At once we must make another assumption. Do we assume that foreign growths would be excluded from the United States? It seems a certainty that exclusion of all foreign growths except limited amounts of certain special fiber lengths would continue.

But what are we to assume concerning our exports abroad of both raw and manufactured cotton products? Let us begin by assuming that there are no export subsidies, no special governmental loans or grants to make up for deficits in the balance of payments of European countries. But what are we to assume with respect to our barriers to trade?

---

which ran for a time around five billion dollars per year. Only through this gigantic general export subsidy were the nations of Western Europe able to purchase essential goods from the United States.

[17] It has been pointed out that at full employment domestic consumption of cotton would probably be around eight to nine million bales per year.

Remember that all prices assumed are intended to show relationships of various prices, quantities and costs and are not forecasts of actual prices.

[18] The support price as of August 1, 1949, for 7/8″ middling was 27.23 cents per pound. However, the support price for 15/16″ middling, which is more commonly thought of as "the price of cotton" was 29.43 cents per pound.

TABLE *LXXXII*   PARITY PRICES, AND FARM PRICES OF COTTON, IN CENTS PER POUND, UNITED STATES, 1940–49

YEAR BEGINNING AUGUST 1	AVERAGE PARITY PRICES
1940	15.62
1941	17.86
1942	19.34
1943	20.71
1944	21.20
1945	22.20
1946	26.91
1947	30.38
1948	30.63
1949	—
	PRICES RECEIVED BY FARMERS[1]
1940	9.89
1941	17.03
1942	19.04
1943	19.88
1944	20.73
1945	22.52
1946	32.64
1947	31.93
1948	30.10
1949	—
	MIDDLING 15/16" IN TEN SPOT MARKETS
1940	11.00
1941	18.31
1942	20.14
1943	20.65
1944	21.86
1945	25.96
1946	34.82
1947	34.58
1948	32.15
1949	—

Cotton Branch, Production and Marketing Administration.
[1] Annual averages are crop-year average prices, by States, weighted by sales, including an allowance for unredeemed loans at estimated average loan value.
SOURCE: *The Cotton Situation*. Bureau of Agricultural Economics, Oct. 1949.

Are increased imports of textiles to be allowed through the reduction of our import duties? In each of these cases different assumptions might be made. To begin with let us assume that there are no increased imports of textiles into the United States.[19]

[19] Imports of cotton textiles, largely on account of our tariff, have never been very important. During the last forty years they have generally been less than 50 million yards, and only twice have they been more than 150 million yards. Our exports have frequently been above 500 million yards. In 1947, due to abnormal circumstances they reached almost 1,500 million yards. See *The Cotton Situation*, Oct., 1949. Table *LXXXIII*.

TABLE *LXXXIII* COTTON CLOTH: EXPORTS FROM UNITED STATES, 1920–1948[1]

CALENDAR YEAR	TOTAL[2]
	Million sq. yds.
1920[3]	818.8
1921[3]	551.5
1922	587.5
1923	464.5
1924	477.8
1925	543.3
1926	513.3
1927	565.0
1928	546.8
1929	564.4
1930	416.3
1931	367.0
1932	375.4
1933	302.0
1934	226.3
1935	185.6
1936	200.5
1937	236.3
1938	319.6
1939	367.5
1940	357.9
1941	586.7
1942	447.8
1943	538.5
1944	638.1
1945	672.8
1946	774.9
1947	1,474.8
1948[4]	940.4

Compiled from *Monthly Summary of Foreign Commerce of the United States* and reports of the Bureau of the Census.
[1] Includes duck, tire fabrics, all other cotton cloths, bleached, unbleached yarn dyed and colored, and mixtures made largely of cotton yarns.
[2] Totals were made before figures were rounded to millions.
[3] Linear yards.
[4] Preliminary.
SOURCE: *The Cotton Situation.* Bureau of Agricultural Economics, Oct. 1949.

If we assume full employment in the United States, continuation of our textile cloth exports at a somewhat reduced rate, and no increased imports of textiles, we might expect a domestic mill consumption of raw cotton at full employment of some eight or nine million bales. With no export subsidies of either a general nature or applicable in particular to cotton, at a price of 30 cents per pound we might expect to export eventually practically no cotton at all. If cotton production were limited to domestic consumption of eight million bales, total income thus derived would be $1,200,000,000. *Thus looked at purely in terms of dollars received by the growers of cotton,* substantially the same dollar return would be received in this case of governmentally supported prices from the sale of eight million bales of cotton on the domestic market alone, as was received from 13 million bales sold at 17 cents per pound on both the domestic and foreign market under favorable assumptions with respect to export markets and without direct governmental price supports and crop controls. It is roughly twice as much as would be received as under the assumptions in the first alternative of no crop controls, no support price, and no export subsidies either general or specific. *As far as the cotton farmer is concerned,* the advantage assuredly would appear to be with the policy of governmental price support.

The two situations of no-governmental crop control vs. governmental crop control and price supports would differ sharply in other respects, however. Somebody has to pay the difference between 12 cent, 17 cent and 30 cent cotton. With the higher prices, under the assumptions of support prices and crop control, American consumers would have to pay higher prices for the cotton textiles which they purchased than under the alternative situation of no control. Furthermore, it would be next to impossible to keep cotton production as low as eight million bales with the price of cotton as high as 30 cents. Almost impossibly high benefit payments to growers at heavy cost to tax payers would be required to induce them to restrict production to anything like this level. If one is to consider the interests of other southerners as well as of other citizens of the United States it must be remembered that the higher returns to southern growers under this control situation would be paid by their fellow citizens North and South and, of course, by cotton growers themselves in their roles as tax payers and textile consumers.[20]

Fourth Alternative: Continuation of Present Program with Controls, Price Support, and Export Subsidies. There is practically no likelihood, however, that we should ever actually reduce cotton production through governmental controls to the eight or nine million bales re-

20 On the other hand one would have to consider what would be done with the land, labor and other resources which would have been used in producing the five million bales which would by assumption have been produced and shipped abroad if there had been no control program and if exports had been maintained by general export subsidies. Would this land, labor, and capital be unemployed? If these production factors were all employed what would be the value of the product? Whatever the value of the product, if the resources were used at all, it would be some offset to the loss sustained by paying higher prices for cotton textiles and higher taxes under the control program. The two amounts are practically incommensurable.

quired for domestic consumption. If we have a price support program with crop control, as it now seems certain that we shall, there is the strong likelihood that such a program would be combined with specific export subsidies on cotton, plus some generalized export subsidies through continuation of loans and grants by the United States Government to foreign countries. Thus it seems that we are quite likely to see a price support and control program under which some 13 million bales might be produced, *with the whole amount sold at prices which would bring the grower as much as 30 cents per pound.*

Under this likely set of circumstances we could assume a domestic consumption of eight or nine million bales plus an export of some three or four million bales. These would have to be disposed of on the world market through some combination of direct and indirect export subsidies which might amount in their total effect to as much as 10 cents per pound. In addition, cotton growers would be receiving benefit payments to induce them to restrict their production and these payments would come out of general receipts of the U. S. Treasury.

Under these circumstances southern cotton producers would fare far better under governmental control plus price support than they would producing cotton under free competition. They would be receiving 30 cents per pound on the three million or four million bales shipped abroad in addition to their other receipts. If one added $450 million thus received from exports to what was obtained from the sale of eight million bales for domestic consumption, plus an additional sum, of say, $100 million for benefit payments, the dollar advantage might be as much as $700 million dollars, as compared with no controls or price supports but with freer international trade plus a general subsidy on our exports. There would be an advantage of as much as $1,260 million dollars over no controls and no price support and with no subsidies for exports.

Realism thus compels the admission that a system could be set up by which the price of cotton would be supported by government loans or other price supports at a level at which the total receipts from cotton sold on the domestic market alone would not be below and might be substantially above the total receipts from a substantially greater crop of cotton sold partially at home and partially abroad without price supports or production controls. *With a substantial export subsidy it would be possible to place an additional amount on the*

*foreign market by means of a differential and lower price so that the
total amounts of cotton produced on American farms might well be
substantially larger under crop controls than without controls.* Under
such circumstances the advantages of crop control and price supports
from the special point of view of cotton growers would be very great.

It has been pointed out that it would be possible to pay for the restriction of production through benefit payments and for export subsidies on cotton out of general receipts of the United States Treasury.
Under these circumstances, there can be no denying that the immediate economic interests of the cotton grower would be served by a
policy of control of production plus price supports and export subsidies. *Yet the whole of this economic advantage would come out of
an additional price charged to domestic consumers plus a subsidy
from tax payers to cover the cost of the export subsidy and the benefit
payments for acreage restriction.* It would be as though the government had levied a combined excise tax on cotton goods and an income
tax sufficient to raise a billion dollars more or less and had distributed
this amount among cotton growers.

There can be no doubt that an export subsidy as high as that assumed would arouse sharp resentment among growers in foreign countries competing on the international cotton market. A subsidy on a
particular commodity such as cotton is resented in a way which is not
true of a general subsidy on all our exports such as is in effect under
the Marshall Plan. It would consequently appear highly desirable, if
the policy of production controls and price supports for cotton is in
fact to be combined with a high subsidy on exports of cotton, that
some device should be developed for blending such specific subsidies
into a general fund. This could be used to make up some part of the
persistent deficit in the balance of payments of the rest of the world
with the United States.

It has been pointed out that we have been in effect disposing of
American grown cotton on the foreign market ever since the early
days of World War II by allowing cotton to participate in the general
subsidy of our exports represented at different times by Lend-Lease,
UNRRA, the British Loan, and the Marshall Plan, supplemented by
special subsidies on cotton exports during a part of this time. A combination of export subsidies and benefit payments of the order of a
billion dollars plus increased costs to consumers might appear a much

heavier charge than would be politically borne for the benefit of cotton growers. Yet all these costs are not at once visible nor is their incidence apparent.

A large part of the subsidy cost could probably be made to appear as part of a program of foreign aid. For some time, direct export subsidies could be at least temporarily avoided by allowing stocks of cotton to pile up in the vague hope that if there were to be a war or other extraordinary situation, they could somehow be liquidated without being "charged against the grower." Perhaps the benefit payments could be blended into a program of payments to farmers for "soil improving practices." In these ways the apparent cost of a program of price supports and production costs could be minimized and the benefits to cotton growers perhaps made politically attainable. It is thus once more hard to avoid the conclusion that governmental price supports and production controls offer far greater immediate advantages to growers than would unrestricted and unaided production and marketing of cotton, although at heavy long-term costs to the national economy.

There is little doubt, on the other hand, that the removal of price supports and production controls would increase the proportion of cotton grown on larger farms and outside the traditional cotton growing area and probably stimulate the movement of rural population towards industry and away from the uneconomically small farm. Conversely, a program of price supports and production controls such as provided for in the Agricultural Act of 1949 is almost certain to call for controls of acreage taken out of cotton production to prevent its use in the production of other crops which are likewise to be price-supported and production-controlled. This would put a sharp brake upon the change-over from cotton production to dairy, meat animal, and general type farming which is already underway and which offers so much promise in increasing per capita income in southern agriculture.

Fifth Alternative: Compensatory Payments. Since there seems little possibility of restoring a really old-style free market economy, accompanied by full employment in the United States, the possibility of removing all price supports for cotton, as for other crops, seems to be actually out of the question. Upon this assumption the application to cotton of something like the Brannan Plan but at much lower support levels, would have substantial advantages over the present system of price supports and production controls plus the inevitable concomitants described above.[21]

Such a program would mean, in assence, the application of some of the principles of the Brannan scheme as worked out for perishable crops to the staple crops, such as cotton, as well. The price of cotton would be allowed to sink to whatever level would be required to move the annual crop into consumption. This would mean lower prices to the consumer and would prevent surpluses piling up which would be unsalable at existing prices. The producer would be compensated by paying him the difference between the market price and an estimated "normal price" in addition to what he received from market sales.

The important departure from the Brannan Plan which the national interest would seem to dictate would be to set the "normal price" at a level low enough so that on the average the grower would receive an income which would induce the production of a "normal sized crop" and no more. This would go far to remove the need for direct production controls. Ascertaining such a "normal price" and such a "normal sized crop" is much easier said than done, of course. Such a "normal price" would be substantially lower than that now current or contemplated under most circumstances in the Agricultural Act of 1949.[22] Cotton growers would probably not greet such a "normal price" with enthusiasm.

Supporting grower income through guaranteeing prices at some stated per cent of normal would cost the government money which would have to come directly out of taxes. This would be in contrast with the present system which uses higher prices to consumers, together with more or less concealed governmental subsidies, as the financial source of payments for the cost of the plan. If all economic costs were entered on the ledger, however, a system which guaranteed normal prices to growers through governmental compensatory payments, while allowing prices to remain uncontrolled so that consumer prices would be lower than at present, would have a lower aggregate

---

21 See also Chapter XII, Agricultural Policy.
22 According to this Act, under certain circumstances, the level of support prices for cotton could go (but is not *required* to go) as low as 75 per cent of the newly defined parity price if the "supply percentage" is as high as 130. The parity price of cotton as computed in November 1949, for "Ilustrative purposes" by the BAE was 27.88 cents per pound. However, after allowance for grade and staple length, parity prices for the bulk of cotton would probably be about two cents above this. This is about two cents per pound lower than under the old parity formula.

cost to the consumer-taxpayer than would the present system. Such a program would also avoid freezing the production pattern in southern agriculture. It would not interfere with a type of agriculture already in course of development which affords the southern producer an opportunity to attain a higher real standard of living, with the minimum of conflict with the interests of consumers and taxpayers.

XIV THE TOBACCO SITUATION

Tobacco is an unusual and fascinating crop in many respects. Among its many other characteristics, it has engaged the attention of governments from its earliest days.

The Virginia Assembly, in August 1619, when this the first legislative body on the continent was not more than a few days old, passed an act requiring the inspection of tobacco and the burning of the leaf of poor quality.[1]

Later the colony designated tobacco as money. In these and in many other forms, the tobacco problem was often in the legislative halls. In its manufactured forms, tobacco has long been a favorite object of heavy taxation and several governments use it as a vehicle for profitable fiscal monopolies.

Tobacco is of special significance to the South. It is the region's second most important agricultural crop and has been a dynamic factor in the southern economy during the past 20 years. Since 1929 it has made a greater contribution toward increasing southern agricultural income than any other crop.

One comparison will indicate the magnitude of the changes which have occurred. In 1929 the South's tobacco crop was worth about $234 million, or about one sixth of the value of the cotton crop. By 1946 the value of the tobacco crop had almost quadrupled and stood at $861 million, or about two thirds of that year's cotton crop. But during the next two years the tobacco crop declined slightly in value while the cotton crop rose sharply, leaving the tobacco crop equal to about 38 per cent of the cotton crop in 1948 (see Table *XXXIV*).

Tobacco is a significant crop in only seven of the 13 southern states

[1] Joseph C. Robert, *The Story of Tobacco in America*, New York, Alfred A. Knopf, 1949, p. 33.

and usually takes up less than 10 per cent of the acreage covered by cotton. In 1929, tobacco accounted for 7.5 per cent of all cash farm receipts in the South; by 1939 this had risen to 11.2 per cent; by 1946, to 13.7 per cent, from which point it fell to 10.4 per cent in 1948. In North Carolina, the leading tobacco-producing state, the increase was from 37 per cent in 1929 to about 57 per cent in 1946, from which point the figure declined to 48 per cent in 1948.

The purpose of this chapter is to relate the principal facts in this story of spectacular change and to tell, at least in part, how and why it came about.

TABLE *LXXXIV* BASIC DATA ON TOBACCO PRODUCTION IN THE SOUTH* AND THE NON-SOUTH FOR SELECTED YEARS, 1929–1948

(Absolute Amounts—Three-Year Averages)

	SOUTH			NON-SOUTH		
	1929–31	1936–38	1946–48	1929–31	1936–38	1946–48
Acreage (000 acres)	1,796	1,446	1,610	235	152	178
Production (Million lbs.)	1,339	1,211	1,917	243	162	220
Yield Per Acre (lbs.)	746	837	1,190	1,034	1,065	1,236
Crop Value ($ millions)	170	260	870	37	28	116
	Relatives (1929–31 = 100)					
Acreage	100	81	90	100	65	76
Production	100	90	143	100	67	91
Yield Per Acre	100	112	160	100	103	120
Crop Value	100	153	512	100	76	314
Value of Tobacco Crop as Per Cent of Total Cash Farm Income*	17.7	25.5	26.0	0.5	0.4	0.5
South as Per Cent of U. S.:						
Acreage	88.4	90.5	90.0	—	—	—
Production	84.6	88.2	89.7	—	—	—
Value of Crop	82.1	90.3	88.2	—	—	—

* In this table the South consists of the seven states of Virginia, North Carolina, South Carolina, Georgia, Florida, Kentucky, and Tennessee.
SOURCES: Computed from reports of the U. S. Department of Agriculture.

Changes in Crop Values. From $234 million in 1929, the value of the South's tobacco crop fell drastically to $91 million in 1932—a decline of 61 per cent compared with a decline of 69 per cent in the value of the cotton crop. From that low point tobacco came back, in value terms, probably more rapidly than any other major crop. By 1934 it was back to 93 per cent of its 1929 value while cotton was at 56 per cent. In 1937 it was 24 per cent above the 1929 level, and in 1939 it was slightly above, while cotton was some 60 per cent below its 1929 level. The war years brought great increases, and by 1946 the tobacco crop was up in value by 268 per cent over 1929 while cotton had not quite regained the 1929 level. In 1948, the tobacco crop was 257 per cent above the 1929 level in value while the cotton crop was up by 53 per cent.

Total Production. For the three years 1929–31, tobacco production in the South averaged 1,339 million pounds per year. By 1936–38, the average was down to 1,201 million pounds, and thereafter it rose to 1,917 million pounds in 1946–48, which represented an increase of about 43 per cent over 1929–31. Thus increased production accounted for only a minor part of the increase of almost 260 per cent in crop values which took place during this period.

TABLE *LXXXV*   PRICES RECEIVED BY FARMERS—INDEXES FOR CERTAIN MAJOR COMMODITY GROUPS

(Aug., 1909–July, 1914 = 100)

Year			Group			
	TOBACCO	COTTON	FOOD GRAINS	MEAT ANIMALS	DAIRY PRODUCTS	ALL GROUPS
1929	174	144	116	160	164	149
1932	86	47	45	65	86	68
1935	174	94	97	116	114	109
1938	176	67	75	115	114	97
1941	159	107	97	146	139	124
1944	354	164	165	200	198	195
1946	382	228	201	256	242	233
1947	380	261	271	340	269	278
1948	387	259	250	371	97	287
Per Cent Increase, 1929–48	122	80	116	132	81	93

SOURCE: *Agricultural Statistics,* 1948, p. 584; *Survey of Current Business,* 1949, Statistical Supplement, p. 26.

Price Movements. Since the volume of production explains only a minor part of the growth in crop values, the remainder of the explanation must lie with prices. Table *LXXXV* shows the movement of tobacco prices for selected years since 1929 in comparison with the price movements of certain other major agricultural commodity groups.[2] It shows that tobacco prices in 1929 were higher, in relation to the 1909–14 base, than the prices in any other group. Of more significance

[2] The index used for tobacco prices here covers tobacco prices in the whole United States, but since the South grows about 90 per cent of the nation's tobacco this does not cause any substantial error.

for this story, it shows that after 1929 tobacco prices were consistently higher in relation to the 1929 level than the prices in any other group except those for meat animals in 1948. In 1948 they were 122 per cent above the 1929 level in comparison with an increase of 93 per cent for all groups.

In absolute terms, average season prices for the two leading types of tobacco—flue-cured and burley[3]—varied as follows for certain years in cents per pound:

YEAR	FLUE-CURED	BURLEY	YEAR	FLUE-CURED	BURLEY
1929	18.0	21.8	1935	20.0	19.1
1930	12.0	15.5	1936–45 (Average)	29.1	30.8
1931	8.4	8.7	1946	48.3	39.7
1932	11.6	12.5	1947	41.2	48.5
1933	15.3	10.5	1948	49.6	46.0
1934	27.2	16.9	1949*	47.0	—

* Preliminary.

Between 1929 and 1948, tobacco prices, on the average, increased by considerably more than 100 per cent; in the case of flue-cured, by more than 150 per cent. During the same period of time, production increased by less than 50 per cent. Thus the principal factor which caused the increased income from tobacco was the rise in prices. Since supply and demand are still major factors in determining prices, we turn now to data on those factors.

Consumption. The end-use of tobacco falls into two principal categories—exports and domestic consumption. During the period under consideration, the domestic consumption of tobacco products in the United States increased greatly. This growth of demand was concentrated entirely on the product which uses flue-cured and burley tobacco, and further, which uses the most expensive grades of those types, namely, the cigarette. The use of all other tobacco products showed a net decline. As a result, these two types of tobacco showed the greatest increases in prices and rose from 74 to 85 per cent of U. S. total production.

The increase in the consumption of cigarettes was truly phenomenal. After small declines in 1931 and 1932, the number of cigarettes manu-

3 Flue-cured is grown exclusively in the South—principally in Virginia, the Carolinas, Georgia, and Florida—and accounts for about 60 per cent of all tobacco grown in the United States. Burley is grown principally in Kentucky and Tennessee and accounts for about 25 per cent of total United States tobacco production.

factured increased every year, and during the war years the increase was quite large. From an average of 121 billion in 1929–31, the number rose to an average of 369 billion in 1946–48—an increase of 205 per cent. There were declines in the noncigarette uses of flue-cured and burley tobaccos, however, and total domestic consumption increased from 526 million pounds in 1929–31, to 1,181 million pounds in 1946–48, for an increase of 124 per cent (see Table *LXXXVI*). In the latter years, domestic consumption was somewhat greater than total domestic production in the earlier years.

TABLE *LXXXVI.* PRODUCTION AND DISAPPEARANCE OF FLUE-CURED AND BURLEY TOBACCO IN THE UNITED STATES, 1929–31 AND 1946–48

(*In Millions of Pounds, Farm-Sales Weight*)

	AVERAGE, 1929–31	AVERAGE, 1946–48	PER CENT INCREASE
Production	1,132	1,820	60.8
Disappearance:			
Exports	450	478	6.2
Domestic Consumption	526	1,181	124.5
Total Disappearance	976	1,659	70.0

While the domestic market flourished under an expanding demand fed by rising incomes, the foreign market was subject to recurrent crises and shortages of purchasing power. First there was the prolonged crisis of the early 1930's, then the abrupt suspension of British purchases at the outbreak of war in 1939 (which was effectively relieved only by lend-lease), followed by the wartime restrictions on shipping, and, finally, the curtailments caused by dollar shortages in the postwar years. The net result was that exports in 1946–48 showed only a modest increase of 6.2 per cent over 1929–31 and that shaky and uncertain increase rested entirely upon Marshall Plan dollars.

The far-reaching changes in the consumption pattern for U. S. leaf tobacco in the past 20 years has been briefly summed up as follows:

In 1949, it is estimated that a record quantity of 1.2 billion pounds (farm-sales weight) of tobacco will be used in the manufacture of cigarettes. This is about . . . 4¾ times the 1924–28 average. . . . During the late twenties, exports provided an outlet for 45 per cent of United States leaf . . . In 1949, however, . . . exports estimated at around 525 million pounds . . . will account for only 25 per cent of the total. The share going to cigarettes is nearly 60 per cent, compared with only about 20 per cent in 1924–28.[4]

[4] BAE, U. S. Department of Agriculture, *The Tobacco Situation,* Oct., 1949, p. 1.

Total disappearance of flue-cured and burley in 1946–48, (the sum of exports and domestic consumption) amounted to 1,659 million pounds, which was 70 per cent greater than in 1929–31. This compares with an increase in production over the same period of 60.8 per cent. In the years 1929–31 production was 16 per cent greater than disappearance; in those years incomes were falling fast and tobacco consumption was declining slightly after a long period of growth. As a result, leaf tobacco prices fell more than 50 per cent between 1929 and 1931. In 1946–48, production was ahead of disappearance by 9.7 per cent; but in those years incomes were rising and tobacco consumption was increasing steadily. Under those conditions, tobacco prices retained the gains they had made over the previous four years. In this connection it must be remembered that tobacco is bought two years or more before it is used. When the trend of consumption is strongly upward, tobacco companies must buy more tobacco than they use, and hence production must exceed disappearance if adequate stocks are to be maintained.

Tobacco Acreage. Between 1929–31 and 1946–48, the average annual acreage of flue-cured and burley tobaccos declined from 1,538,-000 to 1,525,000 acres. The reason for this stability of acreage in the face of much higher prices was the tight control of acreage which was maintained throughout the war, the details of which are explained in a later section. During most of the years from 1934 to 1943, total acreage was kept substantially below the 1929–31 level. One great exception was 1939, when there were no controls. In that year the acreage of flue-cured jumped from 909,000 to a record of 1,270,000; burley acreage rose from 407,000 to 425,000.

Despite the fact that tobacco requires more hand labor per acre than almost any other crop, sufficient labor was forthcoming throughout the war to cultivate the allotted acreage. There is a normal working margin of about 7 per cent between allotments and actual acreage, but this was about the same during as before the war. This is in striking contrast with the situation in cotton, where acreage fell drastically even without controls. This would indicate, among other things, a great difference in the profits to be realized by growing the two crops.

Yields per Acre. While acreage was strictly controlled, farmers could and did increase the average yield per acre. In the 50 years before 1930, the average yield of tobacco per acre in the whole United States had changed little; it rose from an annual average of 740 pounds per acre in 1876–80 to 771 in 1926–30, an increase of only 4.2 per cent. But after 1930 it rose sharply; the increase for each five-year period was as follows: 5.2 per cent, 12.0 per cent, and 13.6 per cent. The average annual yield per acre in 1941–45 was 1,033 pounds—34 per cent higher than 15 years earlier.[5]

The increase in yields was most striking in the cases of flue-cured and burley—the two types which were under the strictest and most continuous acreage control and which realized the greatest price increases. From 1929–31 to 1946–48, the average yield per acre of flue-cured increased from 710 pounds to 1,168 pounds, an increase of 65 per cent. With burley the increase during the same period was from 797 pounds to 1,268, or 59 per cent. By comparison, the increases in yield for fire-cured and Maryland—the two next most important types of volume—were, respectively, 44 per cent and 21 per cent during the same period.

There is not adequate analysis showing just how these increases in yield were accomplished. There are special difficulties connected with increasing the yield of tobacco. If more fertilizers are applied indiscriminately or if production is shifted to heavier, more fertile soils, the result is likely to be a rank growth which lowers the quality and hence the selling price per pound. One analyst states that the increased yield of flue-cured "has resulted mainly from advancing knowledge of fertilizers which permits increased yield without rank growth of poor leaf, and from the development of better varieties." Elsewhere he mentions as causes, "improvements in farming techniques, more careful choice of fields, better seed varieties, and copious use of better fertilizers."[6] The improved techniques might include the practice of closer planting to produce the lighter, thinner, and milder leaf which is more and more in demand for use in cigarettes. The individual leaves are lighter, but the increased number more than offsets this and gives a higher yield per acre.

As for other improvements, many millions of dollars have been spent, mainly by agencies of the Federal Government, on research to overcome diseases and pests and to develop more resistant and higher-yielding varieties. While much remains to be done, this research has

---

[5] U. S. Department of Agriculture, *Tobaccos of the United States,* Washington, 1948, pp. 6–7.

[6] William H. Fisher, *Economics of Flue-Cured Tobacco,* Richmond, Federal Reserve Bank of Richmond, 1945, pp. 33, 34.

scored a number of important victories over pests and diseases and growers have been quick to adopt and follow the methods or remedies found to be effective.

THE TOBACCO CONTROL PROGRAM

Production and marketing controls have been a major factor in bringing about the higher prices and the great expansion in the value of the tobacco crop. A brief case study of the development and operation of those controls may be instructive for several reasons. In respect to basic economic factors, tobacco has been in a better situation than almost any other major agricultural crop. As noted above, domestic consumption has more than doubled since 1929; that demand is more stable than the demand for most agricultural products since the commodity is habit-forming and has a low unit price. Dependence on exports, which are less stable, has been reduced substantially since 1929.

The existence of such a dynamic demand provided an unusually favorable situation for carrying out any needed adjustments in the production of tobacco. If the New Deal's agricultural program was one of "adjustments" as its name implied, then tobacco should have completed its adjustments and dispensed with governmental controls long since. On the contrary, we find that tobacco has been more continuously under acreage control and restrictions than any other crop. Such controls have been in force every year except three since 1934 and were used throughout the war—which was true of no other crop. Congress has given special legislative attention to tobacco on several occasions. Nearly every type of control has been used on the crop and they have been combined into a system of controls which is more elaborate and complicated than is used on any other crop. Thus it may be fair to say that federal policy in relation to tobacco epitomizes and magnifies federal policy in relation to agriculture generally.

The Original AAA. The agricultural program of the New Deal was started with a special provision for tobacco. In the first Agricultural Adjustment Act of 1933 the basis of computing the parity price for all other farm commodities was prescribed as the period from 1909 to 1914; for tobacco it was the postwar period from August, 1919, to July, 1928. Official figures do not show the exact effect of this shift of base but computations based on the parity formula indicate that it raised the parity prices of flue-cured and burley tobaccos by amounts ranging from 3½ to 4 cents per pound, or about 25 or 30 per cent.

It is not entirely clear why the postwar period was chosen for tobacco. One investigator, writing shortly after the event, gives this explanation:

> Those engaged in drafting the bill also gave attention to the question of how it would work out when applied to tobacco and made trial computations of "fair exchange value" using the pre-war base period then contemplated. These investigations showed that . . . current prices for several kinds of tobacco were above the pre-war parity and could not be increased through operation of the bill then under consideration. After several proposals for meeting this difficulty had been considered, it was determined that use of a post-war base period would give the desired result. Accordingly, the ten-year period August, 1919, to July, 1929, was finally designated, although for all other commodities August 1909, to July, 1914, is used.[7]

The views of two legislators who participated in this action, given several years later, tend to corroborate this view and also give a significant indication of their concept of parity. Speaking in 1940, Representative Flannagan said that in 1933 ". . . we found it impossible to find a base period that would give tobacco growers parity."[8] Representative Chapman stated that "we set up a ten-year post-war base period for tobacco; otherwise AAA would have been inoperative for burley and flue-cured tobacco." [9]

The only other reason which has been advanced for the selection of the postwar years as a base period for tobacco is that price data for tobacco in the prewar years were not adequate to permit the use of that period. That is a technical question which could be answered satisfactorily only by a few people who are thoroughly familiar with the statistics of the U. S. Department of Agriculture. In response to a request, one official of that Department gave this reply:

> The only data we have available on average prices per pound received by farmers for the different types of tobacco in the period of 1909–14 are as follows: Flue-cured 12.9 cents; Burley, 10.8 cents; Maryland, 8.2 cents; Fire-cured and Dark Air-cured, 7.6 cents; Pennsylvania type 41, 8.6 cents; Cigar filler and binder, 12.9 cents.[10]

7 Harold B. Rowe, *Tobacco Under the AAA*, Washington, The Brookings Institution, 1935, p. 17. Copyright 1935 by The Brookings Institution.
8 *Cong. Rec.* 76th Cong., 3d Sess., Vol. 86, p. 13474 (Oct. 9, 1940).
9 *Ibid*, p. 13477.
10 Letter dated October 28, 1948 from J. E. Thigpen, Chief, Tobacco Branch, Production and Marketing Administration, U. S. Department of Agriculture.

A priori, it would seem that those data provided a sufficient number of bases from which interpolations could have been made, using 1919–28 pattern of prices, to establish satisfactory base prices for all types and grades of tobacco.

Background. The developments of the three or four years preceding 1933 may have had some effect in causing the action on tobacco. From 1929 to 1932 the price of leaf tobacco fell by more than 50 per cent, and the income of tobacco growers declined accordingly. But the price of tobacco products did not reflect this decline. In fact, the average wholesale price of cigarettes rose steadily from $5.40 per 1,000 in 1929 to $6.04 in 1932.[11] With all costs declining, led by the precipitous fall in leaf tobacco prices, the profits of tobacco manufacturing companies set new high records in those depression years. Rowe presents figures showing "total gross amounts received by farmers for tobacco used in domestic manufacturing and the total profits available for distribution by the 34 leading manufacturers" for certain years. The amounts, in millions, were as follows:

	1923	1925	1927	1929	1930	1931	1932
Farmers Receipts	174	141	149	174	136	96	68
Manufacturers Profits	76	100	115	134	145	147	146[12]

With prices behaving in this fashion and tobacco manufacturers taking advantage of it to realize the highest earnings in their history at a time when nearly all other segments of the economy were experiencing losses, the tobacco growers had a strong case on general grounds of equity, regardless of the theory of the agricultural adjustment program.

The Control Program. The agricultural program got under way too late in 1933 to influence tobacco planting for that year. There was no "plow-up" program for tobacco as there was for cotton, so when the marketing season opened in August, 1933, there had been no limitation of production and there was no specific plan for such control. Prices for the early sales were very low; around ten cents per pound

11 *Statistical Abstract of the United States,* 1934, p. 288.
12 Rowe, *op. cit.,* p. 84. As a matter of fact, profits in 1932 were probably higher than in 1931. There are indications that the companies, by methods available in those pre-SEC days, deliberately reduced their stated profits to avoid showing record earnings in that disastrous year. One large company set aside a "reserve" of several million dollars for the next year's advertising and reduced its stated earnings accordingly.

for flue-cured, or about seven cents below the newly established parity. Farmer discontent mounted as the low prices continued, and finally there was a mass meeting in Raleigh, N. C., in which growers called on the AAA to take certain definite actions to remedy the situation and "called upon the Governor of North Carolina to declare a marketing holiday and under martial law to close all tobacco warehouses in the state."[13] The Governor acted as requested and the Governor of South Carolina took similar action.

While this holiday was in effect, two major actions were taken. First, within two weeks 95 per cent of the growers of flue-cured tobacco signed agreements to limit acreage for the next year. Second, an agreement was negotiated with the leading tobacco buyers governing amounts of tobacco they would buy from the 1933 crop and the prices they would pay. The average price was to be 17 cents per pound, or approximately parity. Similar actions were taken later in respect to burley tobacco. The markets were then opened and sales and prices were satisfactory for the remainder of the season. Average prices for the season were 13.1 cents for flue-cured and 11.8 cents for burley.

In 1934, the acreage reduction prescribed for flue-cured tobacco was 30 per cent from the base acreage and, in addition, each grower was limited as to the number of pounds he could market. Burley growers could reduce acreage by either 50 per cent or 33⅓ per cent, with differences in benefit payments. Reductions in acreage of 25 or 30 per cent were designated for other types of tobacco. The actual reduction in acreage from 1933 to 1934 was about 28 per cent for flue-cured and 40 per cent for burley.

Growers of flue-cured tobacco who signed contracts for production control might qualify for any of four types of benefit payments: rental payments for land excluded from cultivation; adjustments payments based on the market price of tobacco in 1934; deficiency payments for tobacco production below allotments; and price equalizing payments for certain tobacco sold in 1933. Essentially similar payments were provided for other types of tobacco. On the other hand, growers who did not sign contracts or who grew beyond their allotments had to pay a tax of from one fourth to one third of the market price under the Kerr-Smith Act, passed in June, 1934. This was similar to the Bankhead Act for cotton.

13 *Ibid*, p. 101.

With the aid of both payments and penalties, tobacco production was effectively controlled in 1934 and 1935 and prices of flue-cured and burley ranged well above parity as measured by the postwar base period. After the *Hoosac Mills Case* in early 1936, Congress repealed the Kerr-Smith Act and only payments were available for use in controlling the 1936 and 1937 crops. Growers of flue-cured and burley uniformly voted for controls by large majorities (85 per cent or more) in every referendum held to approve quotas. Prices continued above parity although Congress, in 1935, had prohibited "any action designed to maintain prices to farmers above the 'parity' level."[14] The 1937 crop was large and growers asked Congress for control machinery under which penalties could be imposed for marketing in excess of quotas. Such machinery was provided in the Agricultural Adjustment Act of 1938 which provided penalties of ten cents per pound for flue-cured, burley, and Maryland tobacco marketed in excess of quotas, and five cents per pound for other types.[15]

The 1938 AAA. In addition to providing penalties the new act made other important changes. The definition of parity price was amended to include freight rates in the list of payments made by farmers.[16] But another change made the whole concept of parity price unimportant except for support purposes. In determining whether marketing quotas shall be proclaimed for any type of tobacco, the Secretary of Agriculture is required to compute a figure for the "reserve supply level" for that type. If the total estimated supply exceeds the reserve supply level, "a national marketing quota shall be in effect."[17]

A referendum is then held among the growers of that type of tobacco, and unless more than a third of those voting disapprove the quota, it remains in effect.[18] It should be noted that the use of quotas is not directly connected with or dependent on price. Technically, it would seem that quotas could be proclaimed and production be curtailed even though prevailing prices were two or three times parity

14 E. G. Nourse, J. S. Davis and J. D. Black, *Three Years of the Agricultural Adjustment Act*, Washington, The Brookings Institution, 1937, pp. 36–37; *Stat. L.* 750.
15 52 *Stat. L.* 48. This was amended in 1946 to provide a penalty of 40 per cent of the average market price of the preceding year for all types of tobacco. *P. L.* 302, 79th Congress, Feb. 19, 1946.
16 Statisticians pointed out that they were already included automatically in the index number of prices paid for commodities.
17 52 *Stat. L.* 46.
18 This throws the burden of the initiative on the opponents of quotas.

prices. Indirectly, there is some connection with prices, since presumably prices could not rise to extreme levels so long as actual supplies exceed reserve supply levels.[19]

Control Program under the 1938 Act. Growers of flue-cured and burley tobacco voted to make the penalties under the 1938 Act effective on the 1938 crop and as a result production in that year was considerably below that for 1937. But the 1938 program was worked out hastily and there was "irritation on the part of growers arising out of difficulties encountered in (its) administration . . ."[20] Also, the high prices which had prevailed over the past four years had made many of them impatient with the strict controls of production. As a result, only 57 per cent of flue-cured growers and 59 per cent of burley growers voted in favor of controls for the 1939 crop. Since a two-thirds favorable vote was required, there were no controls for that year.

With controls removed, the acreage of flue-cured jumped by 40 per cent to a record of 1,270,000 acres and at the same time the yield per acre rose somewhat. The result was a crop of 1,170,000 pounds, larger by far than any other crop produced to that time. The production of burley also increased, but not nearly so much. Then came the war in Europe and for a time British buyers suspended purchases entirely.

The wartime loss of such an important part of the demand caused the flue-cured markets to shut down, and it was not until the second week in October that buying was resumed. During this interval, flue-cured growers approved, by referendum, a marketing quota for their 1940 crop, and the Commodity Credit Corporation through a purchase and loan agreement restored to the market the buying power of the purchasers for the British trade.[21]

Under the agreement, the Commodity Credit Corporation bought about 175 million pounds of flue-cured tobacco in 1939. The agreement was extended the following year and resulted in the purchase of

[19] When the consumption of tobacco products is increasing rapidly, as in the past 10 years, the connection is not at all close. The reserve supply level concept is based upon consumption for the preceding ten years, "adjusted for current trends in such consumption." When consumption is changing rapidly, those adjustments, of course, become of major importance, but no criteria are prescribed for them. In effect, legislative power is thereby delegated to the Secretary.

[20] U. S. Department of Agriculture, *Agricultural Adjustment, 1938-1939*, Washington, 1939, p. 66.

[21] U. S. Department of Agriculture, *Agricultural Adjustment, 1939-1940*, p. 46. The vote in favor of controls was 90 per cent for flue-cured and 83 per cent for burley.

about 200 million pounds. After that, provisions were made for supporting the prices of flue-cured and burley at 85 per cent of parity. That, together with the reimposition of controls and the coming of lend-lease and the defense program soon solved the problem and moved most of the tobacco surplus. The emergency actions and the reimposition of controls in 1939 greatly alleviated the price decline in that year. The average price of flue-cured fell from 22.2 cents in 1939 to 14.9 cents in 1939—a decline of about one third. In 1940 the average was 16.4 cents and in 1941 it was up to 28.1 cents.

Shifting the Parity Base. In 1933, tobacco had obtained a more favorable base period for computing parity price than had other farm commodities. In the fall of 1940 the base for flue-cured and burley was again boosted by some 25 per cent. The story of how that was accomplished provides an interesting and significant study of legislative strategy.

On September 30, 1940, the Senate was considering a routine bill affecting tobacco. Senator Barkley offered an amendment to change the base period for flue-cured and burley from 1919–28 to 1934–38. He gave only one significant argument in favor of the amendment. He stated there had been a change in production methods ". . . which results in the farmer producing and handling for cigarette purposes less tobacco per acre than formerly."[22] This was an ambiguous statement. If it meant that the production per acre was less, then it was wrong, for yields per acre had been rising steadily for several years. On the other hand, if it meant that production per worker was less, than it might have been correct, although even that is doubtful. Production had been shifting in the direction of those grades which require more labor but that tendency was offset, at least in part, by the use of better varities, closer planting, and the other practices which gave higher yields per acre. In any event, no data were given to support the argument.

The only other argument advanced was that the Department of Agriculture had sent the bill over with its approval. After a few perfunctory questions and a few minutes of consideration, the Senate passed the bill.

On October 3, 1940, Representative Flannagan in the House asked for unanimous consent to suspend the rules and consider this bill out

[22] *Congressional Record,* 76th Congress, 3d Session, Vol. 86, p. 12833 (Sept. 30, 1940.)

of the regular order. He admitted that there had been no hearings, that the Committee on Agriculture had not considered it, and that there was no report on it. He contended only that the Department of Agriculture and tobacco growers wanted this bill. The amendment would ". . . only change the base period from 1934 to 1939 (sic!) due to the fact that in tobacco we have found that the cost of production has greatly increased."[23] There was objection, so the bill could not be considered.

Representative Flannagan again brought the bill up in House on October 9, 1940. This time unanimous consent was given and the bill was debated for about 40 minutes. Still there had been no hearings, no committee consideration, and there was no report. The only copy of the bill available was the one on the Speaker's desk. The arguments were the same as those used earlier; in order to produce the thinner, lighter leaves suitable for use in cigarettes, growers had to space the plants closer together and "you get less poundage per acre."[24]

The only objections to the bill came from other members of the farm bloc who feared that tobacco growers might share in future appropriations for parity payments. There were complaints, however, against the irregular procedure in bringing up the bill without hearings, committee consideration, report, or even copies of the bill itself for House members.[25] In partial explanation, it was stated that the bill had received full consideration in the Senate. On a roll-call vote, many members abstained from voting. The bill received a majority but not the two-thirds majority required for bills considered under a suspension of the rules, so it failed to pass.

On November 18, 1940, the bill was again brought up under a suspension of the rules. This time there was no mention of hearings, committee action, or report. After a very brief debate, it was passed without a roll call.[26]

The new parity prices were 22.4 cents per pound for flue-cured and 21.8 cents for burley, or roughly 25 per cent higher than parity prices under the old formula. On a 1909–14 base, parity prices would have

[23] *Ibid*, p. 13119.
[24] *Ibid*, p. 13474. At no time were any statistics or other factual information given to support the agruments concerning costs of production and yields per acre.
[25] The same tastics were used in 1945 to obtain an increase in the parity prices for dark tobaccos. Charles M. Hardin, "The Tobacco Program: Exception or Portent?" *Journal of Farm Economics*, XXVIII (Nov., 1946), 934 fn.
[26] *Ibid*, p. 13638.

been, respectively, 15.7 cents and 13.2 cents; the new prices were 43 per cent higher for flue-cured and 65 per cent higher for burley.

The Control Program during the War. After the disastrous experience of 1939, tobacco acreage was reduced sharply in 1940. In flue-cured, the reduction was about 40 per cent; in burley, about 15 per cent. Acreage was held at about the same level in 1941 and increased slightly in 1942. Demand increased rapidly and as a result average prices rose about 150 per cent between 1939 and 1942; from 14.9 cents to 38.4 cents for flue-cured and from 17.3 cents to 41.8 for burley. The sharp rise in prices led to the imposition of price controls by the OPA at the end of August, 1942. Controls remained in effect for the remainder of the war, during which average prices for flue-cured rose from 38.4 cents in 1942 to 43.6 cents in 1945.

As consumption of cigarettes rose rapidly during the war, stocks of flue-cured tobacco, in relation to consumption, fell sharply.

"At the end of 1941–42, stocks were sufficient for only 30.5 months' manufacture; and by July 1, 1943, they had fallen to enough for only 23.8 months' manufacture. . . . When it is remembered that the normal supply of tobacco runs about 36 months' equivalent at going rates of manufacture in order to allow proper aging of the leaf, it is clear that the increase in wartime consumption has forced manufacturers to use less-aged leaf in their recent products."[27]

This shortage was considered so acute that the War Food Administration, on August 13, 1943, issued an order bringing the flue-cured crop under rationing and prescribing a formula for its allocation.[28]

At this time the reserve supply levels of flue-cured and burley tobaccos were below the expected total supply and the Secretary of Agriculture was therefore not authorized to proclaim marketing quotas. But Congress, in an act passed July 7, 1943, provided that notwithstanding the terms of the Agricultural Adjustment Act governing quotas, "National marketing quotas for burley and flue-cured tobacco for the marketing year 1944–45 shall be proclaimed."[29] This was later amended to include the marketing years 1944–45 and 1945–46.[30] The reason given for this action was "to assure that there will be available for the production of essential food and fiber the land, labor and

27 Fisher, *op. cit.*, pp. 81–82.
28 *Federal Register* 11331 (Aug. 17, 1943).
29 57 *Stat. L.* 387.   30 58 *Stat. L.* 136.

equipment which will probably be devoted to the production of tobacco in the absence of any assurance that marketing quotas will be in effect for the 1944 crop" and to enable growers to plan their 1944 farming operations.[31] Thus by the fall of 1943 there were, in respect to flue-cured tobacco, price controls to hold down its price, rationing controls to limit purchases and insure its equitable distribution, and marketing quotas to limit its production.

In the first year after the war, total available supplies were still below the reserve supply level. Early in 1946, growers were afraid that there would be no quotas for the *1947* crop, so they prevailed upon Congress to enact quotas "even though the supply of burley and flue-cured tobacco is less than the reserve supply level." The argument was that, "during the war foreign stocks of flue-cured tobacco were exhausted or seriously depleted. Supplies on hand in this country are inadequate to satisfy needs in foreign countries which normally buy U. S. flue-cured tobacco." But 1946 quotas were up by 10 per cent over 1945 and this was expected to make up the deficiency and make it necessary to reduce the acreage in 1947.[32] Congress accepted these arguments and passed the legislation extending quotas.[33]

Stabilization Corporations. Another control device which apparently is unique with tobacco and naval stores is the "Cooperative Stabilization Corporation." There is one each for flue-cured and burley tobacco. They are cooperative organizations of growers who contributed the initial capital funds. On the one hand they are agencies for the cooperative marketing of the tobacco of their members. On the other

---

[31] *House Report 622*, 78th Cong., 1st Sess. About the same time (July, 1943) spokesmen for the growers were presenting a contrary view before another Congressional committee. In opposing a proposed increase in the federal excise tax on cigarettes (which they did successfully), they stated that the higher tax would reduce the amount of tobacco they could sell and thus force them into dairying or the growing of other crops, such as food and feed crops. They would thus be forced into competition with farmers in other parts of the country. Both they and the members of the Committee on Ways and Means appeared to regard that possibility as highly undesirable. *Hearings before the Committee on Ways and Means, House of Representatives,* 78th Cong., on Revenue Revision of 1943, pp. 1414–18.

Still another view was expressed by a spokesman for the tobacco growers in 1948 when he stated: "We have about 2,000,000 acres of tobacco of all varieties. That is about one-half of 1 per cent of our total crop land in this country that is in tobacco. What we do with those acres if and when we adjust up or down, Senator, does not amount to much in the aggregate as we look at production in this country." *Senate Hearings on Agricultural Act of 1948* (S. 2318), p. 426.

[32] *House Report 1476,* 79th Congress, 2nd Session, pp. 1–3.

[33] *P. L.,* 302, 79th Congress (Feb. 19, 1946).

hand, they are the agencies used by the Commodity Credit Corporation to carry out the official price-support operations for these two types of tobacco. Funds used in purchasing (or making loans on) tobacco, together with overhead, administrative, and carrying costs, are borrowed from the C.C.C. on nonrecourse loans. Nearly all the funds contributed by the members of the Flue-Cured Corporation, are invested in U. S. Government securities.

Official data show that for the three years 1946–48, the C.C.C. financed loans on some 399 million pounds of flue-cured and some 264 million pounds of burley tobacco.[34] Considerable amounts of the tobacco had been withdrawn and the loans repaid, but on October 31, 1949, loans of $150 million were outstanding on 364 million pounds of tobacco.[35]

The Agricultural Act of 1948. The Agricultural Act of 1948 combined certain temporary provisions with what was designed to be a permanent agricultural program. The principal temporary provision extended price support until June 30, 1950, at the rate of 90 per cent of parity to cooperators who produce basic commodities. Incidentally, the base period for computing parity prices for Maryland tobacco was changed from 1919–29 to 1936–41.[36]

The most important of the permanent changes, to go into effect in 1950, was a change in the definition of parity price. The new parity price for any commodity for any year is based upon the average price received by farmers for that commodity during the ten years immediately preceding; certain adjustments will be made to relate it to the 1909–14 base period and to prices currently being paid by farmers for the things they buy.[37]

The effect of the new definition of parity differs greatly with different commodities. For most basic commodities the new parity prices are lower, but for tobacco they are higher. As of June 30, 1948, parity prices computed by the old and the new formulae would have been as follows:[38]

[34] U. S. Department of Agriculture, *Annual Report on Tobacco Statistics,* 1948, p. 43; *The Tobacco Situation,* Feb., 1949, pp. 15, 18.
[35] *The New York Times,* Jan. 6, 1950, p. 31.
[36] *P. L.* 897, 80th Congress, Title I.
[37] *Ibid,* Title II.
[38] U. S. Department of Agriculture, "Summary of 'Agricultural Act of 1948'" (n.d.), p. 6.

	WHEAT	CORN	OATS	PEANUTS	COTTON	TOBACCO FLUE-CURED	BURLEY
	PER BUSHEL			PER POUND		PER POUND	
Old Formula	$2.22	$1.61	$1.00	12.0¢	31.1¢	48.8¢	47.3¢
New Formula	$1.82	$1.42	$0.82	9.3¢	27.0¢	50.2¢	50.7¢

Expressed as percentages of the prices prevailing in the 1909–14 base period, the parity prices under the new formula as of June 30, 1948, would have been as follows: wheat, 206; corn, 221; oats, 206; peanuts, 194; cotton, 218; flue-cured tobacco, 389; burley tobacco, 469. Again tobacco benefited because it had had a better than average performance in the past.[39] To the extent that future market prices will be determined by parity prices, the new act has perpetuated that advantage.

The new act also provides a system of support prices varying from 60 per cent to 90 per cent of parity, depending upon the supply situation. The higher the supply in relation to normal consumption, the lower will be the support level. But a special provision of the act Sec. 202(a) states:

> Notwithstanding the foregoing provisions of this section, the level of price support to cooperators for any crop of tobacco for which marketing quotas are in effect shall be 90 per centum of its parity price . . .

And still another part (Sec. 208) states:

> . . . The Secretary shall proclaim a national marketing quota for each marketing year for each kind of tobacco for which a national marketing quota was proclaimed for the immediately preceding marketing year . . .

Since quotas are now in effect for all important types of tobacco except the cigar types, this means that so long as this provision remains in effect there will be quotas on tobacco from now on, regardless of price or supply considerations unless two thirds of the growers disapprove. The two sections together mean that, regardless of what happens to other prices, tobacco prices will be supported at 90 per cent of parity prices which are, for the two leading tobacco types, about twice as high in relation to the 1909–14 base period as are comparable prices for other basic farm commodities. In the hearings and the re-

---

[39] One writer has described this process in these words: "control programs that tend to raise prices are introduced; prices rise; then the new prices are made into a new base for the calculation of support prices." Hardin, *op. cit.,* p. 937.

ports which preceded this legislation no reasons were given why this special treatment should be accorded to tobacco except that the growers desired it.

The Agricultural Act of 1949. Before the permanent provisions of the Agricultural Act of 1948 became effective on January 1, 1950, they were amended by the Agricultural Act of 1949.[40] Perhaps the most important changes were the inclusion of farm wage rates among the prices paid by farmers in computing parity and a provision that, for the four years beginning on January 1, 1950, the parity price of any basic commodity "shall not be less than its parity price computed in the manner used prior to the enactment of the Agricultural Act of 1949."[41] The index of farm wage rates in 1949 (on a 1910–14 base) stood at 428 compared with 88 in 1933. The 1949 figure was approximately 77 per cent higher than the index of all prices paid by farmers in that year (242) and so its inclusion raised the average appreciably.

Based on prices paid and received by farmers in September, 1949, the new parity prices of flue-cured and burley tobaccos authorized by the 1949 Act and comparable prices computed by the old method, in cents per pound, were as follows:[42]

FLUE-CURED		BURLEY	
OLD	NEW	OLD	NEW
46.5	49.5	44.8	49.7

The new parity price for flue-cured as of that date would have been approximately equal to the highest average price ever received for that type for any season; for burley, it would have been approximately one cent above the highest seasonal average. These prices were further changed and reduced slightly (to 48.8 cents in each case on the basis of prices paid and received in January, 1950) by revisions in the indexes of prices mentioned below.

When the permanent provisions of the 1948 and 1949 Acts went into effect in January, 1950, the Department of Agriculture published a revision of the indexes of prices paid and received by farmers, which are the basis for the computation of parity prices. In the case of the prices paid, the principal changes were: a shifting of the base period for weights from 1924–29 to 1937–41, the addition of a number of

[40] *P. L.* 439, 81st Congress, 1st Session.
[41] *Ibid,* Sec. 409 (c).
[42] U. S. Department of Agriculture, *The Tobacco Situation,* Oct., 1949, p. 19.

new commodities, the inclusion of wage rates as noted above, and a reduction in the weights of taxes and interest.[43]

The index of interest payable had dropped from 164 in 1933 to 76 in 1949 and the index of taxes payable had risen from 220 to 275 in the same period. The combined weight of these two series was reduced from 12.2 per cent to 6.8 per cent and cash wage rates were added with a weight of 8.0 per cent of the total. The effect of these and other changes was to increase the index of total prices paid by farmers for 1949 from 242 to 250 and to reduce the parity ratio of all commodities from 104 to 100.

The 1949 Act retained the provisions for flexible support levels varying from 75 per cent to 90 per cent of parity for all other basic commodities and the flat 90 per cent level for tobacco. If producers of any other basic commodity reject marketing quotas, the support level becomes 50 per cent of parity, but " . . . no price support shall be made available for any crop of tobacco for which marketing quotas have been disapproved by producers."[44]

Effect of Control on Land Values. It is apparent from the above that tobacco growers have a vested interest in the control of tobacco acreage and in the allotments which determine how much tobacco each grower can cultivate. Those allotments are valuable hereditaments which Congress has created and, thus far, has carefully protected. Since the allotments generally go with the land, it is inevitable that they should be incorporated into the value of the land. Available data indicate that they have been so included and that they have contributed materially to the increase in farm land values which has been going on for the past ten years.[45]

It is difficult to determine the exact influence of allotments on land values because of the relatively small acreage of tobacco, both in total and per farm, and the practice of selling farms as units. Even in North Carolina, by far the most important tobacco producing state, total tobacco acreage is only about 13 per cent of total crop land and less than 3 per cent of the total land area. The average amount of tobacco

43 U. S. Department of Agriculture, *Agricultural Prices,* Jan. 31, 1950, pp. 29–32.
44 *P. L.* 439, 81st Congress, 1st Session, Sec. 101 (d) (3).
45 See John E. Mason, "Acreage Allotments and Land Prices," *Journal of Land and Public Utility Economics,* Vol. 22, pp. 176–81 (May, 1946) for examples and a discussion of this point. He cites several instances in which "buyers and sellers of land consider the allotment of sufficient importance to specify its size in land deeds and contracts."

acreage per farm growing tobacco is less than three acres, although the average for flue-cured is somewhat higher—perhaps nearer five acres. But it is usual to sell a farm ranging in size from 30 to 50 acres which may carry with it a tobacco allotment of three or four acres. Thus the value of each acre of tobacco allotment is spread over many other acres which carry no allotment. In addition, in the statistical series which report value of farm real estate, the figures for tobacco farms are merged with the figures for other farms which raise no tobacco. Thus the value of the allotment is greatly "watered down" by the time it appears in the indexes.

In the principal flue-cured tobacco areas it has been accepted practice for several years, in appraising ordinary small tobacco farms, to base the whole value on the size of the tobacco allotment. A rule of thumb has been to value good tobacco land at $1,000 per allotment acre or more and "throw in" the incidental acreage and buildings if they are of the usual amount and quality. Mason, apparently considering both flue-cured and burley areas, arrived at the conclusion that, "a majority of the farms in the tobacco area that were sold in 1945 and which had appropriate tobacco allotments were enhanced in market value by from $300 to $600 for each allotment acre."[46]

The value of the allotments shows up distinctly in the usual indexes of farm land values despite the extent to which they are diluted. Tables *LXXXVII* and *LXXXVIII* have been compiled from the indexes regularly published by the Bureau of Agricultural Economics, U. S. Department of Agriculture. Table *LXXXVII* gives index numbers for farm real estate by states for the five leading tobacco states on a 1912–14 base. In 1930, the average for the tobacco states was 13 per cent above the U. S. average, but in 1946 and 1948 it was 51 per cent higher. In 1948, North Carolina had an index number of 324; no other state in the country had an index above 270. All five of the

---

46 *Ibid*, p. 181. A very brief consideration will show why prices of $1,000 or more per "allotment" acre for tobacco land may well be justified on economic grounds. Agencies connected with N. C. State College have compiled figures, based on 1948 yields and prices, to show typical "Estimated Costs and Returns to Landowner and Tenant per Acre for Flue-cured Tobacco." These show that the landowner would have had gross receipts of $311.25, total expenses of $81.04, and a net return of $230.21 per acre. The tenant, after expenses and an allowance for labor at 44 cents per hour, would have had a net return of $61.04 per acre. These data are based on the assumption that the landowner furnished all power and equipment, that the tenant provided all the labor, and that all other expenses were shared equally. Department of Agricultural Economic, N. C. State College and N. C. Agricultural Experiment Station, *Cost of Producing Farm Products in North Carolina*, Raleigh (Aug., 1949), p. 15. (Mimeographed.)

TABLE *LXXXVII* INDEX NUMBERS OF ESTIMATED VALUE PER ACRE OF FARM
REAL ESTATE BY STATES FOR CERTAIN YEARS, 1930–1948

(1912–14 = 100)

STATE	1930	1940	1944	1946	1948
Virginia	134	112	146	200	226
North Carolina	158	138	193	268	324
South Carolina	104	89	136	172	208
Kentucky	127	113	165	221	264
Tennessee	123	108	160	213	258
Average	129	112	160	215	256
U. S. Average	115	84	114	142	170
Average of Tobacco States as Per Cent of U. S. Average	113	133	140	151	151

SOURCE: BAE, U. S. Department of Agriculture, "Current Developments in the Farm
Real Estate Market," April 1, 1948, pp. 6–7.

tobacco states had index numbers above 200, most of them by wide
margins, while in all the remainder of the United States only seven
states had figures above 200.

TABLE *LXXXVIII* INDEX NUMBERS OF ESTIMATED VALUE PER ACRE OF FARM
REAL ESTATE BY TYPE OF FARMING AREAS FOR CERTAIN YEARS, 1935–48

(1935–39 = 100)

TYPE OF FARMING AREA	1935	1940	1944	1946	1948	PER CENT INCREASE, 1935–1948
Tobacco	89	109	170	217	255	185
Cotton	96	101	137	173	223	132
Corn	97	102	143	175	231	138
Winter Wheat	94	96	136	183	268	185
Spring Wheat	106	84	113	137	182	72
Dairy	94	99	131	158	188	100
General	97	104	141	191	254	162
All Areas	95	102	138	171	205	116

SOURCE: BAE, U. S. Department of Agriculture, "Current Developments in the Farm
Real Estate Market," Apr. 1, 1948, p. 10.

Table *LXXXVII* shows index numbers of the value of farm real
estate by types of farming areas. The index for the tobacco area was
the lowest of all in 1935, but it quickly forged ahead and remained
well ahead of all other areas until 1948, when the winter wheat area
went slightly ahead by a sudden spurt. The increase for the tobacco
area between 1935 and 1948 was 185 per cent compared with an increase of 166 per cent for all areas.

It does not necessarily follow that the value of tobacco allotments have accounted for all the differences in the two tables. Aside from possible shortcomings in the methods of computing the index numbers, there are many and complex factors which influence land values. But it is a reasonable conclusion from the data shown in these two tables that the value of tobacco allotments was a significant factor in the great increase in general farm real estate values. If that is correct, then it follows from the facts pointed out above that the increase in value of the relatively few acres on which tobacco is actually grown was many times as great.

This conclusion is greatly strengthened by a general deductive analysis of the economic process which has been operating. From the facts presented earlier in this chapter, there can be little doubt that tobacco farming has been, in the past 15 years, considerably more profitable than most other types of farming. That margin of differential profit is protected only by a strict system of acreage control and allotments. There are some provisions for new producers to enter the field, but in the very nature of the case there can be nothing approaching free entry.[47] Consequently, new producers can gain entrance to the field generally only by the payment of a large entrance fee in the form of a high price for land with an allotment. The normal economic process for determining the price of that land would be to take the "normal" price of the land—that is, its value for unrestricted use—and to add to it the present discounted value of the differential profit to be made from growing tobacco on it for all years in the future, in so far as such profit can be foreseen and estimated. To the extent that this process works out, all present and expected future special advantages to tobacco growers accrue to present landowners; workers who rent land now or buy it in the future get only the normal return for their work. Over the years, as tobacco land changes hands, the new buyers come to have a very real "vested interest" in the continuation of the control program. If Congress should abandon or sub-

---

[47] The Secretary of Agriculture is directed to provide ". . . for the allotment of *not in excess of 5 per centum* (italics supplied) of the national marketing quota . . . to new farms and to increase acreage alloted to small farms." Not more than 75 per cent can go to new farms, so the maximum that can be assigned to new farms in any year is 3.75 per cent of the total quota. 52 *Stat. L.* 47. Between 1940 and 1946, the number of flue-cured allotments increased from 196,014 to 201,401 or by 2.8 per cent. In the same period, the allotments of flue-cured acreage increased from 760,562 to 1,257,106, or 65.3 per cent. *Annual Report on Tobacco Statistics,* 1947, pp. 33–34.

stantially reduce that program, those owners would accuse Congress of "robbing" them. Such a change, would, indeed, present very real problems and probably produce more candidates for congressional relief.

It may be questioned whether it was the original intention of Congress to create such an elaborate structure of artificial values. But now that it has been created and has become imbedded in land values, it gives rise to tremendous pressures for its protection and continuation.

CONCLUSION

The developments related above indicate that the term "parity prices," at least as it is used in connection with tobacco, now has a meaning substantially different from that which it had at the beginning of the New Deal agricultural program. It now represents primarily the highest price which representatives of growers, by using all the parliamentary devices at their command, have been able to persuade Congress to accept as the basis for governmental price support. Under the Agricultural Acts of 1938, 1948, and 1949, the growers now have an effective monopoly, operated through the agencies of the United States Government, enforced through federal laws and regulations, and financed in part by federal funds. Congressman Hope, a member of the House Committee on Agriculture, has said that "it is not only a closed shop proposition but it is a closed union with a closed shop."[48]

It is pertinent to ask how the other interested groups, principally manufacturers and consumers, were affected by the growers' monopoly and the high tobacco prices. Table *LXXXIX* sums up some of the relevant data for the years 1939–46. These data are not comparable to those quoted earlier from Rowe since they show total farmer receipts from flue-cured and burley tobacco rather than the cost of tobacco which went into domestic production. Profits of cigarette manufacturers include profits of seven leading companies. The comparison is shown between gross receipts of growers and net profits of manufacturers simply because no data are available on net profits of growers; if such were available, however, they probably would show a greater relative increase than gross receipts. Data on profits of

48 Quoted in Hardin, *op. cit.*, p. 920.

TABLE *LXXXIX* VALUE OF TOBACCO CROP, MANUFACTURERS' NET PROFITS, AND CIGARETTE PRICES, 1939–1946

	VALUE OF FLUE-CURED AND BURLEY TOBACCO CROPS		NET PROFITS OF CIGARETTE MANUFACTURERS[1]		TOTAL CORPORATE PROFITS[1]	MANUFACTURERS' PRICE PER 1,000 CIGARETTES[2] (END OF YEAR)
YEAR	AMOUNT ($ MILLIONS)	INDEX	AMOUNT ($ MILLIONS)	INDEX	INDEX	
1939	242.6	100	83.9	100	100	$2.51
1940	185.2	76	86.5	103	129	2.51
1941	280.9	116	75.6	90	187	2.51
1942	455.4	188	69.9	83	188	2.51
1943	496.2	205	67.4	80	207	2.51
1944	721.2	297	62.9	75	198	2.51
1945	739.0	305	64.9	77	179	2.51
1946	897.0	370	85.5	102	251	3.01

[1] Net profits after taxes.
[2] Price of "standard" brands net of federal excise taxes and discounts.
SOURCES: Value of tobacco crops—U. S. Department of Agriculture; Prices of cigarettes and net profits of cigarette manufacturers—Division of Tax Research, U. S. Treasury Department, "Federal Excise Taxes on Tobacco," pp. 7, 18; Total corporate profits—*Statistical Abstract of the United States, 1948*, p. 276.

all corporations are from the national income estimates of the Department of Commerce; they are not strictly comparable with the data on profits of cigarette manufacturers but are close enough for a rough comparison.

Cigarette manufacturers suffered a considerable decline in net earnings during the war while corporate earnings generally were rising rapidly. However, even at the low point, they were earning nearly 10 per cent on net worth and this increased substantially after the removal of price control. If their earnings (before taxes) had increased greatly during the war, the excess profits tax would have taken most of them. So, while cigarette manufacturers did not receive an "equitable" share of the tobacco profits in those years, they did not suffer greatly.

For their part, consumers have fared quite well. Manufacturers' prices (net of excise taxes) did not rise at all during the war and have risen only 34 per cent since then. Even after numerous tax increases, state and federal, cigarette prices to the consumer have risen much less than most other prices.

How was it done? How were manufacturers able to make any profit at all when cigarette prices remained stationary for so long in the face of an increase of more than 150 per cent in leaf tobacco prices and increases of 100 per cent or more in wages and other costs?[49] The answer lies in a tremendous increase in production. The production of cigarettes more than doubled between 1939 and 1948, and the greater volume brought reductions in the unit cost of producing cigarettes which went far to offset the higher wages and tobacco prices.

Large profits were inherent in the great increase in cigarette production and the manufacturing technology involved. If leaf tobacco prices had risen only as much as other commodities in these years, if wages in the cigarette factories had risen in line with wages generally, and if manufacturers had made the same return on their investment as at the beginning, there would have been a large differential profit somewhere along the tobacco line, even if cigarette prices had remained constant, and even larger profits if they had risen in line with the general price level. It might be said that consumers got a part of these profits in the relatively small increase in cigarette prices. But the growers appropriated much the greater part of these profits and, during the war years, reduced somewhat the normal profits of the manufacturers.

During most of the years covered above, the Federal Government was searching desperately for additional revenue to finance rearmament, war, and the "cold war." The differential profits, as defined above, which were largely created by federal legislation, would have been a logical and relatively painless source for such revenue. Instead, they went in the main to tobacco growers and the owners of tobacco land. They appeared in the form of higher market prices for tobacco, and these higher prices were used in the 1948 Act to raise parity prices for tobacco to a new high level; in the 1949 Act they raised the support level for tobacco to a record high and are designed to maintain it in that relative position permanently.

Two features of the legislative strategy employed in the tobacco program are worthy of note. The first was to obtain benefits, or bring about changes in the tobacco program, some years before they were made for the agricultural program as a whole. Then when similar changes were made in the general program they automatically applied to tobacco and thus compounded the advantages. For example,

---

49 Three-year average (unweighted) prices of flue-cured tobacco rose 161 per cent from 1938–40 to 1946–48; for burley, the increase was 155 per cent. Total wages paid by cigarette manufacturers increased by 111 per cent from 1939 to 1947.

the two changes in the base period for parity prices for tobacco permitted higher prices during the war and those higher prices were automatically translated into still higher parity prices by the 1948 and 1949 Acts. As a separate proposition, this increase in the parity prices of tobacco at a time when most other parity prices were being reduced could not readily be justified and probably would not have been proposed; as the result of the application of a general formula, it was established automatically and with little notice.

The second feature, in line with traditional monopolistic practice was to give special attention to restricting the entry of new producers in the field. As we have seen, restriction of production is the keystone of the whole tobacco program. Those who shaped that program evidently did not want to leave the matter of controls to the voluntary and spontaneous action of growers from year to year. The 1948 Act (Sec. 208) provides that the Secretary of Agriculture *shall* proclaim marketing quotas for every year in the future for each type of tobacco now under quota. Such quotas remain in effect unless they are disapproved by more than a third of the voters voting in a referendum on the question. Voting is limited to those who grow tobacco in the current crop year. Thus, quotas could be ended only by the growers taking the initiative to defeat an existing measure under which they have profited greatly.

XV POLICIES FOR INDUSTRIAL DEVELOPMENT

The income of southerners would have to be increased by about 50 per cent to make it roughly equal to the income of non-southerners. Twenty years ago it would have required an increase of more than 100 per cent. Thus progress is being made in reducing the southern lag. The crucial question now is how that progress can be maintained and even increased. From what sources—from what types of economic activity and from what sectors of the economy—can we expect to realize the increased income?

It is not logical to look to agriculture as the major source of the higher income. Preceding chapters have shown that we probably can not expect total agricultural income, in real terms, to rise greatly above its present level. If agriculture were extensively mechanized, the per capita income of farmers could be raised very substantially but hundreds of thousands, if not millions, of workers now on farms would have to find work elsewhere. In practice it probably would not take place unless there was a market, such as industry could provide, to absorb the displaced workers. Higher farm incomes could be realized by the development of dairying, poultry and cattle raising, and truck farming, but these activities depend heavily upon a strong and steady demand in the nonagricultural sectors of the economy. While agriculture will probably remain an important part, and perhaps a fairly profitable part, of the southern economy, it is not likely to provide the major impetus for higher per capita incomes.

The other extractive industries—mining, drilling, fishing, forestry, and the exploitation of natural resources generally—are also significant parts of the southern economy. In many cases they can and should be extended and developed. In some instances they provide

364

substantial amounts of income. But the nature of these activities and the South's mineral reserves do not offer much promise of substantially higher average incomes from those sources. The early stages of extractive processes nearly always provide only low-paid jobs; the real profit lies in the more advanced processing of the products. Those later stages of processing can be performed only by a fairly well developed industrial system. Further, the South's supply of mineral resources today is dominated to a considerable extent by petroleum and natural gas. Over the coming decades these are likely to be depleted and activities depending upon them are likely to diminish. Extensive increases in other fields would be required merely to offset this decline. Finally, there is the general principle that extractive industries are subject to decreasing returns or increasing costs; the best resources are used first. Unless there are some striking new discoveries or technological developments, we would not be justified in expecting this sector of the economy to provide the means of raising per capita income substantially.

Another large area of the economy is made up of wholesale and retail trade, finance, transportation and communication, and the services—personal, professional and governmental. In general, income in these activities is dependent upon, and is determined by, the income in other sectors of the economy rather than the reverse.[1] In terms of generating new primary income, a nation or a region can increase its total income by activities of this kind only by performing these services for outsiders or by performing for themselves services for which they have formerly paid outsiders. Here the South has two opportunities for gain. First, it can perform for itself more of the banking and related financial services for which it has often in the past depended upon the large centers of the North and East. Second, it could and probably will continue to develop its facilities for entertaining vacationers from outside the region.

These could well be important items, especially for certain localities, but they are hardly likely to amount to a major net source of income for the region as a whole. Of course, the South may also increase substantially its income, as it has done, by enlarging the volume of services performed by its own labor for its own consumers,

[1] We are omitting from consideration here the possibility that governments, through their fiscal policies, may affect the level of income by changing the amount of purchasing power in the hands of consumers.

but the demand for such services has its origin in the purchasing power generated in the primary occupations. There is a certain legitimate income to be earned by laundries, but we cannot expand our incomes indefinitely by "taking in each other's washing."

THE DESIRABILITY OF FURTHER INDUSTRIALIZATION[1]

Both the above considerations and the history of nations over the past 150 years strongly suggest that if the South is to realize higher per capita income it will have to look to industry. In the modern world, manufacturing industry constitutes the dynamic heart of the economy which, to a very great extent, determines the level of income for the economy as a whole. It is unusual for any nation or region to enjoy a high income unless its activities are based rather directly upon some fairly well developed system of manufacturing.

There are, it is true, great differences in manufacturing. There are factories of the sweat-shop variety which require only a minimum of skill, produce cheap and coarse goods, and afford little better than a subsistence level of living. Even that income may be higher than that enjoyed by some tenants and sharecroppers, but such industries are not desirable in the long run. They may well develop into communities so unattractive that they repel more desirable industries later.[2] The South needs, particularly at this stage of its development, those industries which carry further the processing of goods, which have relatively large amounts of capital equipment per worker, and

---

[2] It is obviously in the best interest of any area to follow the principle of developing those industries in which it has the "best comparative advantage" or the "least comparative disadvantage." This means that a country or an area with a high ratio of labor to capital and natural resources will first develop those industries using a large volume of labor in proportion to capital and natural resources. This will be reflected in low wages per worker which keep the price of the products of industry and agriculture low enough so that they can compete with those produced by countries or areas having higher ratios of capital and natural resources to labor supply. This is what has happened in the South historically and is illustrated by the development of cotton and tobacco culture and the textile industry.

With capital in far greater actual and potential supply than ever before and with the factor of unalterable natural resources of less importance than previously, the South is no longer condemned in perpetuity to dependence upon low ratios of capital and land to labor. The situation is affected also by the possibility of controlling the price at which the products of industry are sold. Southern industry may thus be able to exploit as well as be exploited through the use of quasi-monopoly power. This, of course, complicates but does not at all invalidate the principle of comparative advantage. Tobacco prices under governmental support and control illustrate this.

which produce a large value of output per worker. Those are the only industries that can raise per capita incomes in the amount required. Fortunately, many of the industries which have been established in the South since World War II have been of that type.[3]

There are unpleasant and undesirable aspects to the process of industrialization; it is not an unmixed blessing. Some factories give off unpleasant odors, noises, and waste matter; streams get polluted; living quarters may be crowded and slums may develop; there may be friction and strife between labor and management; workers transplanted from the countryside may lose some of their individuality and sense of responsibility; the mill community may not provide as good an environment as the farm for rearing children; etc. Some southerners have looked at those unpleasant aspects and have decided that they do not wish to see the South industrialized.[4] This is understandable. But those men may have been comparing the seamy side of an industrial society with the better and somewhat idealized aspects of a rural society; they may have forgotten that we have rural slums and that squalor and poverty can be as degrading in the country as in the town.

There are two sides to the question and it is necessary to establish some minimum standards to see that industry does not become a liability rather than an asset. Considering the trends of the past 20 years and the kinds of industrial plants which have been established in the South in the past four years, however, there can be little doubt that there is a large net advantage on the side of industry and that industrialization provides the principal means for raising incomes in the South.

[3] See, for example, the discussion of the changes in the pattern of southern industry in Chapter VI and the footnote showing relative earnings in the lumber, furniture, and paper industries in Chapter XII.

It is obvious that the very type of industry with high "value-added per worker" ordinarily requires larger capital investment per worker than do industries characterized by low value-added per worker. Consequently, per dollar of capital invested, industries which produce a high value-added per worker will probably provide less additional employment than those with low value-added per worker. Nevertheless, under present circumstances the South is likely to obtain more benefit from additional investment in industries such as those producing automobiles, chemicals, and paper and pulp rather than in a further extension of the textile and garment industries. If we follow the policy of lowering our tariffs which our general national interest seems to indicate, our textile industry is likely to meet stiff competition in years to come from those areas with labor in such large supply that their "least comparative disadvantage" would be found in developing that industry.

[4] See Twelve Southerners, *I'll Take My Stand,* New York, Harper Brothers, 1930.

EFFECTS OF CONSCIOUS POLICIES ON INDUSTRIALIZATION

In our economy, decisions concerning the development and location of industrial plants are made by owners and managers. As a rule, those decisions are made with primary reference to basic economic factors which are subject to little, if any, change by man-made decisions, at least in the short run. These factors are discussed briefly below. It is well to keep this principle in mind and to recognize that any sound industrial development must rest upon the advantages offered by the basic economic characteristics of the region.

That is not to say, however, that conscious policy can have no influence on industrialization. It can affect the basic economic factors in two ways. First, science and research can change the significance and value of existing assets by finding new ways of using them. The present uses of cottonseeds and southern pine are outstanding examples. Second, proper policies can, in the long run, greatly affect the availability of some of the basic factors. The timber supply can be increased by good forest policies, water supply can be protected by preventing stream pollution, labor skill can be increased by education, raw materials can be made more available by good highways, and so on.

There is the further fact that modern industry is affected more and more by man-made laws, institutions, and conditions. General corporation laws, anti-trust laws, minimum wage laws, maximum hour laws, tax laws, labor union laws—all of these and many others go to make up the general economic climate in which industry must operate. These laws and the way in which they are administered can do much to encourage or discourage the development of industry.

RESPONSIBILITY FOR POLICY FORMULATION AND ADMINISTRATION

If there is to be a conscious, deliberate policy, who shall have the responsibility for formulating and administering it? For activities requiring such broad and general powers, governments—national, state or local—naturally come to mind.

In many respects the Federal Government has the greater powers in this field and thus is able to exert the most influence on industrial development. The Federal Government, however, has neither the responsibility nor the right to make any special effort to promote the industrial development of any given region unless that is required by the national interest.[5] It does have the positive duty to avoid policies which discriminate unfairly against any region. The South should not ask or expect favors from the Federal Government; any industrial development based on invidious legislation or policies would be vulnerable to political attack and subject to change with changing political fortunes. In the main, the South must look to its own efforts to encourage industrialization.

As between state and local governments, the states have great advantages in this field. They cover greater areas, they have a larger perspective, they enact general legislation and, in general, control local governments. They have greater financial powers and are increasing their relative financial strength steadily. In so far as industrialization is to be encouraged by public action, the states must carry the bulk of the work and responsibility.

In the nongovernmental field there are many agencies which can influence the development of industry. These include the Federal Reserve Banks, commercial banks, railroads, public utilities, and many organizations of business men such as chambers of commerce, trade associations, and local community development corporations. In this field the principal problem is to see that the policies advocated are sound in the beginning and that they do not conflict or overlap. Local groups are prone to have narrow perspectives, to adopt shallow policies, and to compete with each other so that their efforts cancel out.

TECHNIQUES FOR IMPLEMENTING POLICIES

Once the decision to promote industrialization has been adopted, it must be implemented. What are the techniques available? In this discussion it is assumed that direct government ownership or operation of industry, or both, are not practicable alternatives. This assumption is made because government ownership or operation of manufacturing enterprises (in peacetime) would be inconsistent with the

[5] In the past, the fact that the South was the "Nation's Number One Economic Problem" may have justified special action by the Federal Government designed to raise income in the South, but as that income rises, the justification disappears; it stops far short of the income level most southerners would like to see.

philosophy on which our economy is organized. Furthermore, many of our states now have constitutional provisions which prohibit state or local governments from participating in, or lending funds to, private business enterprises. (As used here "industry" means primarily manufacturing industry and what is said above is not meant to rule out the possibility of governments or government corporations operating public utilities or developing hydroelectric power.)

If direct governmental participation is excluded, then any policy for influencing industrial development must operate by affecting the decisions of private owners and managers. There are three general methods for influencing those decisions. The first is through publicity and information; by advertising and by assembling, analyzing and making available to private enterprises pertinent data on the economic resources of a given region or locality. The second method is the use of special inducements such as bonuses, the donation of land and/or buildings, tax exemptions, etc. The third method is to attempt to create a more favorable economic environment; to attempt to change or modify the basic economic factors which largely determine industrial development and location. Each of these methods is discussed more fully below.

DETERMINANTS OF INDUSTRIAL
DEVELOPMENT AND LOCATION

The factors which determine industrial development and location are many and complex.[6] They vary in importance from one industry to another and often are interdependent in a most complicated way. In some cases one factor is so important that it dominates the decision as to whether there will be a plant and where it will be located; in other cases, the factors are so evenly balanced that even a minor factor may swing the decision one way or the other. Neither time nor space permit anything approaching an exhaustive discussion of these factors here; rather a mere listing with a few comments must suffice.[7]

6 Actually, development and location are two separate problems and the factors which govern them vary somewhat. But for this brief discussion they are discussed together.

7 For a recent and comprehensive discussion of this subject see E. M. Hoover, *The Location of Economic Activity*, New York, McGraw-Hill, 1948. For an excellent and pertinent study which applies these factors to 88 specific cases in the South in recent years see Glenn E. McLaughlin and Stefan Robock, *Why Industry Moves South*, National Planning Association (NPA Committee of the South Report No. 3), Washington, 1949.

Major Factors. For a large majority of industry the three major factors which determine development and location are the three M's— *men, materials, and markets.* In other words, when considering a new location, industrialists give most attention to the available labor supply and its ability and intelligence; to the availability of raw materials and their cost and quality; and to the location of the markets for their finished products. In any given case one or the other of these factors is likely to be dominant, according to the nature of the industry, and thus we have market-oriented industries, materials-oriented industries, and labor-oriented industries. It should be noted that none of these factors is susceptible of any appreciable change in the short run; even in the long run changes are likely to be slow, difficult, and small.

McLaughlin and Robock found that the expanding southern market was the most important factor which attracted industrial plants to the South in the first three years after World War II.[8] Since the demand for industrial products is largely determined by the level of income, this fact is understandable in the light of what has been happening to southern incomes in recent years. Total income depends largely upon the rate of activity in the economy as a whole, so there is little that any promotional policy can do directly to affect it. Since markets depend upon income and income depends in considerable part upon industry, it is to some extent a problem of lifting one's self by one's bootstraps. However, there is one favorable aspect; when the movement once gets started, as it now seems to be in the South, it tends to feed on itself. That is one of the most encouraging signs on the southern horizon at present.

Raw materials constitute another important factor affecting the location of industry and the one which has been second in importance in attracting industry to the South in recent years. The list of raw materials is a long one including: mineral resources; forest products; livestock and dairy products; vegetables; fuel and power in the form of coal, natural gas, petroleum and electric power; and, last but not least, abundant supplies of usable water.

It may be contended that the South has had these resources all along. Why is it that they are just now exerting their influence to attract industry? Why has industry not taken advantage of them before? In the main, these resources *have* been here all along, although in some cases considerable effort was required to provide adequate

[8] *Op. cit.,* pp. 26, 32.

supplies of electric power at low rates and to assure food-processing plants of adequate supplies of dairy products and vegetables. But the important change which has taken place in recent years is that the importance or significance of these southern resources to industry has increased with changing conditions. For example, southern forest resources have become more important as the nation's supply dwindled, as the production of synthetic fibres increased, and as it became possible to produce newsprint from pine trees. Natural gas and petroleum become more important as industrial raw materials when it is possible to produce from them synthetic rubber and a host of other commodities. Many modern techniques of production, especially in various branches of the chemical industry, require enormous amounts of water, and thus the South's abundant water supply becomes important.

Most raw materials are not readily amenable to change by promotional efforts. In some cases important new uses for certain materials can be found. Intelligent long-run policies will be helpful in protecting the water supply, providing cheap power, and conserving scarce natural resources.

The labor supply was the third most important factor in attracting industry to the South in recent years. As with raw materials, the question might well be asked as to why labor has exerted its drawing power only recently. The South has had an abundant supply of labor for a long time; why has it not attracted industry earlier? Further, we might ask what aspect of the labor supply has been most significant; low wages, the absence of labor unions, more training and skill on the part of workers, or the mere availability of labor?

Again, the answer seems to be that the added attraction has been due more to changes which took place outside the region rather than to anything which happened within the South. Over the past ten years there has been a great increase in industrial employment throughout the whole country. Employers have often found that workers simply were not available in the cities and in the large industrial centers, but that they could be found on the farms and in the small towns of the South. In the recent boom years, with their tight labor market, the mere availability of labor has been the South's principal advantage in this field.[9]

9 *Ibid*, p. 67 ff.

Of course, a labor supply must be more than a certain number of adult human beings. Potential workers must have a certain ability plus a minimum training or the aptitude to acquire it quickly. As was noted earlier, southern labor has made a good showing as to innate ability and productivity.

Low wages and the comparative weakness of labor unions have undoubtedly attracted some industrial plants to the South, but in general these considerations have not been major factors influencing industrial location. Some employers pay lower wages in the South, but most of them expect the North-South wage differential to continue to decline and perhaps to disappear. "In any event, with few exceptions, company executives pointed out that they could not justify a large investment based on such an uncertain matter as a North-South wage differential."[10] Most employers apparently are not greatly concerned over the prospect of dealing with unions, although some of them say that they are interested in getting away from radical and irresponsible labor leadership and from the congested industrial centers where operations are likely to be interrupted by labor disturbances arising outside their own plants.

One conclusion drawn by McLaughlin and Robock is pertinent to this discussion: ". . . it is no longer necessary to base promotional efforts on low wage rates, as many of the southern development groups are realizing."[11] The labor supply is another factor which is not susceptible to much change in the short run. In the long run it can be improved by such things as more technical training in the schools, sound and fair state labor laws, and other similar measures.

Minor Factors. In addition to the three major factors discussed above, there are a host of minor factors which help to determine industrial development. They vary in number and importance with the different industries. They include such things as transportation services, availability of capital, taxes, governmental services, the availability of land and buildings, corporation laws, the attitude of state and local governments, living conditions, climate, and others. Most of these factors (with the outstanding exception of climate) can be changed within a reasonable time and by fairly direct action. Only in rare cases is any one of them decisive. If any promotional policy is to depend on these

10 *Ibid*, p. 70.   11 *Ibid*, p. 120.

factors, it should operate through several of them if it is to be effective in exerting any influence on decisions.

PUBLICITY AND INFORMATION AS AIDS TO INDUSTRIALIZATION

Now that we have discussed techniques generally and have described the channels through which they must operate, it is appropriate that we should consider in greater detail some particular techniques and evaluate their usefulness.

Advertising. About 12 or 15 years ago, several states began to make appropriations for state advertising. In many cases it was a combination of industrial and recreational advertising. Since the war there has been a substantial increase in such activities. At the present time eight southern states are spending amounts varying from $10,000 to $250,-000 per year, in addition to administrative costs, for industrial advertising. The total is probably between $750,000 and $1,000,000 per year and apparently rising.

Advertising is not designed to affect any of the basic economic factors which determine industrial location. Its purpose is to persuade businessmen—to "sell" them on locating in a certain area. Apparently it is based on the assumption that businessmen decide on the location of industrial plants in the same way that individuals decide on the purchase of consumer goods. The whole theory of state advertising needs a close and critical examination, which apparently has not been made.

There is need, also, for a careful evaluation of the results obtained from industrial advertising by states. So far as can be learned, no such study has been completed. Such fragments of evidence as are readily available appear to provide little justification for the practice. McLaughlin and Robock found that ". . . for the large manufacturing companies included in this survey, advertising campaigns are reported to have had little effect upon locational decisions."[12] In one state, an analysis of advertising expenditures showed that advertising costs per inquiry received varied from about $65 to over $100 for certain specified periods. Over a four-year period, the cost was about $200 per inquiry and no locational decision could be traced directly to the advertising. In another southern state, it has been estimated that advertising costs per inquiry received varied from about $700 to almost

12 *Ibid*, p. 110.

$1,000 for different periods.[13] Operating on an annual advertising budget of $30,000, a Louisiana department reported that in a period of between a year and a half and two years (not stated specifically) "over 600 bona fide inquiries" were received as a result of the ads. This would indicate a cost of between $75 and $100 per inquiry. As for actual results, "Since the beginning of our advertising program, over 250 industrial projects have started in Louisiana."[14] It is not stated whether any of the new projects were traceable to the advertising. While there may have been results which did not show up in inquiries received, these figures are so striking that they should raise serious question concerning the usefulness of industrial advertising, especially since the number of inquiries itself may be almost meaningless as an indicator of actual results achieved.[15]

There are at least three dangers for the future in connection with advertising programs. The first is that advertising agencies, in order to get the business, are likely to exert their persuasive influence for larger appropriations without much regard for the results which those programs have achieved. The second is that businessmen and others who believe in the potency of advertising in private business will approve of state advertising on the assumption that the two are comparable. The third danger is that state departments which administer the programs may demand higher and ever higher advertising budgets because other states are spending heavily and thus the states will become engaged in a competitive race in which their efforts very largely cancel out.

Providing Locational Data. The second part of a publicity program is to provide pertinent data on the economic resources of a given area to

---

13 These data are based on statements made to Mr. W. D. Ross during personal interviews.

14 *Report of the Department of Commerce and Industry,* State of Louisiana, for the Biennium 1946–1948, p. 10.

15 In the Mississippi BAWI program, "about 3,800 inquiries and propositions were received (a considerably smaller number than had been anticipated). . . .

"The initial screening or sifting process brought the 3,800 proposals down to 300 that appeared worth while. The investigative work then began. . . .

"The 300 propositions were in turn brought down to about 100. The work then involved a concentration upon those 100, with the result that 60 manufacturing concerns became sufficiently interested to send their representatives into the state. . . .

"Out of the final 60 firms . . . came the issuance of 21 certificates . . . (and) 12 plants were eventually established under the BAWI plan.

"For the original 3,800 proposals, there was an over-all mortality of 99.7 per cent. For the 300 propositions that seemed fairly promising, the mortality rate was 90.1 per cent." Ernest J. Hopkins, *Mississippi's BAWI Plan,* Federal Reserve Bank of Atlanta, Georgia, 1944, pp. 23–24.

interested parties. General data are usually assembled, analyzed, and kept on file. Special analyses or surveys may be conducted to meet the needs of a particular industry.

There is definite justification for such activities if the work is thorough and accurate. The data provided are in the nature of "market information" and those who decide on locations must have all the information possible if they are to make intelligent decisions. Small companies have almost no means of obtaining this type of information for themselves and even the large companies never have enough of it.[16] McLaughlin and Robock found that activities of this kind had been ". . . important in calling the attention of concerns to certain local possibilities, although . . . (they) were minor elements in the final choice of locality." In most cases the companies preferred to get their information from railroads, public utilities, and state planning boards, several of which were found to be very good in this respect. "Usually, however, prospective producers preferred to get information on local industrial conditions from local manufacturers and other businessmen."[17]

As a result of their study, McLaughlin and Robock offer a suggestion to promotional agencies in this respect.

If an agency first makes an inventory of its locational attractions, and second, . . . determines the specific types of plants for which it offers the greatest advantages, its development efforts . . . may become more effective. Instead of using the shotgun technique of general advertising, the agency could then concentrate efforts on securing those types of industries suggested by local resources. . . .

In order to impress a prospective producer with the advantages of local resources, a development agency should be able to present to him comparative costs of getting together the required elements in production. Such briefs can be prepared only by men having familiarity with the industry under study.[18]

SUBSIDIES OR SPECIAL INDUCEMENTS

Many communities, especially small ones, eager for industrial development, attempt to attract industrial plants by some type of special inducement. These may take the form of: (1) cash bonuses; (2) local participation in financing; (3) free building sites and/or buildings or

16 See Hoover, op. cit., pp. 266–67.
17 McLaughlin and Robock, op. cit., pp. 110–111.
18 Ibid, p. 118.

very low rentals; (4) tax exemptions; or (5) advance agreements on utility rates and services. They may be used separately or in combination. These are the most immediate and most obvious techniques for attracting industry. But they do not affect any major locational factor and only in rare cases can they be decisive in a locational problem. One or more of these devices are now in use in more than half of the southern states.

Donations. Although cash bonuses are sometimes given, the most usual forms of donation are building sites and buildings themselves. Frequently the building is rented at a nominal figure for a period of years, after which the industrial company gains title if it has met specified conditions. Usually the land and buildings are paid for from the proceeds of bonds issued by city or county governments. Over a recent ten-year period the Tennessee legislature authorized the issuance of almost three millions dollars of such bonds, although the state constitution prohibits the practice.[19]

This practice is almost universally condemned by those who have studied the question thoroughly, yet its persistence is evidenced by its continued use even in the face of constitutional prohibitions. Perhaps one explanation is that the leaders of a community, frequently businessmen and landowners, see a chance to make a profit while the cost is paid by taxpayers as a whole, many of whom derive no benefit from the transaction. The rank and file of the taxpayers may have no leadership, or they may be ashamed to oppose the measure since it is presented as a "progressive" move.

A large majority of the companies studied by McLaughlin and Robock were opposed to special inducements.

> Corporate executives are generally convinced that it would be poor business on their part to accept any special concession from a local community. It was often indicated that to accept local gifts would make it more difficult to work in harmony with the community. . . .
> Another reason why manufacturers were usually not impressed by local concessions was that the offered grants consisted mainly of free sites or payments on buildings, which accounted for only a small proportion of total plant cost. Very rarely among the large concerns investigated did the site itself account for more than a few per cent of the total plant investment and even where the building was included the cost was usually less than that for the machinery. Several manufacturers indicated that it

[19] Tennessee State Planning Commission, *Subsidies for Industries in Tennessee,* Nashville, 1947, p. 1.

would be taking advantage of the local community to accept gifts because a gift could not affect the locational decision. . . .

In three instances the firms accepted a local concession as evidence of the cooperation of the community and returned the funds to the community at the opening of the plant.[20]

Subsidies of this kind are not likely to attract to the community either the right kind of companies or the right kind of industries. Responsible businessmen do not ask for charity from the community in which they expect to operate. As the Tennessee State Planning Commission states, "A request by an industry for gratuitous aid is generally a danger signal, for sound enterprises do not seek outright gifts."[21] Further, when communities indulge in this practice they are lending themselves to the game practiced by the railroads in the nineteenth century when they played one community off against another to see which would make the highest bid. Since the funds involved are public funds, the individuals doing the bidding are not limited by the usual restraints.

The industries which accept subsidies of this kind are usually those which have relatively low investment in equipment, produce a low value per worker and pay low wages. Shoe and garment factories are outstanding examples. While at the moment those industries may be better than none in a given community, they are not likely to become elements of strength in the community. ". . . One community which had obtained a garment plant in part by local contributions . . . was trying to raise another fund for a shoe factory. When asked to contribute to the new plant, the garment plant refused."[22] The Tennessee State Planning Commission concludes with a strong recommendation that ". . . this uneconomic and dangerous practice be discouraged."[23]

Tax Exemptions. Some degree of tax exemption is probably a more prevalent form of subsidy than outright donations. At the present time, eight southern states—Alabama, Arkansas, Kentucky, Louisiana, Mississippi, Oklahoma, South Carolina, and Tennessee—allow tax exemption in some form. In Tennessee, a number of local units grant exemption although it is contrary to the state code. Three other states —Florida, Georgia, and Virginia—have recently repealed tax exemption provisions or allowed them to expire. That leaves only two

20 McLaughlin and Robock, *op. cit.,* pp. 112–13.
21 *Op. cit.,* p. 3.
22 McLaughlin and Robock, *op. cit.,* p. 114.
23 *Op. cit.,* p. 16.

states—North Carolina and Texas—which have not experimented with this device.

In most cases the exemptions are granted by local governments, under power of state law, with little or no supervision by the state. In Louisiana, however, each exemption is granted by a department of the state government in the form of a contract. The period of exemption varies from five to ten years. Exemptions usually do not extend beyond property taxes and may not include all of them.

Most of what was said above about gifts will apply also to tax exemptions. Exemptions are the more insidious in that they do not require any cash outlay and so, apparently, do not cost anybody anything. However, it has been pointed out that

> ... addition of a new industry increases the financial burdens of a community: increased charges for extension of sewers and lights, new streets needed, added costs for fire and police protection, and increased costs for health, education, protection, and relief services for the additional acquired population.[24]

This may well raise the rates for existing taxpayers and lay the basis for ill will against the newly acquired industry. Sometimes that results in "soaking" the industry when the exemption expires.

Again, there is little evidence that tax exemptions have had much appreciable effect, at least on the location of important industrial units. "The policy of using tax subsidies, judging from evidence at hand, has no material influence on industrial development."[25] McLaughlin and Robock found that "with respect to tax concessions, manufacturers have rarely located a plant primarily to obtain the concessions. . . ."[26] The Georgia exemption feature, which was in effect from 1923 to 1945, ". . . produced no very striking results. Nearly all of the exemptions . . . were centered in three towns, and only 20 specific instances were found in which new industries had been attracted by the exemption."[27]

Among the broader aspects of the problem, several observations are pertinent. First, state and local taxes constitute only a minor factor affecting the location of industry; exemption from them for a relatively short period could not logically be expected to produce any substantial

[24] Tennessee State Planning Commission, op. cit., p. 3.
[25] Ibid., p. 5. [26] Op. cit., p. 114.
[27] R. P. Brooks, "Taxation of Manufacturing in Georgia," in Southern Manufacturer's Tax Bill, Bulletin of The Bureau of Business Research, University of Kentucky, Lexington, 1947, p. 21.

results. Second, there is no available record of any significant area in which a large amount of industrialization has been induced by tax exemptions. Third, three of the southern states which have had exemptions have given them up; apparently results did not justify continuing them. Finally, the two southern states which have had the greatest industrial development—North Carolina and Texas—have never granted tax exemptions.

Mississippi's BAWI Plan. Perhaps the most significant effort to stimulate industrialization in the South in recent years has been the Mississippi BAWI—Balance Agriculture With Industry—Plan. The first plan operated from 1936 to 1940; a second and essentially similar plan was started in 1944 and still continues. Both plans combined donation of building with tax exemptions. It is not feasible either to explain or discuss the plans here; Hopkins' little booklet gives an excellent discussion of the first plan.[28]

During the four years of the first plan, local communities issued almost a million dollars in bonds to assist in the establishment of 12 new industrial plants. These included one shipyard which soon came to exceed, in number of employees and wages, all the others combined. Four of the plants were hosiery mills and three were garment plants; all were branches of outside companies. About the middle of 1941, when all plants were in operation, total employment was about 5,000. The one distinctive feature of the plans was the strong state commission which closely supervised their operation. It investigated thoroughly all applicants for aid and approved all projects. Without doubt, it was instrumental in weeding out many unsound and unfit projects.

Hopkins does not offer any opinion on the over-all success or failure of the first plan. In any event, the advent of the war soon after the plants were established would make such an appraisal almost meaningless. The state commission approved 21 projects. In one case voters failed to approve the bonds and in another the sale of bonds was enjoined. In five cases industrial companies refused to go through with the deals after bonds had been approved, and in one case the company established the plant but refused the aid. In the end, 13 aid projects were consummated, 11 for new plants and two for expansion of old plants. Two of the original establishments failed to fulfill the terms of their contracts and were replaced by others. While the plan

28 Ernest J. Hopkins, *Mississippi's BAWI Plan,* Federal Reserve Bank of Atlanta,. Atlanta, Ga., 1944.

was certainly not a complete failure, it was also certainly far from the success its proponents hoped and expected.

POLICIES TO CREATE A FAVORABLE
ECONOMIC ENVIRONMENT

The policies described above are not likely to have much effect in encouraging industrialization. Most of them are superficial and temporary; they do not influence the major factors which determine industrial development and location. Some of them are unsound and dangerous. A sound industrialization policy must include action to affect the more permanent and basic factors of location in so far as that is possible. Some suggested elements of such a policy are discussed below. Since there are several of these, only a very brief discussion of each can be given. No attempt has been made to arrange them in the order of their importance.

Honest, Efficient Government. To a considerable extent, honest and efficient government, at both the state and local level, is a matter of tradition. Good government is an important factor in industrial growth. McLaughlin and Robock found that "Among the concerns covered all were interested in the costs and efficiency of local government."[29] Naturally, those companies were most interested in governmental policies and attitudes affecting business. But those are not unrelated to honesty and efficiency. The dishonest, inefficient demagogue is likely, sooner or later, to have financial difficulties. Further, strong business organizations, especially those with headquarters outside the state, are not so likely to pay toll to his "machine." Under such conditions there are likely to be charges against "Big Business," "Wall Street Interests," and "Northern Capitalists," and attempts to "soak" them by discriminatory taxes and other punitive measures.

Recently, for example, one of the departments of the State of Louisiana referred to ". . . our greatest handicap, which is our past reputation of antagonistic state government attitude toward industry."[30] It was proposed to offset this handicap with tax exemptions. One can doubt both the advisability and the efficacy of the proposed remedy.

[29] *Op. cit.,* p. 108.
[30] *Report of the Department of Commerce and Industry,* State of Louisiana, Biennium, 1944–46, p. 54.

A Sound Labor Code. Although federal labor regulations are dominant in many respects, there are still many phases of labor management relations, especially for small companies, which are controlled by state law. These include regulations governing maximum hours, night work, safety precautions, workmen's compensation, and the suppression by law enforcement agencies of illegal activities by labor or management. The larger companies which have established plants in the South in recent years have not been interested primarily in avoiding labor unions, as such, any more than they have been primarily interested in low wages. Probably most of these companies consider the unionization of their plants inevitable anyway. They *have* been interested in avoiding labor racketeering and ". . . keeping away from labor disturbances which might affect labor generally within a large population area."[31] Thus they are more likely to be interested in assurances of evenhanded enforcement of law and order than in anticlosed shop legislation by states.[32]

Water and Electric Power. The supply of water and the quantity and cost of electric power available are of significance to all industries and are of critical importance to some. A discussion of these factors, with some recommendations, is given in the chapter on policies in relation to natural resources.[33]

Good Forest Management. The chapter on Forestry explained the far-reaching economic significance of good forestry management. It is important to industry because it would insure the supply of important industrial raw materials, protect the water level, and regularize stream flows. A suggested forest program to achieve these and other goals has already been outlined.[34]

A Sound, Fair Tax System. In popular discussion high and discriminatory taxation is perhaps more frequently cited as a deterrent to industrial growth than any other cause. There are several reasons for this; taxes are an obvious factor, they are universally unpopular—and perhaps existing companies hope to gain by a move made for the ostensible purpose of attracting new industry. The conclusion about taxes is often based upon a comparison of the rates of two or three specific taxes. But Professor Heer has shown with remarkable clarity how

---

[31] McLaughlin and Robock, *op. cit.,* pp. 71, 100.
[32] For a discussion of other phases of this question see Chapter XVI, "Labor and Wage Policy."
[33] See Chapter X.   [34] See Chapter XI.

complex the problem is and how difficult, if not impossible, it is to say that one state's tax system is more favorable to business generally than another. Among other things, the state and local tax burden depends upon the composition of a firm's assets, its rate of earnings, and the level of federal taxation.[35]

Generally, state and local taxes have not been a major factor affecting industrial location. In recent years they have been declining in importance for two reasons. First, state and local governments have been depending less and less on property taxes, one of the main levies paid by industrial concerns. Second, federal taxes—principally the corporate income tax—have more and more dominated the corporation's tax bill. For the usual profitable company, federal taxes are now considerably more than state and local taxes combined. Rates under the federal corporate income tax are now approximately three times as high as they were 20 years ago. Not only are state and local taxes a much smaller part of the total tax bill, but they are usually deductible in computing taxable income for the federal income tax. Thus, if a corporation is liable for a federal income tax, for every dollar it pays in state or local taxes, it saves from 24 to 38 cents in federal income tax. This reduces considerably the significance of tax differences between states.

Two recent studies indicate that southern states have a slight advantage in the matter of taxation. McLaughlin and Robock found that, ". . . northern companies consider the lower level of manufacturing taxes in the South an advantage in plant location. Usually the property tax was also lower, though there were a few notable exceptions."[36] Professor Martin, summarizing the results of tax studies in seven southern states, arrived at these conclusions: (1) manufacturing taxes in the South "are in general relatively low as compared with those on other sorts of business activity"; (2) "The general level of state and local taxation is slightly lower in the South than in the average other state, but the differential is unimportant"; and (3) "The tax differentials between states in the South or between these and the remainder of the country are an unimportant factor affecting the rate of industrial growth."[37]

[35] Clarence Heer, *Tax Bill of A Selected Manufacturing Corporation in Six Southeastern States,* Committee on Taxation, North Carolina State Planning Board, Raleigh, 1945 (Mimeographed).
[36] *Op. cit.,* p. 107.
[37] James W. Martin, *Southern Manufacturer's Tax Bill, op. cit.,* pp. 2–4.

While taxes usually are not a major locational factor, nevertheless it might be well for southern states to study their tax systems to see that they do not penalize industry. It is not feasible here to attempt to outline a desirable tax system, but a few comments are in order. First, the number of taxes levied on corporations should be reduced and the states should attempt to standardize and coordinate the regulations and forms used in administering taxes so as to reduce the work involved in preparing tax returns. Second, administrative provisions and practices may be more important than tax rates. Such provisions would include the statutory rules for assessing property and the formulae for allocating capital used, or income earned, within the state. Fair and sound administrative practices can be insured only by competent and impartial administrative personnel. Third, since southern states are still largely rural states, special care should be taken to prevent farm pressure groups from relieving rural areas of taxes at the expense of urban dwellers and industry. For example, a plan for financing the public schools which was seriously considered in North Carolina in 1949 would have discriminated greatly against urban areas. Fourth, the size of corporate earnings in itself is no sound criterion for levying taxes. If in a few prosperous years, a $100-million company earns $10 million per year, that is no indication that it is making exorbitant profits or that it has any unusual taxpaying ability. Labor and farm pressure groups are likely to press for taxes directed against large incomes as such. On the contrary, attention should be given to amount of capital invested, the risk involved, and average earnings over the course of a business cycle.

Professor Heer has suggested that southeastern states should agree upon a uniform plan for taxing manufacturing enterprises and thus ". . . to cut manufacturing concerns loose from all general state and local taxes and to segregate them in a special class for tax purposes." He states that:

All of the elements of taxable capacity tapped by existing taxes could be reached just as well by only two taxes and there would appear to be no real need for manufacturing concerns to deal with more than one tax administration.

In line with the above ideas the proposed uniform plan might be reduced to the following simple elements:

1. A uniform classified property tax to be administered by the states and shared with their localities on whatever basis seemed expedient in each state.

2. A uniform state administered net income tax which might or might not be shared with the localities according to the decision of each state.[38]

Perhaps the prospective stability and the protection against discrimination by any particular state in such a plan as this would be as attractive to business concerns as any rates which might be set.

Industrial Development Corporations. The lack of capital funds has frequently been cited as an important obstacle to industrial growth in the South. Both the legitimate demand for investment funds and the supply of such funds are very difficult to determine. What is needed first is an intensive analysis of this problem, in one or several localities, to determine whether such a shortage exists and, if so, how the funds might be provided. To make a valid and worthwhile study of this kind would be a long, difficult, and costly task. It would have to be made by a group of outstandingly competent men from many walks of life. It would require much field work and a rigorous and thorough analysis of the results obtained. Preferably it should be sponsored by some nongovernmental agency or group such as one of the large philanthropic foundations, the Federal Reserve Banks, an insurance association, or a group of bankers' associations. But if it is not done otherwise, some state might well authorize its planning board to arrange for and supervise such a study.

To provide investment funds, if a study of the kind described above should show they are needed, or to test the market on an experimental basis if no study is made, at least two types of precedent are available. The first is provided by the Louisville Industrial Corporation.[39] This concern has functioned for more than 20 years as a nonprofit organization and has considerable success in financing new small business units in and around Louisville, Ky. It has turned over its funds several times and has not only maintained them intact but has added to them. Its capital was supplied originally by businessmen of Louisville.[40]

An English precedent is provided by the Industrial and Commer-

38 Heer, *op. cit.*, pp. 20–21.
39 For an excellent description of the work of this Corporation see Ernest J. Hopkins, "Louisville Industrial Foundation, A Study in Community Capitalization of Local Industries," Federal Reserve Bank of Atlanta, Atlanta, Ga., 1945.
40 For further comment on the Louisville Industrial Corporation and a discussion of other community development corporation in southern states see Buford Brandis, *Industrial Development by Community Corporation,* an unpublished study made for the Committee of the South.

cial Finance Corporation, Limited. This company was formed in 1945 by the commercial banks of England and Scotland, banks subscribing roughly in proportion to their deposits. Total authorized capitalization is £45 million, one third in share capital and two thirds in loan capital. Only £6 million of share capital and £5 million of loan capital had been called up and issued to September, 1948.

The purpose of the company is to aid in the financing of small and medium-sized business units in England, Scotland and Wales. According to its Chairman, the company begins "where the banker leaves off" and leaves off "where the public investor begins."[41] Through September, 1948, the company had actually advanced some £13¼ million; about 60 per cent was in loans and 40 per cent in share capital, the latter represented mostly by preferred shares. Loan rates varied from 3½ to 5½ per cent. Advances varied from £5,000 to £220,000 and averaged about £45,000. In the third year of its operation the company made a small profit and reduced its accumulated deficit to £113,249. The Chairman believed that "the first stage of building up this new financial instrument—the achievement of viability—has been accomplished," and that revenues would continue to cover operating expenses with a margin for reserves.[42]

The similarity of conditions affecting the financing of small business in England and in the United States may be indicated by two short quotations. In England:

. . . the private investor in local and private business. . . has played an important role. In recent decades, his numbers have been depleted by two factors. One is high personal taxation. This has depleted his resources, because the capacity of the individual to accrete capital has been savagely cut back. It may also have diminished his appetite for a private risk. . . . Secondly, the opportunities for investment in negotiable securities have increased; and improved marketing technique has brought home these opportunities to the man who in the past would have invested a thousand or two in a neighbor's business.[43]

In the United States:

. . . the migration, urbanization, and industrialization of our society

41 Lord Piercy, "Long Term and Permanent Finance for Industry," London, 1948, p. 2.
42 Statement by the Chairman, Third Annual General Meeting, Dec. 7, 1948.
43 Lord Piercy, op. cit., p. 4.

during the last half century have tended to break down the personal ties of family and neighborhood that gave rise to the informal pools of risk funds with which many a nineteenth-century enterprise was launched. The present-day equivalent of Uncle Bill and Aunt Susie must be found in a more impersonal source of capital funds—the more so since tax levels on business and individual incomes have slowed the rates at which earnings can be plowed back for business growth.[44]

More Technical Training and Research. An industrial economy of the first magnitude requires a wide distribution of the more elementary technical and mechanical skills among that part of the population making up the labor force; it requires facilities for giving more advanced technical training to foremen and advanced technicians; it requires one or more centers which can provide absolutely the best training in technology and business administration for those who will be technical experts, officials, and policy makers; and finally, it requires adequate research centers, properly equipped and staffed, to solve production problems and advance the frontiers of technical science. To enumerate these requirements is, to a considerable extent, to indicate the South's deficiencies, despite considerable progress which has been made in recent years. If the South is to increase *both* the quantity and the quality of its industry it must give attention to removing these deficiencies.

The first basic requirement can be met by vocational courses in the public schools and by elementary technical schools which offer short, intensive courses.[45] Particular attention should be given to making this training available in rural areas which supply much of the industrial labor force as well as the operators of future mechanized farms. Intermediate technical training can be provided in special technical schools or in state agricultural and mechanical schools. The principal need is to see that offerings are in keeping with the requirements of an expanding industry.

The South is most deficient in the last two basic requirements; they are the ones which are most important in advancing industry for they generate the technical "know-how" which is the spirit of industrialism. There is need for at least one outstanding graduate school of tech-

[44] A. D. H. Kaplan, *Small Business: Its Place and Problems*, New York, 1948, p. 151. Chapter VII of this study, which was made for the Committee for Economic Development, suggests a number of ways in which funds might be provided for small business.

[45] Several southern states are already making considerable progress along these lines.

nology and one of business administration in the South.[46] They would not, at least for some time, be large schools. They would set rigorous standards for selecting their students and would aim at giving them a training second to none in the world. If possible, they should aim to inculcate in the students something of "the spirit of entrepreneurship" and give them the widest possible outlook. Such schools are very expensive to establish and operate, especially if tuition costs are to be kept within reach of those who should attend. No single state and no existing university could afford such schools. Perhaps this would be an appropriate project for six or eight southern states joining in a cooperative undertaking to establish a regional university. Or perhaps some wealthy industrialists might wish to make this contribution to advancing industry in the South.

Available data indicate that less than 5 per cent of the nation's industrial research facilities are located in the South. This is due in considerable part to the fact that the large national companies which have branch plants in the South maintain their research work near their non-southern headquarters. Southern plants benefit from those facilities, but nonetheless there is urgent need for more research in the South, particularly for the many small and medium companies which cannot maintain their own research staffs. There are two possible solutions. One is more public-supported research, especially in connection with state universities. The other is to encourage the growth of independent research associations, either on a mutual, nonprofit basis or on a commercial basis or on some combination of the two. Some beginnings have been made in this field and preliminary results are encouraging.

Good Highway Facilities. More and more, industry is using trucks, and some of the newer industrial communities are almost completely dependent on this form of transportation. Good roads give industry more freedom in choosing the location for their plants and more flexibility in scheduling their work. Good highways, properly maintained and with reasonable regulations for their use, are thus of considerable importance in attracting industry. The South has one inherent advantage in this respect in that the weather permits year-round use of the highways with few interruptions.

46 These two schools could, and probably should, be parts of one major university or institution. There are distinct advantages in integrating advanced training in technology and in business administration.

In general, southern states have built adequate road systems, even though it has been at the cost of high motor fuel taxes. On the basis of land area, the South has almost as many miles of paved roads as the rest of the country.[47] Two or three states have built up large and unwieldly highway debts which may be a threat to adequate maintenance and expansion in the future. In a few other states the highway organization has, at times, been a tool of politics; this could easily lead to trouble.

Avoid Trade Barriers. During the depression of the 1930's, many states resorted to a type of mercantilism. In some cases this took the form of arbitrary restrictions on the use of highways, in others it appeared as discriminatory taxes and license fees, and in still others as preferential purchasing by governmental units. In times of severe depression, there is always a temptation to "protect the home market" and we may see a recurrence of these barriers and restrictions.

It was noted above that the expanding southern market has been one of the most important causes of industrial growth in the region in recent years. Barriers of the type described above would seriously limit that market. It is to be hoped that southern states will not yield to the pressure of narrow and short-sighted groups which might clamor for such restrictions in any future period.

Dependence of Industrial Expansion upon the National Level of Business Activity. It has been pointed out that the future economic development of the South is vitally dependent upon the further expansion of investment in industry. Upon this development the employment of perhaps a million workers who will probably become available to industry through the further mechanization of agriculture during the next decade must largely depend. The same is true with respect to employment opportunities for a large fraction of natural increase in population during the same period. Furthermore, the increase in value of product per worker and hence of an increase in wage rates in the South must largely depend upon the expansion of capital investment in industry also.

It is true that with an increase in the general level of income in the South, a considerably smaller fraction of the working population released from agricultural employment and of the natural increase in population need depend directly upon employment in industry. With

[47] See Chapter IX.

the increased use of power machinery of all kinds in agriculture, the labor of women and children will no longer be so badly needed. Probably the majority of this type of labor will not go into commercial channels when released from agriculture. Children will spend a larger proportion of their time in school and the women will, for better or worse, spend their time in household duties or in attendance at the movies, viewing television, and the like.

Even more importantly, with a higher level of income there will be a much larger proportion of people employed in secondary and tertiary "industry." Retail and wholesale trade, transportation and communication, education, garages, libraries, barber shops, beauty parlors, restaurants, soft drink stands, movies, pool halls, road houses, "beer joints," as well as establishments purveying harder drink, and the like will absorb a large amount of labor. Employment in these "service trades" is not wholly but largely dependent upon the prior development of the more basic industries and of capital investment therein. On the one hand, there appears to be a fairly definite limit on how far the service trades can expand without the sustenance of purchasing power provided by production in the more primary industries. On the other hand, once the basic sources of income exist in the form of the primary industries much can be done to expand total employment and to raise per capita income through the maximum exploitation of the potentialities of the complementary and supplementary industries and the service trades.

Thus we come back to the necessity for sustained and expanded investment in southern industry. It has been pointed out elsewhere in this volume that the expansion of capital investment in the South, as in the rest of the nation, depends upon the maintenance of a dynamic demand for the products of industry which exists only during periods of substantially full employment. Indeed, as has been pointed out, the South in the past through the medium of the terms of trade with the rest of the national economy, has suffered disproportionately from economic depressions.

The desirability, indeed the necessity, for high levels of employment in the national economy presents a difficult paradox and conceivably a dilemma. It has been true in the past that the Federal Government often did not take action soon enough and on sufficiently massive a scale to maintain the purchasing power of the economy and thereby prevent deflation and mass unemployment. It was the failure of the previous administration to prevent mass unemployment which brought the New Deal to power and it was the degree of success that the New Deal had in creating employment through deficit financing which kept it and its successor, the Fair Deal, in power.

The crude measures by which economic depressions can be prevented and a high level of purchasing power for the products of industry maintained are now well known. It is precisely because this is so that the paradox-dilemma arises. The danger that the Federal Government will not take the right measures soon enough to prevent an economic depression, does indeed, still exist. *That measures will be taken which will result in inflation instead of depression is probably now the greater danger, however.*

Once politician-statesmen have learned the efficacy of even very crude measures in preventing depressions and unemployment, deficit financing becomes a most tempting way to meet the manifold and constantly growing expenses of government and to satisfy the demand of pressure groups for ever larger governmental subsidies, either outright or concealed. Furthermore, higher wages, higher farm prices, and higher industrial profits can always be permitted or even encouraged if the government stands ready to maintain purchasing power by sufficiently massive deficit financing. If this process is pursued without restraint all the devastating evils of inflation will arise.

This means that there is the most urgent need for the development of an adequate economic theory as well as adequate economic mechanisms and procedures for the maintenance of a reasonably adequate level of economic activity in the economy. There are immense needs in this area. What is more important, however, is that politician-statesmen should learn that the powers of the Federal Government to maintain adequate levels of employment must be used with restraint and with the greatest care. This means that the economist must depend upon the politician-statesman to resist the painfully efficient pressures of special interest groups if he is to have a chance to aid in keeping the economy on an even keel. Upon the successful solution of this problem of the maintenance of employment in the economy without inflation the future of capital investment in industry in the South and indeed in the whole nation depends.

XVI LABOR AND WAGE POLICY

THE PERIOD 1929–1947

Statistical data showing the essential elements in the industrial wage and labor situation in the South from the peak of prosperity in 1929 through depression and recovery to the outbreak of the war in 1939 were shown in Chapter VI. Additional data, showing the changes brought about by the war were also given in the same chapter. By way of quick summary of these data it may be pointed out that from 1929 to 1939 the number of wage earners in manufacturing in the South was almost exactly the same at the end of the period as at the beginning, 1,338,000 in 1929 and 1,349,000 in 1939. Value of product, value added by manufacture and total wages paid in manufacturing likewise showed little change in dollar terms for the period. The first showed a negligible change of from $8,215,000,000, to $8,253,-000,000, the second a similarly insignificant change from $3,199,-000,000, to $3,124,000,000 and the third a change from $1,182,-000,000, to $1,065,000,000. These slight alterations in dollar values obscure a substantial increase of some 20 per cent in real value of product, however, since the price level in 1939 was lower than in 1929.

One way of looking at what had happened to the relative position of the South is to see what changes had taken place in the Non-South for the same period. At the end of this ten-year period before the war the Non-South had 13 per cent fewer wage earners in manufacture, total wages were 23 per cent lower, value of product was 22 per cent lower and value added was 24 per cent lower than at the beginning. Thus the South had improved its position by some 20 per cent as measured by these indices during the period 1929–1939, with about the same number of wage earners at the end of the period as at the beginning. The Non-South, on the contrary, after correcting for differences in the price level had barely regained its 1929 level of output and of total wages by 1939, while its number of wage earners was 13 per cent lower.

Thus, although number of wage earners, wages paid, value of product and value added by manufacture in the South were in dollar terms almost the same at the end of the period as at the beginning, the importance of the South in manufacturing in relation to the rest of the country had increased during the period. The South's percentage of the nation's wage earners had increased from 15.1 per cent to 17.3 per cent. The South's percentage of wages paid in the nation increased from 10.2 per cent to 12.1 per cent, of value of product from 11.7 per cent to 14.5 per cent and of value added by manufacture from 10.2 per cent to 12.7 per cent.

World War II expansion and subsequent contraction of the number of persons employed in manufacturing in the South followed the same pattern as that of the United States as a whole. The South's percentage of total employment in the United States was nearly the same in 1947 as in 1939. In both the United States as a whole and in the South the increase in employment in manufacturing from 1939 to 1947 was around 50 per cent with the increase for the United States as a whole slightly above that of the South.

According to the *Census of Manufactures,* average annual wages in the South rose 149 per cent from 1939 to 1947, while the average increase for the Non-South was 122 per cent.[1]

Over the whole period from 1929 to 1945, all important wage groups in the southern economy, except farm workers, increased their *aggregate* wage income much faster than those in the rest of the country.[2] For the South the increase in aggregate wages and salaries from 1929 to 1945 was 145 per cent. For the rest of the country the increase was 79 per cent.

THE NORTH-SOUTH WAGE DIFFERENTIAL

In answering the question of the relative position of wage earners in the South in comparison with that of the North, both at the present

[1] Source, *Census of Manufactures, 1947.*
[2] *Labor in the South,* Bulletin No. 98, Bureau of Labor Statistics, p. 51. The increase of the *aggregate wage income* for the South is at a much higher rate in relation to the country as a whole than is true for *annual wage rates in manufacture* because wages in other branches of industry besides manufacturing are included in aggregate wage income and because the proportion of wage earners in the South engaged in the more remunerative war time types of employment increased greatly.

and through time, it is essential that the problem of the wage differ-ential between North and South be analysed. Almost all aspects of labor and wage policy can be analysed in terms of this differential which exists between wage rates in the South and those in the rest of the country. The differential is most extreme when comparisons are made between wages in the South and in the Far West but a sub-stantial differential exists between southern wages and those paid in all other regions. Of particular interest is the differential between wages paid in the South and those paid in the important industrial northeastern region with which a considerable portion of southern industry is directly competitive. According to a recent study, if wage rates in the Northeast be taken as 100, in 1945–46 wage rates in the South were 85, in the Middle West 101 and in the Far West 115.[3]

Historical Trends. It is striking to note that if the average differential as it existed in 1907 be compared with the average differential as it existed in 1945–46, there would apparently be no significant change in the relation of an average of wage rates for all occupations in the South to similar wage rates in the Northeast, or indeed between wage rates in the South and wage rates in the entire country. Thus wage rates in the South were 86 per cent of those in the Northeast in 1907 as compared with 85 per cent in 1945–46.[4] The gap in the differential had widened during the Depression of the Thirties but it had nar-rowed again so that over a period of almost forty years the differential had returned to its former point.

The North-South wage differential has narrowed from the period when the upturn from the Depression of the Thirties began to the present time. This apparently constitutes a new trend towards the eventual disappearance of the differential, although this cannot be forecast with certainty. It is impossible to separate out the influences of N.R.A. legislation, the Fair Labor Standards Act, the increased

---

[3] *Monthly Labor Review,* p. 375, April, 1948.
[4] Measuring the North-South wage differential by comparing the medians of the averages of wage rates for a series of occupations which are carried on in the different areas, as was done by the Bureau of Labor Statistics in arriving at the data quoted above, tends to understate the size of the North-South wage differen-tial from the standpoint of average income of wage earners. Thus, if the total wage income in manufacturing for each area is divided by the number of workers in each area, annual wage income in the South is only about three-fourths that of the Non-South.
See Table *XLVII,* Chapter VI.

bargaining strength of labor unions in the South, and general economic forces operating during the recovery from depression and during the war and postwar boom, in causing the progressive diminution in the differential.

TABLE *XC* MEDIAN REGIONAL DIFFERENCES IN OCCUPATIONAL WAGE RATES IN MANUFACTURING INDUSTRIES, BY SKILL AND SEX, SELECTED PERIODS

OCCUPATIONAL CATEGORY AND PERIOD	MEDIAN RELATION TO NORTHEAST* (*in per cent*)		
	SOUTH	MIDDLE WEST	FAR WEST
All occupations:			
1907	86	100	130
1919	87	97	115
1931–32	74	97	113
1945–46	85	101	115
Men's occupations:			
1907	88	100	131
1919	88	98	117
1931–32	74	97	114
1945–46	84	102	115
Men's skilled occupations:			
1907	93	99	131
1919	95	98	(1)
1931–32	83	96	(1)
1945–46	91	101	113
Women's occupations:			
1907	(1)	(1)	(1)
1919	81	92	(1)
1931–32	73	(1)	(1)
1945–46	87	98	114

(1) Number of occupations covered too small to justify selection of median.
* The New England states and Middle Atlantic states are both included in the designation Northeast.
SOURCE: *Monthly Labor Review*, p. 375, April, 1948.

Nature of Differential. Lumping all occupations together tends to obscure the differences in regional wage rate differentials between occupations. In general the regional differentials were less for skilled occupations than for unskilled. However, as Lester points out,

Wage differentials between the South and the North vary widely and irrationally from industry to industry, from locality to locality, and from firm to firm. In most industries the differential is greatest for unskilled workers; it practically disappears for skilled workers in such lines as iron and steel, paper and pulp, and building. However, in cotton textiles and some other low-wage industries, markedly affected by minimum wage determinations, the differential is greatest for skilled occupations.

There has been practically no South-North wage differential during recent years in the automobile, railroad, aircraft, oil, paper, seamless hosiery, and men's and women's cotton-garments industries. Yet in other industries like lumber, furniture, rubber, fertilizer, soft drinks, and food, wage rates in the South have averaged at least twenty-five per cent below Northern averages for comparable jobs.[5]

TABLE *XCI*　PER CENT SOUTHEAST AVERAGE STRAIGHT-TIME HOURLY EARNINGS ARE OF UNITED STATES AVERAGES FOR SELECTED SKILLED AND UNSKILLED JOBS IN 28 INDUSTRIES

INDUSTRY	SKILLED JOB	UNSKILLED JOB
Ferrous foundries	70	63
Nonferrous foundries	71	70
Power laundries	85	79
Footwear, other than rubber	86	85
Electric light and power	87	81
Limited price variety stores	89	88
Clothing stores	78	73
Machinery, miscellaneous	89	69
Paperboard mills	92	79
Fabricated structural steel	93	72
Upholstered wood furniture	92	88
Department stores	96	77
Power boilers	98	74
Seamless hosiery	100	98
Paper mills	102	83
Women's and misses' dresses	43	72
Men's and boys' dress shirts	73	86
Overall and industrial garments	83	85
Work pants	85	91
Work shirts	87	96
Sheet metal	87	89
Pulp mills	100	127
Structural clay products	69	74
Bakeries	71	78
Telephone	72	99
Wood furniture, not upholstered	82	91
Cigars	82	94
Full-fashioned hosiery	86	92

SOURCE: *Monthly Labor Review*, October, 1946, p. 524.

Causes of Differential. There is some evidence that the North-South wage differential may be to some extent a differential between wages in large cities and wages in small cities. The South has relatively fewer large centers of population than the Non-South. Consequently the in-

[5] Richard Lester, "Must Wages Differ North and South," *Virginia Quarterly Review*, Winter, 1946, pp. 21–22.

fluence of this factor alone could account for some part of the North-South wage differential.[6] One cannot, however, leap to the conclusion that the North-South wage differential is almost wholly a matter of large city vs. small city differential. When relative levels of straight-time hourly earnings in 22 cities, in 1945–46, were compared, the six Southern cities included were at the bottom of the list, ranking from 17th to 21st.[7]

This long existing wage differential on the one hand has been violently attacked as a disgrace to the South which should be wiped out by governmental action, or by collective bargaining, or by a combination of both, without further ado. It has on the other hand been stoutly defended as one of the precious assets of the South in its effort to increase productivity and the standard of living of its people through the acceleration of industrialization. In an effort to subject this controversy to analysis it is inevitable that one should begin by seeking the causes of low wages in the South as compared with other areas.

Many reasons have been advanced to explain low wages in the South. There seems little validity in one of the reasons most commonly advanced to explain the wage differential, namely differences in cost of living. Edgar M. Hoover, Senior Staff Economist, Council of Economic Advisors, states, "Under present circumstances in the United States, for instance, it appears that geographical differentials in living costs cannot account for any major part of the existing differentials in wages."[8] He cites a number of different studies in support of this contention. The only consistent regional differential, North and South, has been found in fuel costs, reflecting climatic conditions. Living

6 The study of C. S. Sufrin, A. W. Swinyard, and M. F. Stephenson indicates that in market areas having large populations, the North-South wage differential was very small, while in market areas having a low concentration of population the differential was considerable. *The Southern Economic Review,* October, 1948, pp. 184–190. In addition to the effect of community size upon wage differentials, the proportion of Negroes and whites in the population has been advanced as a partial explanation. There is no general agreement on this subject, however.

See Herbert E. Klarman, "A Statistical Study of Income Differences Among Communities," Part Six in *Studies in Income and Wealth,* Vol. VI, National Bureau of Economic Research, New York, 1943, p. 226.

See also comments by Gerig, Wendt, and Yntema in the volume cited above, pp. 226–235 and Henry M. Oliver, Jr., "Income, Region, Community-Size and Color," *The Quarterly Journal of Economics,* Vol. LX, Aug., 1946, p. 594.

7 "Inter-City Wage Differences," *Monthly Labor Review,* June, 1948, p. 601.

8 Edgar Hoover, *The Location of Economic Activity,* New York, McGraw-Hill, 1948, p. 106.

costs do tend to be somewhat lower in small cities than in larger ones. To the extent that the South does not possess many large cities, living costs would be somewhat lower for this reason.

Edgar Hoover further points out that contrary to the generally held belief, "In a country with high living standards, only a small part of consumer expenditures consists of remuneration to farmers; so access to surplus food producing areas has far less to do with over-all living costs than it does in poorer countries. Even the food we eat is so highly processed that it costs the same all over the country." Consequently there is less advantage in terms of lower costs of living for those workers employed in cities and towns having easy access to agriculture than might be supposed.

A different type of analysis is more pertinent. The higher rate of population increase in the South as compared with the remainder of the United States naturally makes for a plentiful supply of labor. The population of the South which predominantly first sees the light of day in the rural areas, when it reaches laboring age finds southern agriculture as its most obvious source of employment. Southern agriculture has been traditionally carried on under circumstances of low ratios of fertile land and capital equipment to labor. Consequently the productivity and wages of agricultural labor are low.[9] Educational facilities are more limited in the South than in other parts of the country and the opportunity for acquiring industrial skills is likewise less. The substantial proportion of Negroes among the population is held to accentuate the other causes of low productivity. All these basic factors in the situation seem entirely consistent with those by means of which economists have traditionally accounted for low labor productivity and low wages.

The alternative to employment in agriculture is in manufacturing or in the distributive or service trades. Both the remuneration and the number of openings in the distributive and service trades largely depend, however, upon the level of income of labor employed in manu-

[9] In all references to the productivity of labor in relation to wages, "productivity" is as nearly as possible used in the sense in which economists have used the term "marginal productivity." Unhappily economists have not always meant the same thing by this term. In general, economists have used it to refer to the value-productivity of labor "determined at the margin of use," as affected by the quantities of natural resources, capital equipment, industrial "know-how" and entrepreneurial and managerial capability used in proportion to the quantity of labor employed. It is measured in terms of the loss of production which would occur if a single homogeneous unit of labor were added or removed. Statistically this method of measurement is not very practicable, however.

facturing and agriculture. Thus the alternative to employment in low-productivity and low-wage agriculture practically becomes employment in industry.

The productivity of labor can be raised by labor moving out of southern agriculture to jobs in northern industry or by capital moving long distances from the North to the South, there to furnish employment to the southern laborer who has abandoned agriculture. Both movements have been going on for a long time. It is only in this way, say the defenders of wage differentials, that wage differentials between North and South can eventually be eliminated.[10]

So long as the productivity of southern agriculture remains low, so long as a high rate of population increase continues in the South, progress towards elimination of the differentials depends upon moving labor to industrial capital or industrial capital to labor. Lowering the wage differentials by legislative action or by collective bargaining, so the argument goes, would reduce the incentive for industry to locate in the South, would prevent labor productivity from increasing and would accentuate the tendency of the southern laborer to move North as the only feasible way to remedy the low productivity which is the cause of his low wages.[11]

[10] The outstanding exponent among economists of the position that the North-South wage differential is advantageous to the South as a means of affording increased employment in southern industry to laborers who would otherwise have to depend upon lower paid and less productive employment in southern agriculture is Dr. J. V. Van Sickle. His position is substantially that taken traditionally by most orthodox economists. It can be found in his "Dissenting Statement on Wages and Wage Policy," p. 688, *Study of Agricultural and Economic Problems of the Cotton Belt,* Hearings before Special Sub-Committee on Cotton of the Committee on Agriculture, House of Representatives, Eightieth Congress, First Session, and in his other writings on this subject.

The opposing position among economists has been stated most forcefully by Dr. Richard Lester in a series of articles which have appeared in the last few years: "Diversity in North-South Wage Differentials and in Wage Rates Within the South," *The Southern Economic Journal,* Jan., 1946, Vol. XII, No. 3, pp. 238–262; "Effectiveness of Factory Labor: South-North Comparisons," *The Journal of Political Economy,* Feb., 1946, Vol. LIV, No. 1, pp. 60–75; "Shortcomings of Marginal Analysis for Wage-Employment Problems," *The American Economic Review,* March, 1946, Vol. XXXVI, No. 1, pp. 63–82; "Trends in Southern Wage Differentials Since 1890," *The Southern Economic Journal,* April, 1945, Vol. XI, No. 4, pp. 317–344; "Wage Diversity and Its Theoretical Implications," *The Review of Economic Statistics,* August, 1946, Vol. XXVIII, No. 3, pp. 152–159.

[11] Lester has shown, however, that there is no very general correspondence either in trend or in yearly changes in the North-South wage differential in those industries in the South, such as cotton textiles, furniture and hosiery, in which competition with agriculture for the labor supply would naturally be expected. ("Must Wages Differ North and South," *The Virginia Quarterly Review,* Winter, 1946, p. 22.) He states, "There seems to be a surprising lack of relationship between the South-North textile and farm wage ratios, especially during the past two decades. The lack of

As a further extension of the argument that low productivity is a cause of the wage differential, it has usually been claimed that labor has a low productivity in southern industry as well as in southern agriculture. It is significant here to distinguish between the productivity of labor *in the same industry,* North and South, and the productivity of labor *in different industries,* North and South. The industries in the South which account for the greater part of the employment of labor are generally industries having lower labor productivity in terms of value of products per laborer than those which account for the greater part of employment in the North.[12] An effort to account for this is made a little later.

The argument that labor productivity would naturally be lower in the South than in the North *in the same industry* seems to have its origin in a somewhat naive application of the marginal productivity theory held by orthodox economists. If labor is in plentiful supply, relative to capital, and can consequently be hired at relatively low wages it will be combined with capital equipment in proportions which economize the use of capital and which utilize large amounts of labor, it has been maintained. According to this argument an industrial plant in the South would be expected to employ greater numbers of laborers in proportion to capital equipment, with the result that productivity per laborer would be lower.

The application of this principle to southern agriculture has been noted. The low wages of labor in southern agriculture can undoubtedly be explained in large degree by the low ratios of fertile land and capital to labor. But the situation in industry is usually not analogous to the situation in agriculture. Particularly in those industries in which large amounts of modern, complicated machinery are used, there is limited opportunity to vary the ratio of men to machinery. The same type of machinery is used in a southern plant which is used in a north-

---

such relationship is also notable within the South, where the rank of states in terms of textile and farm wages has seldom corresponded. Furthermore, for the past half century there is little tendency for the South-North ratios in different industries to rise and fall together." ("Trends in Southern Wage Differentials," *Southern Economic Journal,* Vol. XI, April, 1945, p. 337.)

12 As is pointed out later, the lower value of product may be due in considerable degree to the less favorable terms of trade under which the products of these industries are sold than to actually lower productivity if such could be measured purely quantitatively. For numbers of wage earners in the most important manufacturing industries in the South see Chapter VI, Table XLII.

See also Jesse W. Markham, "Some Comments upon the North-South Differential," *Southern Economic Journal,* Vol. XVI, No. 3, Jan., 1950, pp. 279–283. Markham makes essentially this same point.

ern plant and the number of men required to operate the machinery is likely to be a "built-in" characteristic of the machinery which cannot be altered at will.

There is evidence, presumptive rather than conclusive, that in industries which operate both in the North and in the South, the machinery in the southern plants is likely to be as new and as efficient as that in northern plants and that the ratio of men to machinery does not and probably could not vary widely between the two areas. It is significant in this connection to note that average expenditure for new plant and equipment per production worker in major industry groups was higher in 1947 for the South than for the Non-South. Direct and conclusive statistical evidence is hard to obtain with respect to the relative productivity of labor North and South in the same industry. There is evidence, however, which casts serious doubt on the belief in a generally lower labor productivity in the same industry in the South when compared with the North.[13]

The Differential in Relation to Value Added by Manufacture. If there is no substantial difference in North-South labor productivity within the same industry, while an appreciable wage differential exists, the natural inference would be that the returns to capital and management must be larger in the South than in the North. The ratio between the average annual wage per worker and the average value added by manufacture per worker in the South was about the same as the ratio in the Non-South in 1929. For the decade 1929–1939, value added by manufacture per worker increased somewhat more rapidly, in relation to wages paid, in the South than in the North. The same trend continued at a slightly diminished rate from 1939 to 1947. During the whole period from 1929 to 1947 the ratio of wages per worker to value added per worker changed very little in the South. In the Non-South the ratio of wages per worker to value added per worker increased somewhat, that is, from 37 per cent to 41.1 per cent—roughly 10 per cent. Thus the inference is that in the South the division of value added per worker in manufacturing between labor and property ownership apparently remained substantially unchanged. In the Non-

---

[13] For data on expenditures for new plant and equipment per production worker in the South and Non-South see Table *XLV*, Chapter VI. See also Lester, "Effectiveness of Factory Labor: South-North Comparisons," *The Journal of Political Economy*, Feb., 1946, Vol. LIV, No. 1, pp. 60–75. See also *Why Industry Moves South*, by Glenn E. McLaughlin and Stefan Robock, Committee of the South, National Planning Association, Washington, 1949.

South the division changed during the period to the advantage of labor.[14]

There is also evidence that interest rates are somewhat higher in the South than in the North,[15] and that salaries, at least in the textile industry, are probably higher than in the North. In other words, in general the distributive share of the product going to labor is apparently

CHART *XII* AVERAGE ANNUAL WAGE AND AVERAGE ANNUAL VALUE ADDED PER WORKER IN MANUFACTURING, SOUTH AND NON-SOUTH, SELECTED YEARS, 1929–1947

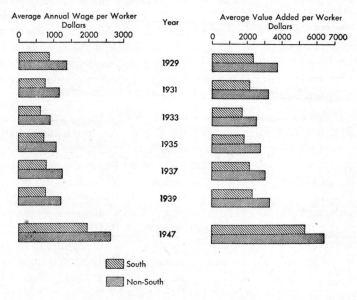

somewhat less in the South than in the North.[16] The defendants of wage differentials would no doubt argue that these higher returns to capital and higher salaries to management are precisely what is needed to attract additional industrial investment to the South.

Value Productivity vs. Physical Productivity in Relation to the Differential. The proposition that labor productivity does not apparently differ markedly North and South within the same industry seems flatly contradicted by the evidence offered by statistics of the value added

[14] See Table *XLVII*, Chapter VI.   [15] See Chapter VIII, pp. 178–180.
[16] This point is also noted by Sufrin, Swingard, and Stephenson, *op. cit.,* p. 188.

by manufacture per worker in the North compared with the South. Value added by manufacture when reduced to a per worker basis is substantially larger in the North than in the South.[17] The greater value added by manufacture per worker in the North seems, however, rather to reflect the differences in average value productivity between southern and northern industries rather than differences in worker productivity within the same industry as such. That is, the South has far less employment in manufacturing industries with high value added per worker than does the North. For example, value added by manufacture per worker in South Carolina in 1939 was $682. Value added by manufacture per worker in the same year in Michigan was $3443. It has been too hastily assumed that this difference simply reflects differences in the marginal productivity of labor in the two areas and that these differences were caused only by differences in labor skills and ratios of labor to other factors.

It would of course be difficult to make a valid comparison of the physical productivity of the average worker in the same industry in Michigan and in South Carolina, since the industries which are important in one state are not of major significance in the other. However, the *value* productivity of a worker in the automobile industry in Michigan was indeed far higher than the productivity of a worker in the textile industry in South Carolina and this was reflected in the huge difference between the two states in value added per worker.

The higher productivity of the worker in the automobile industry in Michigan as compared with the textile worker in South Carolina is attributable to a number of factors. It would not be very useful to try to account for the difference by saying that the automobile worker is the more skilled, since an objective basis of comparison of the different skills would be difficult. It is quite true that the value of capital equipment, entrepreneurial ability, and engineering skill associated with each laborer is much higher on the average in the automobile than in the textile industry, so that if the ability of the laborers in both industries were the same, one would naturally expect the value of product per laborer to be higher in the automobile industry.

So far this is entirely consistent with what economists have understood to be the cause of differences in the productivity of labor, since these differences are held generally to depend more upon the quantity

17 This point is emphasized by Van Sickle, *Economic Problems of the Cotton Belt*, p. 392.

and efficiency of the industrial equipment and upon managerial "know-how" with which labor works than upon any innate qualities of the labor force itself. It does, however, raise the question of why the automobile industry remains in Michigan and pays the high wages customary there rather than migrating to South Carolina, if the industry could employ labor at the going rate paid labor in the textile industry by moving to that state.

To raise the question is, of course, almost to answer it. It is obvious that almost no wage rate, however low, could attract any large part of the automobile industry to South Carolina, since factors other than wage rates are of overwhelmingly great importance in determining that the automobile industry is to remain in Michigan rather than to migrate to South Carolina. If, however, historical and locational factors affecting raw materials supply, markets and the like *were* as advantageous for the automobile industry in South Carolina as in Michigan, it seems entirely probable that in case the industry *did* move to South Carolina it would develop a labor productivity quite as high as that which the industry enjoys in Michigan. Since the historical and locational factors which caused the industry to locate in Michigan do not exist in South Carolina this conclusion, of course, has no importance whatever in indicating an early change in the location of the automobile industry but it does have significance for the understanding of the problem of wage differentials.

In the case of a new industry, which is not bound by superior locational factors to areas where industries which pay high wages determine the general wage level, there might be a very substantial advantage in locating in an area where wages are low, because the level of wages which would have to be paid by the new industry would be determined by those being paid in industries which cannot sell their products at unusually favorable terms of trade. This advantage is likely to be much larger than that which would be measured by the application of a wage differential of the magnitude of 15 per cent which is roughly the average wage differential between North and South within the same industry and which when applied to total costs might amount to less than 5 per cent.

Such a new industry might find that it could obtain its labor if it located in South Carolina for perhaps no more than 50 per cent of the wage rate it would pay in Michigan, since it would be competing with the textile industry rather than with the automobile industry for the supply of labor. In such a case, the saving in labor cost might be enough to influence substantially the choice of the location of the industry even though labor costs were no more than, say, 30 per cent of the costs of production of the industry in question. The ability to produce goods at 15 per cent less (50 per cent of 30 per cent) would be of an order of magnitude which might well be determinative. The advantage would, of course, be even greater in the case of an industry in which labor costs were a still higher proportion of total costs of production.

The Differential in Relation to Terms of Trade. To pursue the comparison further, the products of the textile industry and indeed of most of the industries which traditionally have furnished the larger part of the volume of employment in the South, have in the past been sold under conditions which at least approached the kind of competition assumed by the classical economists. Even though the process of consolidation and integration of industry is changing this situation in the South to some extent, a significant sectional difference still exists. In industries such as the textile industry, characterized by the degree of competition inherent in production carried on by many competing manufacturing concerns, it is much more difficult to maintain price by controlling output than it is in the automobile industry in which such a large percentage of production is put on the market by a very few large producers.

It is not only quasi-monopoly and "administered" prices which are responsible for high rates of value added by manufacturing, however. Naturally enough, industries characterized by an unusual rate of technological progress will be in a position to show high ratios of value added by manufacture to number of workers under circumstances in which active competition does not compel the advantages of technological progress to be passed on fully to the consumer. Dynamic advertising, which stresses product differentiation rather than cheapness of product, further facilitates marketing of the product without the painfulness of price cutting to obtain a high volume of sales.

Industry-wide unionization of such an industry may be the final capstone which completes the beautiful structure of quasi-monopoly which is reflected in a high value added by manufacture per worker in the industry. Through industry-wide bargaining by the labor union in the industry, protection is obtained against "cut-throat competition" which might unsettle the whole price structure if one employer were free to sell his product more cheaply by means of wage cutting. Under these circumstances a high labor value-productivity inevitably is the result, but viewed in its true light, this high value-productivity simply means that the factors which are used in production are combined and their product sold at very favorable prices so that the factors of production, including labor can be well compensated. Industry-wide wage bargaining thus both facilitates the maintenance of favorable prices for the product and insures that labor will not fare poorly in the distribution of the proceeds received for the product.

This means that industries in their sale of products are characterized by varying "terms of trade" much as are countries. The circumstances which enabled the British for generations to sell manufactured goods to the raw material-producing countries in exchange for their products at favorable rates are complex, just as are the circumstances which determine whether the textile industry or the automobile industry can dispose of its products at more or less relatively favorable terms and consequently at more or less favorable rates of payment for the productive factors employed in the industry. It seems to be a rather general rule that the more highly fabricated and specialized the product, the less exposed the product to price competition, the more highly organized the industry (both on the labor and on the management side), the more favorable the terms of trade are likely to be for industry and for the country or geographical area possessing the industry.

In such industries having favorable terms of trade it is common to speak of the "productivity of labor" as high. In a sense this is quite true but the consequences in terms of guiding principles for social policy are a good deal different than in the case of the productivity of labor where no consideration to the principle of the relative terms of trade has to be given.[18]

18 In general this doctrine is consistent with the theories rather generally held concerning the stages of industrial development through which countries progress as they move from the colonial stage, characterized by the extreme preponderance of the extractive industries producing largely staple commodities, towards the more advanced stages of industrialism. In a sense, the South is advancing through the stages from colonial industrialism to full-fledged industrialism and is meeting the problem of adverse terms of trade on the way. It is probable that the diminution of the North-South wage differential in the textile industry in recent years reflects, in some degree, an improvement of the terms of trade under which the southern textile industry sells its products. Wage increases obtained by trade union action and by governmental wage intervention through the Fair Labor Standards Act were factors which probably had some effect in raising the prices at which southern textile products were sold in the nation.

The Differential as an Industrialization Bonus. The proponents of the wage differential have argued that even if the productivity of labor in the South were as high in a given industry as in the North, it would still be advantageous to the South to have southern wages lower than in the North, so long as there exists a large reservoir of labor employed in agriculture at still lower wages than those paid in southern industry. There can indeed be no doubt, all else being equal, that the prospect of being able to get labor at less than its "productivity" would increase the potential profitability of an enterprise and hence the attractiveness of a southern location to an industrialist who was considering building a plant in the South.

Indeed, in so far as a wage differential is depended upon as a "bonus-incentive," payable to induce the more rapid industrialization of the South, it is obvious that the industrialist *must* be able to get his labor at less than its productivity if he is to have any *special* low wage "premium" to induce him to locate in the South. A lower wage which reflected no more than the lower productivity of southern workers would constitute no special advantage. If he has to pay workers the full amount of their productivity he would have no greater reason to locate in the South than elsewhere, labor wage rates alone considered. *He would have just as much incentive to locate in the South as elsewhere, however.*[19]

Stated even more simply and bluntly, this becomes practically a tautology . . . If goods of equal quality can be sold at the same price then the manufacturer with lower labor costs can make larger profits. In its simplest form, then, the argument for wage differentials is that the South must offer a bonus in terms of lower labor costs if it is to achieve as high a rate of industrialization as is desired.

By a similar line of reasoning *any* area which wished to attain a higher rate of industrialization or which like New England, for example, was intent upon not losing industry to some other area, other advantages being equal, would have to compete for industries by keeping its labor costs lower than those of some other geographical

---

[19] If the industrialist could combine his labor with other factors of production so that he used more labor in proportion to capital equipment than in the North, with a consequent lower "marginal productivity" per worker he would, it is true, be able to earn higher profits even if he paid southern workers their "southern marginal productivity." It has been pointed out that the opportunity to profit in this way is sharply limited by the technological circumstance that equipment used in both the North and the South would necessitate in all probability the use of about the same ratios of men to machines.

area which might be a competitor for its industries. It would, of course, be logical to argue that the South has more reason to offer wage rates lower than marginal productivity of labor in industry since alternative employment in agriculture in the South is less productive than in most other areas in the United States.

The Case against the Differential. Those who have maintained that wage differentials should be abolished naturally have insisted that the wage differentials are not essential to the further progress of industrialization of the South. As a second line of defense, they have argued that the current wage differential is too high a price to pay for the more rapid industrialization of the South and that the differentials should be abolished even if this slowed down the rate of industrialization.

These opponents of wage differentials argue in support of their case that, since labor costs in a given industry are only, say, 30 per cent of total costs for a particular plant in an industry, a wage differential which averages 15 per cent as between the South and the Northeast, will make a difference in labor cost embodied in the sales price of the product of only 4½ per cent (30 per cent of 15 per cent).[20]

Furthermore, there are wage differentials for the same type of employment or occupation within areas which are as great and even greater than those between areas and nevertheless the industries with the higher wages are not forced out of business. Consequently, it is argued that wage differentials must not be a major factor in determining the profits of industry or at least in determining the ability of a particular plant to stay in operation.[21]

[20] This type of argument is legitimate for any one manufacturing establishment, but it is quite illegitimate when it is argued that a 15 per cent increase in all wages on the national scene would only raise wages 4½ per cent. Since the wage costs of one industry appear as a part of the materials cost of another, it is probable that a 15 per cent "round of wage increases" nationally would raise prices by at least 75 per cent of 15 per cent, or 11¼ per cent since total labor costs must be reckoned at some 75 per cent of all manufacturing costs. Indirectly the additions to the price of the product might even approach the full 15 per cent or temporarily even surpass the full amount of the increase. In the case of a manufacturer who was comparing labor costs in one area with another he would, however, have no reason in general to think that his decision to locate in a low wage area would effect the price of his raw materials or other elements in his costs at all. Consequently, in this case it would be legitimate to compute the effect of the difference in wage rates on his costs at some 30 per cent of 15 per cent or 4½ per cent.

[21] Thus Lester says, "The differential between South and North is now far less significant than is popularly assumed. There is no such differential today in a number of industries, and in many skilled trades. Where there is an average differential

This argument has been further supported by the contention that manufacturers are not able to compute closely the relation between the productivity of their workers and the wages which are paid them. This amounts to saying that if the wage differential affects cost of production no more than, say, 5 per cent, this amount is less than the margin of error of the manufacture in computing the productivity of his workers anyhow. To which it might be replied that however inexactly an industrialist computes his costs he is not likely to disregard a 4 or 5 per cent reduction in these costs even if he is not able to compute them precisely.

The opponents of wage differentials further argue that lower wages in the South result in lower purchasing power for the products of industry. They also contend that lower wages are a cause of lower efficiency of labor and that higher wages would compel southern manufacturers to become more efficient instead of relying upon the wage differential to enable them to compete successfully.

The first contention assumes that wages in the hands of laborers are more dependable as purchasing power than profits in the hands of industrialists. It further assumes that the higher wages will not result in less employment but indirectly in more employment. To this it must be said that under certain circumstances the argument is sound. Under some circumstances it is indeed possible to increase wages without diminishing employment. Under other circumstances the contrary may be true. During a period of depression or threatened depression the incomes of workers are more certainly spent than are the incomes of corporations and of stockholders of corporations. Under inflationary circumstances, however, it may be undesirable to have consumer income increased in relation to investment or indeed to have money incomes increased at all.

The argument that manufacturers would be compelled to increase the efficiency of management if wages were raised by wiping out the differential obviously assumes that the manufacturer *has* been influenced by the wage differential. The assumption must be that some southern manufacturers had been making a rate of profit acceptable to them while enjoying the ease of conducting their affairs in a more

---

for an industry, a number of Southern plants usually can be found that pay wages as high as those of their Northern competitors. In such industries, differentials in wage levels between firms in the same labor market or local area in the South are generally much greater than the average South-North wage differential." "Must Wages Differ North and South," *The Virginia Quarterly Review*, Winter, 1946, p. 30.

"slip-shod" manner than their northern competitors. Some southern industrialists could have been making use of the opportunity afforded them by the North-South wage differential to make higher profits instead of enjoying the privilege of being slip-shod. If this is conceded then one would have to admit likewise the incentive value in some degree of wage differentials in the acceleration of the industrialization of the South.

It would seem a simple approach to the problem of the importance of wage differentials as an incentive to the industrialization of the South to ask southern manufacturers and thus find out. This has indeed been done by several investigators.[22] The general tenor of the replies does not afford a solid support for the contention that lower wages have been a major cause for the location of industry in the South rather than elsewhere. But this evidence is, on the face of it, unreliable. In the modern day and age, few manufacturers are going to admit, perhaps even to themselves, that they have sought what economists had always assumed they would seek, the lowest possible labor costs, all else being equal.

Nevertheless, the preponderance given by industrialists to other reasons for their decision to locate in the South helps to support the case for the proposition that the wage differential would not of itself furnish a sufficiently strong incentive to an industrialist to locate his plant in the South. Whether or not he is going to be able to be in a favorable position with reference to his market and to his raw materials, whether he is likely to have a dependable labor supply as well as other considerations, seem to take precedence over wage differentials themselves in locational decisions of the typical industrialist. Perhaps the main reason industrialists appear no longer to find major significance in wage differentials is that they have so little confidence that they will be able for long to resist labor union insistence upon the elimination of the differentials. Industrialists have stated that they would not feel justified in making heavy and permanent investments on the basis of what they consider only a fleeting advantage.

It is of some significance to see what has happened with respect to employment in states and industries in the South having higher or lower average annual wages. Table *XCII* shows what happened by states between 1939 and 1947. Table *XCIII* shows what happened by industries. These data do not indicate that the most important

22 McLaughlin and Robock, *op. cit.*

TABLE *XCII* AVERAGE ANNUAL WAGE PER PRODUCTION WORKER IN MANUFAC-
TURING, 1947, AND PERCENTAGE INCREASES IN NUMBER OF PRODUCTION WORKERS,
1939–1947, IN THE SOUTH BY STATES

STATE	AVERAGE ANNUAL WAGE	PER CENT INCREASE IN WORKERS
Oklahoma	$2380	57.1
Texas	2303	93.6
Kentucky	2156	76.2
Louisiana	2069	56.3
Virginia	2013	44.7
Alabama	2006	60.3
Florida	1937	31.4
Tennessee	1923	46.6
Arkansas	1889	61.1
South Carolina	1886	39.7
North Carolina	1833	30.1
Georgia	1767	44.2
Mississippi	1643	52.2
All states—South	1968	50.0

SOURCE: Computed from *Census of Manufactures, 1947.*

expansion in number of workers took place either in the states or
industries where wages were lowest. While too many other factors
are involved to warrant definite conclusions, the data do indicate
that the greater percentage increase in number of workers between

TABLE *XCIII* AVERAGE ANNUAL WAGE PER PRODUCTION WORKER IN MANU-
FACTURING, 1947, AND PERCENTAGE INCREASES IN NUMBER OF PRODUCTION
WORKERS, 1939–1947, BY MAJOR INDUSTRY GROUPS IN THE SOUTH

MAJOR INDUSTRY GROUP	AVERAGE ANNUAL WAGE	PER CENT INCREASE IN WORKERS
Petroleum and Coal	$3275	70.0
Transportation Equip.	2721	209.1
Printing and Pub.	2609	48.4
Machinery (Exc. El.)	2464	166.7
Paper and Products	2455	78.4
Chemicals	2333	66.7
Fabricated Metals	2288	110.7
All Other	2192	84.4
Stone, Clay, and Glass	2000	65.7
Textiles	1921	16.4
Food Products	1847	60.3
Furniture and Fix.	1787	53.1
Tobacco Mfg.	1758	51.2
Lumber and Products	1438	47.3
Apparel	1385	58.5
All groups	1968	50.0

SOURCE: Computed from *Census of Manufactures, 1947.*

1939 and 1947 tended to be in the states and industries where wages were higher than the average. (The coefficient of correlation [rank] is .593 for states and .643 for industries.)

LABOR UNIONS

Accurate figures on the total number of labor union members in southern industry are not available. In 1928, four of the principal manufacturing industries of the South — furniture, cotton textiles, lumber and steel—were almost entirely unorganized, although there had been numerous craft organizations and unionization of railway transportation was very nearly complete. By 1938, the effect of N.R.A. and the Wagner Act had changed the situation materially. The cigarette branch of the tobacco industry had become organized. A substantial beginning in the organization of the textile workers had been made. Furniture and lumber remained almost entirely unorganized.

Another decade later, by 1948, the rate of progress in unionization of the workers in industry in the South apparently had been only about that which had prevailed in the rest of the United States during the same period. A study by Dr. Frank deVyver of the changes in membership of 48 unions comprising all but three of the unions having any degree of activity in the South, indicates that the increases in membership for these unions had been at just about the same rate as that for the total membership of labor unions in the United States.[23] During the period total union membership in the United States had increased from eight million to fifteen million, or an increase of 87 per cent. For the 48 unions studied by Dr. deVyver the increase in membership in the South has been 88 per cent. Thus, in spite of the organizational drive of the CIO carried on under the name of "Operation Dixies" and the similar drive by the A F of L, the South had not, during the decade following the outbreak of World War II, done much towards "catching up" with the rest of the country in the field of collective bargaining.

The number of organized workers in the textile industry in the South is probably not much more than one out of five of all workers employed in the industry. The cigarette branch of the tobacco industry on the other hand is almost completely organized, as it already was in 1938. Furniture and lumber remain largely unorganized. Most

23 See F. T. deVyver, "The Present Status of Labor Unions in the South, 1948," *The Southern Economic Journal*, Vol. XVI, No. 1, July, 1949, p. 3.

southern workers in bituminous mining are organized. From 80 to 100 per cent of the workers in the United States in the following industries, which have substantial numbers of workers in the South, were organized—aluminum, breweries, cement, men's clothing, women's clothing, newspaper printing and publishing, rubber products, and basic steel products. Presumably the extent of union organization in the South did not deviate greatly from that of the rest of the country in these industries.

With the impetus which is likely to be given to unionization by the participation of labor unions in the victory of President Truman in the election of 1948, it appears probable that the ratio of organized to unorganized labor in southern industry will begin once more to advance. It seems likely that it is only a matter of time until the level existing in the rest of the country will be reached. Such a development which would match the power of organized labor against organized industry would be fraught with serious consequences. When such a development had reached its culmination it would be idle to talk any longer of prices and costs, profits and wages as determined primarily by the action of the free market, if indeed it is appropriate to talk in this way now. The resultant enhancement in importance of the role of the state in the economy would in turn offer problems the solutions of which are not apparent. These are problems for the nation as well as for the South.

Probably most industrialists who build new industrial establishments in the South are not very optimistic about "escaping" from labor unions for long. As one large manufacturer has stated,

There is no doubt that by moving South we only escape from trade unionism for the moment. I pay wages as high as the union scales now and there is no doubt that in a few years my plant will be organized. But it is supremely important to me that in the years during which I am organizing this new industry and training labor in the plant that I should not have to operate within the straight-jacket of union rules and regulations with respect to seniority, feather-bedding practices and the like. I recognize that these rules and regulations are developed in the main to protect the worker, even though they often limit efficiency without any proportionate protection for the worker. Sometime I will have to accept these rules and regulations. But I will have got my plant going well by then. The rules and regulations will of necessity conform in some degree to the actual routine of operation which I will have established by that time. Then let the union come and organize my men, as come it will.

It has by no means been true, however, that the progress of unionization of industry in the South has always been accompanied by a
fall in labor productivity or even by freezing labor productivity at
existing levels. On the contrary, in the textile industry, for example,
in their efforts to resist unionization of their plants, the managements
of unorganized mills have quite generally met increases in wages in
unionized mills by equal increases in their own mills. Union leaders,
feeling the necessity of keeping total weekly wages in unionized plants
at levels which would compare favorably with those in nonunionized
plants, have countered this strategy with their own. They have agreed
to the incorporation of incentive clauses in the contracts which they
negotiate with the management of unionized mills so that increased
productivity is compensated for on particularly favorable terms. Mill
managements in nonunion mills have encouraged the belief among
their workers that the unionization of the mills really means the
introduction of the hated "stretch-out." The anti-union slogan "Join
the union and get stretched-out" has thus become popularized.

What then, are the practical conclusions which would appear to
follow from this analysis of the North-South wage differential with
respect to current controversies? In particular, what would be the
effect of eliminating or at least reducing the wage differential through
collective bargaining or through action by the Federal Government?
Probably some decrease in the differential could take place without
placing southern industry at a disadvantage profit-wise in relation to
northern industry. The reduction in profits of southern industry which
increased wages might cause, might be limited to some extent by
relatively higher prices for the products of southern industry sold in
the national market. It is consequently doubtful whether a substantial
further decrease in the North-South wage differential would reduce
current employment in the South appreciably.

On the other hand, it would be idle to argue that with the prospect
of no more than equal rates of profit on investment, if this were to be
brought about by the reduction in the wage differential, the motives
for the location of industrial plants in the South would be as precisely
strong as ever. Furthermore, if the elimination of wage differentials
meant, as it sometimes would, that a manufacturer who was contemplating locating in the South a plant which was part of an industry
hitherto located exclusively in a high wage paying area of the North
would have to pay just as high wages in the South, the motivation for

locating in the South would be substantially weakened.[24] The prospect of being able to pay lower wages, at least during the period while the process of production was being organized and local labor trained, has probably been a factor of some significance in accelerating the industrialization of the South. With the elimination of the wage differential the South would have to depend, in the competition for additional capital investment in industry, upon its advantages of climate, of location in reference to raw material, of labor supply, and of nearness to consuming markets and the like, just as do other areas of the United States.

FEDERAL WAGE LEGISLATION

A case can be made for setting by federal action a minimum wage as high as that justified by the marginal productivity of labor in the national economy, on the grounds that if some employers do not or even cannot pay so high a wage the national interest would be better served by having laborers in such enterprises migrate to better paying jobs or even go temporarily on relief. The payment of substandard wages may in some cases serve as a threat to the wage and price structure in an industry and even to the maintenance of a stable economy for the nation. The payment of substandard wages may even retard the movement of labor to more productive employment. In the main, however, the case for a minimum wage must rely upon the assumption that the majority of employers are able to pay the minimum wage or higher, and that those who are not can raise wages to the required level through increasing the efficiency of production or, in special cases, by raising prices. Such a minimum wage should not be so high as to cause so considerable a volume of unemployment that total production in the entire nation would be appreciably lowered or that unemployment would be greater than the resources of the public purse could sustain.

There can be little question that the labor legislation of the New Deal was responsible for substantial improvement in the bargaining power of southern labor. Without the Wagner Act, the organization and maintenance of labor unions in the most important industries of

24 In many cases, however, the manufacturer even now has little advantage in trying to escape from high wage areas in the North to low wage areas in the South, since the union usually pursues him inexorably and compels him to maintain the wage rate he has previously been paying in the North.

the South would have been almost impossible. The Walsh-Healy Act and the Fair Labor Standards Act played some role in raising wages in industry but were doubtless less effective than was the newly won power in collective bargaining of the unions themselves. It would require a great deal of hardihood for anyone to argue that real wages would be as high as they are in the South had there been no federal labor legislation at all.

It is clear enough that the rise in wages which did take place over the last fifteen years or so did not cause unemployment in southern industry. It is, however, possible that employment did not expand as much as would have been true had wages not increased. Changes in the general demand for goods in our national economy from 1933 to the present time have almost completely "swamped" any changes in potential employment in southern industry which might have been caused by changes in wage rates in the South. This period, was, on the whole, one of greatly increasing demand for goods, engendered first by the expansionary money and credit policies of the New Deal and later by the effects of deficit spending for war. Under these circumstances, southern industrialists could pay the increased wages without serious difficulty at a time when their own profits were generally increasing.

Given national full employment and the concurrent dynamic demand for consumption goods, those branches of industry which are well established in the South are no longer dependent upon low wages in order to be able to produce for the national market. For example, by the beginning of 1949 the differential in the textile industry between minimum wages paid in large plants in the South and similar mills in the North had shrunk to less than 10 per cent.[25]

If one judged by the past experience of the South with federal minimum wage legislation, one would find additional evidence to conclude that the recent increase in minimum wages to 75 cents would not seriously curtail employment in southern industry. The 40-cent minimum wage was taken by southern industry "in its stride." It has been pointed out, however, that the general increase in employment and price level caused by the war almost completely obscured any economic effects for which the increase might otherwise have been responsible.

[25] In most industries the differential in the minimum wage continued to be substantially larger.

There seems little doubt that if high levels of industrial activity were to continue and if the price level remained substantially unchanged, the new federal law enacted in 1949 providing 75 cents per hour can be paid without producing a significant volume of unemployment. We know that a large proportion of southern industry could pay a minimum wage as high as 75 cents per hour without difficulty, since the minimum wage in most plants is already above this level.

In the larger and more efficient textile mills, for example, the actual minimum wage paid is already above 90 cents per hour.[26] On the other hand, there are small plants which would probably be put out of business if the hourly wage were increased even to 60 cents per hour, but the volume of employment involved is probably quite small. It is possible that employment in small southern lumber mills may be adversely affected by the increase in the minimum wage to 75 cents per hour. In some cases the only alternative to persons who may be thrown out of employment would be a return to much lower-paid employment in submarginal agriculture.

The closing of some small and inefficient industries might be offset, at least to some extent, by increased employment in the more efficient and larger plants which would now have to be depended upon to supply the goods formerly produced in the plants which had had to close because of an increase in the minimum wage.

Even in the case of some of the small sawmills, the result of the increase in minimum wages might be partially to lower the price paid to owners of timber and partially to increase the price which would be charged for grades of lumber produced in the South rather than to make the entire adjustment by reducing employment or going out of business.

PROBLEM OF THE DISTRIBUTION
OF THE SOCIAL PRODUCT

It is obvious that a minimum wage should not be set independently of movements in the general price level. While a minimum wage probably has some effect in maintaining a "floor" under commodity

---

[26] The Secretary of Labor, acting under authority of the Walsh-Healy Act has determined that the "prevailing wage" which must be paid labor employed on government contracts in the textile industry in the South is not less than 80 cents per hour for beginners and not less than 87 cents per hour for all others.

prices if these prices did decline substantially, it might be essential that the minimum wage be adjusted downward if the general price level did decline and stayed lower for a considerable time. It would be just as true that a minimum wage level should have upward flexibility in case the general price increased.

It is less well recognized that there is also a problem which might be called that of the "maximum wage." The problem of determining the maximum wage which a given industry can pay without inequitably raising prices to consumers and without discouraging expansion of industry—while permitting adequate contributions to the costs of government through taxation of the profits of industry—has not yet been solved. General wage policy—like the maintenance of full employment, the prevention of inflation, and the determination of a proper price and production policy for agriculture—is fundamentally a national rather than a regional problem.

Here again is a clear necessity for the development of a national policy in the interest of the country as a whole, which would prevent the unrestricted use of economic power by industrial corporations or labor unions in order to obtain an undue proportion of the national income for particular economic groups and subgroups.

It is not at all apparent, moreover, that even if equalization of bargaining power could be attained, the problem of setting wages which would be "reasonable" and neither much "too high" or much "too low" would be solved at all. Equality of bargaining power might only insure stalemate in wage negotiations. It is not of much help, for example, if both sides can afford to wait, say, three months and no more before coming to an agreement. The public interest is not served if, for example, the railroads and the railway unions are both powerful enough so that the only alternative to interruption of service through strikes would be both wage and rate increases.

Equalization of bargaining power would likewise not constitute any very dependable assurance that wage rates in southern industry would be set as high as they could be without substantially interfering with the expansion of southern industry and no higher. All that can be said is that here is a field in which our national economic policy is not yet at all clear. Whether the substitution of collective bargaining for the individual wage bargain inevitably leads to some sort of comprehensive intervention in the fixing of wages by the Federal Government only time will tell.

So long as our economy was characterized by almost complete laissez faire, with unlimited competition of producers in the sale of their products and of workers and employers in the sale and purchase of labor power, one could avoid the embarrassing necessity of taking sides on such a question as to whether wages should be higher or lower. One would logically have had to take the position that such was not a proper matter of national or regional concern. Whatever wage the market set would be the "best" rate, whether there was a differential or not. Any interference with that rate by the government or other association of men would be contrary to the greatest good of the greatest number.

In an economic world in which laissez-faire capitalism has undergone serious structural changes, in which quasi-monopoly and quasi-monopsony characterize the sale and purchase of both goods and the factors producing them, entrepreneurs and labor leaders and sometimes politicians do have to take positions as to whether wages in a plant, in an industry, or in the whole economy should be higher or lower than elsewhere, and if so, by how much. The time is already here when it is essential that both management and union executives give far greater attention to the general public interest in working out the wage bargain than is now the case. We are still going on assumptions with respect to the role of competition in protecting the interests of all nonparticipants in the wage bargain in an era in which competition can no longer be wholly depended upon. The public interest is even more involved in the question of whether and by how much an increase in wages will raise the price of a particular product to consumers than it is in the question of geographical wage differentials. Under existing circumstances, equal pay in industry for equal skills, equal responsibility, and equal productivity would appear a goal as desirable as it is difficult and rare of attainment.

In collective bargaining the question of whether or not there should be a wage differential is not usually the most important consideration. Labor union executives are concerned with getting wages as high as they can, all circumstances considered, and industrialists are concerned about keeping labor costs as low as possible, all things considered. There seems no overriding reason why there should be either a conscious public policy to maintain or to eliminate regional differentials. We can hope for a satisfactory solution to the problem of geographical wage differentials only when we are ready to tackle the much more basic problem of how the value product of a particular industry can most effectively and fairly be divided between the workers in a particular industry and the other claimants—management, furnishers of capital, and consumers—to what is really a social product.

Fortunately the social product to be divided among the various claimants has been growing during the past decade at a truly impressive rate. According to one measure, total national income of the nation increased from some $72 billion in 1939 to around $225 billion in 1949.[27] A more significant figure which takes into account such factors as the rise in the price level and the increase in population during the decade is per capita disposable income. By this measure the increase in per capita real income during the period was slightly more than 40 per cent.[28]

Labor participated in this process of expansion of the national income. Total salaries and wages increased from a level of around $45 billion in 1939 to around $135 billion in 1949.[29] Deflated to take care of the increase in cost of living, but not for increase in population, this would amount to an increase in real terms of around 75 per cent. Average hourly earnings increased from about sixty-three cents per hour to about one dollar forty cents per hour in 1949. After also deflating average hourly earnings to allow for the increase in the cost of living the increase is reduced to about 30 per cent.[30] Labor, like almost all the other claimants to shares in the national income, fared well during the period.

Some five years of this period can be considered "war years" when the demand for labor might inevitably be expected to be high in relation to the supply. Even after hostilities came to an end, however, substantially full employment continued. Consequently labor, as in the case of the other elements in our society, has benefited, not merely by higher real rates per hour, but by steady employment for substantially all the members of the family who wished to work.

It has been pointed out that southern labor has shared fully in this decade of unprecedented prosperity and has been steadily improving its position relative to labor in the rest of the nation. It has been

27 These figures are from "National Income By Distributive Shares," the *Federal Reserve Bulletin*, Jan., 1950, p. 96.
28 Based on data from *Economic Indicators*, Jan., 1950, p. 25.
29 *Federal Reserve Bulletin, op. cit.* It is extremely difficult to compare the increase in the share of the national product which accrues to labor with the shares going to other claimants.
30 *Economic Indicators*, p. 25.

pointed out that what is true for labor is generally true for the rest of the southern economy as well. The moral seems to be that difficult as the problem of dividing up regional or national income between the different claimants may be, disputation about the size of the shares should not be allowed seriously to interrupt the production of that income. So long as national production is allowed to expand, the size of the national income "pie" grows impressively bigger each successive decade. The evidence indicates clearly that it is much more sensible to strive for a larger slice by assisting in baking the larger pie than to concentrate all energy in the self-defeating effort of each group to maximize the size of its individual slice. Once more the urgent need for the development of a social policy and machinery by which conflicting claims for shares in the national product can be peaceably resolved is emphasized.

XVII INTERNATIONAL TRADE POLICY

FREE TRADE VS. PROTECTION; HISTORICAL ATTITUDE

It is an interesting commentary on the perversity of men and events that the United States, which has been historically a protectionist country, should have become the current leader of the movement to lower international trade barriers. Indeed, almost no other country has shown pronounced enthusiasm for the movement. The United States has a far less vital economic stake in the maximization of the international trade than does Great Britain, Japan, Italy, Germany, or Belgium, for example. Yet, the United States has "hit the sawdust trail," even though very belatedly, and embraced the policy always advocated by orthodox economists at a time when most other countries were showing a decided preference for exchange controls, bilateralism, import quotas, and other features of a controlled and managed foreign trade.

In contrast with the rest of the nation, the South, historically, has staunchly supported free trade. It is true that the sugar planters of Louisiana always formed a protectionist outpost in an otherwise free-trade society. It is true, too, that our textile industry has been glad to profit from the protective tariff imposed at the insistence of the northern wing of the industry. But these were particular aberrations which did not materially hamper us in our castigation of northern industrialists for their "shameless exploitation" of the South through the device of the protective tariff.

Our case, as it has usually been presented, was simple and logical. The protective tariff raised the price of the industrially-produced consumer goods which we bought. It likewise lowered the price for which

422

we could sell our cotton and tobacco by limiting the purchasing power of potential or actual European sellers of manufactured goods on our domestic market. Thus the protective tariff was held to be primarily responsible for the low per capita value product of the South and for a standard of living much below the national average. The question was rarely asked whether the production of cotton and tobacco by existing prodigality in the use of manual labor could have afforded a standard of living as high as the national average even if there had been no tariff.

The Agricultural Adjustment Act of 1933 was "sold" to southern farmers principally on the argument that it was the best practicable substitute for a lower tariff, which would have been preferable but which was ruled out by political considerations. Many southerners still believe that the elimination of the protective tariff would insure prosperity for southern cotton and tobacco growers and remove the need for crop controls, price supports, or, for that matter, for further industrialization of the South.

TABLE *XCIV* VOTES OF SOUTHERN MEMBERS* OF THE UNITED STATES HOUSE OF REPRESENTATIVES ON TARIFF BILLS

PERCENTAGE OF MEMBERS VOTING FOR BILLS TO RAISE TARIFFS		PERCENTAGE OF MEMBERS VOTING FOR BILLS TO REDUCE TARIFFS	
1816	40	1832	60
1824	18	1833	97
1828	20	1946	74
1842	13	1857	97
1875	34	1870	83
1883	21	1872	85
1890	18	1894	94
1897	17	1913	88
1909	11		
1922	15		
1930	25		
1947	29		

*For the years through 1909 "Southern Members" includes members from the 11 states of the Confederacy; after that date it includes, in addition, members from Kentucky and Oklahoma.
SOURCES: For years through 1909, M. Ogden Phillips, "The Tariff and the South," *The South Atlantic Quarterly*, Oct. 1933, pp. 385–86; for years after 1909, *The Congressional Record*.

With increasing industrialization the South has nevertheless lost some of its unrestrained enthusiasm for free trade. This is evidenced by the propaganda of many trade and industry groups and is reflected to some extent in the votes of southern congressmen. Table *XCIV* shows how southern congressmen have voted on important tariff bills since 1816. (The 1947 bill was a minor one raising the tariff on wool; it is included only because of its recent date.) This table shows that the number of southern congressmen voting for protective tariffs rose from 11 per cent in 1909 to 25 per cent in 1930 and 29 per cent in 1947, higher figures than were registered at any time after 1816 except for the reconstruction year of 1875. These figures might suggest that the South no longer presents a solid front in its opposition to protective tariffs.

Even this limited tendency towards a stronger but still small minority supporting tariff protection is, however, by no means conclusive as indicating a trend. It is offset in large measure by the pronounced tendency of southern congressmen to support the original Reciprocal Trade Agreements Act and its subsequent renewals. Under that Act our tariffs have been reduced to levels lower than they have been since 1913. As a result of the multilateral negotiations carried on at Annecy, in 1949, our tariff has been lowered substantially below the level of 1913. Southern congressmen as a group have strongly supported this policy of tariff reduction through reciprocal agreement.[1]

No economist would question the validity of the free trade doctrine under the assumptions which were part of the doctrine. Since, however, we are living in a world in which fully collectivized, controlled, and semicontrolled national economies are the rule rather than the exception, it is at least questionable whether we shall ever have the degree of freedom in international trade which existed in 1914 or even in 1929. It is, therefore, appropriate to re-examine the South's stake in international trade, particularly with reference to the extent to which the prosperity of the southern economy is dependent upon national and international trade policies.

[1] These agreements have largely been reciprocal in name only. The United States has no balance of payments problems and consequently has no fears that the total of its imports will exceed its exports. The real problem is how the total of imports is to reach a level which will enable other countries to pay for their exports from the United States. European countries, on the contrary, literally dare not allow their nationals to import all that they would be willing to pay for in their own currencies. Consequently to the extent that we induce other countries to agree to a mutual reduction in their tariffs they are generally faced with the necessity for substituting some other trade barrier to keep out imports from the United States. This the escape clauses in the agreements permit them to do. This does not at all reflect bad faith on the part of these countries but simply necessity.

DIMINISHED DEPENDENCE UPON FOREIGN TRADE

Let us see what has been happening to southern exports. Since exports from the United States are not designated as to the regions from which they come, we must estimate the proportions coming from southern states. In the following computations it has been assumed that all the raw cotton, leaf tobacco, naval stores, and sulfur exported from the United States originate in the South. This is not strictly true with respect to cotton and tobacco but any of those products coming from outside the South will be offset by southern products not included in our table. Further, one half of the value of manufactured cotton goods and two thirds of the value of manufactured tobacco are included, since these proportions are roughly equal to the South's share of United States production in these lines. Forty per cent of the value of exports of wood and wood products and 60 per cent of

TABLE *XCV* EXPORTS OF PRIMARY INTEREST TO THE SOUTH FOR SELECTED YEARS, 1926–1948

(Dollar Amounts in Millions)

COMMODITY	AVERAGE, 1926–1929 EXPORTS	% OF TOTAL	AVERAGE, 1936–1939 EXPORTS	% OF TOTAL	AVERAGE, 1945–1948 EXPORTS	% OF TOTAL
Cotton:						
Unmanufactured	$833	56.4	$300	41.2	$438	30.0
Semi- and Manufactured (½ of U. S. total)	56	3.8	29	3.9	246	16.7
Total Cotton	889	60.2	329	45.1	684	46.7
Tobacco:						
Unmanufactured	144	9.8	126	17.3	268	18.3
Manufactured (2/3 U. S. Total)	14	0.9	9	1.2	36	2.5
Total Tobacco	158	10.7	135	18.5	304	20.8
Petroleum Products (90% of U. S. Total)	319	21.6	212	29.0	373	25.5
Wood and Wood Products (40% of U. S. Total)	63	4.3	26	3.6	49	3.3
Naval Stores	32	2.2	17	2.3	30	2.0
Sulfur	15	1.0	11	1.5	25	1.7
Totals	1,476	100.0	730	100.0	1,465	100.0

SOURCES: U. S. Department of Commerce, *Statistical Abstract of the United States Summary of Foreign Commerce of the United States*, 1947 and 1948; U. S. Department of Agriculture, *Agricultural Statistics; Crop Production*, December, 1948.

the value of exports of petroleum products are included since the South produces about 44 per cent of the lumber and a little over 60 per cent of the crude oil of the nation. It is believed that the total of these items gives a fair measure of the exports of southern products. To show trends over the past 20 years, the years 1926–1929, 1936–1939, and 1945–1948 have been selected for comparison.

Table *XCV* shows that for the years 1926–29, southern exports, computed as described above, had an average annual value of $1,477,-000,000, which was 30.0 per cent of all United States exports in those years. Cotton and its products made by far the largest group, totaling $889,000,000, or 60.2 per cent of the total. Petroleum products were next with $319,000,000, or 21.6 per cent, followed by tobacco with $158,000,000 and 10.7 per cent, wood products with $63,000,000 and 4.3 per cent, naval stores with $32,000,000 and 2.2 per cent, and sulfur with $15,000,000 and 1.0 per cent. In volume, exports of raw cotton averaged 8,711,000 bales, or about 58 per cent of average production for those years; for leaf tobacco the figure was 537,167,000 pounds, or approximately 40 per cent of average production. Exports of naval stores were about one half, of sulfur about one third, and of petroleum products about one sixth, of total production in the United States.

In order to understand the significance of these exports to the South's economy we must compare them with certain other economic magnitudes. Table *XCVI* shows that in relation to agriculture, the

TABLE *XCVI*   EXPORTS FROM THE SOUTH AND FROM THE NON-SOUTH AND THEIR
RELATION TO CERTAIN OTHER VALUES FOR SELECTED YEARS, 1926–1948

	SOUTH			NON-SOUTH		
	1926–29	1936–39	1945–48	1926–29	1936–39	1945–48
Exports of Region ($ Millions)	1,477	730	1,464	3,438	2,245	10,194
Exports of Region as Per Cent of:						
Total U. S. Exports	30.0	24.5	12.6	70.0	75.5	87.4
Cash Farm Receipts of Region	49.2	33.1	21.1	43.4	37.8	51.7
Total Income Payments in Region	11.9a	6.4	4.2	4.9a	3.9	7.0
Wages Paid in Manufacturing in Region	128.2b	54.5c	36.8d	34.1b	27.2c	38.8d
Value Added by Manufacturing in Region	45.3b	23.9c	13.6d	13.0b	10.3c	16.0d

aBased on total income payments for the single year 1929.
bBased on average figures for the years 1927 and 1929.
cBased on average figure for the years 1937 and 1939.
dBased on figures for the year 1947 alone.
SOURCES: Publications cited in preceding Table; U. S. Department of Commerce, *Census of Manufactures; Survey of Current Business.*

total value of exports was equal to about one half of cash farm receipts in the South. They were slightly greater in value than the total cotton crop (including cotton seeds) in 1929, which was worth $1,434,012,000.

In relation to manufacturing in the South, based on figures from the Census of Manufactures for 1927 and 1929, the value of exports was equal to 128 per cent of wages paid and 45.3 per cent of the value added in manufacturing. Figures for income payments by states are available only for the year 1929. Average exports for 1926–1929 were equal to about 12 per cent of income payments in southern states for that year.

It is obvious that exports were vitally important to the South in this period. As a rough approximation, it might be said that, in value, exports were equal to 20 or 25 per cent of the value of all economic production in the region. It was no great exaggeration to say that at that time the South had to export or die.

Ten years later the picture had changed considerably. The value of southern exports in the years 1936–1939 was $730,000,000, or just about half of the 1926–29 figure. It had declined somewhat more than total U. S. exports since it now represented only 24.5 per cent of the U. S. total, compared with 30 per cent earlier. Cotton exports fell by more than 60 per cent in value, declining to $329,000,000 or 45.1 per cent of the South's total. In contrast, tobacco exports fell only about 15 per cent and amounted to $135,000,000 or 18.5 per cent of the total. Exports of petroleum products were still in second place with $212,000,000, a decline of about one third. Wood and wood products had, like cotton, declined in value by more than 60 per cent. Naval stores and sulfur also showed very large value declines but they were unimportant in the total.

In physical terms, average exports of cotton in this period were 5,258,000 bales or about 38 per cent of average production, while exports of leaf tobacco averaged 449,719,000 pounds, or about 28 per cent of production. These were sharp reductions compared with the earlier period. The other commodities showed only moderate declines in this respect.

In relation to other economic values, exports dropped sharply in the 10-year interval. In relation to cash farm receipts, they declined by about a third, although agricultural values themselves were substantially reduced. But the decline was even greater in comparison with manufacturing; here the drop was equal to 50 per cent or more. Exports were equal to only little more than 6 per cent of total income payments, contrasted with almost twice that proportion 10 years earlier. Again, if a rough approximation had to be made, we could say that exports were now equal in value to about 12 or 14 per cent of the value of all economic production in the region.

The latest figures available are for the years 1945 to 1948. These figures must be accepted with considerable reservation since this was a period of violent fluctuations, especially in prices. For these two years southern exports averaged $1,464,000,000, which was very near the 1926–29 average. This figure, however, was only 12.6 per cent of the U. S. total instead of the 30 per cent of the earlier period. Cotton and its products were still in first place with $684,000,000 although their relative importance was reduced to 46.7 per cent of the total from the 60.2 per cent of exports from the South which they represented during the 1926–29 period. Furthermore the total value of the exports of cotton and its products were swollen both by the high prices for raw cotton during the immediate postwar period and a totally abnormal volume of export of cotton cloth and other manufactured cotton goods.

Petroleum products still held second place in value although they were closely followed by tobacco, which attained a total more than twice either the 1926–29 of the 1936–39 averages and reached $373,000,000, or about 25.5 per cent of the total. Naval stores and wood products gained in dollar value but lost ground relatively, while sulfur almost doubled in dollar value but barely held its own in relation to the total.

In physical terms, raw cotton exports dropped further to an average of 2,968,000 bales and this level was maintained only by drawing heavily on accumulated stocks, since domestic consumption was high and the 1945 and 1946 crops were among the lowest in 50 years. Production increased sharply in 1947, in 48 and 1949 so that by 1948 exports were no longer limited by stocks but were again limited by dollars available for their purchase. Tobacco exports rose substantially to an average of 503,000,000 pounds, slightly below the 1926–29 average but this rate was drastically reduced in the spring of 1947 by Great Britain's efforts to conserve dollars.

While southern exports made sweeping recoveries from the 1936–39 levels in value terms, and (except for cotton) in physical terms, they continued to decline in relation to other economic values. They were equal to only 21.1 per cent of cash farm receipts and 36.8 per cent of the wages paid in manufacturing in the year 1947. Export values were equal to only 4.2 per cent of total income payments in southern states. A rough guess now would be that exports are equal to somewhat less than 10 per cent of the value of all economic production in the South.

Table *XCVI* also shows the values of exports originating outside the South and some ratios between those values and other economic magnitudes for the non-southern part of the country. From this table it will be seen that between 1926–29 and 1936–39 exports did not decline nearly as much in relation to other economic values for the United States outside the South as they did in the South. Further, since 1939 non-southern exports have risen in relative importance in three of the four comparisons available and declined very slightly in the other one. Finally, from a study of Table *XCVI* it would seem to be a fair generalization that exports are now no more important to the southern economy than they are to the economic life of the rest of the nation; perhaps they are actually of less importance.

Even a superficial inspection of the above tables shows that during the past 20 years exports have declined greatly in their importance to the southern economy. They have declined by more than a half and probably by almost two thirds in the relative importance. It is true that these have been unusual times and we must exercise great caution in using them as a basis for generalization. Nevertheless, two facts would seem to be significant. First, the decline in the relative importance of exports has continued during both depression and boom. Second, the South has attained its period of greatest prosperity, both absolutely and relatively to the nation, in a period when exports were relatively smaller than at any other time in recent years and probably in its entire history.

Limitations of space do not permit any adequate examination of the causes of this significant change. Undoubtedly American tariff policy has been one factor causing the decline in exports. Another factor was the world-wide decline in international trade, particularly during the early thirties, which partly caused, and was partly caused by stringent quotas, embargoes, and currency controls. A third factor was our domestic policy of supporting the price of agricultural products, especially cotton, and its accompanying allocation of acreage.

It is significant that even at the depth of the Great Depression and after the Tariff Act of 1930 had been in effect for some time, our exports of cotton, in physical volume, were actually above the level of the 1920's. For 1931–32, exports were 9,193,000 bales; for 1932–33, 8,895,000 bales.[2] The big decline came in the two following years, after the crop control program was started. Of course, in dollar terms cotton exports fell sharply, beginning in 1929, because of the decline in cotton prices. Finally, it should be noted that, whatever the causes of the decline, it does not necessarily follow that the former levels of international trade would be restored by removing them or at least by removing the American part of such causes. When cotton and tobacco culture have been greatly expanded in other countries, it is not logical to expect that we could, within the foreseeable future, regain our former level of exports by any predictable action, whether unilateral or multilateral. Nor does it necessarily follow that it would be to our best interest to regain the former level of exports in these lines. If there are other lines of production which yield higher per capita incomes and which are less wasteful of manpower, more economical of natural resources, and less dependent on foreign markets than the raising of cotton and tobacco, then it would be advantageous for the South to shift to them. World conditions do change, and it is doubtful whether the comparative advantage which the South had in raising cotton and tobacco 100 years ago still really exists.

Instead of the particular regional interest in foreign trade of an earlier day, it is true that the South retains the same interest as the rest of the country in the expansion of world trade. It is through the expansion of world trade that international division of labor can aid in raising the standard of living of all countries. This is particularly important in the case both of backward countries and of highly industrialized countries deficient in foodstuffs and raw materials, such as the United Kingdom and Japan, which must literally import or die.

For the South, as for the rest of the nation, alternative policies which might be followed in foreign trade by the Federal Government are not matters of life or death in their immediate economic effect. Indirectly, on account of our stake in the economic well-being and political stability of other countries, they may almost amount to that. If the United States were to follow a policy of high protective tariffs accompanied by export subsidies, to use an extreme example, we

[2] Bales of 500 pounds gross weight. *Agricultural Statistics* 1946, p. 72.

would probably render impossible the development of freer international exchange of goods, with possibly disastrous results to the rest of the world, and, indirectly to ourselves. On the contrary, a foreign trade policy which effectively promoted the expansion of international trade would contribute immensely to world political stability and economic well-being. At the same time, under favorable circumstances, such a policy would contribute to our economic well-being through an increase in imports which would permit foreign countries to pay in goods for the huge excess in exports which we have been sending abroad for years.

It would not be impossible, it is true, to absorb these excess exports or their equivalent at home by expanding domestic purchasing power but it would raise complex problems. Our own standard of living does not directly and basically depend upon the particular organizational form which international trade happens to take, whether free or controlled. The raw material imports which are the only ones of critical importance to our economy are likely to be available regardless of the organization of world trade.

THE SOUTH AND EXPORT SUBSIDIES: "EXPORT DUMPING"

It is worthy of particular note that the South is presently receiving what amounts to a substantial subsidy on the export of its cotton and tobacco through America's free grants to countries of Western Europe and to the other countries under the Marshall Plan, just as the rest of the nation is simultaneously receiving and paying for, in effect, similar export subsidies on other American products shipped abroad. It seems highly unlikely, for example, that the current price of cotton of about thirty cents per pound could be maintained in the absence of the general subsidy now provided by the Marshall Plan, unless the government substituted a specific and direct subsidy upon the export of cotton or took even greater amounts of cotton than at present "under the loan" at the support price.

It would be no more sound for the South to count upon international trade as a means simply of dumping "surplus" production in foreign countries than for the country as a whole to make a similar calculation. The concept of the United States producing a net "surplus" of commodities beyond our ability to consume is not only nonsense—but thoroughly mischievous nonsense. Such ideas lead to export subsidies to assist in dumping "surplus" commodities abroad and to tariff and other barriers against the import of goods which are the only sound way to pay for our exports. A policy of export subsidies combined with import barriers not only works to the economic detriment of the United States but arouses the maximum of resentment against the United States.

It is not generally recognized that a policy of extending a very large volume of uncollectible loans and gifts to foreign countries, if not wisely administered and if not limited to the emergency period following the war, amounts in effect to a generalized subsidy on our exports. Such a policy, very much as in the case of particular export subsidies, can arouse great resentment abroad and can be used as the basis for charges of "imperialistic pushing of American trade."

Considerable conflict of interest has already arisen, for example, in the case of the sale of American tobacco in Europe under the Marshall Plan in competition with Greek and Turkish tobacco. The representatives of southern farmers argued that since we were providing free grants for the purchase of commodities from the United States under the Marshall Plan, these funds should certainly be used for the purchase of our surplus commodities. The Turkish and Greek representatives argued that if American tobacco displaced their own in European markets, they would never be able to pay for their imports from the United States through the sale of their tobacco in the export trade.

Extraordinary financial aid to foreign countries such as the Marshall Plan is overwhelmingly justified by existing economic and political considerations as a four-year program. It would most emphatically not be justified if it degenerated into a scheme for "getting rid of surpluses" without any terminal date.

It must be recognized that the South is likely to be more susceptible to schemes for export-dumping than the rest of the country. For the country as a whole, a billion dollars appropriated by the U. S. Government for Social Security, for building roads, hospitals, and the like, has just as great effect in maintaining demand for the products of American industry and agriculture as does a billion dollars given as a grant-in-aid to, say, the Patagonians to enable them to pay for imports from the United States. In the case of the agricultural staples, such as cotton and tobacco, however, it must be admitted that an additional

billion dollars given away to foreigners by our government is likely to
have a somewhat greater effect in increasing the demand for these
commodities than is an equal amount spent domestically for relief, or
for public works, or the like. This is likely to be true because of a
somewhat greater elasticity of demand for these commodities by foreign consumers than at home, when sufficient money to alleviate any
so-called dollar shortage is provided by the United States Government without cost to the recipient governments.

Nevertheless, even though the South might have a special interest
in subsidized exports of cotton and tobacco it is unsound economically
for our government to finance the disposal of our goods on the foreign
market, under normal circumstances, by any other means than by
full payment—which means payment through our receipt of goods and
services produced abroad.[3]

INCREASED IMPORTS AS PAYMENT
FOR EXPORTS

It would be idle to maintain that there are not very substantial difficulties in the way of our receiving additional quantities of goods and
services in payment for this country's exports. Certainly if we fail to
maintain a state of substantially full employment it would prove
almost impossible for us to allow larger quantities of goods to come
into the United States at the same time that our own factories and
laborers were idle. The answer to this, however, lies not in erecting
barriers against imports but in taking appropriate measures to maintain domestic full employment. Consequently, the interests of the
South—like those of the rest of the country—are likely to be served
best by extending the program for facilitating payment for our exports through enlarged imports under our reciprocal trade agreements
policy.[4]

[3] This, of course, includes payment through the use of the proceeds of American
loans made abroad under circumstances in which these loans can be serviced by
the import of goods and services into the United States.
[4] The principal factor determining the volume of our imports is the level of our
own industrial activity. Consequently both hopes and fears which stem from the
effect on the volume of our imports of reducing our protective tariff are largely
exaggerated. See also footnote 1 with reference to reciprocal trade agreements.
There can be no doubt that the long-time trend of the deficit in the balance of
payments of Europe with the United States represents a problem far more basic
than one which could be cured by changes in our own tariff policy. See "Europe
After 1952, The Long Term Recovery Problem," by John H. Williams, *Foreign
Affairs*, April, 1949, pp. 426–448.

By 1952, when the Marshall Plan is supposed to come to an end, our economy must have made the necessary adjustments so that export subsidies—either specific or indirect and general—will no longer be needed. Viewed from the standpoint of our whole national economy, the problem is difficult but by no means insoluble. If five or six billions of dollars annually were no longer needed for foreign aid, taxes on lower incomes in the United States could be reduced by that amount. Five or six billions of additional dollars in the hands of our lower income receivers would function as purchasing power almost as well as when it is turned over to Europeans for the purchase of American goods. It would probably be necessary, in addition, to expand social security payments financed by the Federal Government very substantially and to expand other types of desirable federal expenditures, and even to pass over to deficit financing to offset any possible fall in the demand for goods if we did not need any longer to give away these billions of dollars in foreign aid.

If viewed as a fraction of our annual national income of substantially over $200 billion, additional imports of five or six billion dollars necessary to balance our goods and services accounts with the rest of the world do not loom very large. An increase in imports amounting to no more than some 2½ per cent of our national income would appear easily capable of absorption. The difficulty largely arises because increases in imports could not possibly consist of 2½ per cent of every kind or variety of goods and services making up the national income. Increases would have to be much higher in some categories than others and particular industries would feel foreign competition much more than others. Some indeed, would not have to meet any increased competition at all.

There is likely to be strong resistance throughout the country to allowing increased imports of manufactured goods to enter the country. It is quite likely that this sentiment may develop in the South in case the competitive situation between our textile manufacturers and those of countries exporting to our domestic market should become difficult.

In the light of international trade doctrine, one would expect a large part of the rest of the world to have a potential comparative advantage in the production of textiles. According to orthodox doctrine the United States should specialize in the production of commodities requiring heavy capital investment, such as automobiles, both for domestic use and for export. Commodities embodying large quantities of relatively low-skilled labor should be imported in exchange. This doctrine would appear to forecast an ominous future for the textile industry of the United States and particularly for the South where that industry furnishes such a large proportion of the volume of employment.

Current data do not support such a gloomy forecast. In the years immediately following the war there has not been much question of competitive imports of cotton textiles. During this period British cotton textiles, for example, were priced substantially above most American produced goods. During the year 1948 we exported the equivalent of almost a million and a half bales of cotton in the form of textiles.

It is true that the immediate postwar period was an abnormal one in which Japanese, Italian, and German competition was temporarily destroyed by the war and British production has not been able to attain prewar levels. It is true, likewise, that our exports of finished textiles during and immediately after the war were financed largely by Lend-Lease, UNRRA, the Marshall Plan, and similar extraordinary financial aid. We were, however, able to export substantial amounts of cotton textiles even before the war while our imports of textiles have always been relatively negligible. It is true that textile imports were kept at such low levels largely by our tariff. Our exports of cotton textiles afford, however, some measure of our ability to compete on the international market without tariff protection, at least in particular types of textiles.

The orthodox doctrine holds that the advantages of international division of labor are to be gained precisely by exposing to international competition those industries which are so uneconomic as to have high costs and allowing them to be eliminated while expanding low cost industries. This doctrine is unlikely to be accepted as a guide to governmental policy in the case of any industry which is long established and which employs a substantial percentage of the national labor force. The textile industry of the South would probably be able to compete with foreign producers on our domestic market even if the protective tariff were further reduced. If there ever were any question of a substantial fraction of that industry being put out of business by foreign imports, it is unlikely that this would be endured without swift protective action by the Federal Government.

Just as in the case of our agricultural policy, it is essential that we should not plan our foreign trade policy on the assumption that we are going to have a serious economic depression. It would be impossible to plan a rational economic policy in international trade on the assumption of wide-spread unemployment in our own economy. It seems quite certain that no government could allow large-scale unemployment to continue for any long period without taking the most heroic measures to overcome it. If these measures are taken too soon or are on too grandiose a scale the possibility of slipping into an inflationary upsurge cannot, of course, be discounted. Nevertheless, since the means of offsetting deflationary forces are now so well known it is almost a certainty that, whatever the dangers, these means will eventually be used, not only by our own government but by substantially all governments throughout the world.

FUTURE PROSPECTS IN FOREIGN TRADE:
PROBLEMS, DIFFICULTIES, RECOMMENDED
POLICIES

The problems of carrying on international trade between countries which, like our own, are still characterized by a large degree of free enterprise, and countries which have wholly or largely state-controlled economies, are many and serious. The problem of overcoming the persistent deficit in the balance of payments of most of the rest of the world with the United States is also an extremely difficult one. Its solution depends not only upon the economic policy of our own government but even more upon the policies of the governments of the countries having the deficit in their balance of payments. In order to expand their exports in the dollar area these countries must keep the prices of their exports down, measured in dollars. This can be accomplished in the short run by the devaluation of their currencies in relation to the dollar. In the long run it means keeping cost of production down, also measured in dollars. This, in turn, means keeping real wages from increasing too rapidly. This is likely to be politically very difficult.

During the postwar period, some of the most difficult economic problems of these countries have been rooted in inflationary policies. While there is some evidence that inflationary tendencies are being brought under control in these countries, it does not seem likely that any country in Europe or elsewhere is likely to persist in deflationary policies should serious unemployment begin to appear. This means that the inflationary danger is likely to be the more chronic problem, although there well may be serious deflationary interludes. Thus the expansion of European exports to dollar areas faces discouraging prospects. Curtailment of imports from dollar areas of supply and increased bilateralism in trade in order to push sales in nondollar areas may turn out to be inevitable.

The conclusion that the existence of long-continued, large-scale unemployment is not one of the conditions upon which our policy in foreign trade should be based seems thus to be strongly reinforced. The safeguards in the Charter of the proposed International Trade Organization and in the Reciprocal Trade Pacts against injury to our domestic industry, which might result from a heavy influx of imported manufactured goods at a time when our own industries were having to curtail production owing to the lack of demand during a depression, seem as adequate as could be devised under the circumstances. On the other hand, the use of the safeguard clauses in order to curtail imports serves to that extent to curtail the expansion of world trade.[5]

Once more we come to the conclusion that the maintenance of adequate demand for the products of the economy of the United States is a necessary condition for a sound policy in international trade, just as it is for a sound policy in our domestic economy. If this highly complex problem—how full employment in our economy is to be maintained without succumbing to the evils of inflation—can be solved, we could reasonably expect that overcoming the lag of the South in economic well-being need not be critically hampered by future developments in international trade.

It is true that at the present time the whole international trade policy of the United States hangs in the balance. Following World War II, the United States Government elected to follow what might be thought of as an extension of the Cordell Hull policy which had been instituted following the Democratic victory in 1932. This policy had consisted of turning our backs on our high tariff policy of the past and trying to induce the other countries of the world to join us in removing both government controls of, and barriers to, foreign trade.

---

[5] Whether the general program of freeing international trade from national controls and restrictions as is contemplated by the I.T.O. will actually become operative remains in doubt, as is pointed out below.

It has been pointed out that after World War I, international trade had not returned to the patterns which characterized it before 1914. The gold standard, in a real sense, was not restored. Barriers to trade and controls of trade which had come into existence during the war were not completely removed. Just at the time when a Democratic victory in 1932 brought Cordell Hull into office and he began his Jeffersonian crusade on behalf of free-trade, the Great Depression was at its worst. The depression spawned whole categories of additional controls and barriers. Exchange control, import quotas, bilateral agreements, and bulk purchases by governments became all but universal outside the United States. Even the United States was by no means wholly innocent of such measures. These developments were caused primarily by two factors. First, each country by means of trade controls could take action to maximize employment within its own boundaries, even if this meant "exporting unemployment" to other countries. Second, by means of trade controls, each country strove to protect its balance of payments and to insure that whatever foreign exchange was earned by the sale of its products would be devoted to paying only for those imports which were considered most essential to the national interest. This complicated machinery of national controls of foreign trade was still in existence when World War II swept normal international trade out of existence.

As World War II drew to a close, the United States joined with other countries in setting up the International Monetary Fund and the International Bank for Reconstruction and Development, in an effort to aid in developing new institutions which it was hoped could deal with the new conditions in international trade. The United States during the post-World War II period contributed many billions of dollars through UNRRA, the International Monetary Fund, the International Bank, the Export-Import Bank, the British Loan, and the Marshall Plan in order to aid world economic reconstruction and development. One declared purpose of all these "billionaire" aid programs has been to facilitate, and even to induce, all countries to remove controls and barriers in world trade. Greatly doubting, the recipient countries nevertheless joined in commitments to expand international trade and to relax controls and remove barriers. This movement culminated in the Havana Conference in 1948, when over fifty nations wrote the "Charter for an International Trade Organization."

The Economic Cooperation Administration has had a remarkable degree of success during its first two years of operation in carrying out the purposes of the Marshall Plan. By the time of the outbreak of the war in Korea, agricultural production in Western Europe had been restored to prewar levels. Industrial production was almost a third greater than in 1938. Even the persistent deficit of Western Europe in the balance of payments with the rest of the world showed signs that it might be brought under successful control by 1952 and 1953, when the program was supposed to be terminated. The tremendous rearmament program associated with the outbreak of the Korean war introduced new uncertainties but these did not seem to threaten and indeed might even facilitate improvement in the balance of payments situation. The problem of whether an equilibrium in the balance of payments of the rest of the world with the United States can be maintained without discrimination against our exports is likely, however, to continue to plague us indefinitely.

It is still a question whether there is a good prospect for returning to a world which would be as nearly free of trade controls and barriers as the world of 1914. The development of giant corporations, industry-wide collective bargaining, managed currencies, deficit-financing for full employment, and the like, had fundamentally changed the character of the economic systems of most important industrial countries even before the further development of collectivized economies. This can be clearly seen in the case of a country like the United Kingdom, or still more plainly in the case of Soviet Russia, but it is true in considerable degree of all modern industrialized countries. Almost no country is willing any longer to allow its prices and wages to move freely under the influence of international economic forces. The free movement of exchange rates and the movement of gold, together with the free movement of internal prices, was what made the old-fashioned international trading system work wonderfully well without governmental direction. These movements compelled countries adhering to the gold standard to keep their price levels in international alignment and their wage levels consistent with the productivity of their labor.

In a world in which the currents of international trade have been violently disrupted by two world wars and one greatest-of-all depression, in a world in which the beneficial exchange of manufactured commodities by Europe for food stuffs and raw materials from the

United States has become seriously difficult of consummation, there remains doubt whether the development of world trade is going to be along the lines advocated by the United States. It becomes a question of whether we shall not have to accustom ourselves to a world of continued exchange control, bilateral agreements, barter agreements, and the like.

Fortunately, neither the South nor the United States as a whole need be affected catastrophically by the purely economic effects of such a development. It has been pointed out that regardless of the organizational forms which international trade assumes in the future, we are not likely to have difficulty in obtaining essential imports. Our total volume of both exports and imports is likely to be less should these developments occur.[6] Our exports would almost certainly be less than under conditions like the present, when through gifts and loans abroad some one third of our goods shipped abroad are unrequited exports.

If such a development should take place, the South would face a difficult problem in continuing to sell abroad the current amounts of tobacco and cotton. It should not be forgotten, however, that this problem must be faced in the near future in any event, since only very large financial aid amounting to gifts enables the current volume of exports to be maintained.

It is highly desirable that the gross disparity between our exports be brought somehow into balance. It was hoped that by our policy of attempting to restore free international trade, our balance of payments could be brought into balance while both imports and exports were expanding. If this policy proves unsuccessful and our exports have to be adjusted to our imports, it will be even more essential that alternative sources of domestic demand be developed to absorb the equivalent of our current unrequited exports. Fortunately, as has been pointed out, the reduction in the relative importance of foreign trade to the South has at least rendered the South not much more vulnerable to current developments in international trade than is the rest of the country.

6 The abandonment of the attempt to restore "free trade" and the recognition that a system of bilateral agreements, barter agreements between countries, and the like, constitutes the actual method of international exchange, would not be *certain* to reduce the volume of world trade below what it is under the existing hybrid system. It must be remembered that this system is sustained at present, by a vast program of generalized dollar subsidies provided by the United States Government.

SELECTED BIBLIOGRAPHY

Note

For a work of this kind, a complete bibliography would make a sizeable volume in itself. Almost every chapter deals with a subfield of Economics different from that considered in every other chapter and requires a different set of reference works and different sources of data. Below is a selected bibliography of the sources and reference works which were most useful in the preparation of this study.

As the titles below indicate, we have relied heavily upon the statistical series published by various federal agencies; it is doubtful that a book of this kind could be written without the wealth of data they provide. Most important of all for a wide-ranging study of this kind are the various volumes of the *Statistical Abstract of the United States,* compiled by the Bureau of the Census. Only slightly less useful have been such publications as: *Agricultural Statistics* by the Bureau of Agricultural Economics; the *Census of Manufactures,* and the various publications of the decennial censuses, by the Bureau of the Census; *The Federal Reserve Bulletin* by the Board of Governors of the Federal Reserve System; the call reports and the annual reports of the Federal Deposit Insurance Corporation; the *Minerals Yearbook* and other publications of the Bureau of the Mines, Department of the Interior; the publications of the Forest Service, U. S. Department of Agriculture, especially the series comprising the *Report on the Reappraisal of the Forest Situation* which were issued in the years 1946–1948; and the data on income payments by states prepared by the National Income Division of the Department of Commerce.

Special mention should be made of three sources which have been especially helpful, two of which were devoted entirely to the South. The first is the series of *Situation* reports, prepared and published at frequent intervals by the Bureau of Agricultural Economics. They are both timely and comprehensive; they are most useful in dealing with particular commodities and special phases of the agricultural economy. We have used extensively the *Agricultural, Cotton, Farm Income,* and *Tobacco* reports. The second source is the publications of the Special Subcommittee on Cotton of the House Committee on Agriculture (the so-called Pace Committee). The large volume of *Hearings* in 1944 and the equally large volume issued in 1947 containing nine research studies (*Study of Agricultural and Economic Problems of the Cotton Belt*) each contain a wealth of data and analysis on cotton particularly and the South generally. The third source is *Labor in the South,* by the Bureau of Labor Statistics of the Labor Department. This first appeared as a feature article in the October 1946, *Monthly Labor Review* and was later published separately as Bulletin No. 98 of the Labor Department. It is an excellent study, particularly of industrial developments during World War II.

UNITED STATES GOVERNMENT DOCUMENTS

AGRICULTURE, DEPARTMENT OF

American Tobacco Types, Uses and Markets, by Charles E. Gage, circular 249, 1933; Revised Ed., 1942

Agricultural Adjustment Agency
 Reports (Irregular, 1933–34 to 1944–45)

Bureau of Agricultural Economics
 Agricultural Prices (Monthly)
 The Agricultural Situation (Monthly)
 Agricultural Statistics (Annual)
 Annual Report on Tobacco Statistics
 Cash Receipts from Farming by States and Commodities, Calendar Years 1924–44, Jan. 1946
 Changes in Farming in War and Peace, by Sherman E. Johnson, 1946
 The Cotton Situation (Irregular)
 Current Developments in the Farm Real Estate Market (Quarterly)
 Crop Production (Monthly)
 Experience in 1945 with Mechanical Cotton Pickers in California, Oct., 1946
 Farm Employment and Related Data
 The Farm Income Situation (Irregular)
 The Farm Real Estate Situation (Annual)
 Income Parity for Agriculture (VI Parts; Publication began in 1938)
 Livestock on Farms, Jan. 1 (Annual)

Livestock and Poultry on Farm, January 1; Number, Value per Head, Total Value; Livestock and Poultry by Classes. Revised Estimates, 1940–45 by States, Feb. 1947

Looking Ahead with Cotton (Miscellaneous Publication No. 584) Dec., 1945

Net Income and Parity Reports, 1943 and Summary for 1910–42, July, 1944

Readjustments in Processing and Marketing Citrus Fruits, July, 1946

The Tobacco Situation (Quarterly)

Tobaccos of the United States, 1948

(With Southeast Regional Land Tenure Research Committee)

Farm Tenure Situation in the Southeast, Preliminary Draft, 1948

Farm Security Administration

Inter-Bureau Coordinating Committee on Farm Tenure
Farm Tenure Improvement, July, 1940

Forest Service

Basic Forest Statistics for the United States as of Beginning of 1945, 1946

Biennial Reports of the Southeastern Forest Experiment Station, Asheville, N. C.

Economics for our Southern Forests, by E. L. Demmon, Southern Forest Experiment Station, occasional paper No. 62, New Orleans, 1937

Place of Forests in a Land Use Program for the South, by E. L. Demmon, Southern Forest Experiment Station, occasional paper No. 59, New Orleans, 1937

Report on Re-Appraisal of the Forest Situation:
No. 1—Gaging the Timber Resources in the United States, 1946
No. 2—Potential Requirements for Timber Products in the United States, 1946
No. 3—The Management Status of Forest Lands in the United States, 1946
No. 4—Wood Waste in the United States, 1947
No. 5—Protection Against Forest Insects and Diseases in the United States, 1947
No. 6—Forest Cooperatives in the United States, 1947
Forests and National Prosperity, Misc. Pub. No. 668, 1948

Forest Taxation Inquiry

Forest Taxation in the United States, by F. R. Fairchild et al., Misc. Pub. No. 218, 1935

BOARD OF TRUSTEES OF POSTAL SAVINGS SYSTEM

Annual Reports on Postal Savings System

CIVILIAN PRODUCTION ADMINISTRATION

Facilities Expansion, July 1940—June 1945

COMMERCE, DEPARTMENT OF
  State Income Payments, 1929–37, by R. R. Nathan and J. L. Martin,
    1939
  Bureau of Census
  Age—Adjusted Death Rates in the United States, 1900–1940
  Census of Agriculture (Quinquennially)
  Census of Governments, 1942
  Census of Manufactures (Biennial to 1939; quinquennially beginning
    1947)
  Census of Population (Decennial)
  Cotton and Rayon Mill Machinery in the United States, 1942
  Cotton Production and Distribution (Annual)
  Current Population Reports
  Economic Characteristics of Migrants (Internal Migration 1935 to
    1940, 16th Census, 1940), 1946
  Historical Review of Local and State Government Finance, 1948
  Government Employment
  Revised Summary of State and Local Government Finances, 1942,
    1948
  Social Characteristics of Migrants (Internal Migration 1935 to 1940,
    16th Census, 1940), 1946
State Finances
Statistical Abstract of the United States (Annual)
Vital Statistics Rates in the United States, 1900–1940
  Bureau of Foreign and Domestic Commerce
  Income Payments to Individuals by States (Published annually, usu-
    ally in the August issue of Survey of Current Business)
  Office of Business Economics
  Survey of Business
  Commission on Organization of Executive Branch of the Government
  Task Force Report on Water Resources Projects (Appendix K), 1949
CONGRESS
  Congressional Record
  Public Laws
  Statutes at Large
  House of Representatives
    Subcommittee of Committee on Agriculture, 78th Congress
      2nd Session
      Hearings on Cotton, December 4 and 9, 1944
    Subcommittee on Cotton, 80th Congress, 1st Session (Pace Com-
      mittee), Study of Agricultural and Economic Problems of the Cot-
      ton Belt, July 7 and 8, 1947
    Committee on Ways and Means, 78th Congress, 1st Session, Hearings
      on Revenue Revision of 1943
    House Report No. 622

Joint Committee on the Economic Report
  Economic Indicators (Monthly beginning May 1948)
Senate
  A National Plan for American Forestry
    Senate Doc. No. 12, 73rd Congress, 1st Session, 1933
  Cotton Textile Industry
    Senate Doc. 126, 74th Congress, 1st Session (Cabinet Committee
    Report), 1935
  Export Trade in and By-Products Users of Tobacco
    Senate Misc. Doc. No. 39, 76th Congress, 1st Session, 1939
  Sub-Committee of Committee on Public Lands, 80th Congress, 1st
  Session
    Mineral Position of the United States (Printed as an Appendix in
    "Hearings on Investigation of National Resources," May, 1947)
    Hearings on Agricultural Act of 1948, Senate Document No. 2318,
    80th Congress, 2nd Session
COUNCIL OF ECONOMIC ADVISERS
  The Annual Economic Review (Annual)
FEDERAL DEPOSIT INSURANCE CORPORATION
  Annual Reports
  Assets and Liabilities, Operating Insured Commercial and Mutual Sav-
    ings Banks (Usually three issues each year, including data for June
    30 and Dec. 31)
FEDERAL RESERVE SYSTEM
  Federal Reserve Bulletin (Monthly)
FEDERAL SECURITY AGENCY, OFFICE OF EDUCATION
  Biennial Survey of Education in the United States
PUBLIC HEALTH SERVICE
  Infant Mortality by Race and by Urban and Rural Areas, 1947, 1949
  United States Abridged Life Tables, 1939, 1947
FEDERAL WORKS AGENCY
  Public Roads Administration
    Highway Statistics: Summary to 1945
    Highway Statistics (Annual)
INTERIOR, DEPARTMENT OF THE
  Bureau of Mines
    Minerals Yearbook (Annual)
  Fish and Wild Life Service
    Fishery Statistics of the United States
INTERSTATE COMMERCE COMMISSION
  Interstate Commerce Reports
LABOR, DEPARTMENT OF
  Bureau of Labor Statistics
    Labor in the South (Bulletin No. 98), 1947 (Also appeared in
    Monthly Labor Review, Oct., 1946)

Monthly Labor Review
State and Regional Variations in Prospective Labor Supply (Bulletin
     No. 893), 1947
THE NATIONAL ARCHIVES
Division of Federal Register
Federal Register
NATIONAL RESOURCES PLANNING BOARD
Bibliography of Reports by State and Regional Planning Organizations,
     1942
The Southern Forests, 1940
SOCIAL SECURITY BOARD
Social Security Bulletin (Monthly)
Social Security Yearbook (Annual)
TARIFF COMMISSION
Cotton Cloth, 1936, Report 112, 2nd Series
TEMPORARY NATIONAL ECONOMIC COMMITTEE
Agriculture and the National Economy (by A. L. Meyers) Monograph
     23, 1939
Hearings, Part 28
TENNESSEE VALLEY AUTHORITY
Annual Reports of the Tennessee Valley Authority
TREASURY, DEPARTMENT OF THE
Annual Report of the Secretary of the Treasury on the State of the
     Finances
Treasury Bulletin (Monthly)
Bureau of Internal Revenue
Annual Reports of the Commissioner of Internal Revenue
Statistics of Income (Annual)

OTHER PUBLIC DOCUMENTS

ILLINOIS
University of Illinois
The Tax System and Industrial Development, by George Steiner, Uni-
     versity of Illinois Record, Vol. 35, No. 58, Urbana, 1938
KENTUCKY
University of Kentucky
Southern Manufacturers Tax Bill, James W. Martin, Ed., Bulletin,
     Bureau of Business Research, Lexington, 1947
Southern State and Local Finance Trends and the War, by James W.
     Martin, Bulletin of the Bureau of Business Research, No. 10, Lex-
     ington, 1945
LOUISIANA
Department of Commerce and Industry

Louisiana's 10 Year Tax Exemption Plan for New Industries, Baton Rouge, n.d.

Reports of the Department of Commerce and Industry, Baton Rouge (Biennial)

Forestry Commission

The Louisiana Forestry Plan (3 pt.), Baton Rouge, 1948

MISSISSIPPI

University of Miss.

Cotton's Way Forward, by M. K. Horne, Jr., Bureau of Business Research, Oxford, 1949

NORTH CAROLINA

North Carolina State College

Mechanical Harvesting of Cotton in North Carolina, by J. Gwyn Southerland and H. Brooks James, Information Series No. 22, Raleigh, 1950

North Carolina State College and N. C. Experiment Station

Cost of Producing Farm Products in North Carolina, Raleigh, 1949

North Carolina State Planning Board

Tax Bill of a Selected Manufacturing Corporation in Six Southeastern States, by Clarence Heer for Comm. on Taxation, Raleigh, 1945

University of North Carolina

Taxation in North Carolina, U.N.C. Extension Bulletin, Vol. XII, No. 4, 1932

SOUTH CAROLINA

State Planning Board

Is New Industry Tax Exemption Effective? Pamphlet No. 4, Columbia, 1943

TENNESSEE

State Planning Commission

Partners; Industry and the Tennessee Community, Nashville, 1947

Subsidies for Industries in Tennessee, Nashville, 1947

Tennessee Is Making Plans, Nashville, 1947

University of Tennessee

An Analysis of State Industrial Development Programs in the Thirteen Southern States, by Paul Barnett, The University of Tennessee Record, Vol. 47, No. 1, Knoxville, 1944

Industrial Development in Tennessee; Present Status and Suggested Program, by Paul Barnett, Univ. of Tenn. Record, Vol. 44, Knoxville, 1941

UNITED KINGDOM

Board of Trade

Working Party Report on Cotton, His Majesty's Stationery Office, London, 1946

UNITED NATIONS

Food and Agricultural Organization

Forestry and Forest Products, World Situation 1937–1946, Washington, 1947

World Fiber Survey, Washington, 1947

Yearbook of Food and Agricultural Statistics, 1947, Washington, 1947

VINER, JACOB

Trade Relations between Free-Market and Controlled Economies, League of Nations, II, Economic and Financial, II, A, 4, 1943

WHITE, JR., BENNETT S.

Trends in Demand for Tobacco of the Southern States, Kentucky Agricultural Experiment Station, Bulletin 431, Lexington, 1942

BOOKS

BACHMAN, JULES and M. R. GAINSBOROUGH, Economics of the Cotton Textile Industry, N. Y., National Industrial Conference Board, Inc., 1946.

BARGER, HAROLD and HANS H. LANSBERG, American Agriculture, 1899–1939, N. Y., National Bureau of Economic Research, Inc., 1942.

BLAKEY, ROY G. and VIOLET JOHNSON, State Income Taxes, Chicago, Commerce Clearing House, Inc., 1942.

BRANDT, KARL, The Reconstruction of World Agriculture, New York, W. W. Norton, 1945.

BROOKS, R. P., The Industrialization of the South, Athens, University of Ga. Press, 1929.

DEMING, FREDERICK L. and WELDON A. STEIN, Disposal of Southern War Plants (NPA Committee of the South Report No. 2), Washington, National Planning Association, 1949.

DUBLIN, LOUIS I., ALFRED J. LOTKA and MORTIMER SPEIGELMAN, Length of Life, Rev. Ed., New York, The Ronald Press, 1949.

DUERR, WILLIAM A., The Economic Problems of Forestry in the Appalachian Region, Cambridge, Harvard Univ. Press, 1949.

FRIEDMAN, MILTON and SIMON KUZNETS, Income from Independent Professional Practice, New York, National Bureau of Economic Research, Inc., 1945.

FISHER, WILLIAM H., Economics of Flue-Cured Tobacco, Richmond, Federal Reserve Bank of Richmond, 1945.

HEER, CLARENCE, Income and Wages in the South, Chapel Hill, Univ. of N. C. Press, 1930.

HERRING, HARRIET L., Southern Industry and Regional Development, Chapel Hill, Univ. of N. C. Press, 1940.

HOOVER, E. M., The Location of Economic Activity, New York, McGraw-Hill Book Company, Inc., 1948.

JOHNSON, CHARLES S., EDWIN EMBREE and W. W. ALEXANDER, The Collapse of Cotton Tenancy, Chapel Hill, Univ. of N. C. Press, 1935.

JOUBERT, WM. H., Southern Freight Rates in Transition, Gainesville, Univ. of Fla. Press, 1949.

KAPLAN, A. D. H., Small Business: Its Place and Problems (A Study for the Committee for Economic Development), New York, 1948.

KUZNETS, SIMON, National Income and Its Composition, 1919–1938, National Bureau of Economic Research, Inc., 1941.

LEVEN, M., Income in the Various States, Its Sources and Distribution, 1919, 1920 and 1921, New York, National Bureau of Economic Research, 1925.

LEVEN, M. and K. R. WRIGHT, Income Structure of the United States, Inst. of Ec. Pub. No. 74, Washington, The Brookings Institution, 1938.

MCLAUGHLIN, GLENN E. and STEFAN ROBOCK, Why Industry Moves South (NPA Committee of the South Report No. 3), Washington, National Planning Association, 1949.

NOURSE, E. G., J. S. DAVIS and J. D. BLACK, Three Years of the Agricultural Adjustment Act, Washington, The Brookings Institution, 1937.

ODUM, H. M., Southern Regions of the United States, Chapel Hill, Univ. of N. C., 1936.

ODUM, H. M. and KATHERINE JOCKER, In Search of the Regional Balance of America, Chapel Hill, Univ. of N. C. Press, 1945.

ODUM, H. M. and H. E. MOORE, American Regionalism, New York, Henry Holt & Co., 1938.

RATCHFORD, B. U., American State Debts, Durham, Duke Univ. Press, 1941.

ROBERT, JOSEPH C., The Story of Tobacco in America, New York, Alfred A. Knopf, 1949.

ROWE, HAROLD B., Tobacco Under the A.A.A., Washington, The Brookings Institution, 1935.

SHEPHERD, GEOFFREY S., Marketing Farm Products, Ames, Iowa State College Press, 1946.

SHEPHERD, GEOFFREY S., Agricultural Price Control, Ames, Iowa State College Press, 1945.

SHEPHERD, GEOFFREY S., Agricultural Price Analysis, Ames, Iowa State College Press, 1947.

SCHULTZ, THEODORE W., Agriculture in an Unstable Economy, New York, McGraw-Hill Book Company, Inc., 1945.

SLAUGHTER, JOHN A., Income Received in Various States, 1929–1935 (No. 234 N.I.C.B. Studies), New York National Industrial Conference Board, Inc., 1937.

TWELVE SOUTHERNERS, I'll Take My Stand, New York, Harper Brothers, 1930.

VANCE, RUPERT B., Human Geography of the South, Chapel Hill, Univ. of N. C. Press, 1932.

VANCE, RUPERT B. (In collaboration with Nadia Danilevsky), All These People, Chapel Hill, Univ. of N. C. Press, 1945.

VAN SICKLE, JOHN V., Planning for the South, Nashville, Vanderbilt Univ. Press, 1943.

VAN SICKLE, JOHN V., The Stake of the Cotton South in International Trade, Berkeley, Univ. of Cal. Press, 1945.

WESTERFIELD, RAY B., Money, Credit and Banking, Rev. Ed., New York, The Ronald Press Company, 1947.

WILCOX, WALTER W., The Farmer in the Second World War, Ames, Iowa State College Press, 1947.

WOOFTER, T. J., The Plight of Cigarette Tobacco, Chapel Hill, Univ. of N. C. Press, 1931.

ARTICLES

BISWELL, H. H., J. E. FOSTER and B. L. SOUTHWELL, "Grazing in Cutover Pine Forests of the Southeast," Journal of Forestry, XLII, 195–198 (Mar., 1944).

DEMMON, E. L., "Forests in the Economy of the South," The Southern Economic Journal, III, 369–380 (Apr., 1937).

deVYVER, F. T., "The Present Status of Labor Unions in the South, 1948," The Southern Economic Journal, XVI, 1–22, (July, 1949).

FESLER, J. W., "North Carolina's Local Government Commission," National Municipal Review, XXX, 327–334 (June, 1941).

FULMER, JOHN L., "Factors Influencing State Per Capita Income Differentials," The Southern Economic Journal, XVI, 259–278 (Jan., 1950).

GEE, WILSON, "The 'Drag' of Talent Out of the South," Social Forces, XV, 343–346 (March, 1937).

GEISERT, H. L., "The Trend of the Interregional Migration of Talent: Southeast, 1899–1936," Social Forces, XVIII, 41–47 (Oct., 1939).

HARDIN, CHARLES M., "The Tobacco Program: Exception or Portent?" Journal of Farm Economics, XXVIII, 920–935 (Nov., 1946).

HEATH, MILTON S., "The Rate Structure," Law and Contemporary Problems, XII, 405–415 (Sum., 1947).

HERZEL, WM. G., "State Tax Legislation in 1947," National Tax Journal, I, 79–90 (March, 1948).

JOHNSON, KEITH W., "Natural Gas Industry of the Southwest and Its Significance to Industrial Development," Monthly Review of Federal Reserve Bank of Dallas, XXXIV, 33–41 (March 1, 1949).

KLARMAN, HERBERT E., "A Statistical Study of Income Differences Among Communities," Studies in Income and Wealth, Vol. VI, part 6, National Bureau of Economic Research, Inc., New York, 1943.

KOHLER, E. L., "The TVA and Its Power Accounting Problem," The Accounting Review, XXIII, 44–55 (Jan., 1948).

LESTER, RICHARD A., "Diversity in North-South Wage Differentials and in Wage Rates within the South," The Southern Economic Journal, XII, 238–262 (Jan., 1946).

LESTER, RICHARD A., "Effectiveness of Factory Labor: South-North Comparisons," The Journal of Political Economy, LIV, 60–75 (Feb., 1946).

LESTER, RICHARD A., "Must Wages Differ North and South?" Virginia Quarterly Review, XXII, 20–31 (Winter, 1946).

LESTER, RICHARD A., "Shortcomings of Marginal Analysis for Wage Employment Problems," The American Economic Review, XXXVI, 63–82 (March, 1946).

LESTER, RICHARD A., "Trends in Southern Wage Differentials since 1890," The Southern Economic Journal, XI, 317–344 (Apr., 1945).

LESTER, RICHARD A., "Wage Diversity and Its Theoretical Implications," The Review of Economic Statistics, XXVIII, 152–159 (Aug., 1946).

LEVY, MARK, "Lease-Back Financing Expanding," Best's Insurance News, Life Edition, L, 37–42 (June, 1949).

LIPPERT, T. W., "Cerro Bolivar: Saga of an Iron Crisis Averted," Journal of Metals and Mining Engineering (Feb., 1950).

LOWRY, ROBERT E., "Municipal Subsidies to Industries in Tennessee," The Southern Economic Journal, VII, 317–29 (Jan., 1941).

MARKHAM, JESSE W., "Some Comments upon the North-South Differential," The Southern Economic Journal, XVI, 279–283 (Jan., 1950).

MASON, JOHN E., "Acreage Allotments and Land Prices," Journal of Land and Public Utility Economics, XXII, 176–181 (May, 1946).

MCFERRIN, JOHN B., "Resources for Financing Industry in the South," The Southern Economic Journal, XIV, 46–61 (July, 1947).

OLIVER, HENRY M., JR., "Income Region, Community-Size and Color," Quarterly Journal of Economics, LX, 588–599 (Aug., 1946).

PALMER, E. Z., "Sources and Distribution of Income in the South," The Southern Economic Journal, II, 47–60 (Jan., 1936).

RATCHFORD, B. U., "New Forms of State Debts," The Southern Economic Journal, XIII, 459–478 (April, 1942).

RATCHFORD, B. U., "Public Debts in the South," The Southern Economic Journal, II, 13–25 (Jan., 1936).

RATCHFORD, B. U., "The Work of the North Carolina Local Government Commission," National Municipal Review, XV, 323–327 (June, 1936).

RATCHFORD, B. U. and K. C. HEISE, "Confederate Pensions," The Southern Economic Journal, V, 207–217 (Oct., 1938).

SPENGLER, J. J., "Population Problems in the South," The Southern Economic Journal, III, 393–410; IV 1–27, 131–153 (April, July, and Oct., 1937).

SHRYOCK, JR., HENRY S. and HOPE TISDALE ELDRIDGE, "Internal Migration in Peace and War," American Sociological Review, XII, 27–39 (Feb., 1947).

SUFRIN, C. S., A. W. SWINYARD and F. M. STEPHENSON, "The North-South Differential—A Different View," The Southern Economic Journal, XV, 184–190 (Oct., 1948).

TAYLOR, CHARLES T., "Transportation on the Tennessee," Monthly Review, Federal Reserve Bank of Atlanta, XXXIV, 13–19 (Feb. 28, 1949).

(Unsigned). "TVA's First Audit by GAO Points Way to Businesslike Evaluation," Journal of Accountancy, LXXXIII, 507–510 (June, 1947).

WELCH, FRANK J., and D. GRAY MILEY, "Mechanization of the Cotton Harvest," Journal of Farm Economics, XXVII, 928–946 (Nov., 1945).

PAMPHLETS AND MISCELLANEOUS WORKS

BRANDIS, BUFORD, "Industrial Development by Community Corporations," (Unpublished study) Washington, NPA Committee of the South.

BRYAN, MALCOLM, "The Supply of Funds in the South, 1946," (A speech before the Georgia Bankers Association) December 11, 1946.

HEBERLE, RUDOLPH, "The Impact of the War on Population Redistribution in the South," Nashville, Institute of Research and Training in the Social Sciences, Paper No. 7, Vanderbilt Press, 1945.

HERRING, HARRIET L., "Southern Resources for Industrial Development," Richmond, Monograph 2, Southern Association of Science and Industry, 1948.

HOPKINS, ERNEST J., "Louisville Industrial Foundation: A Study in Community Capitalization of Local Industries," Atlanta, Federal Bank of Atlanta, 1945.

HOPKINS, ERNEST J., "Mississippi's BAWI Plan, An Experiment in Subsidization," Atlanta, Federal Reserve Bank of Atlanta, 1944.

KORSTIAN, C. F. and LEE M. JAMES, "Forestry in the South," Richmond, Monograph 1, Southern Association of Science and Industry, 1948.

MOLONEY, JOHN F., "Cotton in Peace and War," Nashville, Institute of Research and Training in the Social Sciences, Paper No. 6, Vanderbilt Univ. Press, 1944.

MOLYNEAUX, PETER, "Economic Nationalism and Problems of the South," Dallas (Arnold Foundation Studies in Public Affairs), 1933.

National Cotton Council of America, "Report of Proceedings of the Beltwide Cotton Mechanization Conference," August, 1947.

PIERCY, LORD, "Long Term and Permanent Finance for Industry," London, 1948.

Southern Regional Council, "The South: America's Opportunity Number One," Atlanta, 1945.

STEPP, JAMES A., "Rural Industrial Development in Four Southern States Since World War II," (Unpublished study) Washington, NPA Committee of the South, 1948.

VANCE, RUPERT, "Research Memorandum on Population Distribution within the United States," New York: Social Science Research Council, 1938.

VAN SICKLE, JOHN V., "Public Works, Economic Stabilization and the

Rural South," Nashville, Institute of Research and Training in the Social Sciences, Paper, No. 2, Vanderbilt Univ. Press, 1942.

WILLIAMS, EDITH WEBB, "Research in Southern Regional Development," Richmond, Monograph 3, Southern Association of Science and Industry, 1948.

WORSHAL, J. NORMAN, "Financial Operations of Cooperative Marketing of Forest Products by the Farmers Mutual, Inc., in the Vicinity of Durham, North Carolina," Unpublished Thesis, Duke University, 1949.

"The Coming of Industry to the South," Annals of the American Academy of Political and Social Science, Vol. 153, (Jan., 1931).

NEWSPAPERS, PERIODICALS AND OTHER SERIALS

Best's Insurance News, Life Edition, Alfred M. Best Company, Inc., New York

Best's Life Insurance Reports, Alfred M. Best Company, Inc., New York

Daily News Record

Davison's Textile Blue Book, Davison Publishing Co., New York

Monthly Letter on Economic Conditions, Government Finance, National City Bank of New York

Monthly Review of the Federal Reserve Bank of Atlanta

Monthly Review of the Federal Reserve Bank of Dallas

Monthly Review of the Federal Reserve Bank of Richmond

Monthly Review of the Federal Reserve Bank of St. Louis

Municipal Bond Sales (Annual), The Bond Buyer, New York

The New York Times

Proceedings, Annual Meetings of Life Insurance Association of America

Proceedings of the Association of Life Insurance Presidents, (Annual)

Savings and Loan Annals (Annual, 1939–1941; formerly Building and Loan Annals), U. S. Building and Loan League, Chicago

Tax Systems, Commerce Clearing House, Inc., Chicago

Trends in North Carolina Banking, N. C. Bankers' Association

INDEX

industry in, 116, 132f., 254n., 276, 411
mineral production of, 9f.
power in, 136
public finance of, 199, 210, 222
taxes in, 274n., 378, 380
TVA in, 242
Missouri, 307
Mobile, 14, 162, 246
Mortgages, 94, 107, 166, 187, 189, 190
Motor vehicles, 17f., 82, 107, 197, 199f.
Municipal Bankruptcy Act, 205

National Recovery Administration, 54, 394, 412
Naval stores, 16, 160, 254f., 280, 352, 425ff.
Navigation, inland, (*See also* Transportation, water), 231f., 240
Negroes, 19ff., 24ff., 35f., 41, 109, 398
New Deal, 283, 308, 311, 317, 360, 391, 416, 437
New England, 140ff., 154
New Hampshire, 275
New Mexico, 307f.
New Orleans, 14, 218
North Carolina,
  agriculture in, 284n., 301f.
  banking in, 167, 169
  cotton in, 307
  crop land in, 297, 356ff.
  fertilizers used in, 106
  income in, 50, 104f.
  industry in, 116, 119, 122, 132f., 138, 145, 151, 154, 155, 159, 411
  mineral production of, 9, 13
  population of, 22
  power in, 135f.
  public finance of, 196, 200, 201, 203, 206, 219, 220, 221
  recreation facilities of, 7
  taxes in, 274n., 378ff., 384
  tobacco in, 100, 277n., 337, 356ff.
  water supply in, 234
Nourse, E. G., 347n.
Nylon, 153

Office of Price Administration, 145f., 351
Official Territory, 78ff.
Ohio, 230n., 297
Oil (*See* Petroleum)
Oklahoma,
  agriculture in, 99
  as different from rest of South, 2f., 15
  banking in, 169
  cotton in, 307f.
  education in, 210
  federal aid to, 225
  income in, 50, 104f.

industry in, 132f., 378, 411
mineral production of, 9f.
population of, 22, 35
public finance of, 197, 204, 210ff., 222, 378
rainfall in, 6
research in, 77
transportation in, 14
Oleomargarine, 156f.
Oliver, Henry M., Jr., 397n.
Ostrom, Carl E., 280n.
Ownership, absentee, 74ff., 146, 192f.

Paper industry, 15, 71, 118, 126f., 128, 130f., 193, 232, 235, 253f., 263f., 411
Peanuts, 58n., 95, 96, 97, 98, 103f., 157f., 354
Pennsylvania, 230n.
Pensions, Civil War, 205, 210
Petroleum and petroleum products,
  as raw material, 12, 371f.
  consumption of, 12, 13, 247ff., 365
  export of, 425ff.
  policies concerning, 247ff.
  prices of, 248
  production of, 8ff., 11, 247
  refining of, 116, 123f., 126f., 129f., 161, 232, 235
  reserves of, 10, 11, 72, 247ff.
  taxes on, 204, 251
  wages paid in industry, 411
Phillips, M. Ogden, 423
Piercy, Lord, 386n.
Population,
  age composition of, 23, 27f., 31, 41
  characteristics of, 27ff.
  composition of, 20, 21, 27, 41
  education of, 29ff.
  growth of, 19ff., 26, 398f.
  health of, 29ff.
  migration of, 20f., 26ff., 34ff., 41f., 69f., 90, 120, 399
  pressure, 36f., 70
  rural, 23, 25, 27, 41, 89f., 91, 114
Postal Savings deposits, 184f.
Power,
  electric, 14, 72, 135f., 229f., 237ff., 241, 243, 371f., 382
  equipment, 134f.
  produced by TVA, 14, 72, 135, 162, 230ff., 236ff.
  water, 12, 14f., 71f., 229ff., 238
Price control, 145f., 148f., 158, 248, 286f., 345ff., 353ff.
Price supports, 106, 108, 283ff., 289ff., 317ff., 327, 345ff., 353ff.